Soldiers of Empire

How are soldiers made? Why do they fight? Reimagining the study of armed forces and society, Tarak Barkawi examines the imperial and multi-national armies that fought in Asia in the Second World War, especially the British Indian Army in the Burma campaign. Going beyond conventional narratives, Barkawi studies soldiers in transnational context, from recruitment and training, to combat and memory. Drawing on history, sociology, and anthropology, the book critiques the "Western way of war" from a postcolonial perspective. Barkawi reconceives soldiers as cosmopolitan, their battles irreducible to the national histories that monopolize them. This book will appeal to those interested in the Second World War, armed forces, and the British Empire, and to students and scholars of military sociology and history, South Asian studies, and international relations.

TARAK BARKAWI is Reader in the Department of International Relations at the London School of Economics and Political Science.

Soldiers of Empire

Indian and British Armies in World War II

Tarak Barkawi
London School of Economics and Political Science

CAMBRIDGE
UNIVERSITY PRESS

CAMBRIDGE
UNIVERSITY PRESS

University Printing House, Cambridge CB2 8BS, United Kingdom

One Liberty Plaza, 20th Floor, New York, NY 10006, USA

477 Williamstown Road, Port Melbourne, VIC 3207, Australia

314-321, 3rd Floor, Plot 3, Splendor Forum, Jasola District Centre, New Delhi - 110025, India

79 Anson Road, #06-04/06, Singapore 079906

Cambridge University Press is part of the University of Cambridge.

It furthers the University's mission by disseminating knowledge in the pursuit of education, learning and research at the highest international levels of excellence.

www.cambridge.org
Information on this title: www.cambridge.org/9781316620656
DOI: 10.1017/9781316718612

© Tarak Barkawi 2017

First published 2017

A catalogue record for this publication is available from the British Library

Library of Congress Cataloging in Publication data
Names: Barkawi, Tarak, author.
Title: Soldiers of empire : Indian and British armies in World War II / Tarak Barkawi, London School of Economics and Political Science.
Description: Cambridge; New York : Cambridge University Press, 2017. | Includes bibliographical references and index.
Identifiers: LCCN 2017001511| ISBN 9781107169586 (hardback : alk. paper) | ISBN 9781316620656 (paperback : alk. paper)
Subjects: LCSH: World War, 1939–1945 – Participation, East Indian. | Great Britain. Army. British Indian Army – History – World War, 1939–1945. | Sociology, Military – India – History – 20th century. | World War, 1939–1945 – Campaigns – Burma.
Classification: LCC D767.6 .B27 2017 | DDC 940.54/1254–dc23
LC record available at https://lccn.loc.gov/2017001511

ISBN 978-1-107-16958-6 Hardback
ISBN 978-1-316-62065-6 Paperback

For mama and papa

No one who saw the 14th Army in action, above all, no one who saw its dead on the field of battle, the black and the white and the brown and the yellow lying together in their indistinguishable blood on the rich soil of Burma, can ever doubt that there is a brotherhood of man; or fail to cry, What *is* Man, that he can give so much for war, so little for peace?

– John Masters, *The Road Past Mandalay*

Contents

Illustrations

Maps

Acknowledgments

This project germinated in an assignment David Little gave to me while I worked as his research assistant at the United States Institute of Peace in Washington, D.C. in 1991–1992, before I started my Ph.D. at the University of Minnesota. David was working on a series of books on religious conflict and wanted a brief on Sudan. While researching it – perhaps rather further back than David intended – I discovered that Muhammad Ali Pasha, the modernizing Ottoman ruler of Egypt, had an army of enslaved Sudanese trained by French veterans of the Napoleonic wars. The combination of foreign manpower disciplined by the regular military stuck with me. The model of a university scholar in a beltway think tank, David offered me impromptu seminars on Max Weber, and encouraged my efforts at connections between Muhammad Ali's Sudanese and the colonial armies of the Europeans or the client armies of the Cold War superpowers.

At Minnesota, my advisor Bud Duvall taught me how to think seriously, while other members of my dissertation committee gave me a great deal to think about, as this project originally took shape as a Ph.D. dissertation. Ron Aminzade and Barbara Laslett showed me what it meant to do history and sociology together, while James Farr and Mary Dietz did the same for social and political theory. Minnesota offered an extraordinary environment to do interdisciplinary work. I am especially indebted to the Department of Political Science and the MacArthur Interdisciplinary Program on Peace and International Cooperation for financial support and for the thriving communities of graduate students they sustained. Mark Laffey offered constant intellectual comradeship and endured and commented on many early versions of this project. For their companionship, teaching, and more or less ruthless critique, I am grateful to Kristen Misage, Himadeep Muppidi, Jutta Weldes, Lisa Disch, Ido Oren, Jeff Legro, John Tambornino, Martha Easton, Brett Mizelle, David Blaney, Diana Saco, Hans

Nesseth, Karin Fierke, Margaret Wade, Jen Spear, Helen Kinsella, Shampa Biswas, Andy Davison, Joel Grossman, and Joel Olson.

A MacArthur-funded consortium between the Universities of Minnesota, Wisconsin-Madison, and Stanford brought me in touch with Lynn Eden of Stanford's Center for International Security and Cooperation. Her hard-headed thinking, generosity of spirit, and vast knowledge about military organizations proved crucial at various stages in the development of this book. Doctoral fellowships from Harvard's Olin Institute of Strategic Studies and the SSRC-MacArthur Program on International Peace and Security allowed me the time to master literatures and conduct sustained archival research. While attached to the Department of War Studies at King's College London (KCL), I was supervised by Christopher Dandeker who guided me through military sociology and helped knock my ideas into more definite shape. I have greatly appreciated his wise advice and counsel over the years. At KCL, I followed Brian Bond's seminar on the "Face of Battle" two years running and learned a great deal. Also at KCL, Tim Moreman patiently guided me through the London archives of the Indian Army, generously giving me the benefit of his many years as an archive hound. It was with a great sense of achievement that I was able later to provide him with archival materials on the First Arakan that I had sniffed out in the way he taught me.

I kept working on this project over the first two decades of my career. Colleagues and graduate students at the institutions I held posts at provided invaluable commentary and critique. I would like to particularly thank the late Paul Hirst of Birkbeck College, who showed me that radical social theory and fascination with things military were not incompatible. Paul was an angel on my shoulder while I navigated the shoals of the UK academy. At Aberystwyth, I thank Michael Williams, Jenny Edkins, Patricia Owens, Pinar Bilgin, Maja Zehfuss, Stephen Hobden, Priscilla Netto, John Baylis, Ken Booth, Andrew Linklater, and Collin McInnes. At Birkbeck, I thank Sam Aschenden, Dionyssis Dimitrakopoulos, Jason Edwards, David Styan, and Robert Singh. At Cambridge, I thank Brendan Simms, Duncan Bell, Charles Jones, Stef Halper, Yezid Sayigh, Pervaiz Nazir, Chris Bayly, and George Joffe. At New School, I thank Banu Bargu, Nancy Fraser, and Vicky Hattam. At the London School of Economics (LSE), I thank Martin Bayly, Peter Trubowitz, Chris Coker, John Sidel, and Bill Callahan. I am grateful for financial support from the Department of International Politics and the

College Research Fund, University of Wales, Aberystwyth; the Department of Politics and Sociology, Birkbeck College; the Centre of International Studies, Cambridge University; the Department of Politics, New School for Social Research; and the Department of International Relations, London School of Economics and Political Science.

Scholarship is a collective enterprise as much as it is an individual struggle. It is impossible without intellectual comradeship. Here, I am especially thankful to Shane Brighton for his friendship and support over many years. We have had so many conversations on the theme of "critical war studies" that I no longer know where my ideas end and his begin. Devon Curtis and Susan Carruthers provided invaluable criticism and patient commentary at many junctures. Darryl Li and George Lawson read and commented on the penultimate draft of the book and gave me what proved to be crucial reactions. Other friends and mentors who provided intellectual and emotional support over the years include Rosy Hollis, Mark Hoffman, Martin Shaw, Hew Strachan, Hugh Gusterson, Martin Coward, Debbie Lisle, John Conant, Julian Reid, Terrell Carver, Jan Honig, Louiza Odysseos, Stephen Elbe, Bob Vitalis, Rob Walker, Peter Mandaville, Mustapha Kamal Pasha, Anna Stavrianakis, Rob Dover, Patrick Porter, Dorothy Noyes, Srdjan Vucetic, Josef Ansorge, Alex Anievas, Lisa Smirl, Tim Kubik, Fiona Adamson, Alex Cooley, Russell Bentley, Iver Neumann, and Alex Wendt.

I am especially thankful to the serving soldiers, marines, airmen, and sailors who have so generously shared their knowledge and experiences with me. For their friendship, advice, and patient responses to my many questions, I would like to particularly thank Dom Biddick, Michael Hart, Joe Hatfield, Dave Beall, Paul Edgar, David Buckingham, Simon Diggins, Andrew Sharp, Paul O'Neill, Paul Newton, Hamish Tetlow, Jonathan Worthington, Scott Roberts, Kalesh Mohanan, Leland Burns, and Sam Long. I also thank the many British and U.S. officers who I taught over nearly ten years on the M.Phil. in International Relations at Cambridge. They schooled me as much if not more than I schooled them.

An earlier version of the manuscript was reviewed by Cornell University Press. I would like to particularly thank the editor there, Roger Haydon, and two anonymous reviewers. This project would not have taken the form it has without their collective criticism. I greatly appreciate it.

Presenting this project at two symposia on "Renewing the Military History of Colonial South Asia," held at Greenwich in August 2013 and Kolkata in January 2014, helped me to crystallize the book's argument. I am deeply indebted to Gavin Rand and Kaushik Roy for organizing these events and for their many penetrating comments. I am grateful to Alan Jeffreys, who attended both meetings and whose voluminous knowledge of the Indian Army saved me from many errors. For their conversations and reactions to my trial arguments, I thank Indivar Kamtekar, Anirudh Deshpande, and Peter Stanley. I would also like to thank Sudipta Kaviraj, who gave me invaluable comments when I presented an early chapter at School of Oriental and African Studies (SOAS) many years ago. Thanks also to Dennis Showalter for his comments on the manuscript.

LSE's International Relations department provided support for a "book scrub" seminar to critique a near-final draft. I am particularly grateful to Tony King and Kaushik Roy for reading and commenting on the entire manuscript. For their comments on chapters, contributions to the discussion, and other assistance, I thank Alan Jeffreys, Gavin Rand, Martin Coward, Shane Brighton, Paul Kirby, David Killingray, Chris Coker, Martin Bayly, Patricia Owens, Jan Honig, Christopher Dandeker, and Patrick Porter.

Thanks to John Haslam, Amanda George, Amy Lee, and Katherine Law at Cambridge University Press, and to four anonymous reviewers for their very helpful comments. Thanks also to Vijay Bhatia, Litty Santosh, and N.K. Sreejith for their help in the final preparation of the manuscript.

As other scholars will know, I am deeply indebted to the archivists and librarians who have assisted me. I am particularly grateful to Steven Mahoney who handled with aplomb and companionship a particularly high volume of ILL requests while I was at Aberystwyth; to Gavin Edgerly-Harris at the Gurkha Museum; to Brian Owen at the Royal Welch Fusiliers Museum; to Paul Evans at the Royal Artillery Museum; to the staff who assisted me at the Oriental and India Office Collection, British Library; the Imperial War Museum; the National Army Museum; the Liddell Hart Centre for Military Archives; the Churchill College Archives; the Cambridge Centre for South Asian Studies; the South Wales Borderers Regimental Museum; the Durham University Library; the Public Record Office (as it was); and the (now defunct) British Empire and Commonwealth Museum. I thank also

Irene Hindmarsh of Durham University for helping me track down the Louis Allen story.

My wife, Jennifer Luff, has soldiered by my side as this book was brought to completion, and done so with the care and empathy only a fellow scholar can offer. I am grateful for her giant spirit and unstinting support, and for her laughter and love. I am thankful also for our two cats, Hannibal and Penelope, who journeyed with this project from Ely, Cambridgeshire, to Astoria, Queens, and finally to Phoenix House in County Durham. There, this book finally went out to pasture along with the hundreds of mice Hannibal and Penelope have done for. Their stately beauty and insistent purrs reassured when nothing else could.

I dedicate this book to my mother, who taught me to love books and inadvertently introduced me to the subject of war through her passion for John Wayne films, and to my father, whose very existence made me aware from a young age of the wider world and its armed conflicts.

Acronyms

AA	Anti-Aircraft
ALFSEA	Allied Land Forces Southeast Asia
BO	British Officer
C-in-C	Commander-in-Chief
CO	Commanding Officer
EA	East African
ECO	Emergency Commissioned Officer (British)
EICO	Emergency Indian Commissioned Officer
GHQ(I)	General Headquarters (India)
GO	Gurkha Officer (Gurkha equivalent of VCO)
ICO	Indian Commissioned Officer
IJA	Imperial Japanese Army
INA	Indian National Army
IOR	Indian Other Rank
KAR	King's African Rifles
KCIO	King's Commissioned Indian Officer
LMG	Light Machine Gun
MG	Machine Gun
MT	Motor Transport
NCO	Non-Commissioned Officer
OC	Officer Commanding
OR	Other Rank
PoW	Prisoner of War
RAF	Royal Air Force
RWF	Royal Welch Fusiliers
SEAC	Southeast Asia Command
VCO	Viceroy's Commissioned Officer
WA	West African

Abbreviations Used in the References

BEC   Museum of the British Empire and Commonwealth, Bristol, UK

CC   Churchill College Archives, Cambridge, UK

CSAS   Cambridge Centre of South Asian Studies, UK

DL   Durham University Library, Durham, UK

GM   Gurkha Museum, Winchester, UK

IWM   Imperial War Museum, London, UK

LH   Liddell Hart Centre for Military Archives, King's College London, UK

NAM   National Army Museum, London, UK

OIOC   Oriental and India Office Collection, British Library, London, UK

RWF   Royal Welch Fusiliers Regimental Archives, Caernarfon, Wales, UK

SWB   South Wales Borderers Regimental Archives, Brecon, Wales, UK

TNA   The National Archives, Kew, UK

WA   Firepower, Royal Artillery Museum, Woolwich, UK

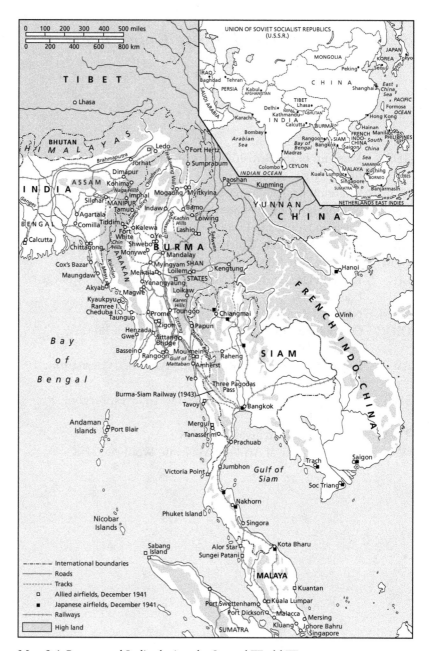

Map 0.1 Burma and India during the Second World War

Introduction

Decolonizing the Soldier

How are soldiers made? Why do they fight? This book takes up these central questions of military history and sociology. It does so with the soldiers of a multicultural, imperial army who fought a great but obscure campaign against Japan on the forgotten fronts of British Asia during the Second World War. With few exceptions, inquiry into these questions has concerned the national armed forces of Western states. Wherever one stands in the debates over "combat motivation," the object of study is usually a national army, and most likely US, British, or German.[1] The nature, character, and course of these debates, which began in earnest during the Second World War, have been fundamentally shaped by the Western and national contexts of both the researchers and the armed forces they studied. Early explanations drew on organizational and social psychological theories and presupposed the nation-state. Later scholars looked to national society and culture, and to national racisms and ideologies, for new thinking.[2] The conceptual vocabulary and historical materials with which we think about soldiers and war are drawn nearly entirely from Western political modernity.[3]

In the terms of such Eurocentric military inquiry, the British Indian Army should hardly have functioned.[4] It was an ethnically diverse conglomeration in which few soldiers operated in their primary language.

---

[1] Key and representative texts include: Creveld, *Fighting Power*; Kellett, *Combat Motivation*; Kindsvatter, *American Soldiers*; King, *Combat Soldier*; Moran, *Anatomy of Courage*; Moskos, *American Enlisted Man*; Shils and Janowitz, "Cohesion and Disintegration"; Stouffer, *American Soldier*, 2 vols.
[2] Bartov, *Hitler's Army*; Cameron, *American Samurai*; Chodoff, "Ideology and Primary Groups"; Fritz, *Frontsoldaten*; Janowitz and Wesbrooke, *Political Education of Soldiers*; McPherson, *Cause and Comrades*.
[3] A point Chakrabarty made about the social sciences in general in *Provincializing Europe*, Chapter 1, pp. 27–46.
[4] For a general introduction and historical overview, see Mason, *Matter of Honour*.

It was divided and ruled down to the company level by the regional, religious, and caste distinctions of the Raj, and it was organized around Victorian ideas about martial races in ways that compromised combat efficiency. By the time of the Second World War, the British Indian Army had become a political and military contradiction confronting the colonized world's most advanced mass independence movement. Colonial control was its *raison d'être*, yet it commissioned nationalist Indian officers in increasing number. A late colonial army, it fought in a total contest of nations and ideologies, while suppressing a nationalist uprising in India. In the "race war" against Japan, it participated on the white man's side, under his command, in engagements as intense and replete with violation as those on any Pacific island battlefield.[5] On the eve of the globalization of the nation-state, the British Empire's cosmopolitan ranks evoked both the multiracial hosts of antiquity and the multinational peacekeeping and coalition forces of the times to come.

This book uses the Indian Army and other British and imperial forces in the Asia-Pacific Wars to rethink army–society relations. It develops a postcolonial perspective on how soldiers are created and come to participate in combat. Most writing about soldiers and battle, across a range of disciplines and genres, presumes the nation-state, or a serviceably equivalent polity, as the political container of relations between armed forces and society.[6] A key premise of this book, by contrast, is to take as ordinary an imperial context in approaching questions of politics, society and army, and their collective envelopment in war. Ordinary not only in the sense that the imperial, with its transnational hierarchies and multicultural formations, is more representative of historical experience than the nation-state.[7] But also because the imperial offers greater insight into the nature of the army as such.

Historically, soldiering in organized warfare exceeds the modern West and its national armies. Yet, the study of soldiers and armies

---

[5] Cf. Dower, *War Without Mercy*.

[6] See e.g. Huntington, *Soldier and the State*, p. 65: "There is no necessary reason why nation states should be the only socio-political groups maintaining professional forces. But with a few peripheral exceptions, this has been true. The military man consequently tends to assume that the nation state is the ultimate form of political organization."

[7] Cooper, *Colonialism in Question*, Chapter 6.

has been profoundly shaped by the histories and sociologies of nation-states in Europe.[8] That is the field against which these subjects are generally imagined. Western experience constitutes the generic categories of inquiry, which then are applied to the histories and societies of others. The national and territorial state, mass society and ideology, democracy and citizenship, bureaucracy and atrocity, even the Greco-Roman origins of the West, underlie scholarly, as well as popular, imaginings of soldiers and wars.[9] Soldiering, an ancient and cosmopolitan vocation, is conceived in provincial terms. But what soldiers are and why they fight are not best understood in modern and national frames like "citizen soldiers." Such categories close off the ways in which soldiers, Western or otherwise, are other than their terms allow.

The problem is not that inquiry and theory based on Western historical experience are somehow intrinsically wrong or misguided. On the contrary, it is deeply insightful.[10] It is that provincial experience overwhelms the general categories and terms of analysis. A particular social and political context – the nation-state – is taken for granted, sets the terms. What happens when we proceed from alternate first premises? What general categories would we develop then?

British and imperial armed forces in the Second World War offer contrapuntal materials – between nation and empire – with which to begin.[11] Through comparative study of British, British Indian, and British imperial forces before and during the war against Japan, this book develops three lines of inquiry that collectively reformulate the terms of debate about armed forces, society and war with respect to infantry battle.

The first is a co-constitutive approach to army–society relations, which serves as both critique of the "army or society" thinking of

---

[8] See e.g. Black, *Rethinking Military History*; Bobbitt, *Shield of Achilles*; Bond, *War and Society in Europe 1870–1970*; Mann, *States, War and Capitalism*; Parker, *Military Revolution*; Tilly, *Coercion, Capital, and European States*.

[9] See e.g. Ambrose, *Citizen Soldiers*; Browning, *Ordinary Men*; Cohen, *Citizens and Soldiers*; Hanson, *Carnage and Culture*; Krebs, *Fighting for Rights*.

[10] Chakrabarty remarks: "The everyday experience of third-world social science is that *we* find these [Eurocentric] theories, in spite of their inherent ignorance of 'us,' eminently useful in understanding our societies." *Provincializing Europe*, p. 29. See also Burton, "On the Inadequacy and the Indispensability of the Nation"; Kaviraj, "The Imaginary Institution of India."

[11] Said, *Culture and Imperialism*.

conventional military sociology and a replacement for it. Military organizations transform social and cultural fields to create soldiers, and encounter frictions and resistances in doing so. Armed forces and society relate dynamically, shaping one another. The constitution of regular military forces has both general and historically particular dimensions; it is the local realization of general techniques. In this sense, national and colonial armies are instances of the same kind of process, rather than the latter being a derivative or imperfect instance of the former, as in narratives of the diffusion of the Western military to the periphery.[12]

That credible regular infantry soldiers can be constituted from diverse populations, in different times and places, speaks to the cosmopolitan character of the army and its disciplinary powers. Thinking about battle, about why soldiers fight, how hard they fight, whether they commit atrocity, and so on, should begin from an anthropological premise: these are general capacities realized in historically specific ways. Regular soldiering and combat are human potentials, not evidence of cultural or national essences, as much writing on armies imagines. Accordingly, the book's second line of inquiry conceives military discipline and the will to combat in terms of rituals, totems, and sacrifices, practices comparable across time and place. It develops a structural account of battle as a force that grabs and transforms participants on both sides, encouraging them to behave in comparable, even similar ways, whatever their national conceits.

These analytic possibilities are difficult to pursue in the traditionally Eurocentric study of Western armies, where soldiers appear as modern citizen-agents who make war and history in distinctive national ways. Battle is seen as a product of the contest of nations, manifesting the contestants' natures. By contrast, an implication of the first two lines of inquiry – co-constitution and anthropology – is that armed forces and war have powers to remake social contexts and their human bearers, even if they do not do so just as they please. Military discipline and battle activate and shape potentials for sacrifice, experienced through the lived categories of time and place. Battle, for soldiers, can generate energies for its own reproduction.

The third line of inquiry – theory – is to think through some of the consequences of the postcolonial perspective for the study of soldiers,

---

[12] See e.g. Ralston, *Importing the European Army*.

including national ones. Soldiers' actions and soldiers' accounts –
reports, testimonies, memoirs – are foundational data for scholarly
debate over the "face of battle" and the nature of military service. They
are key also to efforts, public and private, to find meaning and purpose
in wartime experience. Such accounts often focus on differences with
enemies, as soldiers make sense of their experiences with the cultural
materials they have to hand. An extraordinary racialization marks representations of the Asia-Pacific Wars, in everything from official documents to letters home. This becomes evidence for the role of specific
national racisms in the making of savage battle, or gets caught up in
debates over the relative significance of ideology and national military
doctrine in the commission of atrocity.[13]

For this book, race hate is not the essential property of particular
national groups, such as mid-twentieth century Germans or Japanese,
or the US Marines. Britain's Indian and African colonial soldiers participated fully in intense, no-quarter engagements, as they did in other
barbarous behavior that marked the Asia-Pacific Wars. How do they
prompt us to think differently about racism and battlefield savagery?
Battle played its own role in generating and shaping racial animus
among participants. The experience of combat created a demand for an
accounting, for reasons and motivations to be assigned to the violence.
The categories of nation and race supplied ready meanings to make
sense of battle, to represent and meaningfully construct it. An account
of the relations between the experience of battle and its *ex post facto*
representation is necessary before soldiers' writings can serve as evidence for their motivation.

The notion that soldiers fight and die for a cause is the red thread
of legitimation that ties together state and nation. This is one reason
why infantry and infantry battle lie at the heart of the idea of the
state.[14] Relations between armed forces and society may appear at first
a specialist matter for military sociology. But the connections between
politics and force are fundamental even if neglected questions in
social and political theory.[15] The idea of soldiers' service and sacrifice
underwrites the nation-state as a sovereign territorial package of state,

---

[13] Cameron, *American Samurai*; Dower, *War Without Mercy*; Fritz,
   Frontsoldaten; Hull, *Absolute Destruction*; Rutherford, *Combat and Genocide*.
[14] Hanson, *Western Way of War*; McNeill, *Pursuit of Power*.
[15] Joas and Knöbl, *War in Social Thought*; Keane, *Reflections on Violence*.

army, and society. Colonial soldiers and imperial armies, however, relate differently to state-society-territory, and to the politics that interconnect them. They tell an alternate story about coercion and legitimacy, one where the value of military discipline – of the army in so far as it is the army – is that it can be relatively autonomous from politics, formally speaking. Colonial soldiers did not serve on the basis of national, democratic, or other political legitimation, but on that of the demands and rewards of their vocation. Their bayonets secured the "dominance without hegemony" that was empire.[16] What have been the consequences of allowing the nation, and other collective political identities, to frame and contain our understandings of the passions and energies of military service and battle?

Co-constitution, anthropology, and theory correspond to the three parts of the book. Part I, "Colonial Soldiers," is about army–society relations as historical process, looking first at the making of colonial soldiers out of colonial society in British India, and then at the ways in which the Second World War unmade the old imperial army. Part II, "Going to War," uses the rebuilding of British, Indian, and imperial forces and their employment on the Burma front to think about drill, ritual, and sacrifice in military organization and discipline. It approaches battle as a sphere of unforgiving constraints on agency but one that creates energies for its own reproduction. Part III, "History and Theory," turns to the consequences for inquiry of the interplay between local histories of soldiering and the common demands of military discipline and combat. What are the relations between the experience of battle and its representation in documents, memoirs, letters, and so on? How does the cosmopolitanism of the regular military make us look anew at Western military histories? What are the wider implications for thinking about politics, armed forces, and society?

In much military sociology and history, an unhelpful framework governs thinking about armed forces and society. They are conceived as distinct but isomorphic domains, existing prior to one another, and exercising independent causal force. Scholars take positions on what explains more of the variation in fighting spirit or combat behavior, army *or* society. Is it what happens to people after they join the military, or is it the cultures, identities, and ideologies recruits carry with

[16] Guha, *Dominance without Hegemony*.

them from civilian society into the military?[17] Armed forces and society are conceived as isomorphic in that state, army, and society come in a nation-state package, coeval with sovereign territory, with conjoined but distinct histories over time. The possibility that state, army, and society may vary spatially – that there are international and imperial aspects to the constitution of armed forces – is largely unattended, except in specialist scholarship directly concerned with colonial armies, so-called "private" military companies, and the like.[18]

The British Indian Army was only one, if perhaps the greatest and most long-lived, of the many indigenously recruited forces that secured and expanded the Western colonial order. Almost wherever the Europeans went they raised local forces in regular style, usually officered by a combination of Europeans and native sub-officers. Local soldiers were cheaper than European troops, less prone to disease, and, depending on their training and equipment, roughly as effective in small war campaigns. They were also a source of troops for imperial purposes outside of the democratic and other constraints of metropolitan politics. By the late nineteenth century, France and Britain had large standing colonial forces, which could be expanded for great power war.[19] The British Indian Army numbered half a million in the First World War and two million in the Second.[20] In the latter conflict, it fought from the China coast to Monte Cassino, sending divisions to East and North Africa, the Middle East, and Italy, while carrying the main burden of Britain's war against Japan in Malaya, Burma, and Northeast India.[21]

For colonial rulers, raising troops from among the colonized was a tricky business, one that often defined the rise and fall of empires.

---

[17] The debate marked out by Shils and Janowitz, "Cohesion and Disintegration," and Bartov, *Hitler's Army*, is representative. See also Lynn, *Battle*; *Bayonets of the Republic*; Moskos, *American Enlisted Man*. Despite this paradigmatic debate, sociologists have explored military-society relations in ways which reflect the constitutive approach taken here. See e.g. Boëne, "How 'Unique' should the Military Be?"; Dandeker, *Surveillance, Power, and Modernity*. In practice, many histories narrate complex amalgams of war, armed forces, and society. See e.g. Hull, *Absolute Destruction*; Merridale, *Ivan's War*; Neitzel and Welzer, *Soldaten*; Sherry, *Rise of American Air Power*.

[18] Barkawi, "State and Armed Force in International Context."

[19] For overviews, see Killingray and Omissi, *Guardians of Empire*; Kiernan, *Colonial Empires and Armies*.

[20] Perry, *Commonwealth Armies*, p. 116; Omissi, *Indian Voices*, p. 4.

[21] Roy, *Indian Army in Two World Wars*.

Colonialism was an outside force dependent upon the sword. This situation necessitated curiously explicit arrangements between army and society, between military organization and local culture, and between soldier and polity. Colonial soldiers were not simply mustered from colonial society but rather made through elaborate processes of selection, recruitment, and training, in ways that transformed culture and society. For the Sikhs, one of the principal martial races of the Raj, military service determined who they were as a peasantry and a people.

Colonial power could organize society for military purposes, even modularly rearrange it, but the way in which this was done had consequences, as Chapter 1, "Making Colonial Soldiers," shows. Once the British Indian Army was organized around the idea of the martial races, its myths and stereotypes took on organizational reality for all concerned. Officers had to make the system work and soldiers had to play their parts. The cultural field with which the British organized the army also could be used by disgruntled soldiers and outside activists to organize resistance, or for more mundane purposes of negotiating conditions of service. An upshot is that conventional military sociology's distinction between army and society loses purchase on army–society relations: the two spheres were not separate but constitutively related.

By the time of the Second World War, the ethnic structure of the Indian Army had become too elaborate to be sustained in a major conflict of long duration, much less one fought on two fronts. With its first line formations sent early in the war to fight Italians and Germans in Africa, its war-raised battalions were run over in 1941–42 by the Japanese juggernaut from Hong Kong to Rangoon, via Singapore. From the remnants of this defeated army, the Japanese recruited an anti-British Indian National Army (INA), which, along with the Imperial Japanese Army, threatened India itself. To rise to this challenge, British, Indian, and imperial forces on the Burma front had to be rebuilt as a fighting army under a fighting general, William Slim.[22]

The pressures of operations and defeats and its massive expansion during the war transformed the army. It was forced to commission ever greater numbers of Indians as officers. Recruitment of other ranks reached beyond the favored "martial classes," as they were termed by World War II. In the field, officers bent and then broke the rigid ethnic rules around which the army was organized, in small and large ways.

---

[22] Marston, *Phoenix from the Ashes.*

The right rations, the right type of recruit, the officer knowledgeable in this or that language or religion, were not always available. In unsettling the Raj's reifications, war served as a great denaturalizing force for Indians and British alike.

The cycle of defeat and remaking had put into motion relations between armed forces, society, and war, and this is the subject of Chapter 2, "Unmaking an Imperial Army." Colonial knowledge, the official orientalism so evident in the ethnic structuring of the army, was less relevant to managing the army at war. In large measure, Indian soldiers went out to fight the Japanese led by a combination of emergency-commissioned nationalists (that is, the new Indian officers) and British officers who were new to India and only recently schoolboys. The martial races handbooks were discarded under the demands of campaigning and fighting. Perhaps more surprising, and revealing of battle's brute nature, is that soldiers did not even require much of a common language to fight effectively together.

Colonial soldiers reverse the political logic that governs much scholarly and popular thinking about armed forces. There, political agents – citizens, national subjects – make war. By contrast, war made many Indian soldiers into political agents, especially those who found themselves in Axis captivity. Among other things, the army had taught them to read and then found it necessary to provide them with propaganda. Instead of providing a foundation for military service, the relations between wartime soldiering and politics were fluid and multivalent in colonial context. This is the topic of Chapter 3, "Politics and Prisoners in the Indian Army," the final chapter of Part I.

By 1943, Indian soldiers found their former comrades arrayed against them in the INA. The British had failed even to promise any concrete steps toward independence for India after the war and famine was consuming millions in Bengal, while ethnic and nationalist strife seethed across the Raj. Despite all this, Indian soldiers did go out to fight, increasingly effectively as the war went on. Along with their African and British co-belligerents, they found themselves engaged in an unforgiving infantry war, entangled in Burma's formidable terrain. Combat's exit valve of surrender was shut tight by merciless antagonism, racially expressed. Yet, political modernity's explanatory armory for such battle has little interpretive utility for British imperial forces. No particular racial ideology united Indian and other colonial soldiers; they themselves were brown and black people. Prior to the war, most of them were uneducated peasants, not enfranchised citizens steeped in national traditions and enmities. They served a distant King-Emperor, not a homeland with their own people, and they fought an enemy who promised them liberation from white colonialism. Indian and imperial soldiers did not compile a combat record anything like that of the *Waffen SS* or the US Marines, but their ability to stand up to and then defeat the Japanese army raises questions about the sources of military obedience and fighting spirit. If not some combination of nationalism, ideology, and racism, what sustains soldiers' resolve beyond effective military training and leadership? Setting aside elite forces, and the extremes of variation between mutiny and high *esprit de corps*, what accounts for even a basic level of combat discipline, much less when fighting someone else's war?

It is in response to these questions that Part II, "Going to War," looks at discipline, training, and the fighting in Burma, and at how these operated upon those involved. The army is a machine for group formation. Under the right conditions, battle assists it by generating solidarity and the will to sacrifice among soldiers. Regular military discipline consists of a set of sturdy and robust ritual techniques, many of which double as training, easily adapted to diverse contexts and cultures. These techniques work more or less anywhere, but are always realized locally, articulated with a particular social, cultural, and political character. Soldiers express themselves in a local idiom, but one organizationally transformed by military life. Militarized masculinity and misogyny, for example, can be tailored to fit native custom and still play a key role in bonding together soldiers. Taken together, the ritual dimensions of military life are myriad, pervasive, and profoundly consequential, especially for the instantiation of solidarity, hierarchy, and authority.[23]

A basic presupposition of the debate over combat motivation, across a range of perspectives, is that casualties corrode and ultimately destroy group solidarity and fighting spirit. For Edward Shils and Morris Janowitz, in military sociology's foundational paper, primary groups break down when casualties and other losses are such that the unit can no longer meet the material or psychological needs of its members.[24] In a devastating riposte, Omer Bartov observed that, in conditions of

---

[23] Ben-Ari, *Mastering Soldiers*; King, "The Word of Command"; McNeill, *Keeping Together in Time*.

[24] Shils and Janowitz, "Cohesion and Disintegration," p. 281.

intense fighting and high casualties, primary groups have an alarming tendency to disintegrate. Therefore, how can primary group theory explain fighting spirit in high intensity combat?[25] For Bartov, only fanatical dedication to racial ideology could sustain German soldiers on the Eastern Front in the face of appalling losses and near-certain death. Other scholars debate the percentage of casualties at which a unit's surviving members start to avoid risk, or the effects of casualty and replacement procedures on morale.[26] The underlying assumption is always that casualties are a problem for maintaining combat motivation.

Without denying the ways in which this might be so, this book argues that the combat motivation debate has inverted the primary significance of casualties. They are the very *fuel* of fighting spirit, through logics of group sentiment, collective sacrifice, and blood debt. Casualties call forth energies for reprisal, and intensify group sentiment among surviving members. Military rituals, symbols, and stories evoke and direct these energies, as when regiments celebrate past victories and mourn the long-dead to build solidarity in the present. In battle, and on campaign, these dynamics are more immediate and chaotic but their effects are similar. Spilt blood regenerates the forces binding together the remaining soldiers. Death's revivification of social bonds occurs on *both* sides of battle, creating a self-generating circuit of battlefield violence.

There is, however, a kind of siren call in focusing too much on "fighting spirit"; it suggests the battlefield is a space of agency, which expresses the individual and collective character of soldiers and their units. This is the site of much popular military historical writing. But battlefields are also places of extreme constraint. They thrust tough choices upon combatants. Dynamic exigencies ensnare both sides and govern their behavior. An ethnic array like the Burma front, where even the Japanese formations were full of Korean soldiers, highlights the ways in which soldiers from different countries and contexts started to fight and talk about one another in comparable terms. From distinct backgrounds, in different organizations, soldiers acted in remarkably similar ways when caught in similar situations. Fighting has its own structure.

---

[25] Bartov, *Hitler's Army*, Chapter 2.
[26] See e.g. Bidwell, *Modern Warfare*, pp. 132–133; Creveld, *Fighting Power*.

Part III, "History and Theory," turns to the consequences of the cosmopolitan nature of military discipline for inquiry into soldiers, society, and war. Representations of soldiers' sacrifice, whether produced by veterans or purveyed by states or popular media, invoke the political and national causes for which soldiers are said to fight and die. These causes are read back and seen as the reasons for soldiers' actions. Representations of this kind lend reality to the very political entities said to inspire sacrifice, of which the nation-state is easily the most significant. The image of the world of nation-states is in part sustained by such representations, by the image of soldiers willing to die for national identities, an idea soldiers can take to the front, and write about afterwards.

In writing of their experiences of war, whether in official documents, memoirs, or other genres, soldiers seek to overcome the disintegrative effects of battle and make sense of the transformative powers of military service. They order what has been disordered. In such writing, the grid of concepts that any particular participant, or observer, brings to bear on experience fails them in systematic ways. In letters, *militaria*, and memoirs, soldier-writers express the vital energies of battle through available repertories and tropes, sometimes monstrous and racial. Officers, and scholars, impose meaningful structures which frame and contain the events and dynamics of engagements. But they risk losing track of the sacrificial powers which make fighting possible and of the brute contingencies which determine its outcomes.

In sum, Part I concerns the specific histories of colonial soldiers in India during the Second World War. Part II looks at how the general techniques of military discipline and the demands of fighting impacted upon, and shaped, those histories.[27] Part III shows how the postcolonial approach can generate non-essentialist histories of metropolitan and national armies as well as of colonial ones. Accordingly, the British Army figures more largely in the book's final chapter.

The constitution of armed force has extraordinary political significance. We ordinarily understand it through territorialized polities, such as the territorial state with its monopoly over legitimate force at the center of Western political thought. Much of this book is an effort to

---

[27] Broadly speaking, and adapted to the realm of the political-military from that of the political-economic, Part I deals with what Chakrabarty has termed History 2 and Part II deals with History 1. See Chakrabarty, *Provincializing Europe*, Chapter 2, "Two histories of capital," pp. 47–71.

unhinge the army from collective political identities and their sovereign territories. This is not because armed forces and war do not play important roles in such identities; they obviously do. It is because raising armies, and getting soldiers to fight, is not dependent upon or reducible to political identities. The regular military is a cosmopolitan institution; it can be used anywhere. States have deployed its powers of cultural adaptation to constitute armed forces internationally, from other societies. In bringing into view the cosmopolitan character of the regular military, postcolonial war studies begin to reveal something about the politics of force and the world order projects they have made possible.

PART I

Colonial Soldiers

1 | *Making Colonial Soldiers in British India*

The Sikhs have many religious customs; we see that they keep them whether they like it or not.

– A British officer[1]

The question of why soldiers fight – and of how they are made – easily lends itself to essentialist thinking. Answers typically fall into one of two domains: "army" or "society." Soldiers do it for the regiment or for the country; the unit or the nation; their comrades or their ethnic group. Each of these terms is reified into something which motivates willing sacrifice from soldiers, and accounts for or explains their actions on the battlefield and elsewhere. Military sociology's debate over the role of social context or military organization in combat motivation reflects such an approach.[2] Is it "society" or "army" that makes soldiers?

Even for experts who have most often answered "both," this way of approaching the matter separates into two parts what is in fact a process, the transformation of recruits from some definite social context into soldiers in some historically specific army.[3] Society and army belong to a single analytic field.[4] This chapter emphasizes the *making* of soldiers, with particular attention to ethnic identity and culture. How did political and military leadership construct armed forces out of particular social contexts? How did military practitioners draw on cultural resources to create *esprit de corps* among colonial troops? How

---

[1] Quoted in Cohen, *Let Stephen Speak*, pp. 116–117.

[2] See Introduction, footnote 17.

[3] Many scholars realize that both the military and society play an important role in shaping soldiers' behavior and so study each domain. Survey research, for example, collects data on the civilian and military backgrounds of soldiers, as in Stouffer *et al.*'s groundbreaking *American Soldier*. Such work, however, still conceives military and society as separate and self-contained categories. See e.g. Henderson, *Cohesion*; Moskos, *American Enlisted Man*.

[4] Cf. Cooper and Stoler, "Between Metropole and Colony: Rethinking a Research Agenda" in Cooper and Stoler, *Tensions of Empire*, p. 4.

was imperial control over these troops maintained? What were the consequences of the chosen solutions?

That army and society were interrelated and mutable was evident to the young British subaltern who provides the epigram for this chapter. Sikh soldiers were *made* to be Sikh-like in certain ways, over and over again, in the school that was the army. The British Indian Army incorporated, and also transformed, local cultural resources in the course of giving its Sikh and other martial classes their distinctive characters. The army was imbricated with ethnicity in ways that fostered *esprit de corps*, but which could also be put to use by Indian soldiers to negotiate conditions of service or organize resistance. Rather than "army" or "society," it was society in the army, and army in society, amid dynamic, co-constitutive relations.

In increasingly formalized and explicit ways, ethnicity defined the post-1857 Indian Army. Regular British officers became amateur ethnologists, supposedly tutored in the language and culture of their troops. They turned ethnic precepts into matters of discipline. They invoked ethnicity to build group feeling and to stoke competition between units. For such military purposes it mattered little that the cultural artifacts and practices in question were constructed, even invented, in the course of the colonial encounter between Britain and India.[5]

The reasons why the Indian Army organized itself around the doctrine of the martial races in the latter decades of the nineteenth century had little to do with military excellence, however, but rather with imperial politics. "There is no doubt that whatever danger may threaten us in India," remarked the nineteenth-century soldier and administrator Henry Lawrence, "the greatest is from our own troops."[6] Imperial powers favored strategies of divide and rule within colonial armed forces as well as between them and colonized society. Ethnicity – in British India, caste, region, and religion – was an obvious basis for such a policy.

Some practitioners, like Lawrence, recognized the mutability of culture. It could construct ethnicized boundaries between military formations just as it could between communities, or between those communities and the troops used to police them. But over time, as officers entered and lived out their careers in an army organized around the

---

[5] Cohn, *Colonialism and Its Forms of Knowledge*; Hobsbawm and Ranger, *Invention of Tradition*.

[6] Lawrence, *Essays on the Indian Army*, p. 25.

martial races, many came to believe in the doctrine they had created. Their troops were loyal, distinctive, and fierce, because they were Sikhs, or Dogras, or Gurkhas, or Pathans.[7] While military practice demonstrated cultural fluidity – Sikhs were disciplined into certain customs – many military practitioners, and often the scholars who studied them, thought in essentialist terms.[8] Sikhs behaved in naturally Sikh ways. Social facts were represented as cultural traits, which then served as explanations for the troops' actions.[9]

In the Indian Army, militarized constructs of indigenous culture informed soldiers' identities and constituted part of the disciplinary backdrop against which their actions, obedient and otherwise, took place. An ethnic field of relations was part of the meaningful context of the army, through which soldiers and officers made sense of their experiences, understood their situation, and acted upon it. Army officials mobilized systems of colonial knowledge and memorialized them in recruiting handbooks and other training aids, compiling information on custom, religion, ritual, demographics, and geography for officers of each class of troops.[10] But just how much knowledge, or even language, was attained by British officers? What did the officers, especially those who led the army in combat in World War II, actually know about their Indian soldiers? What did any gap between official texts and lived experience mean for how the army operated?

The discussion below starts with an overview of ethnicity and military organization in post-1857 British India before turning to the disciplinary processes through which the authorities created an ethnically differentiated army. The chapter closes with reflections on the martial races as a colonial military ideology. What were the strengths and weaknesses of these arrangements? Chapter 2 takes up the fate of this army of martial races in the Second World War.

Ethnicity, Army, and Empire

As a strategy for control over a colonial army, *divide et impera* appears deceptively simple. In essays on military reform written before the 1857

---

[7] Mason, *Matter of Honour*, Part XIV, pp. 313–402; Omissi, *Sepoy and the Raj*, Chapter 3, pp. 76–112.

[8] For Lynn, for example, writing of an earlier period, the East India Company's native regiments were "essentially South Asian" and fought for "South Asian values." *Battle*, p. 164.

[9] Cf. Fassin, *Humanitarian Reason*, p. 172.

[10] Roy, *Brown Warriors*, Chapter 3, pp. 120–144.

revolt of the Bengal Army, Lawrence explained why. If troops were recruited from a single ethnic group, imperial power risked dependence on the chosen minority, to whose demands it would be hostage, a praetorian ethnicity. Were recruitment expanded to some delimited set of groups, a further danger loomed: military service would bind together soldiers from different communities, creating an armed bloc, a nation-in-arms, out of what had been mutually suspicious groups in native society.[11]

Lawrence died of wounds during the siege of Lucknow in 1857 after an extensive military and political career in India in which he developed a reputation as a kind of policy intellectual. He had a realist's clarity in matters of imperial power. Many officers and officials lacked critical purchase on the racial and ideological context of empire. The British sense of superiority, and a corresponding account of Indians as backward, warped their understanding. They saw Indians as the culturally and racially determined products of primitive conditions. India was a place where "religion transcended politics" and "society resisted change."[12]

After the rebellion of 1857–58, Britain formally took over the East India Company's sovereign responsibilities and reorganized the army. Colonial officials increasingly conceived Indian society in ethnographic and communal terms, inherently divided by caste, region, and religion. "Communalism" meant religious bigotry of a fundamentally irrational character.[13] In official terms, the British conceived the mutiny and rebellion as having resulted from Western efforts to reform native society. Missionary efforts to convert Indians, a general lack of understanding of Indian custom and religion, and too much modernization too quickly for a non-Western people had caused the trouble.

This view was evident in Queen Victoria's proclamation assuming the government of the Raj: "We disclaim alike the Right and the Desire to impose our Convictions on any of Our Subjects . . . and We do strictly charge and enjoin all those who may be in authority under Us, that they abstain from all interference with the Religious Belief or Worship of any of Our Subjects, on pain of Our highest Displeasure."[14] Understanding anti-colonial unrest in this way drained it of political and economic meaning by placing it under the sign of

[11] Lawrence, *Essays on the Indian Army.*   [12] Dirks, *Castes of Mind*, p. 60.
[13] Pandey, *Construction of Communalism*, p. 10.
[14] Godfrey, *Copies*, p. 2.

culture, the unreasonable reactions of natives to a well-intended civilizing mission. Effective colonial rule was conceived as requiring adequate ethnographic knowledge of indigenous society along with careful handling.[15] Consequently, the latter part of the nineteenth century was the heyday of colonial anthropology in India. Through study of Indian populations, the government created official ethnic identities.[16]

By the late nineteenth century, officials had organized the army along communal lines, in accordance with a theory of the "martial races."[17] This held that among oriental peoples only select "warlike" groups had martial qualities. In South Asia, these were found in north India and Nepal, while the South was populated with "effeminate races."[18] Official versions of Indian communal identities defined which groups could be recruited and receive the benefits of military service. Martial identities became bound up with colonial governance and economy, and played their own role in shaping culture and society. These official identities interacted with and shaped the communities from which soldiers were recruited. Communalism was a central facet of life in the Indian Army. But it was a communalism produced through colonial power/knowledge and its interaction with Indian society, *not* communalism as a set of truths about how Indian society and Indians really were in themselves, as "endemic, inborn" qualities of Indians.[19]

What Henry Lawrence had understood, unlike many of his fellow officers before and after, was that ethnicity was malleable. As he put it, "A cap, a beard, a moustache, a strap, all in their time, have given offence – *all on pretence of religion*. But by a little management, by leading instead of drawing, almost anything may be done. The man who would not touch leather a few years ago, is now in the words of a fine old subedar, 'up to his chin in it.'"[20] Lawrence conceived of ethnicity as a realm that could be variably managed because in his lifetime

---

[15] Hevia, *Imperial Security State*, Chapter 6, pp. 107–151.

[16] Dirks, *Castes of Mind*.

[17] MacMunn, *Martial Races of India*; Mason, *Matter of Honour*, Chapter XIV, pp. 341–361; Omissi, *Sepoy and the Raj*, Chapter 1, pp. 1–46; Roy, *Brown Warriors*, Chapter 3, pp. 120–144. For an example of a recruiting handbook, see Betham, *Handbooks for the Indian Army: Marathas and Dekhani Musalmans*.

[18] Lord Roberts, quoted in Mason, *Matter of Honour*, p. 347.

[19] Pandey, *Construction of Communalism*, p. 10.

[20] Lawrence, *Essays on the Indian Army*, pp. 206–207. The subedar spoke literally. The collar of the uniform coat to which he was referring had leather stocks to keep it stiff.

East India Company forces had used different models for the military organization of ethnicity, particularly in respect of the differing attitudes toward caste of the Bombay and Bengal armies.[21] While more or less equally effective in military terms relative to their size, these armies differed in their consequences for imperial control, most disastrously so in 1857 when much of the Bengal Army mutinied. Both armies had recruited heavily from the second and third sons of a gentry being squeezed politically, economically, and culturally by Company rule.[22] But the Bengal Army allowed high caste Muslim and Hindu soldiers to negotiate disciplinary and living arrangements on the basis of their caste status. They were allowed space within the army to counter-organize and maintain social cohesion. As the army was recruited from those in native society sharing common grievances against the Company, this proved a volatile mix. By contrast, the Bombay Army, which ignored caste in discipline and living arrangements, did not mutiny. As one Indian soldier who served in both armies commented, "In Hindustan it is pride of caste, in Bombay pride of regiment."[23] What was at issue was not ethnicity *per se*, but its military organization in a given political and social context. How armies drew upon culture proved consequential for imperial rule.

As its classically educated officials were aware, Company military experience in India had ancient antecedents.[24] When the Roman imperial army began to rely heavily on "barbarian" recruits in the second century, it encountered similar problems in the control and organization of foreign legions, and it tried similar organizational expedients to maintain loyalty and fighting spirit.[25] One was to organize the cohorts, or sub-units, of a legion by ethnicity. Each was based on a single conquered tribe, controlled by an overlay of Roman centurions and officers. Soldiers retained a degree of *esprit de corps* serving under their own totems. At the same time, from an imperial perspective, different

[21] Barat, *Bengal Native Infantry*; Cadell, *Bombay Army*.
[22] Stokes, *Peasant Armed*.
[23] Quoted in Cadell, *History of the Bombay Army*, p. 161.
[24] When questioned by the Peel Commission on the post-Mutiny reorganization of British Indian forces, Lord Elphinstone, who had served as Governor of Madras and of Bombay, argued against "mixing" Indian recruits of diverse backgrounds together. "*Divide et impera* was the old Roman motto," he said, "and it should be ours." Quoted in Omissi, *Sepoy and the Raj*, p. 9.
[25] Delbrück, *Barbarian Invasions*, Chapter VIII, pp. 161–200; Southern and Dixon, *Late Roman Army*.

cohorts, each with different identities and histories, seemed unlikely to combine to mount a challenge to the Romans. The instrument of divide and rule – the army – was itself divided and ruled. Following this approach, Lawrence emphasized: it was necessary to "oppose class against class and tribe against tribe" within the army.[26] By doing so, the army could avoid mixing different indigenous soldiers together, creating a combined bloc in the imperial army, while at the same time avoiding reliance on any single ethnic group.

In India, there were two basic strategies for realizing Lawrence's advice. One was to organize major units around single classes, such as a Sikh regiment that would only recruit Sikhs for its battalions, a Rajput regiment that would only recruit Rajputs, and so on. This was Lawrence's preference, the idea being that it was unlikely every ethnicity would become hostile all at once; there would always be a plurality to put down a rebellion.[27] The second way was to divide units internally by class, so that no entire unit would mutiny as each class checked the others. A third option was to pursue each strategy in different regional army commands, as the "balanced recruitment school" argued.[28] Ultimately, the army chose the second option. By the time of the world wars, other than in the Gurkhas, most infantry battalions were organized on a "class-company" basis. In a battalion of around 800 soldiers, each company was composed of a different class, for example, a Sikh company, a Dogra company, a Pathan company, *etc.*

For Lawrence, relying on minority populations for military service had to do with power political considerations rather than racial theories about the Orient.[29] But under the stable and long-lived Raj, later officers and officials lacked Lawrence's experience of different British Indian military systems. They *did* perceive ethnic and racial limits to

---

[26] Lawrence, *Essays on the Indian Army*, p. 229.
[27] Lawrence, *Essays on the Indian Army*. He wanted to add some senior NCOs and VCOs from another class, as a check on the troops and source of information for the British officers.
[28] Roy, *Brown Warriors*, Chapter 1, pp. 35–79.
[29] In an essay written in 1843 that forecasted the events of 1857, Lawrence reminded his fellow officers and officials that Indian soldiers were equally human: "We forget that our army is composed of men like ourselves, quick-sighted and inquisitive on all matters bearing upon their personal interests; who, if they can appreciate our points of superiority, are just as capable of detecting our deficiencies." Harlow and Carter, *Archives of Empire*, p. 413.

military recruitment and discipline, and these were codified in the theory of the martial races which came to dominate (in principle if not always in practice) Indian Army organization. Military recruitment was limited to those populations authoritatively identified as martial.

Making an Army of Martial Races

Before the Indian Army could be divided and ruled, its various official component ethnicities had to be codified, its soldiers organized into the correct categories, bounded off from one another by unit and uniform, regulated by official interpretations of religious practice, diet, holidays, and so on. Caste, religious, regional, and other ethnic relations enabled officials to disaggregate Indian populations into "convenient stereotypes."[30] The British crystallized particular versions of Indian identities and enacted them in Indian populations through governance and discipline. Derived variously from readings of Indian history, religious texts, colonial anthropology and sociology, and other "investigative modalities," officials used these identities to order populations in politics, the economy, and in the army.[31] In turn, Indians pursued projects and interests through their own – as well as official – versions of their identities and tales of right.

The Sikhs are a paradigmatic case.[32] As anthropologist Richard Fox wrote, "The British Indian army nurtured an orthodox, separatist, and martial Singh identity."[33] Sikhism is a syncretic religion that developed out of Hindu and Muslim theology and worship in fifteenth-century north India. In Sikh scripture there were ten Sikh Gurus, the last of which, Gobind Singh, gave Sikhism a militant cast in the face of Mughal persecution in the late seventeenth century. In Singh's Khalsa, or brotherhood of the pure, all were to take Singh as their surname, which means lion, and follow rules of comportment and appearance. Over the next century, Punjabi peasants made use of the Khalsa ideal to shape a distinctive martial culture.[34] Khalsa fighters provided the military basis for the rise of Sikh power in the Punjab as the Mughals

---

[30] Arnold, "Bureaucratic Recruitment," p. 7.

[31] Cohn, *Colonialism and Its Forms of Knowledge*, p. 5.

[32] Cohn, *Colonialism and Its Forms of Knowledge*, pp. 107–111; Dirks, *Castes of Mind*, pp. 177–180; Fox, *Lions of the Punjab*; Tan, *The Garrison State*, Chapter 2, pp. 70–97.

[33] Fox, *Lions of the Punjab*, p. 10.   [34] Dhavan, *Sparrows Became Hawks*.

declined. This culminated in the powerful Sikh state established by Ranajit Singh and annexed in 1849 by the British after two wars.

Like the Romans, the East India Company recruited among those they conquered. The Sikhs had fielded a powerful and well-trained army that impressed the British. Recruitment expanded rapidly during and after the 1857 revolt. By 1911, Sikhs accounted for 1 percent of the Indian population but 20 percent of the army. For the British, the true Sikhs were the Jat Sikhs who they equated with the Khalsa, which in turn was equated with Sikhism. Recruiting handbooks advised officers to recruit Sikhs only among the "tribes" which had "converted" at the time of Gobind Singh: "those tribes who, though they now supply converts to Sikhism, did not do so then, cannot be considered... as true Sikhs."[35] Identifying these "true Sikhs" was no easy matter because Sikhism was a variable amalgamation of Sikh and Hindu practices, something one recruiting handbook acknowledged by noting that "the line between the strictest Singh and a Hindu is but vague."[36] In his 1933 primer on the martial races for young officers and the public, Lieutenant-General George MacMunn told the story of the Sikhs "from the beginning" based on the premise that they are a "martial people."[37] This reconstruction of the Sikhs as essentially martial enabled MacMunn to claim that, in restricting recruitment to true Sikhs and disciplining them accordingly, it was "the British officer who has kept Sikhism up to its old standard."[38]

A turban had not been one of the original items of dress in Gobind Singh's rules of comportment, and early representations of Sikhs show at least two different styles of headdress.[39] But by the late nineteenth century, along with a beard, the distinctive "Sikh" turban had become an emblematic mark of Sikhs who served in the army, and of Sikhs generally. (See Figure 1.1) Army uniform regulations specified a turban for the Sikhs distinct from the one worn by Punjabi Muslims or by Dogras. In the troubles that gripped Sikh units early in the Second World War, the turban became a rallying point for resistance as Sikh soldiers refused to exchange it for steel helmets.[40]

---

[35] Falcon, *Handbook on Sikhs*, p. 65; quoted in Tan, *Garrison State*, p. 72.
[36] Falcon, *Handbook on Sikhs*, p. 16; quoted in Fox, *Lions of the Punjab*, p. 110.
[37] MacMunn, *Martial Races of India*, p. 118.
[38] MacMunn, *Armies of India*, p. 135; quoted in Dirks, *Castes of Mind*, p. 177.
[39] Cohn, *Colonialism and Its Forms of Knowledge*, p. 108.
[40] See below, Chapter 2, pp. 61–62.

Figure 1.1 Retired Sikh VCOs at a recruiting festival in 1944.[41]

The martial Sikh identity the British had done so much to foster was mobilized by the Akali movement among rural Punjabi Sikhs between 1920 and 1925, one of the largest and longest mass protests against colonial rule in the history of the Raj.[42] In the name of a true Sikhism, the Akalis rose up against government-appointed temple officials suspected of syncretism and corruption. Former soldiers played a major role in the movement, and its styles of protest borrowed heavily from the military, with marchers organized in ranks and files, walking to the beat of a military cadence and wearing unofficial uniforms.[43] The cultural field shaped by British rule could be turned against the Raj, while cultural and organizational forms fostered in the army played roles outside it.

In establishing and maintaining the boundaries between classes, the army made use of a range of ethnic instruments, including diet, language, uniform, comportment, and religion. (See Figure 1.2) The

[41] IND 3192, IWM.
[42] Fox, *Lions of the Punjab*, Chapter 5, pp. 79–104; Tan, *Garrison State*, Chapter 5, pp. 187–239.
[43] Fox, *Lions of the Punjab*, pp. 82–87, 95–99.

Figure 1.2 Different turbans: Lord Wavell with two Indian Army soldiers awarded the Victoria Cross in 1944. On the left is a Sikh, Naik (Corporal) Nand Singh, and on the right, a Gujar, Sepoy Kamal Ram.[44]

stereotypes of the martial races were realized through disciplinary power, shaping "recruits in the manner of self-fulfilling prophecy."[45] Sikhs who trimmed their hair or beards, for example, risked discharge from the army.[46] For many Sikh Viceroy Commissioned Officers (VCOs), the five visible signs of faith – hair, white underpants, the bangle, steel dagger, and comb – were important attributes of being a disciplined soldier.[47] A wartime British officer wrote home of his experiences training Sikh troops, "The Sikhs have many religious customs; we see that they keep them whether they like it or not." When queried on whether the troops must wear their silver bangles, his battalion commander had insisted "[o]f course they must wear it, it's part of their religion."[48]

[44] IND3972, IWM.   [45] Fay, *Forgotten Army*, p. 21.
[46] Trench, *Indian Army*, p. 11.
[47] Maj. Gen. Sir John Smyth, Mss. Eur. T 63, OIOC.
[48] Quoted in Cohen, *Let Stephen Speak*, pp. 116–117.

What would be lettered companies in a US or British infantry battalion – "A" company, "B" company – in the Indian Army were designated by class: the Sikh company, the Pathan company. Companies were distinct both as an ethnic class and as a military formation. Each class had its own vernacular language, its own mess, and its own quarters. Commissioned officers, usually just two to a company, often strongly identified with the class they commanded, to the point of changing their own diet and appearance. The most junior VCOs – *jemadars* – commanded platoons, and ordinarily came from the same class as those they commanded. The next most senior VCO – *subedars* – served alongside the company commander, equivalent in many respects to a company sergeant major in Commonwealth forces or a first sergeant in the US Army. He too was ordinarily of the same class as his soldiers. Non-commissioned officers could look forward to promotion to VCO in their own class companies, while the best soldiers would be promoted to NCO ranks over their peers, a "stove piped" arrangement that assured that each class grew its own junior leaders. Each company in the class-company battalions became a class-world unto itself until disrupted by the vagaries of war.

The VCOs were an intermediary class of officers between the commissioned officers and the NCOs and soldiers. They combined the function of junior officers with those of senior NCOs in Western armies. Collectively, they comprised a parallel "native" command structure, from the *jemadars* commanding platoons all the way up to the *subedar*-major of the battalion, who advised the battalion commander. Customarily, there were only two British or Indian commissioned officers per company, including the commander. The VCOs took care of most matters of discipline and handled or assisted direct interaction with the soldiers, including the troops' living and feeding arrangements. Minor infractions of discipline and interpersonal dynamics among the soldiers might never come to the attention of the commissioned officers.

Classes were defined in terms of caste, region, and religion. But culture and religion did not seamlessly map on to military formations and sub-formations, even in peacetime. Companies in the same battalion often had cross-cutting affiliations. There might have been two or more Hindu or Muslim companies in a battalion, for example. These would join together for religious services provided by the appropriate

Figure 1.3 The meal: Indian soldiers ate with others of their "class." Here, Pathan trainees take their lunch together somewhere in Northwest Frontier province, 1942.[49]

battalion religious official, a Hindu guru or a Muslim *maulvi*. VCOs, like commissioned officers, maintained separate messes from the other ranks. In many battalions these were sub-divided by religion, one for Hindus and Sikhs, and one for Muslims.

In the VCO and company messes, meals were regulated by military versions of religiously authorized practices in respect of diet and food preparation. The Indian Army "nourished the caste and religious differences of the men it did admit by paying careful attention to who ate what with whom."[50] Eating together is one of the primary ways of establishing and fortifying social bonds. The messes reinforced the boundaries between those who shared the meals and those who did not.[51] (See Figure 1.3) Religion intertwined with discipline in other ways too. If a Sikh soldier committed a minor infraction, especially one involving an issue of moral character, he could be reported to the battalion's granthi (Sikh religious official) for punishment, which might involve washing the men's feet before they entered the gurdwara

[49] IND 1328, IWM.   [50] Fay, *Forgotten Army*, p. 224.
[51] Lincoln, *Construction of Society*, Chapter 5, pp. 75–88.

Figure 1.4 Religion and discipline 1: Muslim soldiers pray with their *maulvi* toward the end of Ramadan, 1944.[52]

(the Sikh place of worship) for a week.[53] A Muslim soldier discovered sipping water in daylight during Ramadan could find himself hauled up before the company commander and given five days of "rigorous imprisonment."[54] In death, soldiers received the correct last rites for their religion. Military discipline became a religious matter. (See Figures 1.4 and 1.5)

This edifice of difference operated upon its denizens regardless of the character of their beliefs and self-identification. In the fighting formations, all soldiers were classed and existed within a class structure. Whatever their own practices in terms of diet and food preparation, they had to conform to what was expected of their class generally, and in respect of the particularities of any given regiment or battalion. In the official view, Indian soldiers were reduced to essential ethnic types, with inbuilt prejudices and other characteristics. As one Indian officer put it, "the old Indian Army was always meticulous in preserving

[52] IND 2677, IWM.   [53] Peter Gadsdon, interview by the author.
[54] Peter Francis and Tony Banks, interview by the author. "Rigorous imprisonment" was detention with hard labor, a standard form of punishment.

Figure 1.5 Religion and discipline 2: Hindu soldiers at prayers.[55]

orthodoxies and taboos. British officers never in any way tried to emancipate the men from their religious inhibitions."[56]

What was of particular significance was not the degree of ethnographic accuracy in the various classifications of the martial races. What mattered were the consequences for people defined by the authorities as belonging to one group or another, and the social, economic, political, and cultural processes set in train by ethnic governance. As cultural stereotypes, the martial races had a variable basis in indigenous ethnic relations but did not overlap entirely with lived experience. Disciplinary processes created soldiers who apparently embodied these stereotypes. Ethnic military organization also fostered various strategic behaviors. Recruits sought to live up to their expected roles to get into the army and to earn favor or promotion once there.

Martial races discourse often seemed self-evidently true to many British officers because they could see with their own eyes an army organized in its image, a panoply of ethnic soldiers. The army inculcated young officers in the martial races. They came to govern the military class system in accordance with the class prejudices of the

[55] IND2283, IWM.
[56] A.A. Rudra, quoted in Palit, *Major General A.A. Rudra*, p. 262.

regiments they joined. Among regulars and wartime officers these crude stereotypes generally reflected the British colonial view that India was composed of sharply distinct and mutually suspicious caste and religious groups. Eric Stokes, later a Cambridge historian of colonial India, had been in the country less than a year as an officer cadet and subaltern of Indian Mountain Artillery when he wrote home to his sister that his regiment took only "the pick of Indian troops," in this case Sikhs and Punjabi Muslims. "The former are definitely more clever, but the Punjabis are easily the most lovable."[57] The clever, scheming Sikh was a stock martial races trope. Serving later with Ahirs, a class recruited in wartime and not normally considered martial, Stokes describes them as "not soldiers by instinct." Indian soldiers were viewed as dependent and childlike: "There is probably no finer training in responsibility than to command Indian troops, because like a teacher at school, they look to you so utterly for their welfare and happiness."[58] New to India, Stokes had rapidly acquired a working familiarity with the martial races and colonial discourse, making sense of his experiences through them.

Stuck in a reinforcement camp, awaiting deployment to Burma, Stokes was given various responsibilities over soldiers waiting for their assignments. In one affair, a Muslim *havildar* (sergeant), charged with maintaining sanitary standards in the camp's kitchens, inspected a cookhouse used by Gurkhas, who were Hindus. In an infantry unit, officers normally left food preparation to the soldiers of each class to avoid conflicts. The sanitary *havildar* apparently tried to touch some of the Gurkhas' food, creating a ruckus. There was sufficient commotion to call for the officer, Stokes. What was at stake for the soldiers involved? Was it religious feeling over a kitchen now polluted and in need of ritual purification? Was the *havildar* overly officious and insistent on carrying out his duties to the letter? Did combat troops not appreciate being given the once-over by a martinet in charge of sanitation? Whatever the case, there is no ambiguity in Stokes' conclusion: "The old religious trouble flared up in the section today ... To a Gurkha, who is a strong Hindu, a Moslem is almost the devil himself."[59] For the young officer, it was a matter of religious bigotry among natives.

[57] Eric Stokes to Jessie Muirhead, 1 January, 1945, CSAS.
[58] Eric Stokes to Jessie Muirhead, 8 February, 1946, CSAS.
[59] Eric Stokes to Jessie Muirhead, 8 May, 1945, CSAS.

Historian Christopher Bayly, who studied under Stokes, thought that Stokes' experiences in India had convinced him that "castes and religions" were "concrete and sharply defined social units," an idea that informed Stokes' scholarship until he encountered Edmund Leach and Stanley Tambiah in the 1970s.[60] Bayly commented that "much of his later work was directed to modifying and refining his original bald view that whole regional castes were the basic units of analysis."[61] This is testament to the Indian Army's powers of constructing and naturalizing different ethnic groups. In the army, the classes literally took form as distinct units. Ethnicity was a primary context for everyday interaction between soldiers and a constitutive medium for expression of the frustrations of military life. A Jat military policeman scolded a Pathan subedar whose jeep had failed to stop due to faulty brakes. The subedar shouted back, "[d]on't talk to me like that! I am a Pathan, and you are only a Jat."[62]

Language and Empire in the Indian Army

For Tzvetan Todorov's Spanish conquistadors, language was a mechanism of empire. Mastery of communication was the key to dominance.[63] The linguistic order of the Indian Army certainly helped to cement difference among Indian soldiers and between them and their British officers. But mastery was another matter. This order consisted of English for the officers, Hindustani/Urdu as the common language of command, and the native languages of each class of troops. The British had invented Hindustani as a language by codifying dialects spoken in the late Moghul Court and the Delhi Bazaar in the eighteenth century.[64] The language could be declared Hindustani or Urdu depending on whom it was spoken to, and could be written in Roman or Arabic script. Given the large numbers of Muslim soldiers in the Indian Army and the historic association of Urdu as an army or camp language, the army generally referred to Hindustani as Urdu.

Upon commissioning into the Indian Army, British officers began a regime of language instruction and examination in Hindustani,

---

[60] Bayly, "Eric Thomas Stokes," p. 471.
[61] Bayly, "Eric Stokes and the Uprising of 1857," p. 206.
[62] Brett-James, *Report My Signals*, p. 161.
[63] Todorov, *Conquest of America*, pp. 123, 221.
[64] Cohn, *Colonialism and Its Forms of Knowledge*, pp. 33–36.

initially assisted by a private tutor, or *munshi*. In practice, for regulars
as for wartime officers, they generally achieved more or less indifferent
Hindustani only. "[B]ad British Hindustani" could be heard throughout the empire.[65] "I mean the British speaking Hindustani was always
rather a joke" commented one interwar Indian officer.[66] Another officer complained in a service journal that only a "very low standard"
was necessary to get past the compulsory language examinations.[67]
Ralph Russell, a wartime officer who later became a leading scholar of
Urdu, commented of his initial encounter with Indian Army language
instruction: "I was really keen to learn [Urdu] well but within a cou-
ple of weeks I had reluctantly given up because the officer instructing
us didn't seem to know the language – especially the pronunciation –
well, and I knew that I should find it very difficult to unlearn incor-
rect pronunciation."[68] Of his fellow British officer-students, Russell
noted that most of them were "unenthusiastic" about learning Urdu
and "didn't see why they should waste time and effort on this inferior
language."[69]

British officers were also supposed to learn the native language of
the martial class they commanded. Here they were even less successful than with Hindustani. Knowledge of native languages was rare in
the officer corps, and wartime emergency commissioned officers likely
"got to learn a few words" only.[70] A wartime officer commanding a
Pathan company started to learn Pashto "but soon gave it up, from a
lazy disinclination for effort" and because he could get by with Urdu.[71]
By contrast, the VCOs were empowered by the army's linguistic order.

---

[65] Slim, *Unofficial History*, p. 40.
[66] Interview with Rashid Ali Baig and his wife Tara, p. 34, Mss. Eur. T 77–78,
    OIOC.
[67] Nimis, "What shall we Talk?" p. 356. This pseudonymous author writing in
    the Journal of the United Service Institution of India goes on to suggest that
    Esperanto should be considered as a *lingua franca* for the Indian Army.
[68] Russell, *Findings, Keepings*, p. 195.
[69] Ibid., p. 205. Later a VCO in his unit, with whom he had become friendly,
    expressed amazement to Russell that excepting Russell "none of the British
    officers after nine or ten months in India had so much as bothered to learn
    that easily acquired minimum of Urdu without which they could neither
    understand their NCOs and men nor be understood by them." Ibid., p. 259.
[70] As one such officer who commanded Pathans said of his competency in
    Pashto. J.R. Wallis, interview by the author. Other British officers interviewed
    referred to their troops' language as a "country language" or vernacular that
    they did not understand. Clifford Martin, George Coppen, Peter Francis, and
    Tony Banks, interviews by the author.
[71] Close, *Pathan Company*, p. 12.

They had command of Hindustani, and were native speakers of the language of the martial class or sub-class through whose ranks they rose. Moreover, the army had been formally teaching them English since the 1920s, in addition to whatever they picked up along the way. While some commissioned officers would achieve this degree of linguistic mastery, the VCOs were most often the only figures who could communicate with everyone in the battalion, from the private soldiers to the lieutenant colonel. The soldiers also had to learn Urdu as spoken in the army, although some would already be familiar with it. In many cases, the vocabulary of recruits and short-service soldiers consisted primarily of the words of command. As the "lazy" Pathan company commander remarked, "Thus it was that throughout our time together we spoke in what was, on both sides, a foreign tongue."[72]

The idea was that, at least for regular officers, language competence would improve through their careers, depending on dedication and ability. Initially, officers had to cope as best they could on the lower standard they mastered in their immediate post-commissioning training. One ritual for company officers involved being presented with soldiers who had committed disciplinary violations and had to have their cases adjudicated by a commissioned officer. These exchanges occurred in Hindustani (or in Gurkhali for Gurkha regiments). In the 1920s, while commanding a company of the 6th Gurkha Rifles, then-Major William Slim described the experience as akin to an Englishman being tried by a Chinese who spoke only Chinese and a little French: "that's what it amounts to."[73] Everyone was working in a second language. Officers and troops remained as mysterious to one another as Chinese to Europeans, in Slim's orientalist idiom for estrangement and mutual incomprehension. "I'm rather stuck on the language question," he went on, "[i]t makes me much hotter than taking violent exercise, this trying to understand what they say."[74] He worried about the implications for discipline and leadership.

The wartime officer Peter Francis recalled doing interviews with soldiers who had just joined his battalion and knew only the Urdu they learned during recruit training. With the VCO hovering nearby,

---

[72] Ibid.
[73] Field Marshal Sir William Slim, 1/2, Letters to P. Pratt, 26/6/1920, CCA. In addition to their own *lingua franca*, Gurkhali, Gurkha officers and VCOs had also to learn Hindustani to enable them to operate with other Indian army battalions.
[74] Field Marshal Sir William Slim, 1/2, Letters to P. Pratt, 26/6/1920, CCA.

Francis asked a few questions to one such group When no reply was forthcoming, the VCO said forcefully to the soldiers, "Don't you understand what you're being asked? Haven't you learned your Urdu properly? The sahib is speaking perfectly clearly, why don't you answer him?" Another officer, who had passed Urdu exams up to interpreter grade, gave a lecture on chemical warfare to a group of Indian soldiers: "I'm certain they didn't understand a word."[75] Sydney Bolt reports being taken by some Indian friends to hear a comedian send up "Bad British Hindustani." "Even I could enjoy the mimicry of anglicized mis-pronunciation. It was as funny as Peter Sellers doing the same thing in reverse, but I missed the resulting double entendres."[76] One British offi-cer advised his colleagues that they would be better understood if they spoke English with an Urdu accent than if they spoke Urdu with an English accent. "If you must speak Urdu with an English accent, use any dialect or brogue, but never the 'Oxford accent.'"[77]

Moments such as these inspired anxiety for fledgling soldiers and officers alike. One regular officer in the interwar period, H.E.M. Cot-ton, in the Madras Sappers and Miners, tells of being left alone with his company at the beginning of his career and having to give a training lecture to the NCOs in Urdu. He wrote it out in English and asked his *munshi* to translate it into Romanized Urdu. He then read this out to the assembled NCOs, using English pronunciation for the Roman char-acters. The NCOs duly nodded their heads in understanding but Cot-ton "wondered in fact how much they did understand."[78] Bolt com-ments that "In the eyes of most *sahibs* it was undignified to contort the mouth in an effort to observe phonetic distinctions that English had no use for."[79] Cotton reports that only a few British officers who served in the regiment's units for many years without detached postings learned Tamil. He knew of three.[80]

In the headquarters of his Chindit brigade in Burma during the war, Michael Calvert faced even greater linguistic complexity, at one point working with seven different "races," British, Indian, Burmese, Karen,

[75] J.R. Wallis, interview by the author.   [76] Bolt, *Pseudo Sahib*, pp. 225–226.
[77] Col. F.L. Brayne, "Teaching of Urdu," p. 355.
[78] Col. H.E.M. Cotton, British in India Oral Archive Transcript, p. 8, Mss. Eur. T90/1, OIOC.
[79] Bolt, *Pseudo Sahib*, p. 226.
[80] Col. H.E.M. Cotton, British in India Oral Archive Transcript, pp. 8–9, Mss. Eur. T90/1, OIOC.

Chinese, West African, and Gurkha. "I now know why cosmopolitan races gesticulate," he comments after describing a situation in which he gave orders for a troop movement by charades: "...'to that lone tree on the hill,' and I would look forlorn and lonely – 'There is your objective!' and I would make motions to dig in madly."[81] In Calvert's brigade, which distinguished itself at high cost in casualties in the second Chindit operation, there was a Hong Kong Volunteer platoon composed of British, Anglo-Chinese, and Portuguese-Chinese. Other Chinese units under his command had some Filipinos as well as Chinese and European-Chinese soldiers.

Despite linguistic incomprehension, the army functioned. Surprisingly, fluency was not necessary for effective infantry operations of the kind conducted in Burma. One reason why is found in Calvert's charades. Although infantry combat by the Second World War was a complex art, potentially involving many different weapons systems, the basic tasks which any given group of soldiers had to perform were few in number and inculcated by training. Officers provided the intellectual oversight necessary for operations. Orders to cover a given arc, to patrol an area, to hold fire until a certain event, and so on, were relatively simple to communicate. Calvert noted that "every soldier in the British Empire understands the same words of command."[82] The Roman imperial army had proceeded similarly, with Latin as the language of command alongside native vernaculars spoken in the ranks of its non-Romanized soldiers.[83] In the Korean War, the US Army decided that a vocabulary of around one hundred words was sufficient to allow US and South Korean soldiers to serve together at the platoon level.[84]

Of course, for military and disciplinary purposes, as well as for reasons of imperial control, it was better that the officers spoke the languages of their troops. As Slim put it: "It is difficult to know what a man really feels or thinks unless you speak his language," and also, "Knowledge of his language is the closest and strongest link in the bonds between officer and sepoy."[85] Slim learned Gurkhali and Urdu

---

[81] Calvert, *Prisoners of Hope*, p. 41.   [82] Ibid.

[83] Delbrück, *Barbarian Invasions*, p. 163. Writing around the time of the First World War, Delbrück goes on to make the comparison himself: "The present-day English army in India offers analogies to these Roman auxiliaries." Delbrück, *Barbarian Invasions*, p. 163.

[84] Sheehan, *Bright Shining Lie*, p. 555.

[85] Field Marshal Sir William Slim, Editorial, *The Journal of the United Service Institution of India*, Vol. LXII (July 1932), No. 268, pp. 291–292, 4/2, CCA.

in the interwar period, which served him well as a general in his many impromptu visits and talks with the troops in Burma. He expressed concern about the standard of language proficiency among the regular officer corps between the wars, complaining in 1932 that officers were learning only Urdu, not the vernaculars of their troops. How could officers understand the sources of discipline and indiscipline if they could not understand their soldiers?

Slim also pointed to a disciplinary dimension of language beyond comprehension. The effort to learn was in itself a compliment that the Indian soldier deeply appreciated, "evidence of a real effort to understand him, a real desire to learn about his customs and beliefs."[86] As another officer remarked, "Nothing delights the Pathan soldier more than being addressed in his own tongue."[87] Since the army was in fact functioning despite its linguistic limitations, Slim suggested how affective bonds might have been as significant as the detailed communication made possible by linguistic comprehension. On one occasion during the war, Slim spoke to two different battalions in succession, the first of which was a Gurkha unit, which he addressed in Gurkhali. After starting out in Urdu for the second unit, a class-company battalion, he lapsed back into Gurkhali, which those soldiers would not have understood. "The main thing is he is here," commented one of the officers in this second unit, "[n]o one is terribly pushed what language he uses!"[88] Authority humanizes itself by showing concern for, and interest in, those under its sway. Officers use bonds forged at the level of sentiment to get more out of the soldiers.

[86] Ibid.   [87] Close, *Pathan Company*, p. 12.
[88] Quoted in Khan, *Memoirs*, p. 44. Slim tells the story this way: "I remember one day I spoke to a Gurkha battalion, drove a mile or so, and addressed an Indian one. My talk in substance was the same to both of them. When I had finished what I thought was a particularly eloquent Urdu harangue to the Indians, I turned to my A.D.C. and said with some pride, 'That was a pretty good effort, wasn't it?' 'Quite, sir' he replied crushingly, 'but I suppose you know that after the first two sentences you relapsed entirely into Gurkhali!'" Notable in this anecdote is that the Indian soldiers did not let on even inadvertently that their general was speaking to them in a language they could not understand, so much so that Slim had believed he had done a good job when in fact he had been speaking the wrong language. Slim comments: "it was only the innate good manners of the Indian soldier that on many an occasion prevented laughter at some gaffe I made." Indian soldiers were practiced at pretending they understood what their British officers said to them. Slim, *Defeat into Victory*, pp. 185–186.

As will be seen in Chapter 6, few got as much out of the soldiers as the wartime officer George Coppen, who commanded a company of Dogras. He too suggested that bonds between officers and soldiers did not depend on actual knowledge of language and culture. While on route marches his subedar would entertain him with stories from the soldiers' villages. The stories were fantastical, "fairy tales" according to Coppen, and told in a mixture of Urdu and the vernacular of the Dogras, which Coppen could not understand. "I always used to look in the eyes of chaps around, and you could tell in their eyes whether the old man was having me on or not." If he was, "I would turn around and say, Subedar sahib, you're an old rogue, you see. And he would burst out laughing because he realized that he had me fooled all that long, in fun, and he was a gentleman." Coppen's connection with the VCO and his troops evidently did not depend on his linguistic competence. In letting himself be "fooled," he displayed sufficient comfort with his authority to allow it to be momentarily reversed, while the VCO had the chance to demonstrate to the troops his influence over the officer. Coppen closed the anecdote with a stereotype right out of the martial races: "Of course I always reckoned the Dogras were gentlemen as well. The Dogras were some of nature's gentlemen."[89] Coppen's use of this stereotype demonstrates the protean nature of racial categories that could underwrite affection as well as prejudice. Less a sign of close study of MacMunn or the recruiting handbooks, Coppen's "natural gentlemen" was a convenient hook on which to hang his heartfelt sentiments.

Martial Races as Military Ideology

The discussion above gives some idea of how British officials constructed the martial races army and governed its component ethnicities, and of how officers and soldiers made the army work. But how should scholars assess the martial races as a way of organizing and operating a colonial army? What were the consequences for imperial control and for military effectiveness? How did the martial races measure up to the demands of total war?

That the British ended up with an army of north Indians and their notional martial races was in part an accident of the fact that the

---

[89] George Coppen, interview by the author.

East India Company defeated the powers of south India first. Regiments of Madrassis in Company service won many of the early victories in the late eighteenth and early nineteenth centuries, but they were later thought racially unsuited for military service due to a tropical climate and lack of hills. Madrassis were shorter – and darker – than north Indians. As the wars moved north, the south became a backwater of garrison soldiering. The Indian Army progressively disbanded the Madras infantry regiments between 1860 and 1920.[90] Allowance was made for one very distinguished regiment to continue on, Queen Victoria's Own Madras Sappers and Miners, which created an exception to the racial rule that required explanation. A senior Indian Army regular of the interwar era, Lieutenant-General George Molesworth, offered a horse-breeding analogy that recouped martial races reasoning in the face of the exception. He said that the Sappers and Miners were recruited from "special stud farms."[91] Other officers simply dismissed the Sappers and Miners as an anomaly to the fact that there were only two kinds of Indians, martial ones and the rest.[92]

Martial races discourse reflected the popularity of social Darwinism in the Victorian era, as well as the emphasis on "blood" and heredity as determinants of social character.[93] At its core was an orientalist division of humanity. Whereas all Western males potentially could become soldiers, only certain non-Western peoples had the requisite qualities. Non-European peoples needed particular social and environmental conditions to pass down their martial qualities through successive generations. For MacMunn, involved in Indian Army recruiting in the interwar period, India aside from the martial races consisted of a "vast mass of unwarlike people" who lacked "guts."[94] The great exponent of the martial races, Lord Roberts, who held senior Indian Army commands in the 1880s and 90s, put it this way:

In the British Army, the superiority of one regiment over another is mainly a matter of training; the same courage and military instinct are inherent in English, Scotch, and Irish alike, but no comparison can be made between the martial value of a regiment recruited amongst the Gurkhas of Nepal or the

---

[90] Mason, *Matter of Honour*, pp. 345–346, 349–350; Omissi, *Sepoy and the Raj*, pp. 13–16.
[91] Quoted in Douds "'Matters of Honour,'" p. 116.
[92] Bolt, *Pseudo Sahib*, pp. 30–31.   [93] Metcalf, *Ideologies of the Raj*.
[94] MacMunn, *Martial Races of India*, pp. v, 1.

warlike races of northern India and of one recruited among the effeminate races of the South [of India].[95]

He constructed a hierarchy of warrior masculinity between Occident and Orient, but one that made allowance for the recruitment of colonial soldiers under European selection and tutelage.

A major consequence of martial races doctrine was to narrow the number of classes considered suitable for military service.[96] Along with the Gurkhas, a few north Indian classes came to dominate: Sikhs, Jats, Pathans, Dogras, Rajputs, and Punjabi Muslims, supplemented by a changing array of minor classes. The grounds on which particular "races" were identified as martial shifted. They included heredity, characteristic types of physique, climate, geography, socio-economic conditions, religion, and culture.[97] (See Figure 1.6) These could be invoked singly or in combination. As one scholar notes, "The most favoured argument was that we find warlike peoples in hilly, cooler places while in hot, flat regions races are timid, servile and unwarlike."[98] Mac-Munn's 1933 primer refers to the "square-shouldered athletic Mussulman of the Punjab," stringing together physique, religion, and region, while Sikhs were "hook-nosed and heavily bearded" as well as "tall and often of aquiline appearance."[99] Native peoples integrated into modern economies or who lived in cosmopolitan, and especially urban, settings were considered to have lost their martial qualities.[100] "[L]ong years of peace and the security and prosperity attending it had evidently had upon them, as they always seem to have upon Asiatics, a softening and deteriorating effect."[101] Similar reasoning was used in the King's African Rifles by another senior officer steeped in the late imperial era: "[o]wing to the rapid civilisation and over-education in Uganda, there has been a marked tendency in recent years for the fighting qualities

[95] Lord Roberts, quoted in Mason, *Matter of Honour*, p. 347. Bolt notes wryly that "the Tamil Tigers were yet to come." Bolt, *Pseudo Sahib*, p. 31.

[96] Omissi, *Sepoy and the Raj*, pp. 19–21; Roy, *Brown Warriors*, Chapter 3, pp. 120–144.

[97] Narain, "Co-option and Control," Ph.D. diss., pp. 95–103; Omissi, *Sepoy and the Raj*, Chapter 1, pp. 1–46.

[98] Caplan, "Martial Gurkhas," p. 261.

[99] MacMunn, *Martial Races of India*, pp. 1, 251.

[100] See Parsons, *African Rank-and-File*, Chapter 3, pp. 52–103, for a discussion of the application of martial races thinking to East African recruitment which emphasizes these elements.

[101] Lord Roberts, quoted in Mason, *Matter of Honour*, p. 345.

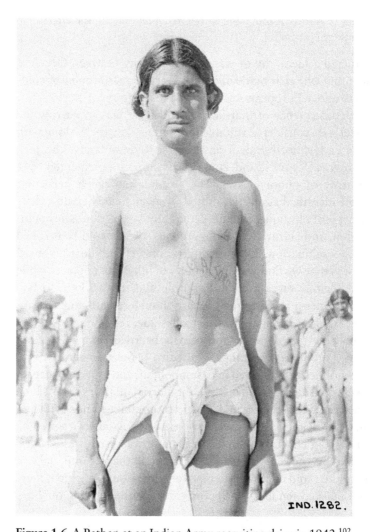

Figure 1.6 A Pathan at an Indian Army recruiting drive in 1942.[102]

of the Uganda native to give place to bible punching, bicycle riding, banana eating gentlemen with no heart for soldiering."[103]

[102] IND 1282, IWM.

[103] Major-General T.H. Birkbeck, "Notes on the History and Organisation of the King's African Rifles and East Africa Command," 83/21/1, IWM. Bananas seemed to have been singled out as the diet of the non-martial, whereas those who preferred grains and meat when available were more likely to be seen as martial. "Bible punching" refers to the view that Christian missionaries led warlike natives away from their martial roots. Killingray, *Fighting for Britain*, pp. 41–42.

While some of the martial races had a warrior heritage, for other groups environmental conditions were sufficient to mark them as recruitable. Rajputs claimed descent from the north Indian warrior aristocracies that had resisted the Mughals and later ruled under their auspices. For many of them, warrior vocations were part of family and cultural lore, although they were a diverse group in civil society.[104] Kumaon and Garhwal, by contrast, were adjacent administrative divisions in the Himalayan foothills of Uttar Pradesh. The Kumaonis and Garhwalis owed their designation as martial classes to their hilly environs and similarity in physique to the Gurkhas, who also hailed from the Himalayan foothills. They were recruited and organized as distinct classes.[105]

A political economy underpinned the martial races as a doctrine of recruitment. In part this stemmed from British attachment to the "yeoman farmer," derived from an imaginary of a romanticized pre-capitalist, pastoral England. The idea was that independent, small-holding peasants were honest, sturdy, and reliable by nature, making good soldiers. As Britain industrialized and urbanized in the nineteenth century, British Army officers preferred rural recruits on grounds they were fit, docile, and amenable to discipline.[106] An interwar era Indian Army officer used the same logic: "The ideal soldier was the sturdy, independent yeoman farmer, be he Rajput, Jat, Sikh or Moslem."[107] Behind the figure of the yeoman farmer in the Punjab and elsewhere were the land settlements by which first the Company and later the Raj made peasants proprietors of small parcels of land responsible for paying taxes and other charges. Indian "yeoman farmers," like the martial races, were products of imperial power and policy. These settlements sought to clear away the feudal array of overlapping rights to land and revenue in India. They created a capitalist agricultural economy in which peasants required cash to pay taxes and for other goods, were often in debt to moneylenders, and were subject to the vagaries of world markets.[108] Cash earnings from wage labor attracted rural people caught in debt bondage. Many Punjabis sought work around the Asian rim and as far away as North America where there were

---

[104] Omissi, *Sepoy and the Raj*, pp. 52–54.
[105] Praval, *Valour Triumphs*, pp. 397–404.
[106] French, *Military Identities*, p. 34.
[107] Trench, *Indian Army*, p. 11. He adds: "The Madrassi soldier was smallish, blackish, and rather low-caste." See also Cohen, *Indian Army*, p. 49.
[108] Fox, *Lions of the Punjab*, Chapter 3, pp. 27–51.

significant expatriate communities, especially on the west coast. Others turned to the Indian Army. As with the Gurkhas, behind the mystique of a warrior race was a rural economy that incentivized migrant labor and cash remittances to hard-pressed families.[109] With only small plots of land at home, one Indian soldier noted, "we had to go to the army to earn a living."[110] Colonial rule produced the peasant recruits the colonial army required.

Martial races discourse represented Indian soldiers as natural warriors, not cash-strapped peasants; politics, economics, and history, imperial or otherwise, were erased. The martial Sikh or the fierce Pathan became an essential type, a character with innate properties, "particular instincts, tendencies, urges," rather than the changing product of certain historical and social contexts.[111] MacMunn cited the "juvenile eroticism" of India in explaining why the majority of its people lacked military qualities.[112] But the mystifying character of martial races thinking should not obscure the ways in which it was a practical and effective guide for the recruitment and governance of colonial armies.

Martial races thinking directed recruiting away from urban populations and toward the peasantry. It did so through a hierarchy of purity, in which those populations most untouched by the civilizing and decadent influences of the city and modern industry made for better soldiers. The underlying strategic logic was sound, however. The Indian nationalist movement proved unable to surmount the urban/rural, economic, and other divisions that separated it from the favored classes of the Indian Army. The martial classes and their home communities continued to see their interests as best served by the British rather than by "national India" and Congress. As Namrata Narain notes of the minorities recruited into the army, "Both regionally and religiously, these dominant minorities had a history of conflict and antagonism with the Hindi heartland. They were unlikely to sympathize with political aspirations postulating majority rule."[113]

---

[109] On the Gurkhas as migrant laborers, see Des Chene, "Relics of Empire," Ph.D. diss., Chapters. VI and IX, pp. 235–260, 335–366.

[110] R.S. Dhatt, interview by the author.

[111] Pandey, *Construction of Communalism*, p. 108.

[112] MacMunn, *Martial Races of India*, p. 2.

[113] Narain, "Co-option and Control," Ph.D. diss., p. 113. Narain's own construction of a Hindi "heartland" is indicative of the depth of the divisions

Martial races discourse could be a fount of *esprit de corps*, flattering Indian soldiers and encouraging their sense of superiority.[114] Military unit identities often involved the idea that each formation was special, unique, or superior. "[A] soldier always believes his own mob is best," remarked an officer of the war-raised Machine Gun Battalion of the 11th Sikh Regiment.[115] Gurkha officers said of their troops that "[t]hey consider themselves vastly superior to any other race on earth."[116] For historian David Omissi, "the purpose of the martial-race theory was not merely to codify but to inspire."[117] The notion that fighting qualities were innate to a "race" provided extra impetus for Sikhs, Rajputs, Gurkhas, etc., to live up to their reputation. One soldier wrote to his family that "As I belong to a martial class, I must not care" for the comforts of home.[118] Another received a letter from home reminding him that "You are the son of a Moghal. Bravo! . . . You should remember that you belong to a Moghal family . . . So you should always bear in mind the tales of our traditional bravery. Never lose heart, obey your officers, and treat your mates decently."[119] Such warrior myths established boundaries of shame and honor. "Let me . . . do my duty and give these blasted Germans what a true Mahratta could do, as so many others have done," one ICO wrote home from North Africa.[120] Were a class to get a "bad name" for indiscipline or mutiny, there was always the threat that the British would stop or reduce recruiting of that class, as occurred with the Sikhs in the early years of World War II. Such threats inspired Sikhs in service to redouble their efforts so as to ensure their good name and, hence, further employment for their families and communities in the army.[121]

within and between Indian nationalism and those who served in the British Indian Army. For an analysis of the divide between the "bourgeois" nationalist movement and the Indian masses, see Guha, *Dominance without Hegemony*, Chapter 2, pp. 100–151.

[114] Cohen, *Indian Army*, pp. 50–51.   [115] Schlaefli, *Emergency Sahib*, p. 137.
[116] Lt. Col. V.E.O. Stevenson-Hamilton, "Some Notes on Gurkhas," LH.
[117] Omissi, *Sepoy and the Raj*, p. 25.
[118] Middle East Military Censorship Fortnightly Summary Covering Indian Troops, No. CLI, 30 June-13 July, 1943, L/PJ/12/655, OIOC.
[119] Middle East Military Censorship Fortnightly Summary Covering Indian Troops, No. CXXXIII, 21 October-4 November, 1942, L/PJ/12/654, OIOC.
[120] Middle East Military Censorship Fortnightly Summary Covering Indian Troops, No. CXXVIII, 30 December–12 January, 1943, L/PJ/12/654, OIOC.
[121] See below, Chapter 2, p. 65.

Martial races thinking was useful for leadership too. The confidence of British officers increased if they believed their troops were natural-born soldiers.[122] Such confidence was an important resource for infantry officers who often had to lead from the front, and confident leadership could evoke active support on the battlefield. Moreover, for all its *faux* ethnography, the Indian Army encouraged officers to familiarize themselves with the culture, religion, and language of their soldiers. Whatever degree of such knowledge actually attained, officers frequently developed warm relations with their troops at a personal level and this kind of intimate knowledge could be employed to inspire and discipline.[123] Many regular Indian Army officers visited the homes and villages of their soldiers, meeting their families and relatives. Officers often identified closely with their troops.[124] One in the 1/11 Sikhs "identified so much with his troops that he grew a full dark beard and rolled it under the chin as did the Sikhs"; only his blue eyes betrayed his origins.[125] Officers in Muslim companies often fasted with their men during Ramadan.[126] That officers thought about and described their men in orientalist and paternalistic language should not obscure the depth of the personal relations that often developed, nor the potential military value of those relations.[127] Combining paternalism and affection, one wartime British officer said of his Indian soldiers "I loved them."[128]

[122] Omissi, *Sepoy and the Raj*, pp. 26–27.   [123] Ibid., p. 25.

[124] According to Field Marshal Auchinleck, who served as Commander-in-Chief of the Indian Army during World War II, officers sometimes made themselves unfit for higher command because of their intense devotion to a particular class of troops. Cohen, *Indian Army*, p. 53.

[125] Major P.H. Gadsdon, untitled memoir of his wartime service, p. 37, 78/6/1, IWM. The officer who grew the beard was well-known to Gadsdon, who reports that he did so out of affection for his men. Other officers in Sikh units may well have grown beards so that they did not present obvious targets to Japanese snipers, in much the same way as British officers in African units blackened their faces before going into action. See Schlaefli, *Emergency Sahib*, p. 109; J.R. Wallis, interview by the author.

[126] Lt. Col. S.P. Fearon, Memoir compiled by Diane Fearon, LH.

[127] See e.g. Brett-James, *Report My Signals*, especially the collection of letters from his former Indian soldiers in the epilogue; Jat Regiment Papers, concerning a post-war reunion between British officers and their former IORs and VCOs, Mss D1196/15, OIOC; Indian Letters Reminiscing about a former Commanding Officer of Skinner's Horse, Misc. 92 (1361), IWM; Col. E.C. Pickard, Letter from ICO dated 28 June, 1946 to Col. E.C. Pickard, 96/8/1, IWM.

[128] Graham Jenkins, interview by the author.

However useful martial races discourse was, making military service both "palatable and profitable" for the recruited minorities, it also had serious drawbacks.[129] For one, it led to complexity and inflexibility in recruitment and administration. Different rations had to be provided to each class; calendars had to be organized around an array of different religious holidays in each battalion; officers had to be trained in different languages; and so on. Such issues could be managed by a stable Raj engaged primarily in low intensity frontier warfare. The world wars were another matter entirely. As with British world power of which it was so much a constituent part, the Raj was ultimately enfeebled by the social, economic, and political consequences of waging them. One such consequence was the unraveling of Henry Lawrence's scheme of a communally organized army.

The reason for this lies in the rate of casualties. In frontier and expeditionary warfare, casualties are suffered for a limited period of time among a few units directly involved in action. As the rate of casualties rises, the ability of the army to replace losses or rotate fresh units becomes stressed, leading to pressures for increased recruitment and compressed training cycles. Ethnically selective recruitment from a small percentage of the population limited the Indian Army's ability to meet the personnel demands of the world wars. The martial races could not supply enough recruits, and a correspondingly more "national" army was recruited in the Second World War, especially in the support services.

The ability to replace casualties or to otherwise deal with the problem of sustained and high losses is a significant factor in maintaining combat motivation. As units dwindle in number over weeks in the line, so too does the willingness of remaining soldiers to vigorously engage in combat.[130] Even if available, the integration of replacements poses problems too, especially if losses are high and time out of active operations for reorganization and training is limited.[131]

The Indian Army was particularly vulnerable to the problem of high casualties over a long period of time. This was so beyond the quantitative problem of finding enough recruits. The infantry battalions were organized around class. The recruiting and replacement system had to

---

[129] Narain, "Co-option and Control," Ph.D. diss., p. 6.
[130] See e.g. Bidwell, *Modern Warfare*, pp. 132–133.
[131] Creveld, *Fighting Power*; Griffith, "The Army's New Unit Personnel Replacement."

be able to provide the number of each class and each rank lost. If it so happened in an action one afternoon that half the Pathan company was wiped out, higher headquarters needed an appropriate pool of replacements if that company was to be brought back up to strength. Junior leader and officer casualties posed further difficulties, especially when taking into consideration the different languages and vernaculars used in the companies. What happened when brigade simply did not have available an officer who spoke Pashto?[132]

The problem could be even more diabolical. Within any given Indian Army martial class, soldiers varied by sub-regions and sub-castes. Regiments had ties with particular districts, recruiting from sub-class clan and village networks. This was the stuff of the recruiting handbooks and of regimental lore. Balances struck in recruitment and promotion in particular units could be undone by casualties, and by centralized provision of replacements at the front that did not take account of regimental preferences and patterns.

An alternative possibility, one realized in many ways small and large in the Indian Army during World War II, was that soldiers and leaders proved more interchangeable than martial races discourse allowed. Lawrence's insight of malleability obtained, especially amid the transformative potential of war to consume and rework culture in all its dimensions. What was decisive, as Chapter 2 will show, was how ethnic difference was organizationally handled, both in general and locally in individual units.

[132] Mason, *Matter of Honour*, p. 341.

2 | *Unmaking an Imperial Army*

I was irked that their religious scruples had not been observed.

> – A British officer, upon discovering Indian soldiers being
> fed sausage and bacon.[1]

The last chapter argued that "army" and "society" should not be conceived as separate realms. Armies and their soldiers are constructed out of fields of social relations, and army–society relations are co-constitutive in historically specific ways. The Indian Army created rigid ethnic stereotypes which it made real through selective recruitment and discipline. What was relatively fluid – a field of ethnic relations – was made putatively fixed.

What the army tried to solidify, the Second World War put into motion. The army had been organized for frontier warfare, internal security, and the provision of imperial expeditionary forces. It was not designed for total war fought on multiple fronts. The war undid the political, military, and economic structures of the Raj, due to the demands made upon colonial society.[2] Britain became indebted to its own colony, having credited India for its wartime expenses.[3] A sub-continent wide uprising began in August of 1942 with the Indian National Congress's demand that the British quit India. The Japanese raised an anti-colonial Indian National Army (INA) from Indian PoWs captured in Malaya and Singapore. Mass famine hit Bengal as wartime price spikes distorted grain markets. The army ran out of martial classes to recruit and commissioned Indian officers by the thousands,

---

[1] Lt. Col. John Peddie, "The Steady Drummer," Chapter VIII, pp. 13–14, 96/17/1, IWM.

[2] Khan, *Raj at War*.

[3] Kamtekar, "Different War Dance." By 1946, Britain owed India more than £1,300 million, one-fifth of UK GNP. Bandyopadhyay, *From Plassey to Partition*, p. 442.

ensuring that the army would not revert to a reliable instrument of colonial control. Soon after the war's end, amid economic crisis at home and a nationalist upsurge in India, the British realized they had lost control of the sub-continent.[4]

While the Second World War saw the unmaking of an *imperial* Indian Army, it was not the undoing of the army as such. This same army fought Rommel's *Afrika Korps* and slogged up the Italian peninsula. In the east, the army recovered from devastating defeats in Malaya, Singapore, and Burma to defeat the Japanese. The army functioned despite the burdens of empire and the disruptions occasioned by war and anti-colonial nationalism.[5] How did a military organization built around a Victorian racial theory that compromised its ability to provide replacements for casualties, or even to communicate on the battlefield, manage to succeed, to the extent it did, in the Second World War? What does it tell us about the making of soldiers and why they fight?

In this chapter and Chapter 3, the focus is on the pressures that unmade the old Indian Army, and what they reveal about military discipline in different contexts. Culture mattered. The army had the capacity to modularly reconstruct difference and rearrange group identity, but the ways in which it did so were consequential and path-dependent. Soldiers' expectations for promotion and perceptions of fairness were shaped by the ethnic order of the army. Wartime improvisations and disruptions in this order were bound to cause trouble.

Yet, the fact that improvisations could be made reveals the transformative powers of military organization. The army was not insulated from society, politics, communalism, and so on, but it could more or less creatively manage and manipulate army–society relations.[6] The army adapted. It continued to raise, train, and prepare units for active service in both the European and Asia-Pacific theaters. Amid the crises of war, of defeat, and, in the next chapter, of capture, officers and organizations formed and trained, and reformed and trained again, successive fighting units.

---

[4] Bayly and Harper, *Forgotten Armies*; Chandra, *India's Struggle for Independence*, Chapters 36–37; Mazumder, "From Loyalty to Dissent"; Voigt, *India in the Second World War*.
[5] Marston, *Indian Army and the End of the Raj*, Chapter 2.
[6] Cf. Rosen, *Societies and Military Power*.

Martial Classes in the Wartime Army

For the Indian Army, the Second World War meant rapid expansion and operations across three continents. From a peacetime strength of about 160,000, it reached a wartime high of approximately two million in 1943.[7] The martial races could not provide sufficient numbers for expansion on this scale. The authorities opened the army to new classes of troops previously not considered suitable for military service. South Indians were brought back in large numbers, especially in service, signals, and artillery units. The fighting arms tried to maintain their martial class composition. But shortages forced them to recruit beyond their preferred sub-regions and sub-groups and stretch the designation of martial. The complexity of the system led to disruption in the class composition of units, often while at the front.[8]

By 1943, much of the Indian Army was fighting in North Africa or Italy, occupying the Middle East, in the INA, or interned in Japanese PoW camps. British officials had to raise new forces to defend India and evict the Japanese from Burma, as well as to supply replacements to the fighting formations. Senior officers worried about new recruits entering service without ties of family and sentiment to the army. They questioned whether the new soldiers would be as loyal as the old martial classes.[9] The army lacked trained cadres that could serve as instructors and junior leaders for the new classes.[10] Punjabi VCOs were foreign to the Madrassis they were now required to instruct.[11] In 1943, General Auchinleck, commander-in-chief of the Indian Army, thought that the greatest obstacle to the effective use of new classes was providing them with VCOs and NCOs of their "own kind."[12] What would happen if soldiers of one class commanded those of another?

---

[7] Perry, *Commonwealth Armies*, p. 116; War Department History, Expansion of the Armed Forces, September 1939–September 1943, Appendix A, L/R/5/273, OIOC.

[8] Wilkinson, *Army and Nation*, Chapter 2, pp. 63–85; War Department History, Expansion of the Armed Forces, September 1939–September 1943, L/R/5/273, OIOC.

[9] See e.g. "Subversive Activities Directed Against the Indian Army," pp. 3–4, L/WS/1/1711, INA, OIOC.

[10] See "Army in India Expansion 1943," L/WS/1/968, OIOC.

[11] War Department History, Expansion of the Armed Forces, September 1939–September 1943, pp. 31–2, L/R/5/273, OIOC.

[12] "A Note on the Size and Composition of the Indian Army," L/WS/1/707, OIOC.

The Raj was at the height of its power and stability when it constructed the martial races army. The military demands of the war exposed the seams and joints of the army's ethnic order. Many officers continued to believe that Indian soldiers had to be organized in separate groups, and that the different customs of each class had to be respected, or soldiers would be unwilling to serve effectively. But the army, in ways large and small, was forced to adapt and devise solutions to shortages of the old classes. Repeatedly tinkering with class organization under wartime pressure made the classes seem all the more artificial. It was not essential, it turned out, to segregate the classes in the army because of the communal bigotry of Indian populations.

A sense of the complexities involved in trying to maintain class segregation in modern war can be gleaned from the Machine Gun Battalion/9th Jat Regiment. Normally, battalions in the 9th Jat were composed of two companies of Hindu Jats, one company of Punjabi Muslims, and one company of Muslim Rajputs, also known as Rangars (a class composition which already involved a mismatch between designation as a "Jat" regiment and half of the troops). After the First Arakan campaign, the MG Battalion was reconfigured as a heavy weapons support battalion, with half of the troops given machine guns and half mortars. It was reorganized from four companies with three platoons each, all equipped solely with machine guns, to three companies with four platoons, of which two had machine guns and two had mortars. How could the new organization accommodate the regiment's three classes of troops, Jats making up 50 percent and Punjabi Muslims and Rangars 25 percent each, and its evenly balanced Hindu and Muslim composition?

After careful thought, the officers decided on one company composed entirely of Jats; one all-Muslim company composed half of Punjabi Muslims and half of Rangars; and one mixed company, which became known as the "chapatti company," composed of two platoons of Jats, one platoon of Rangars, and one platoon of Punjabi Muslims (and so half Hindu and half Muslim in composition).[13] The commander of the chapatti company, Peter Francis, thought that having "three separate castes [sic] in a single company as I had in mine was something of an innovation." But like its nickname implied, the "chapatti company" could be kneaded together through training and effective

---

[13] A chapatti is an unleavened flatbread and a common staple in South Asia.

leadership. "We achieved excellent integration and in the event I believe morale, and pride in the company, was the highest in the battalion."[14] The unconventional class organization of the chapatti company did not prove an obstacle to *esprit de corps*, but rather provided a new identity around which to come together. These sorts of experiences taught the army and its officers to adapt.

In March 1944, the chapatti company was part of a small force sent to face the better part of a Japanese infantry battalion and some INA who appeared at milestone 109 on the Tiddim Road as part of the Japanese Imphal offensive. Milestone 109 was a supply depot situated in an indefensible valley surrounded by forested ridges some eighty miles behind the front. Two companies of MG/9th Jat, one of them the chapattis, were rushed there and tasked with holding off the Japanese long enough for others to retreat. Normally, heavy weapons companies of this kind deployed in support of infantry and other arms, but here they had to fight largely on their own. They did so for four days and nights of Japanese attacks, inflicting over a hundred casualties on their attackers. Francis then ordered his soldiers to render their heavy weapons useless, divide into small parties, and infiltrate out through the surrounding Japanese. To abandon weapons and break into small parties can be a devastating experience. Yet, not only did the chapattis continue to serve as a rear guard once they rejoined friendly forces, they were soon back in heavy action, fighting on the Shenam Ridge on the other side of the Imphal battlefield.[15]

The chapatti company episode shows that while British officers had been indoctrinated in the principles of class division, under pressure they rewrote the rules. British officers took for granted that Indian soldiers came in different ethnic classes which must be kept separate and any interactions carefully regulated. It is this idea which created the problem the officers of the MG/9th Jat felt they had to resolve: how to keep the classes separate given the new organization of the battalion. But when force of circumstance led to the creation of "chapatti-like" arrangements, class proved more flexible in practice than martial races

---

[14] Peter Francis, *Events and Memories*, MS, p. 41; Francis, interview by the author.

[15] Peter Francis, *Events and Memories*, MS, pp. 43–45; Francis and Tony Banks, interview by the author; Grant, *Burma*, pp. 96–101; Allen, *Burma*, pp. 201–202.

discourse allowed. There was no necessary loss of effectiveness when class relations were changed.

Francis was wrong in believing his mixed company was an "innovation."[16] Such expedients emerged throughout the Indian Army in the Second World War. This is not to say that in respect of class anything was possible or that class did not matter. It most certainly did. Once troops were recruited and organized in this way, they had a direct investment in class relations, not least their chances for promotion and their conditions of service as well as the continued well-being of their home communities. While British officers often underestimated the latitude possible in class organization, sticking to their fixed ethnic stereotypes, they were not wrong in fearing the volatility of tinkering with class. The constructed but fateful character of communal relations is something the Indian Army shared with colonized Indian society. In army and society, resistance often took ethnic form because governance managed people and their life chances through ethnic categorizations.[17]

Wartime Officers and Colonial Knowledge

Chapter 1 described some of the limits of the ethnographic knowledge of the professional officer corps. Officers were inculcated in the ideology of the martial races, but for the most part their knowledge of Indian languages and cultures was limited and formulaic. During the Second World War, the Indian Army recruited nearly 30,000 British emergency commissioned officers, or ECOs, to staff its expansion.[18] These self-styled "emergency sahibs" or "pseudo sahibs" hardly had time to master the Indian Army's *lingua franca*, Hindustani, much less the native languages and customs of their particular troops.[19] The ECOs exponentially exacerbated the deficiencies of the regular

---

[16] Peter Francis, *Events and Memories*, MS, p. 41. Even in the pre-war army, the headquarters company in each battalion was by tradition and necessity a mixed unit, composed of a variety of classes from the martial races as well as other classes who served in administrative, logistic, medical, and other such capacities.

[17] Dirks, *Castes of Mind*; Pandey, *Construction of Communalism*.

[18] Marston, *Indian Army and the End of the Raj*, p. 89.

[19] See Bolt, *Pseudo Sahib*; Schlaefli, *Emergency Sahib*. Among other uses, "sahib" was the standard honorific by which Indian soldiers addressed their superior officers. On inadequate language training for emergency commissioned officers,

long-service officers. Yet, the British ECOs more or less successfully led Indian soldiers in combat of far greater scale and intensity than the frontier operations of the peacetime Indian Army and its professional officer corps. It would seem that, for the wartime governance of soldiers, battalion officers needed only an elementary mastery of colonial forms of knowledge.

Just what did British officers know about their soldiers? What did the ECOs learn from the old regulars? Indian soldiers had to be placed in one or another class group, no matter how similar they otherwise seemed. For example, Colonel Hugh Hudson, described at length the attributes of the Sikhs in his unit, the 1/15th Punjab, including their turban, dietary habits, hair, comb, and so on, noting that his regiment only recruited Jat Sikhs, who are "Sikhs by descent." Despite this clear account of who real Sikhs were according to martial races discourse, he goes on to note a few lines further on that: "The Jat Sikhs which we recruited could easily be confused with the Jats, *an entirely different people* who are Hindus." Since both groups were Punjabi peasants and both shared various Hindu practices like the avoidance of beef, he stresses the different pronunciation of "Jat" used for each group in order to underline the distinction.[20] The officer who made himself an authority on a particular class is a stock character in Indian Army memoirs.[21] In the 1/15th Punjab, a Scot was the resident Pathan expert, with good Pashto, knowledge of the different tribes, and time spent in their home areas. "I think he overdid it," remarked Colonel Hudson.[22] In becoming vocal advocates for specific classes, such officers compromised their ability to command formations larger than a class-company and consequently their own chances for promotion.[23]

During the war, officers maintained rigid classifications even when the soldiers themselves desired otherwise. In the 2/13th Frontier Force Rifles, Jats were incorporated into its Sikh company due to wartime

see Marston, *Indian Army and the End of the Raj*, pp. 87–88; Prasad, *Expansion of the Armed Forces*, p. 100.

[20] Col. H.B. Hudson, "A Backward Glance: A Personal Account of Service in the Indian Army 1932–1947," pp. 59–60, emphasis added, CSAS.

[21] See e.g. Major P.H. Gadsdon, untitled memoir of his wartime service, p. 37, 78/6/1, IWM; Col. H.E.M. Cotton, British in India Oral Archive Transcript, pp. 8–9, Mss. Eur. T90/1, OIOC. See also Mason, *A Matter of Honour*, pp. 350–358, esp. p. 357.

[22] Col. H.B. Hudson, "A Backward Glance," pp. 41–42, 66, CSAS.

[23] Cohen, *The Indian Army*, p. 53.

recruitment shortages. The Jats "fitted in well with the Sikhs." When the time came to revert to an all Sikh company toward the end of the war, the Jats asked if they could convert to Sikhism in order to remain with the battalion. The officers felt that if they allowed this request, they would offend community and temple authorities. So the Jats had to remain Jats and leave the battalion, more casualties of the Indian Army's struggle to maintain difference. The 2/13th Frontier Force Rifles were sad to say goodbye to "brave men and good comrades" they had fought with, but were "naturally glad to get back to our pre-war class composition."[24]

While some wartime British officers, and some Indian nationalist officers, groped toward Henry Lawrence's lost insight of ethnic malleability, most worked hard to inculcate the army's vision of an ethnically differentiated order. As in the 2/13th Frontier Force Rifles, officers expressed a general preference for the pre-war martial classes, a preference that led to rigidity in the face of recruitment constraints. "We were all snobs about the Martial Races," noted Hudson.[25] Another officer remarked, "We officers would often speculate on the distinctions and relative merits of the clans and tribes from which we enlisted...unhampered by much anthropological or sociological evidence."[26] When the 15th Punjab Regiment was instructed to raise a new battalion with two new classes of troops, there was "violent dissension" among the regiment's officers, who regarded the imposition of new classes as "mistaken" and a "political" decision. "It was an experiment no one thought worth making."[27]

Officers' courses sought to address the rigidity of class prejudices and preferences among Indian Army officers. In a lecture enumerating and describing the various classes in the army, wartime junior officers heard that despite their personal preferences, "there is little to choose between" the classes.[28] In one exercise, senior majors were asked to list the various classes in order of merit. Which were better, Pathans, Sikhs, Jats, Gurkhas, or some other class? The exercise concluded that, despite officers' preferences for particular classes, and outward signs

---

[24] Brig. A.B. Gibson, Unofficial War History, 2/13th Frontier Force Rifles, p. 73, 1/4, LH.

[25] Col. H.B. Hudson, "A Backward Glance," p. 229, CSAS.

[26] Gilmore, *Connecticut Yankee*, p. 95.

[27] Col. H.B. Hudson, "A Backward Glance," p. 232, CSAS.

[28] Four Lectures by a Commanding Officer for Officers on Joining the Indian Army, Lecture I, L/MIL/17/5/2225, OIOC.

of cultural difference such as language and headdress, "when it came to intelligence and sense of humour and family virtues and sense of devotion to duty," soldiers of all classes "appeared to have the same basic good characters." As Hudson concluded from his own experience, "The remarkable thing about the men, it seems to me, was that they were so alike."[29] They were alike in the sense Hudson probably meant: all were Indian soldiers from similar peasant backgrounds in the same organization, the Indian Army. They were also alike in that each class of soldiers had its own communal coloring, a situation of "sameness in difference."

What is clear from these episodes is that ethnicity does not play the role assigned to it by colonial discourse. There, ethnicity was conceived as a fixed attribute of native peoples, a source of their irrational prejudices and behaviors, and expert knowledge was required for their deft management.[30] On such a view, the secret of the Indian Army was that British officers "knew" their soldiers, with deep knowledge of customs and languages. As the Chapter 1 argued, this was not how ethnic relations functioned in the Raj or its army. Ethnicity was a modality for colonial rule which bureaucratized and stereotyped ethnic identities. Knowledge of languages and indigenous culture, even of the orientalist variety, was not as widespread as might be imagined among British officers, whether regulars or emergency commissioned.

An indication of the cultural knowledge actually attained by wartime officers can be gleaned from Peter Gadsdon of 4/14th Punjab. Although a very successful infantry officer, awarded a Military Cross (MC), he uses the simplest of stereotypes to describe the classes of his battalion:

A Company, the Sikhs, grew their hair long and never cut it during their lifetime . . . [They] also do not smoke, and to offer them a cigarette is an insult. B Company were Dogras, many of them Hindus of the high Brahmin caste. The Cow is a sacred animal to all Hindus, and they were very careful in their eating and drinking habits . . . My Punjabi Mussulmans in C Company held that all pork was defiled and the more strait-laced of them would not touch alcohol. D Company Pathans were also Muslims and held the same views, but, in their case, it was easy to upset them over their honour, about which they could sometimes be touchy.[31]

---

[29] Col. H.B. Hudson, "A Backward Glance," p. 65, CSAS.
[30] Cohn, *Colonialism and Its Forms of Knowledge*, pp. 41–47.
[31] Peter Gadsdon, *An Amateur at War*, MS, p. 29.

Figure 2.1 The Indian Army: A British major gives orders to two Indian other ranks while a VCO, a *subedar*, looks on with his stick. (The 11th Sikhs somewhere in Burma, 1944.[32])

Like Eric Stokes in the last chapter, Gadson understood the basic frame of a communally organized army and how to identify its constituent groups. But what of "knowing the men?"

Simply put, the army did not know its troops as well as its officers imagined. How could the army function in these circumstances? One reason was the role of the VCOs. (See Figure 2.1) Gadsdon had mastered the basic standard of Urdu required by the army within three months of joining his battalion, helped by special tutoring from the subedar in his company. With this he could engage in formal exchanges with the men. But for local knowledge he had to rely on the VCOs. Confronted with a soldier asking for leave to repair his family's house damaged from rains, Gadsdon checked with the subedar to see if there had been rain.[33] Peter Francis, the chapatti company commander, described as avuncular his relationship with the subedar-major of the battalion. "I would go and ask his advice and opinion as would a junior to a senior." He asked either the subedar-major or his company subedar about issues relating to the men, such as promotions and disciplinary

[32] IND 3647, IWM.   [33] Peter Gadsdon, interview by the author.

difficulties, "anything on which I felt I needed a little advice to handle a problem in the company."[34] Company grade officers in Western armies make comments like these about senior NCOs. While formally subordinate, these NCOs are respected for their wisdom, which arises not only from greater length and breadth of service than junior officers but also from closer interaction with the soldiers.

In Western and colonial armies such an intermediary position comes with a degree of power and influence. In the Indian Army this status was boosted by the cultural and linguistic isolation of the wartime British officers. In matters of personnel administration and discipline, officers were often left in the dark. As one officer remarked "It appears I was sometimes not told" by the VCOs about lapses in discipline among the men.[35] "We were really rather figureheads ... the VCOs dealt with everything," remarked another officer, Clifford Martin. The basic barrier was language. "The men spoke a sort of country language. The VCOs you could talk Urdu and understand and the NCOs but after that not that much ... One didn't really know much about the troops, like one would know in a British unit." The result was an overreliance on the VCOs and on those who spoke some English. "You trusted your VCOs. You did trust them. Yes, and the havildar clerk. He spoke very good English."[36]

But the clerk Martin mentioned described a number of disciplinary issues hushed up by the VCOs. One lurid incident concerned soldiers in garrison robbing a pimp while some of their number kept his prostitutes busy. According to the clerk, "In 'A' [company] everyone was aware of this incident except the company commander."[37] Such escapades can be found in any army, but fooling an officer who lacked linguistic competence was all the easier. What is perhaps more interesting, and in need of explanation, is that despite this Martin was an effective and aggressive combat leader of these same Indian soldiers, awarded the MC and wounded in action.

The plain-spoken John Randle, a Pathan company commander in 7/10 Baluch, arrived in India in mid-1941 and did not benefit from the later improvements in training for emergency commissioned officers. He describes the experience of being inserted at twenty years of age

---

[34] Peter Francis, interview by the author.   [35] Close, *Pathan Company*, p. 46.
[36] Clifford Martin, interview by the author.
[37] Mohammed Akram, letter to the author, 30 May 2001.

into a cultural world for which he had few guideposts. "At no time do I ever recall being told about customs...you just had to pick it up." In an incident soon after he joined his company as a newly commissioned officer, in Burma in early 1942 before the Japanese invasion, his subedar produced some fine china on which to have tea. Randle had been keeping a pi-dog as a pet in the village they garrisoned, unaware of the taboo status of dogs among his Muslim soldiers. Randle spilt his tea into the saucer: "In England you put your saucer down and let the dog lap it up and I did this." His Pathan VCO picked up the saucer and smashed it. "I tried to explain look I didn't want to defile anything, I'm just a raw young officer who doesn't know Muslim customs." At the same time as he took responsibility for his ignorance, Randle asserted his authority and told the subedar he could have made the point "a bit more quietly," an indication of how officership functioned across cultural divides.[38]

Randle described the range of tacit knowledge he acquired, from eating with his right hand in front of the men to not letting his shadow fall over the food of Hindu troops. Unlike among British troops, officers took care never to appear naked in front of the men and to deal with their bodily functions out of sight, which meant foregoing chances to bathe in streams in Burma. Randle took along a tommy-gunner to guard him while he furtively defecated in the woods around his company's positions. "This chap didn't actually watch me but he was around," Randle recalled. Randle went on to build a good relationship with his Pathan subedar during hard soldiering over four years. He often took his evening meals with him. Although British officers were provided with bully beef and biscuits, Randle switched to Indian food. "My Urdu had got pretty good by then and we could talk a lot. He was a tremendous chap, a bit of a philosopher and nobody's fool."[39] Randle, like many British officers new to the Indian Army, had learned how to negotiate a world of cultural difference.

Class and Discipline

In maintaining ethnic distinctiveness, the army created space for each class to organize resistance on the basis of caste, region, and religion.

---

[38] John Randle, interview by the author.
[39] John Randle, interview by the author.

Caste could be invoked to avoid distasteful jobs, whether through conviction or calculation. After the 1935 earthquake in Quetta, the 4/19th Hyderabad was sent to bury corpses. Its high caste company of Kumaonis refused to touch the dead on grounds that it would break their caste. They were only convinced to do their share when the British and Indian commissioned officers, among them a Brahmin, set to work first as an example.[40] Accompanied by a mortar unit portered by elephants in Burma in 1945, John Randle's Pathan company in the 7/10 Baluch refused, "for cultural and religious reasons," to remove the tremendous amount of dung produced by the elephants, which attracted flies and left a heavy stench around their positions. Even the company sweeper refused on grounds that his duties involved human excrement only. In persuading the men, Randle provided an argument that both implicated and enabled everyone in the company to get on with the distasteful but necessary duty: he reminded them they had cleaned up mule dung earlier in the war. An elephant was a sort of big mule, he said.[41] These kinds of episodes were localized, but the communal organization of the army made it easy for trouble to spread among troops of the same class in different units.

In the early period of the war, there were a number of instances of unrest in Sikh units.[42] In Hong Kong, the Sikh 20th Anti-Aircraft Battery refused to wear steel helmets. The ostensible reason was religious, that the men were not being allowed to wear their turbans, although investigators thought that a communist or Ghadarite cell was active in the unit, working in league with the granthis.[43] Having given their Sikh troops turbans, the British had also provided them with a totem around which to organize resistance. From a disciplinary point of view, ritual objects with powers of group formation were double-edged. Any Sikh who followed orders and wore his helmet could be seen to have

---

[40] Evans, *Thimayya*, p. 151.   [41] Quoted in Latimer, *Burma*, p. 420.

[42] See Disaffection of Sikh Troops, L/WS/1/303, OIOC; Note on Sikhs, L/WS/2/44, OIOC; Disaffection in Indian Army, WO/208/763, TNA.

[43] The Ghadar Party was founded before World War I and was based in the Punjabi expatriate community on the west coast of the United States. It had a large proportion of Sikhs and had made some abortive attempts at raising the Punjab in armed revolt during the First World War. See Chandra, *India's Struggle*, Chapter 12, pp. 146–158. For a general discussion of patterns of dissent in the Indian Army before 1940, see Omissi, *Sepoy and the Raj*, Chapter 4, pp. 113–152.

violated his religion.[44] When the 2/14th Punjab arrived to reinforce the Hong Kong garrison, the 20th AA jeered its Sikh company for wearing their helmets. The 85 Sikhs in the 20th AA were told that if they did not relent and wear their helmets, they would be tried by court martial. Only two backed down. The next day Sikh quartermasters refused to handle boxes containing steel helmets. Steel helmets were also a factor in unrest among Sikh motor transport companies in Egypt. Grievances that might be local in nature could mobilize other troops of that class through the use of religious and communal symbols. Tensions in the Punjab arising from the Muslim League's goal of an independent Pakistan also fostered unrest in Sikh units, especially among those about to embark for overseas service.[45] The Sikhs feared for their families should the situation in the Punjab turn violent, as it eventually did.

The communal organization of the army created space for communal politics to disturb discipline, conjoining village and barracks.[46] But communalism in the army and communalism in civil society had different valences. The army put its own stamp on the way communalism worked in the ranks, both in general and in local ways in particular units. For reasons of discipline and perceived fairness, the army had to treat equally soldiers who were, in civil society, positioned within hierarchies. Caste relations in civil society, despite variety and fluidity in practice, were hierarchical, as were social identities based on vocation, region, and religion, however disputed the rankings. Yet in the army, it was necessary that each class be treated impartially, in so far as was possible, or risk complaints about discrimination. In any given battalion, classes were acutely sensitive to bias in promotions, perks, and the assignment of difficult duties.

The stability of class composition in the peacetime army made it relatively easy to treat each class equally, as the proportion of classes in a unit rarely changed. This ensured an equivalent number of NCO

---

[44] A similar phenomenon was evident in the greased cartridges affair preceding the 1857 mutiny. Many *sepoys* knew that their cartridges were not greased with pig or cow fat, in some cases because they had made up the cartridges themselves. But the *sepoys* still could not be seen to use them as long as it was popularly believed that the cartridges were greased with animal fat, for fear of social opprobrium. See Kaye, *History of the Sepoy War*, pp. 553–559; Palmer, *Mutiny Outbreak*, p. 6.

[45] There were many desertions in Sikhs units designated for overseas service and one unit collectively refused to embark for the Middle East.

[46] Disaffection of Sikh Troops, L/WS/1/303, OIOC.

and VCO positions, and other perks and promotions, for each class. Wartime disruptions and casualties scrambled such arrangements.

Chauvinism was a volatile force during the war. The NCOs and VCOs of each class or sub-group protected the interests of their troops, generating charges of nepotism, favoritism, and graft organized on a class or sub-class basis. VCOs sought to promote soldiers from their family, village, or community.[47] New officers in the Indian Army were warned about "*bhai bundi,*" or brotherhoodliness, the idea that men with village or kinship ties will watch out for one another.[48] In the 7/10th Baluch one "sub-clan" of the Pathans tried to convince the officers that they were in fact a distinct class of troops, and should have their own separate slots for promotion. "We got a steer from regimental HQ that this was a load of cock," recalled Randle.[49]

Significantly, local conditions in particular units shaped the expression of class tensions and their consequences for discipline. Class mixing in companies could create majority-minority problems, with predominant classes making life difficult for others. When Lieutenant Colonel Tighe took over command of the 4/4th Bombay Grenadiers in 1945, he was given a handwritten document entitled "The Balance of Power" by the outgoing second in command, Major F.S. Owen, which covered "several minor intrigues" and "categories of 'trouble'" based on class differences that might lead to more serious disturbances. In the Jat company resentments arose over the distribution of promotions among two different sub-classes of Jat. Officers were meant to be promoted on the basis of merit, but "all the bright boys" belonged to one sub-class, with the consequence that the other class lost all representation among the ranks of the VCOs and NCOs. This led to friction and discontent, including a "violent quarrel." In another company in the battalion with a mixed class composition, the VCOs and NCOs of the predominant class prevented any promotions from members of the minority. Rifle bolts went missing and were found in ways which implicated members of the minority class. The company commander was "ignorant of the influences at work." These tensions were kept in

---

[47] See e.g. Brig. A.B. Gibson, *Unofficial War History*, 2/13 Frontier Force Rifles, p. 65, 1/4, LH; Evans, *Thimayya*, pp. 195–196; Schlaefli, *Emergency Sahib*, p. 78; Mohammed Akram, letters to the author, 15 and 30 May, 2001.

[48] *Four Lectures by a Commanding Officer for Officers joining the Indian Army*, Lecture IV, L/MIL/17/5/2225, OIOC.

[49] John Randle, interview by the author.

check by senior VCOs who "squashed all trouble." Owen advised the
new commanding officer to "watch this Balance of Power closely."[50]

In the 10/16th Punjab, officers altered the proportion of Sikhs, Muslims, and Hindus due to difficulty recruiting Dogras and Sikhs during
the war. This led to an increase in the percentage of Muslim troops. The
number of Sikh NCOs and VCO slots dropped with the proportion of
Sikh troops, and the chances of the remaining Sikhs for promotion
declined, contributing to Sikh grievances. Sikh/Muslim tensions ran
high in the unit and involved theft of arms.[51] Similar problems arose
in the 4/14th Punjab. Prior to going to Burma, officers were unable
to find enough recruits of the right classes to fill out their Sikh and
Dogra companies. They made up numbers with Jats in the Sikh company and Gujars and Ahirs in the Dogra company. They had intended
to put these new classes in their own platoons under their own VCOs
but, "the men were far too junior to hold anything but lower rank
appointments." They were spread out among the Sikhs and Dogras. "It
was almost inevitable this ended in the greatest dissatisfaction," claims
the battalion history, reflecting the British belief in pre-ordained conflict between the Muslim Gujars and Ahirs and the Sikhs and (Hindu)
Dogras.[52] The new classes were shunned, particularly in the Sikh company, having no VCOs to look out for their interests, and eventually
became "surly and unwilling to fight."[53] Officers averted more serious
trouble by removing first "ringleaders" and then all the Jats, Gujars,
and Ahirs under armed guard in January, 1945.[54]

These majority/minority tensions in Indian Army battalions resem-
ble those found in other militaries and closed social spaces, such as
prison camps.[55] Informal groupings overlay the formal hierarchy of
the institution, and produce competition, conflict, hazing, exploitation, and so on. The local institutional context determines the capacities of these groupings to protect their members, victimize others, and

---

[50] Major F.S. Owen, "The Balance of Power," Tighe Papers, 8206–83–20, NAM.

[51] Note on Sikhs, L/WS/2/44, OIOC.

[52] Major P.H. Gadsdon, "War History of the 4th Battalion of the 14th Punjab
Regiment 1939–45," p. 59, 78/6/1, IWM.

[53] Major P.H. Gadsdon, untitled memoir of his wartime service, p. 129, 78/6/1,
IWM.

[54] Major P.H. Gadsdon, "War History of the 4th Battalion of the 14th Punjab
Regiment 1939–45," p. 59, 78/6/1, IWM.

[55] See e.g. Faulk, *Group Captives*; Meyers and Biderman, *Mass Behavior in Battle
and Captivity*; Shibutani, *Derelicts of Company K*.

generally cause trouble for the authorities. In military settings, commanders can reshape these capacities in ways that aggravate or alleviate disciplinary problems. The kind of trouble described above could be averted by different handling of relations between class groups. For example, the 2/13th Frontier Force Rifles faced the problem of the lack of junior leaders among newly recruited wartime classes. It avoided trouble through promoting men of the new classes despite their short service, giving the new classes advocates among the battalion's leaders. According to this battalion's war history, "The old classes did not approve originally, but, when told that the promotions would go on no matter how much they moaned about numbers being cut, soon shut up."[56] In this unit, minority status did not have a negative bearing on the everyday life of the new soldiers and so it did not become a disciplinary problem.

Class organization could also be a basis for discipline. Many Sikhs realized that the spate of desertions and minor mutinies in the early years of the war could give their class a bad name and lead to a reduction of their representation in the army, on which Sikh communities depended for their livelihood. One Sikh soldier in the 10/12th Frontier Force Rifles entraining for service in the Middle East told a British officer, "[w]e are thoroughly ashamed of desertions that have taken place amongst Sikhs, and it is our intention to wipe out the disgrace." Other Sikhs told their officers they felt "done down" by the Sikh squadron of the Central India Horse (an armored reconnaissance unit), most of whom had mutinied and refused to embark for overseas service at Bombay in 1940. Worried that the whole Sikh community would suffer as a result, they determined to do "all that was in their power to bring back the good name" of Sikhs.[57]

Officers who knew how to do it flipped class disaffection into fighting spirit. In 1944, there were tensions in the demoralized Jat company of the 8/19th Hyderabad in Burma between two sub-classes of Jat, one from East Punjab and the other from Uttar Pradesh, aggravated by VCOs who sought to assert the interests of their respective sub-classes. The battalion commander, Lieutenant Colonel Thimayya, played upon the Jats' collective sense of warrior prowess vis-à-vis the other

---

[56] Brig. A.B. Gibson, Unofficial War History, 2/13 Frontier Force Rifles, p. 73, 1/4, LH.
[57] Note on Sikhs, L/WS/2/44, OIOC.

companies. After a while, the Jats "wanted to be used in an important action so that their bravery would be proved." When the opportunity came, Thimayya told them they now had a chance to vindicate themselves: "I ordered a bayonet charge. That morning the Jats went wild." Afterwards, they were "exuberant."[58] Thimayya had deployed shared masculinity to overcome differences among the men. He created a virtuous cycle in which each company would seek to outdo the others on the battlefield. Rather than being a source of trouble, class – underwritten by gender – became a source of *élan*.

Class differences fostered fighting spirit in the Sikh Light Infantry as well. This was a war-raised regiment. It recruited what was officially considered a lower class of Sikhs than the pre-war regiments. The officers challenged their men to prove that they were the equal of their supposed betters (a standard disciplinary maneuver). The resultant over-enthusiasm led to unnecessarily high casualties in their first major action, suffered during a bayonet charge delivered without regard for enfilading machine gun fire. But they "came back in great heart, having carved the Japs to pieces."[59]

The Indian Army maintained close ties between soldiers and their home communities in ways which were productive of discipline and fighting spirit. The army developed these ties through family and village connections in recruiting, through its role in the economy, and its influence on governance.[60] It sustained the ties through long and generous leave policies. Officers used these connections between barracks and village for disciplinary purposes. Bad behavior was reported to a father or uncle, who often had served in the army as well, and who in turn exerted pressure on the man to conform. Likewise, distinction in battle enhanced a soldier's reputation among his family and community. While much of this communication between unit and village occurred through VCOs, British officers were aware of the disciplinary potential of ties to home communities.[61] Facing a problem with self-inflicted wounds in First Arakan, the commander of 71st Indian Brigade suggested that "[m]uch more must be done to brand the deeds as shameful

---

[58] Evans, *Thimayya*, pp. 202, 211, 222.

[59] Colonel H.R.C. Pettigrew, "It Seemed Very Ordinary: Memoirs of Sixteen years in the Indian Army 1932–1947," p. 163, Mss Eur Photo 182, OIOC.

[60] Tan, *Garrison State*.

[61] See e.g. Four Lectures by a Commanding Officer for Officers on Joining the Indian Army, Lecture III, L/MIL/17/5/2225, OIOC; Beyts, *King's Salt*, p. 27.

and men should be told that self inflicted wounds will be reported and told to their relatives."[62] Other colonial militaries also drew on these kinds of links, a military advantage of recruiting from peasant communities with extended family and clan relations. The commander of 7/Nigeria Regiment insisted on taking along on Chindit operations a fifty-six year-old soldier of over thirty years' service because he knew the fathers and grandfathers of half the men in the battalion. The idea was that if any of the men did badly "it would not end in the battalion."[63]

These examples show that it was neither military organization nor civilian society alone which accounted for the disciplinary problems and opportunities of communalism in colonial armies. What was decisive was the manner in which the authorities structured the relations, ethnic and otherwise, between the army and the communities from which it was recruited, as well as the particular, local ways in which units and leaders responded to the pervasive and changing connections between army and society.

Traveling, Eating, and Boundary Stretching

Ethnicity denotes a nearly infinite elasticity of religion, culture, language, place, and bodily characteristics in the making and unmaking of social groupings. Such groups are composed "of people who feel bound together as a collectivity and, in corollary fashion, feel themselves separate from others who fall outside their group."[64] Not only are groups continually in the process of being remade through evocation of relations of affinity and estrangement, but new groups can be constructed which may encompass previous groups or split them apart. The plasticity of ethnicity is apparent in the ways in which the British created fixed ethnic categories for their Indian troops, who were then required to alter their practices to fit categories ostensibly based on their own civilian identities.

As easily as military service could inscribe ethnic difference, it could also unmake it. Army life involves common conditions and shared

---

[62] "Notes on Lessons from the Operations in Arakan – 1943," p. 3, WO 203/1167, TNA.

[63] Calvert, *Prisoners of Hope*, p. 120. Chindits were air mobile long range penetration forces pioneered by the British in the Burma campaign.

[64] Lincoln, *Construction of Society*, p. 9.

Figure 2.2 Military modernization: The soldier on the left wears a new cap made from water-proof canvas intended for all Indian Army units except Sikhs and Gurkhas. The soldier on the right wears a "traditional" *pugri* made from five yards of material. Picture taken in 1944.[65]

experiences. These conditions and experiences could be the basis for creating groups bound by communal identification, or for overcoming the communal divides of the Raj. Moreover, for soldiers abroad in Burma, North Africa, and Italy, and the many other places from Hong Kong to Teheran where the Indian Army deployed units during the Second World War, military service involved travel and new experiences, exposure to foreign peoples and places. This gave Indian soldiers new frameworks and comparisons by which to imagine themselves and their country's place in the world.

As ever, the local military and unit context set the conditions and latitude for negotiating difference and often hampered adaptation. (See Figure 2.2) An officer commanding an engineer company in the 10th Indian Division registered surprise that many of his men favored tearing down caste restrictions in the unit, citing instances in which food which violated caste was eaten voluntarily. He noted that the old

[65] IND 3302, IWM.

regulars often lagged behind the wartime soldiers: "[p]rewar NCOs and VCOs are apt to be still a little strict not I think alive to genuine religious feeling but to a 'diehard' sense that the Corps always has been run that way and any change is contrary to 'standing orders.'" His surprise derived from inculcation in martial races thinking, but this officer perceived that what the soldiers cared about was unit tradition and identity, not religious feeling *per se*, much less "ancient hatreds." He concluded that "established Corps customs are in retard of contemporary feeling and are restricting any progress."[66]

Elsewhere, British officers were the diehards. When one unit that had not received enough meat was offered mutton, its commander complained "our men only eat goats; never sheep." The teller of this story mocks the commander: "as if that were a proud regimental tradition which must be encouraged!"[67] Some officers were more flexible. Outside the infantry and cavalry regiments (the latter mechanized in the Second World War), it was common to mix rather than separate classes of troops in the Indian Army. Both the Royal Indian Navy and the Royal Indian Air Force were organized on a mixed basis, with common personnel and living arrangements, as were most support branches of the army. The Indian Observer Corps mixed all classes of Hindus together, and used Punjabi and other Muslim troops as cadre for units recruited in Assam and South India, with no serious difficulties arising from religion or caste.[68] Observing all this, and besieged by demands for more of the old pre-war martial classes, officers responsible for recruiting figured out that the class order of the army was socially constructed:

The Recruiting Directorate points out that the pre-war idea that classes would not mix in the Army was erroneous. Vested class interests, bogus caste prejudices, and parochial minded B.O.'s and V.C.O.'s have endeavored unsuccessfully to maintain the narrow class composition on which most of the pre-war Army was based.[69]

---

[66] Middle East Military Censorship Fortnightly Summary covering Indian Troops, No. CL, 16 June–29 June, 1943, L/PJ/12/655, OIOC.

[67] Quoted in Charles, "The Sepoy Overseas – and at Home," p. 300.

[68] Expansion of the Armed Forces in India, Supplement No. 1, October 1943-March 1944, p. 10, L/R/5/273, OIOC.

[69] War Department History, Expansion of the Armed Forces, September, 1939–September 1943, p. 32, L/R/5/273, OIOC.

As noted in the last chapter, the meal is a crucial site at which social groupings coalesce or fracture. Nothing is "more conducive to the integration of society than the ritual of sharing food."[70] This is so both for making exclusionary group identities, creating ethnic difference, as for more inclusionary ones, overcoming divisions. The powers of mealtime rituals to integrate groups and draw boundaries between them are intensified by daily repetition and the existential significance of food. In military life, the break for a meal offers a partial release from hierarchical control for the collective experience of preparing and eating food. The provision of food and occasions to consume it are a key part of the military's social contract with its soldiers. The heavy physical demands of soldiering further magnify the significance of food. Commanders provide special meals and food items when possible to relieve the tedium of rations and as a reward for arduous service or good behavior. New officers in the Indian Army were advised to do their utmost to feed the troops as well they could, and to be seen by their soldiers taking a strong interest in their feeding arrangements.[71]

With its segregated messes and religiously sanctioned rations provided to each class, the Indian Army used food to maintain its order of communal difference. But the powers of food played their role, too, in breaching boundaries and establishing new groupings. Despite the efforts of the army and of individual officers to ensure Indian soldiers ate the "right" foods, wartime conditions and military travel sometimes dictated otherwise. Major John Peddie, commanding a party of Indian soldiers sent to the UK for post-war celebrations, was appalled to find them enjoying a full English breakfast in their temporary RAF mess (with pork sausage and bacon *haram* for Muslims). Although "[s]eemingly nobody was worried" and the senior VCO reported that none of the men had taken offense, Peddie "was irked that their religious scruples had not been respected."[72]

During the Burma campaign, a common and potentially serious problem was that of providing the correct and preferred rations to the different classes of troops, amid uniquely difficult logistical challenges. There were thirty different scales of rations that had to be supplied

---

[70] Lincoln, *Construction of Society*, p. 88.
[71] Four Lectures by a Commanding Officer for Officers on Joining the Indian Army, Lecture II, L/MIL/17/5/2225, OIOC.
[72] Lt. Col. John Peddie, "The Steady Drummer," Chapter VIII, pp. 13–14, 96/17/1, IWM.

to 14th Army in difficult, remote terrain. The "right" rations had to be gotten to the "right" troops among the various British, Indian, and African formations. There were no cold storage or transport facilities beyond Calcutta; fresh meat had to be sent on the hoof. Doctors worried about malnutrition before the logistics situation stabilized in early 1945. For British troops the worst outcome was likely prolonged periods on tinned "bully beef," described as "terribly monotonous and very unattractive in hot weather when it flows half molten from the tin."[73] Indian troops faced more severe shortages. Sheep and goats, the usual source of meat in the Indian Army, did not travel well in conditions on the Assam front and they died in large numbers. The supply situation for meat substitutes, normally milk and ghee, was worse. Indian troops at times went for months without fresh meat. Only belatedly did the Indian Army develop tinned rations of halal and *jhatka* meat, ritually sanctioned equivalents to the British soldier's "bully." These were not available in quantity until 1945. In the meantime, the army was often not able to supply the "right" food to its troops.[74]

Many officers knew that Indian soldiers would eat what was available if the need was sufficiently dire or the temptation great, even in respect of pork and beef.[75] This had been the experience in the First World War. As Omissi observes in surveying Indian soldiers' letters from that war, while the Raj made sure its soldiers fighting abroad "received culturally appropriate food ... the soldiers themselves seem to have become less fastidious as the war went on."[76] During the interwar period, Indian Army officers debated introducing modern tinned and dried rations of the kind that were then standard for Western armies in the field.[77] Modern efficiencies clashed with the communal dietary order of the army. The 14th Army's supply situation forced the

---

[73] Slim, *Defeat into Victory*, p. 173.

[74] Maj. Gen. A.H.J. Snelling, "Administration in the Fourteenth Army," 17/7, Slim Papers, CCA; Slim, *Defeat into Victory*, pp. 173–175.

[75] See Charles, "The Sepoy Overseas – and at Home," pp. 299–300. During the Irrawaddy crossings in January 1945, one Hindu sapper officer found himself isolated for several days with a British unit under Japanese attack. "There was nothing but bully-beef to eat, and after surviving on water for two days, my will-power ran out. All my inhibitions disappeared as I gobbled up the stuff, and the Tommies shook my hand." Lieutenant R.M. Rau quoted in Latimer, *Burma*, p. 383.

[76] Omissi, *Indian Voices*, p. 13.

[77] "Editorial," *The Journal of the United Service Institution of India*, Vol. LXII, April 1932, No. 267, p. 143, 4/2, Slim Papers, CCA.

issue. The army instructed officers on how to persuade Indian soldiers to eat what was available. One memo drew a distinction between "custom, which must be respected, and mere prejudice" against particular or new food items. Troops should be convinced through "deliberate training" to eat various unaccustomed tinned foods, or shifted off rice for chapattis, for example. "No habit is so beset by prejudices as that of eating," cautioned the memo, but even British troops could be made to change their ways. "British stomachs can digest Indian style food, provided the introduction is deliberate and gradual."[78]

Beyond cultural preferences and religious taboos, changing soldiers' diets was risky in disciplinary terms. Food evoked strong feelings. It could turn into a source of complaint and discontent, or be stoked into one by a minority. Soldiers were accustomed to their diets. Rations of dhal and chapattis, for example, were appreciated by the Indian soldiers used to them. British soldiers expected "complex British style rations in all circumstances" and wrote poems to express their dissatisfaction with the hated pork and soya link, an American-supplied item widely available in Southeast Asia Command: "What magic spell of mystic motions/Blended in unearthly brew,/Produced a Rissole, such as you?"[79] Indian soldiers initially had little experience of different foods and were less willing to adapt. Religion underwrote sentiments and preferences regarding food, and was a useful card for negotiating preferred menus. British officers thought about and discussed the problems involved within the terms of colonial discourse, of carefully introducing Indian soldiers to "modern" rations in ways that overcame "caste prejudices." Close observers like Slim saw that a change in rations created an opportunity for a minority who wanted to raise trouble or were otherwise unhappy.[80] Grumbling over food, after all, was a staple of military life. The class order of the army gave additional salience to these complaints.

[78] Jungle Jottings, "Food and Fitness," based on Army in India Training Memorandum No. 23, December, 1943, p. 61–62, L/MIL/17/5/2239, OIOC.

[79] Jungle Jottings, "Food and Fitness," based on Army in India Training Memorandum No. 23, December, 1943, p. 62, L/MIL/17/5/2239, OIOC; Latimer, *Burma*, p. 256. Wingate's Chindits notoriously used "Soya Link" as the code word for failure, while "Pork Sausage" stood for success. Allen, *Burma*, p. 324.

[80] "Editorial," *Journal of the United Service Institution of India*, Vol. LXII, April 1932, No. 267, p. 143, 4/2, Slim Papers, CCA.

Officers often deceived troops to get them to eat what was available. For protein for the 8/19th Hyderabad in Burma, Lieutenant Colonel Thimayya had available at one point only pork and beef kidney soup (and so offensive to both his Muslim and Hindu troops). "It seemed incredible that anyone could be so ignorant as to order such food for Indians. Yet tons of it were everywhere."

Like the soya link, the kidney soup had not been so much ordered as provided by the United States in a self-heating ration tin. Worried about his soldiers' health, Thimayya billed the food as "something special from America," and dwelled on the novelty of the tin's heating mechanism and the tastiness of its contents to convince a small cadre from his battalion to try the new food. They then introduced it to the others, and soon the troops were eating quantities of the stuff. His game was nearly undone by a version of Eric Stokes' sanitary *havildar*, an Indian commissioned officer inspecting messing arrangements. "One look and I recognized the officious type of high-caste Hindu who would be horrified by the soup; he would spill the beans on my deception." Thimayya raised the false alarm of a Japanese attack and had the officer in a jeep on his way back to divisional headquarters before he could figure it out. "It was a close call."[81] Some of Thimayya's troops, and certainly VCOs who knew English, might well have seen through the kidney soup sham or read the labels. But what Thimayya had done was to provide a public narrative by which the soldiers, Muslim, Sikh, or Hindu, could accept the needed nourishment.

The authoritative religious sanctioning of new foods was another route for seeking such acceptance. At one point, 14th Army had available to it a supply of dehydrated whale meat. Some officers lied about what they were feeding their troops, but word got out. Soldiers murmured that it was unlikely that the whales – who were mammals – had been ritually slaughtered in the proper way for either Hindus or Muslims. Officers successfully appealed to the Grand Mufti in Cairo for confirmation that, for ritual purposes, whales were instead fish, and could be eaten freely.[82] They made a justification available for those soldiers who needed it. Collectively, issues with food, and new experiences arising from military travel and logistics, challenged cultural boundaries in small ways and large, giving soldiers new perspectives

---

[81] Evans, *Thimayya*, pp. 204–205. On Stokes, see above, Chapter 1, pp. 32–33.
[82] Bolt, *Pseudo Sahib*, p. 33.

from which to consider their place in the world. But there were also more direct, intentional efforts to overcome those boundaries.

While mealtime rituals reproduce ethnic difference and social hierarchies, meals also can "serve as the instruments with which alternatives are posed to the established order."[83] In the branches of the Indian Army that mixed classes together, the common mess was a significant site for overcoming ethnic and religious differences among the soldiers. In infantry battalions, while class difference gave each company a distinct identity and *esprit de corps*, the battalion itself had to function as an integrated formation. In this context, the separate Hindu/Sikh and Muslim messes of the VCOs were a potential problem. Promoted from the ranks, the VCOs were used to eating among their "own kind." In garrison, their separate messes often were in different buildings, proprietary spaces to retreat to from daily demands. Genuine religious feeling aside, integrating the mess required everyone to surrender some portion of their personal control, a precious commodity in the close conditions of military life. Yet from commanders' perspectives, cohesion among the VCOs would improve units' efficiency and communication. Shared dining arrangements were one route to greater integration.

Slim describes an extended campaign in one regiment that involved first housing the two messes in the same building but in different rooms, then placing two different dining tables in the same room. The VCOs kept the two tables as far apart as the space would allow. During a visit Slim mischievously shoved the tables closer together, only to discover them again separated the next day. He tells the tale in a colonialist manner, the white man helping the natives overcome their irrational prejudices, the British holding the line between mutually suspicious "Mohammadan and Hindu Officers," nudging them toward greater mutual understanding.[84] Whatever the motive, the story makes evident the disciplinary powers of the military to rework and redraw boundaries.

Curiously, in the integration of VCO messes, battalion commanders and nationalist Indian officers shared a common agenda. Captain Prem Sahgal, an ICO in the 2/10th Baluch and after his surrender at

---

[83] Lincoln, *Construction of Society*, p. 88.
[84] "The Indian Army," transcript of broadcast on BBC Home Service, 19th September, 1947, 13/5, Slim Papers, CCA.

Singapore a senior officer in the INA, felt that the separate messes represented the "unnatural barriers which had been built up in the Indian Army to keep Hindus and Muslims apart." He set about overcoming them in his own battalion before the war, in a version of the kind of campaign Slim describes and which also involved the expedient of two tables in one room. At one point, Sahgal was invited to dinner by the Dogra VCOs of "C" Company. He agreed to come only if they would invite the Pathan VCOs of "B" Company as well. "Look," he said to the Dogras, "you are prepared to sit at table with me and eat with me. Yet in some ways I'm worse than those Muslims, because I eat beef and they don't."[85] Everyone dined together.

The INA offers a useful counter-example to the communal order of the Indian Army. Especially under Subhas Chandra Bose, it went out of its way to break down class distinctions and religious prejudices among its former Indian Army soldiers. Rather than ethnic class, unit titles invoked Gandhi, Nehru, and Bose himself among other all-India, nationalist themes. In further examples of the creative articulation of military practice with ethnicity, the INA's common messes served everyone rice or chapattis, dhal, and vegetables. Pork and beef were kept entirely out, but mutton was made available for those who wanted it.[86] Just as the British Indian Army pursued a project of ethnic transformation, producing the martial races through practices of communal ordering, Bose's INA also sought to change soldiers' identities with a nationalization policy.

In the INA, the question of different religions and holidays among soldiers in mixed units was handled by reciprocal celebration and hospitality. Muslim troops arranged the Diwali festivities and Hindus prepared the *Eid ul-Fitr* feast breaking the Ramadan fast. Bose also introduced a new national anthem and flag, replacing Gandhi's spinning wheel on the Indian tricolor with Tipu Sultan's springing tiger, both efforts to seek greater inclusivity between Hindus and Muslims.[87] The cultural politics of Bose's INA differed from the ethnic division fostered in the British Indian Army. But both exemplified the ways in which military institutions could be articulated with the ethnic relations of civil society. The INA had recourse to similar strategies as the army it

---

[85] Quoted in Fay, *Forgotten Army*, pp 55–56.
[86] Ibid., p. 234.   [87] Ibid., pp. 229–234.

opposed. Official army versions of cultural identities were created and fostered in both the INA and the Indian Army.

What was significant for discipline and group formation, for the cultivation of exclusivity and inclusivity, was the particular, often local manner in which armies incorporated, reshaped, and conditioned ethnic difference. Military life could enact or unmake difference, in intended and unintended ways. Despite the deliberate reinforcement of ethnic difference in the army, ethnicity and culture proved continually malleable.

Wartime mobility facilitated the stretching of cultural boundaries. "[T]he present war, with its varied opportunities has driven a ploughshare through many ancient prejudices," remarked one officer who played important roles in developing propaganda programs for Indian soldiers.[88] In this respect, Indian soldiers' experiences were part and parcel of the transnational and global character of their military profession. In Burma, conditions were stark, and new cultural challenges came in the form of kidney soup. But during the First World War, Indian soldiers met French and British civilians, often while in hospital, visiting domestic spaces, eating new foods, and forming romantic attachments. "What is Paris? It is heaven!" one exclaimed in a letter home, while others asked for potions to attract French women or described new sexual experiences.[89] They compared Europe to India, and identified customs that seemed to impede India's development, such as excessive spending on rituals, arranged and child marriages, and poor education. Indian soldiers were especially struck by the contrast between the social roles of Indian and European women. One sent home a picture of an American female aviator to make this point. "I want you to study it and see what the women of Europe and America are doing," he wrote. "The advancement of India lies in the hands of the women."[90]

In the Second World War, Indian soldiers did not serve in number in Western Europe, with the exception of Italy, but there were echoes

---

[88] J.A.H. Heard, "The Indian Soldier Before, During and After the War," lecture to the Rotary Club of Liverpool, 1946, LH. Heard also spent much of the interwar period in business in India.

[89] Omissi, *Indian Voices*, pp. 114, 160, 164. See also Singh, *Testimonies of Indian Soldiers*.

[90] Omissi, *Indian Voices*, pp. 19, 258, 356. See also Omissi, "Europe Through Indian Eyes."

of these earlier experiences. One wrote home, "I am passing some of the happiest hours of my life in a beautiful European island."[91] "[E]nthusiastic descriptions of the countryside" were common in soldiers' mail home.[92] Serving alongside other Allied soldiers exposed Indian soldiers to Western culture of a kind they were unused to in the Raj. Like their fathers on the Western Front in the First World War, they used this exposure to critique social arrangements in India. According to censors' reports on their correspondence, some wanted to see India reconstructed along Western lines, with national and technical education as well as modifications of the caste system.[93] One Indian soldier wrote home from Egypt, "I think the recruitment slogan 'Join the Army and see the World' is quite right."[94] (See Figure 2.3) Military cosmopolitanism springs from such roots and routes, as James Clifford would have it, the military a "traveling culture."[95] Soldiers compared new experiences and places against how things were done at home, broadening their perspectives.[96]

Common Conditions and Military Modularity

The situation of the young John Randle helps summarize the themes of this chapter and Chapter 1. The cultural knowledge he needed to lead effectively was relatively basic and easily learned. The messing practices, taboos, and habits of his troops were the result of indigenous custom maintained and accentuated by a military disciplinary infrastructure. The military placed the soldiers of his Pathan company in a "classed" setting and subjected them to common discipline. It helped that military and indigenous culture overlapped. But, as many of the instances discussed above show, things could be made different, other militarized identities were possible. Messing arrangements could be reorganized, and disciplinary conditions altered. The possibilities for doing so were not unlimited, and each carried consequences. But the

---

[91] Middle East Military Censorship Fortnightly Summary Covering Indian Troops, No. CLIV, 11–24 August, 1943, L/PJ/12/655, OIOC.

[92] Middle East Military Censorship Fortnightly Summary Covering Indian Troops, 21 April–5 May, 1943, L/PJ/12/655, OIOC.

[93] India Command Weekly Intelligence Summaries, L/WS/1/1506, OIOC.

[94] Middle East Censorship Fortnightly Summary Covering Indian Troops, No. CXLIV, 24 March–6 April, 1943, L/PJ/12/654, OIOC.

[95] Clifford, *Routes*, Chapter 1.   [96] Robertson, *Globalization*, pp. 26–29.

Figure 2.3 Join the army and see the world: Indian soldiers take in Roman ruins in North Africa.[97]

military could adapt to social and cultural contexts, producing different army/society amalgams and circuits of relations.

Consider the identity of Randle's regiment, the 10th Baluch.[98] By the Second World War, there were no Baluchis serving in their namesake regiment, as they had ceased to be recruited as a martial class. In the

---

[97] E 7346, IWM.
[98] 10th refers to the place on the list of regiments of the Indian Army after the 1922 reform, not to the tenth of ten or more Baluchi regiments.

battalion in which Randle served, the 7/10th Baluch,[99] "A" company
were Pathans, "B" and "D" Punjabi Muslims, and "C" Dogras, the
last, Hindus serving in a regiment named after a Muslim, Indo-Iranian
people. This situation is not as unusual as it may seem. Those Roman
cohorts titled after defeated tribes that were mentioned in Chapter 1
had to recruit later from different peoples.[100] When the original fighters taken into Roman service began to die off, others from different
tribes were used as replacements. Despite now erroneous unit titles,
the cohorts carried on with a mixture of soldiers of various origin.[101]
The invented character of military identities gives new meaning to the
idea of fighting among one's "own kind" under one's "own totem."
The common conditions of military service could rapidly create new
groups, new embodiments of one's "own kind."

In its ability to subject groups to common discipline, the military
possesses extraordinary capacities of group formation, especially when
creatively articulated with the cultural, social, and political context of
recruits. In fostering different ethnic groups in its infantry battalions,
the Indian Army ensured that ethnicity was a basis for group formation, in ways productive and corrosive of discipline. The powers of
military life to generate group feeling were evident in collective acts
of discipline as well as indiscipline. The little mutinies and resistances
discussed above required cooperation and group feeling to carry out,
just as did vigorous obedience to orders.

The construction and maintenance of ethnic boundaries within units
generated efforts to transgress and overcome them. Sometimes these
arose out of military necessity as when recruits of the "right kind" were
not available. Sometimes they were inspired by nationalist officers who
had come to realize that the British ruled through division. Sometimes
they came from the contingent conditions of military service, in which
different groups suffered common fates.

The Second World War disrupted, disordered, and reordered the
Indian Army, making visible its processes of group formation. Many of

---

[99] The 7 means that the 7/10th Baluch was the seventh battalion raised and
trained by the Baluchi regimental center during the Second World War.
Ordinarily during peacetime Indian Army regiments maintained 4 or 5
battalions, with additional battalions being raised in wartime as needed.
[100] See above, Chapter 1, pp. 22–23.
[101] Southern and Dixon, *Late Roman Army*, pp. 70–71.

the British worries about the martial races and mixing classes proved ill-founded. More prescient were British anxieties for imperial control, arising from the increasing reliance on Indian commissioned officers. They brought Indian nationalism into the colonial army at the very moment total war was undoing the imperial order. Having dwelled largely on the cultural and ethnic dimensions of army–society relations in the first two chapters, Chapter 3 turns with the Indian officers to the politics of war and colonial military service.

3 | Politics and Prisoners in the Indian Army

As for being a mercenary, I will not say a word about it except that I am yet to meet a soldier of any rank and of any nationality who is doing work without accepting any money in return.

– An Indian officer[1]

In the discourse of nation-states, politics define soldiers and their motivations. They serve either "their own" states (the putatively normal situation) or they are "mercenaries," that is, they serve a foreign power or private company for pay.[2] In this classical opposition, fighting for your own people is thought to be a more or less secure basis for loyalty and obedience, while material interest goes only so far in producing discipline and fighting spirit.[3] Political or pecuniary essences are called upon to account for soldiers' behavior.

Drawing on the experiences of Indian officers and soldiers in the interwar period and the Second World War, this chapter deals with the relations between politics and discipline. It compares expectations arising from the world of national polities with the situation of colonial soldiers. In colonial perspective, politics was part of the social field that officials had to negotiate in structuring army–society relations. Like

[1] ALFSEA Morale Reports, August–October, 1944, WO 203/4538, TNA.
[2] The opposition between the official, national soldiers of sovereign territorial states and foreign mercenaries structures much of the literature on historical and contemporary private military companies. See Avant, *Market for Force*; Percy, *Mercenaries*; Singer, *Corporate Warriors*; Thomson, *Mercenaries, Pirates and Sovereigns*; cf. Abrahamsen and Williams, *Security Beyond the State*. This opposition derives from a Eurocentric reading of the rise of national citizen armies in Europe from the eighteenth century which ignores colonial and imperial armed forces raised by Western powers outside Europe. See Barkawi, "State and Armed Force in International Context" in Colas and Mabee, eds., *Mercenaries, Pirates, Bandits and Empires*.
[3] Machiavelli, *Prince*, Chapter XII.

ethnicity, loyalties were variably constructed, divided, and governed.
How did the Indian Army cope with the nationalist, anti-colonial politics it faced? What motivated Indian officers and soldiers to serve their
colonizers? This chapter shows that political disaffection and conditional loyalty were not obstacles to effective and obedient service, even
in a mass army fighting in a total war. In fact, these sentiments often
had little bearing on soldiers' willingness to fight.

Here again, the colonial situation tells us something about how
armies work in general. Discipline and cohesion among officers and
soldiers were not necessarily dependent upon their shared political
beliefs. In combat and other wartime situations, more or less extreme
conditions and constraints determined soldiers' behavior to a large
extent. Motives of expediency, and of the desire for relative comfort
amid deprivation, complicated any essentially nationalist or political
reading of Indian soldiers' actions, even when, as PoWs, they joined
the Indian National Army ostensibly to liberate the Raj.

During both world wars, the Indian Army fought within alliances
formally committed to national self-determination, which the British
imperial authorities were determined to deny to their subject populations. This contradiction fuelled anti-colonial, nationalist politics in
India. The struggle for independence became a national, mass movement in the interwar period, in no small measure as a consequence
of India's participation in the First World War. It reached its violent
climax in the Quit India disturbances in the summer of 1942, as the
British again refused to promise independence in exchange for India's
participation in a world war. Yet, during the war Britain managed to
recruit and operate an army of two million from what was, as one official put it, "in effect an occupied country."[4] By and large, Indian officers
and soldiers served their British rulers effectively, when policing civil
disturbances in India and in the pitched battles of the Second World
War. Crucial to discipline in the Indian Army, it turns out, were the
conditions, not the politics, of service. These extended beyond pay and
pensions to racial discrimination in the officer corps and the impact
of the color lines of colonial society on the army. Service conditions
included also, as Chapter 4 shows, adequate training and leadership
for the tasks at hand, including combat.

[4] Extract from GHQ(I) Letter, Comments on Political and Economic Situation,
Army in India Expansion 1943, L/WS/1/968, OIOC.

The apparent exception, where politics seemed decisive, arose after surrender, amid defeat and the breakdown of military organization. Captured Indian officers and soldiers formed an Indian National Army (INA), under Japanese auspices, in the wake of the invasion of Malaya and the fall of Singapore in February 1942.[5] Many who joined were motivated to struggle against British rule. Their alternative, however, was living in a Japanese PoW camp with its harsh and often deadly conditions. As colonial soldiers, Indians had options that were not generally available to national soldiers in similar straits.[6] The motives and political stakes involved in joining Axis-sponsored forces were complex and multiple. What was immediate and present – deprivation, fatigue, fear for life and limb, for oneself and others – were often far more important in shaping action than the distant high politics of the war. In this, colonial soldiers were little different from national ones.[7]

The discussion below begins by setting the scene with the impact of the world wars on the Indian nationalist movement. It then looks at how the rank and file of the Indian Army reacted to the political and economic events of the Second World War. These reactions reveal the ways in which the Raj structured army–society relations to generate loyalty. The chapter turns next to the great breach in the wall between the army and "political India": the commissioning of Indian officers in the interwar period. At first, the Raj did so in response to nationalist demands for the "Indianization" of the officer corps; later, during the war, the massive expansion of the army necessitated it. Officers familiar with and sympathetic to the nationalist cause entered the army. How did these officers reconcile their anti-colonial politics with obedient and professional service in a colonial army? The chapter closes with a look at the reasons why captured Indian officers and soldiers joined the INA. Indian soldiers' actions in captivity reflected wider commonalities among people subject to similar conditions, constraints, and pressures. Political preferences and national differences were less significant in shaping reactions than at first might seem the case. The PoW cage

---

[5] Fay, *Forgotten Army*; Ghosh, *Indian National Army*; Lebra, *Jungle Alliance*.
[6] With some exception, such as Vlasov's Army, the PoWs of national armies were not counter-organized into fighting formations, although there was individual collaboration of varying degrees. On Vlasov's Army, see Andreyev, *Vlasov and the Russian Liberation Movement*.
[7] See e.g. Farrar, "Nationalism in Wartime"; Linderman, *World Within War*, p. 24.

can be a cosmopolitan site, where people from different places react in comparable ways, and come together in new groupings.

Indian officers and soldiers came from very different social backgrounds, the former generally from princely families or urban elites, the latter from farming villages. Yet once in service, both officers and soldiers, by and large, developed a similar disposition toward the army: deeply invested in their careers and committed to soldiering, but with conditional loyalties toward the Raj and their British masters. The army's powers of modular rearrangement could handle such political contradictions. But just as an army could be raised from colonized populations, so too could PoWs be recruited into new forces to fight their former comrades. For the Raj and for its Indian soldiers, choices had consequences.

The World Wars and Nationalist Politics

During the First World War, India contributed one soldier in ten to those who fought for the British Empire. At a wartime high of 573,000, the Indian Army outnumbered those of Australia and Canada. Some 273,000 Indian soldiers served outside the sub-continent at any one time, and by war's end 1.3 million had served abroad. Of the 947,000 Imperial war dead, 49,000 were Indians.[8] The scale of this effort, and the tide of the Wilsonian moment, led to expectations for positive change in India's political status after the war.[9] In 1919, the British Parliament passed a Government of India Act, which created elected assemblies for the central and provincial governments and established ministerial councils on which Indian members sat. The official idea was that, eventually, India would become a self-governing dominion within the British Empire.

The 1919 Act, however, left "the substance of British power... untouched."[10] The British retained control through a system of "dyarchy" which reserved core powers for the colonial authorities. Already in March 1919, against the objections of elected Indians in the new assembly and council in Delhi, the Rowlatt Act was passed.

---

[8] Perry, *Commonwealth Armies*, p. 158; Omissi, *Indian Voices*, p. 4; War Office, *Statistics*, pp. 68–69.

[9] Manela, *Wilsonian Moment*.

[10] Voigt, *India in the Second World War*, p. 12.

It extended wartime provisions for the suppression of sedition, including summary trials.[11] "This act of the Government was treated by the whole of political India as a grievous insult, especially as it came at the end of the War when substantial constitutional concessions were expected."[12] The First World War had led to a dramatic increase in popular participation in nationalist politics, occasioned by social and economic disruption, as well as by Muslim and nationalist opposition to fighting on the side of those who defeated and dismembered the Ottoman Empire. The Indian Army had played a major role in the campaigns against the Ottomans.

Gandhi responded to the Rowlatt Act with civil disobedience on a sub-continental scale. The violent clashes that resulted led to the Amritsar massacre in April 1919. General Dyer, who commanded the troops at the Jallianwala Bagh, wanted to produce a "moral effect" throughout the Punjab, and so he did.[13] Nearly twenty years of nationalist, revolutionary, and other political activity followed from these developments, including the mass non-cooperation movement of 1920–22 and the civil disobedience campaign of 1930–32. In 1935, a new Government of India Act gave greater autonomy to elected provincial governments, although still reserving British control over law and order among other spheres. By then, much of Indian opinion had moved on to *swaraj*, which Gandhi understood as complete independence from foreign rule, not some form of British dominion.[14]

World War II disrupted any possibility of an orderly transition to dominion status. In May 1939, recalling dashed hopes for self-rule that followed India's participation in the First World War, Congress decided that it would only support the coming war in exchange for a pledge of full independence afterward and a national government during the conflict. This price London was unwilling to pay. When war came in September 1939, the British cabinet declared war on behalf of the dependent parts of the British Empire. Neither the Raj's legislature

---

[11] Pandey, *Indian Nationalist Movement*, pp. 51–52, 108.

[12] Chandra *et al*, *India's Struggle*, p. 181.

[13] Quoted in Omissi, *Sepoy and the Raj*, p. 218. Dyer ordered a scratch company composed of fifty soldiers from the 1/9 Gurkha Rifles and the 59th Scinde Rifles to fire on a crowd, ostensibly to disperse it. At least 400 died and 1,200 were wounded, many in the stampede to escape the firing.

[14] For overviews of the interwar independence struggle, see Bandyopadhyay, *From Plassey to Partition*, Chapter 6, pp. 279–333; Chandra *et al*, *India's Struggle*, Chapters. 13–26, pp. 159–342.

nor the council with their elected Indian members even deliberated the question. The Viceroy, Lord Linlithgow, simply announced that India, too, was at war. "The contrast between the ostentatious adoption of freedom and democracy as British and Allied war aims and the actual maintenance of Imperial rule was not lost on nationalists, or any politically aware person, in the Empire."[15]

Both Gandhi and, especially, Nehru sympathized with the Allied cause, but they remained focused on their primary goal, independence. Their logic was simple and compelling. If the Second World War was a war for freedom and democracy against fascism and aggression, then a free and democratic India would willingly join the struggle. But if it was a war to maintain the imperial system, India could not participate. Congress's provincial ministers resigned in October 1939 over the war issue.[16] Two and a half years followed of diplomatic efforts to reach a compromise formula by which Congress would support the war, while India's war effort continued under British direction. These efforts culminated in the failure of the Stafford Cripps mission in March 1942 and Congress' passage of the Quit India resolutions in August 1942. Cripps was offering only postwar self-determination, hedged with protections for the princes, British economic and strategic interests, and minorities (the protection of "minorities" long one of the principal justifications for continued British rule). Gandhi famously quipped of the Cripps' offer that it was "a post-dated cheque on a failing bank."[17] Although Britain needed India as a base, a source of troops, and as a producer of munitions and war material, Cripps' offer appeared intended to do little more than demonstrate Congress' supposed unreasonableness when it was rejected.[18] Linlithgow declared Congress a "totalitarian organization" and ordered the immediate arrest of the Congress leadership, national and provincial, which spent much of the rest of the war in jail.[19]

Disturbances broke out immediately in Bombay where Congress had been meeting, with the police killing eight and injuring forty-four on the first day. Unrest rapidly spread across India.[20] The uprising took

[15] Jeffery, "The Second World War," p. 314.
[16] Chandra *et al*, *India's Struggle*, pp. 339–340, 448.
[17] Quoted in Collins and Lapierre, *Freedom at Midnight*, p. 73.
[18] Tomlinson, *Indian National Congress*, pp. 141, 156–157.
[19] Bhuyan, *Quit India Movement*, p. 65.
[20] Bhuyan, *Quit India Movement*, p. 67; Pandey, *Indian Nation*.

the form of rioting, attacks on post offices, police stations, and transport. Police opened fire on crowds in numerous instances. There were mass urban demonstrations, attacks on Europeans and government officials, destruction of government property and buildings, and determined efforts to cut rail and telegraph communications, all of which continued on a large scale for six to eight weeks.[21] Thousands of workers in war industries went on strike, with the connivance of Indian owners and managers.[22] By the end of August, Linlithgow reported to London "I am engaged here in meeting by far the most serious rebellion since that of 1857... Mob violence remains rampant over large tracts of the countryside."[23]

Nearly sixty Indian, Gurkha, and British battalions spent the summer and fall of 1942 "aiding the civil power" (the euphemism for military assistance to the colonial government). Along with the police, they killed around 2,500 and detained 66,000.[24] Some Indian officers appeared to have contrived not to shoot at demonstrators, and in at least one case an Indian officer refused to take his unit into a riotous city. He was allowed to resign, and a few other such cases were quietly handled amid fears among the senior Indian officers that courts-martial would lead to mutiny.[25] By and large, however, the army remained under discipline, and with its assistance the big demonstrations were suppressed by mid-September.

Many soldiers criticized the Quit India movement for the disruption it inflicted on their families' livelihoods.[26] For other Indian officers and soldiers then languishing in Japanese PoW cages, Quit India inspired them to finally join the INA. As one recalled, "we felt that after the Quit India resolutions... really India had declared war on the British and that every true Indian should join the fight against the British."[27]

---

[21] Bhuyan, *Quit India Movement*, Chapter 3, pp. 64–102; Hutchins, *India's Revolution*, Chapter 9; Pandey, *Indian Nation*; Voigt, *India in the Second World War*, pp. 159–160.

[22] Bhuyan, *Quit India Movement*, pp. 81–84.

[23] Quoted in Bhuyan, *Quit India Movement*, p. 94.

[24] Bayly and Harper, *Forgotten Armies*, p. 248; Narrain, "Co-option and Control," Ph.D. diss., p. 61.

[25] Interviews commissioned by Trevor Royle and conducted by Gillian Wright for *The Last Days of the Raj*, Mss Eur R 193, OIOC; Palit, *Major General A.A. Rudra*, pp. 252, 256–257; Palit cited in Bayly and Harper, p. 249.

[26] Intelligence Summaries India – Internal, 16 October, 1942, L/WS/1/1433, OIOC.

[27] Prem Sahgal, Oral History Archive, Tape SH7, BEC.

But those soldiers still serving the British carried on with their work, whether fighting in Burma or North Africa, training in India or aiding the civil power. Why?

Politics and the Army Rank and File

During the Second World War, official nationalist politics in India largely came to a standstill once the Congress leadership was removed from the scene in the summer of 1942, not to re-emerge until late in the war. The fact that despite a country-wide uprising, Indian nationalism was unable to suborn the loyalty of the army reveals not only the social basis of the army but also the nature of Indian nationalism. Congress was largely Hindu and urban, while the army rank and file were heavily Muslim and rural. Indeed, some 140,000 new recruits joined the army *during* the two months of protest that marked the height of the Quit India disturbances.[28] The severe economic crisis and famine during the war made military service attractive, but also led to worry among serving soldiers for the well-being of their families back home.

From the point of view of the authorities, there were two blocs of opinion among the rank and file of the wartime army, one formed of the old martial classes and the other of the new classes of wartime recruits.[29] In 1943, the Secretary of State for India characterized the difference as that between two kinds of mercenarism.[30] Calculations of economic exigency were significant for both groups, but took different form. The pre-war regulars and their families and communities benefited from the Indian Army's extensive welfare system and were thought to identify closely with the institution. The new classes of soldiers not only lacked a tradition of military service, they also came from communities which had not benefited from the largesse showered on the martial classes. Their interests in military service were more immediate, arising from the wartime economic crisis.

Many of the pre-war regulars lived in communities which had supplied recruits to the army since the second half of the nineteenth

[28] Bhuyan, *Quit India Movement*, p. 182.
[29] See e.g. M.G. Hallett to Linlithgow, 18 May, 1943, INA and Free Burma Army, L/WS/1/1576, OIOC; Morale Reports, August–October, 1943, L/WS/2/71, OIOC. See also Tuker, *While Memory Serves*, pp. 64–66.
[30] "Subversive Attempts on the Loyalty of the Indian Army," Indian Army Morale and Possibly Reduction, L/WS/1/707, OIOC.

century. Army pay and pensions were a significant source of income for these communities. Given the uncertainties of agricultural earnings, subject to variation in climate and commodity prices, the regularity of army pay and pensions was a significant incentive in itself. The army provided plots of land in irrigated canal colonies to long-service soldiers upon retirement. Through formal and well-organized links with the civil service and its own network of officials in the provinces, the army advocated for its ex-soldiers and their families, who in return assisted in recruiting, provided intelligence on subversive influences, and acted as a conduit for propaganda. Emergency financial aid was made available to veterans and soldiers' families, as was preferential access to the authorities in the case of land and other legal disputes.[31] These communities became dependent upon the army for their livelihood and standard of living. When officers toured Sikh villages after the minor mutinies in Sikh units early in the war, the incidents were loudly condemned "in no uncertain terms" by Sikhs who worried their proportion in the army would be reduced with dire economic and other consequences for their communities.[32]

For these soldiers and their families, the end of British rule could well mean the end of a way of life, and it was from this perspective that they viewed Indian nationalism. After the failure of the Cripps mission, army intelligence noted very little reaction in the army. But among those Indian soldiers who were following events, their main concern was that Cripps had been offering *too much* to the Congress.[33] Senior VCOs in particular were concerned for their career security after the war. It was the non-martial classes that would inherit independent India, and they feared that these "commercial classes" would not appreciate, need, respect, or reward them as had the British.[34] Long-service soldiers felt the same way. For them, the evident strength of Indian nationalism raised concerns about what would happen to the army after the war, with the added worry that their families

---

[31] See Narain, "Co-option and Control," Ph.D. diss., Chapter 4; Omissi, *The Sepoy and the Raj*, Chapter 2, pp. 47–75; Tan, *The Garrison State*.

[32] "Survey of Sikh Situation as affecting the Army," Disaffection of Sikh Troops, L/WS/1/303, OIOC.

[33] "Congress Influence," Miscellaneous Statistics India, L/WS/1/842, OIOC. Indeed, in coming up with the Cripps offer, the British cabinet calculated that too *generous* an offer to the Congress would lead to disaffection in the army. See Voigt, *India in the Second World War*, pp. 118–119.

[34] Intelligence Summaries India – Internal, 17 April, 1942, L/WS/1/1433, OIOC.

might get caught up in civil disturbances while they were away on active service.[35] One report based on extensive conversations with Sikh troops and their families noted that "in the event of a Congress triumph they would stand to lose all that has made them what they are; that the 'non-violent' Congress has no sympathy whatever for the claims of the martial classes" and that they would consequently lose their place in the army to "Hindu classes."[36] That such fears of what would happen under Congress rule were stoked by British propaganda made them no less real.[37]

If fears for the future security of military careers were more likely to be found among the pre-war martial classes, the wartime economic crisis bore down upon all soldiers of the Indian Army. From the beginning of 1942, runaway prices and a shortage of food hit the Indian economy, resulting in widespread famine that lasted for two years. Provinces with agricultural surpluses already had been hoarding grain, while towns and cities began reporting acute shortages. This economic crisis was in part responsible for the widespread popular participation in Quit India.[38] The crisis ramified differently for the army. For many potential recruits, it made military service, with its promise of regular pay and meals, attractive. But for the martial classes, many of whom were farmers and landowners, the crisis created a disincentive for military service, because the high price of grain made working the land very profitable.[39] For serving soldiers, the crisis produced anxiety for their families. This anxiety dominated reports on the morale of Indian soldiers, especially but not exclusively during the middle period of the war when conditions were at their worst.[40] Around three and a half million Bengalis died in 1943–44, amid an inflated wartime economy and

---

[35] Intelligence Summaries India – Internal, 21 August, 1942, L/WS/1/1433, OIOC.
[36] Survey of Sikh Situation as affecting the Army, Disaffection of Sikh Troops, L/WS/1/303, OIOC.
[37] Bhattacharya, "'A Necessary Weapon of War,'" Ph.D. diss., Chapter 5, pp. 156–181; Tan, "Maintaining the Military Districts," p. 868.
[38] Voigt, *India in the Second World War*, pp. 153–154.
[39] See Security Intelligence Report from O.C. 1 R. Jat for September, 1943, Indian Army Morale and Possibly Reduction, L/WS/1/707, OIOC; Narrain, "Co-option and Control," Ph.D. diss., p. 136.
[40] Intelligence Summaries India – Internal, L/WS/1/1433, OIOC; Morale Reports, L/WS/2/71, OIOC; Middle East Military Censorship Fortnightly Summary Covering Indian Troops, L/PJ/12/655 and /656, OIOC; India: Political and Internal Situation August, 1942 – January, 1944, WO 106/3815, TNA; ALFSEA Morale Reports 1 August – 31 October, 1945, WO 203/2355, TNA;

distorted grain market.[41] As one official noted in April of 1943, "Village welfare, in fact, appears to be assuming an increasingly important part in the conduct of the war."[42] Consequently, information on material benefits available to soldiers and their families was a major theme of official propaganda in the Indian Army.[43]

Soldiers serving abroad became aware of the problems their families were encountering through letters. One relative wrote to an Indian soldier: "People are dying of hunger and if this goes on for another two or three months, then you won't find a single soul alive in our village."[44] Families pleaded with soldiers serving abroad to send more money or for increased family allotments, a portion of soldiers' pay that was sent to their families. Many soldiers were already sending as much money home as they could. A mother wrote: "We are facing a great trouble."[45] Families begged soldiers to intervene with the District Soldiers Boards which administered welfare and other programs for ex-soldiers and their families. Such news caused feelings of frustration and helplessness.[46] One censorship report noted in September of 1943 that "[c]onditions in India are producing a progressively demoralising effect."[47] A wife wrote to her soldier husband begging him to come home: "our condition is really miserable."[48] One Indian soldier wrote back to his family: "In all your letters you urge me to come home on leave without any delay. Do you think that to get leave sanctioned is in my power? ... For God's sake don't write me such letters, it drives me mad."[49]

ALFSEA Morale Reports August – October, 1944, WO 203/4538, TNA; SEAC Morale Reports July, 1944 – February, 1945, WO 203/4537, TNA.

[41] Greenough, *Prosperity and Misery*, p.309.
[42] Intelligence Summaries India – Internal, 30 April, 1943, L/WS/1/1433, OIOC.
[43] Bhattacharya, "'A Necessary Weapon of War,'" Ph.D. diss., Chapter 2.
[44] Middle East Military Censorship Fortnightly Summary Covering Indian Troops, No. CLVI, 8–21 September, 1943, L/PJ/12/655, OIOC.
[45] Middle East Military Censorship Fortnightly Summary Covering Indian Troops, No. CLXXXIX, 13–26 December, 1944, L/PJ/12/656, OIOC.
[46] Middle East Military Censorship Fortnightly Summary Covering Indian Troops, No. CLVIII, 6–19 October, 1943, L/PJ/12/655, OIOC; Middle East Military Censorship Fortnightly Summary Covering Indian Troops, No. CLXXXIX, 13–26 December, 1944, L/PJ/12/656, OIOC.
[47] OIOC L/PJ/12/655, Middle East Military Censorship Fortnightly Summary Covering Indian Troops, No. CLVI, 8–21 September, 1943.
[48] Middle East Military Censorship Fortnightly Summary Covering Indian Troops, No. CLXXXIX, 13–26 December, 1944, L/PJ/12/656, OIOC.
[49] Middle East Military Censorship Fortnightly Summary Covering Indian Troops, No. CLXXVI, 14–27 June, 1944, L/PJ/12/656, OIOC.

An ICO serving in North Africa, fed up with hearing complaints about how rough it was on the home front, retorted "let them be bombed...let them experience the torture of fleas on their soft bodies."[50] Indian soldiers also suffered from another fear common among armies overseas, for the fidelity of their wives.[51] News of infidelity was often linked with desertion for troops serving in or near India itself.[52] An Indian soldier returning home from overseas service in 1943 summed up nearly all the sources of frustration: "We come home to our villages to find that food is scarce and high priced, that there are no men to till the land, that our wives have been led astray, and that our land, or portions of it, have been misappropriated."[53] He bitterly noted that those who benefited from the war were those who stayed behind.

Nevertheless, with the partial exception of the Sikh mutinies early in the war, none of these home concerns led to major disciplinary trouble. The Government of India ensured that the recruiting grounds of the Punjab were spared the worst effects of the famine at the cost of worsening conditions elsewhere.[54] Propaganda for the troops continuously referred to the "comfortable conditions" in the localities from which they were recruited.[55] The compensatory advantages and pleasures of military service took the minds of Indian soldiers off the troubles back home. The army offered many soldiers a better standard of living than they had experienced before.[56] One *havildar* wrote back from Italy "[i]n fact we are better off here than we could be in India."[57] The economic security of military service was responsible for a startling difference in the reaction of many Indian soldiers as compared to other Allied soldiers to the prospect of the war's end. British troops in Burma

[50] Middle East Military Censorship Fortnightly Summary Covering Indian Troops, No. CXL, 27 January–9 February, 1943, L/PJ/12/654, OIOC.

[51] As one report on the morale of British troops overseas noted, "[t]he chief concern of all ranks overseas is the increasing number of men with domestic and matrimonial problems." Report of the War Office Committee on Morale: The Army Overseas September–November, 1944, Morale Committee, Minutes of Meetings, L/WS/1/1375, OIOC.

[52] Morale Reports, November, 1944–January, 1945, L/WS/2/71, OIOC.

[53] Intelligence Summaries India – Internal, 15 June, 1943, L/WS/1/1433, OIOC.

[54] Voigt, *India in the Second World War*, p. 204.

[55] Bhattacharya, "'A Necessary Weapon of War,'" Ph.D. diss., p. 73.

[56] India Command Weekly Intelligence Summaries, 27 July, 1945, L/WS/1/1506, OIOC.

[57] Intelligence Summaries India – Internal, 3 March, 1944, L/WS/1/1433, OIOC.

were obsessed about demobilization, the timing and conditions of their return home, and their release from service.[58] But many Indian troops expressed the desire to remain in the service after the war.[59] By April 1945 some units were reporting that as many as 75 percent of their soldiers wanted to remain in the army.[60]

As the foundations of British rule came apart during the Second World War, the Indian Army functioned as a great racially integrated institution able to stamp out the largest rebellion since 1857 and to fight the German and Japanese armies. This was not a result of the intrinsic effects of "army," "society," "economy," or "politics" as separate spheres, but of the particular ways in which the Raj structured army–society relations. In concentrating recruiting among minority populations and providing these populations with benefits, the British created a socio-economic basis for the Indian Army's long-service troops. During the decisive wartime phase of nationalist politics, amid economic crisis, the army held its appeal for new recruits and the martial classes. But what of the literate and educated Indian officers, recruited from middle and upper-class Indians, generally sympathetic to nationalist aspirations, and subject to racist treatment by their British superiors?

Indianization and Discrimination

In the wake of the First World War, Indian nationalists began to demand the Indianization of the officer corps. They wanted an independent India with a national army led by its own officers. The military authorities began to commission Indians on a regular basis, but did so very gradually amid concerns about the reliability and loyalty of Indian officers. Over some number of decades (or in the view of one of its commanders, a century), the Indian Army was to transition into an independent force with indigenous officers, in the manner of the Canadian or Australian forces.[61] The Raj arranged billets at Sandhurst and

---

[58] See e.g. ALFSEA Morale Reports, August–November, 1944, WO 203/4538, TNA; Morale Committee, Minutes of Meetings, L/WS/1/1375, OIOC.

[59] Intelligence Summaries India – Internal, 27 July, 1945, L/WS/1/1433, OIOC.

[60] Intelligence Summaries India – Internal, 20 April, 1945, L/WS/1/1433, OIOC.

[61] Omissi, *Sepoy and the Raj*, p. 163; Gupta, "The Debate on Indianization" in Gupta and Deshpande, eds., *British Raj and Its Indian Armed Forces*, p. 242. See also Barua, *Gentlemen of the Raj*, Chapter 2, pp. 25–43.

other British commissioning schools for Indians, and established an Indian Military Academy at Dehradun in 1932.[62]

Initially, in 1923, the authorities restricted the Indianization scheme to eight units, six infantry battalions and two cavalry regiments. They were responding to opposition among regular British officers, as well as in Delhi and London. Were the experiment to fail, they reasoned, it would not destabilize the entire army. British officers also resisted the idea of having to serve alongside, much less under, Indian ones, a problem that could be contained by restricting the Indian officers to particular units. Many officials feared that the prospect of serving alongside Indians would harm recruitment of British officers into the Indian Army.[63]

Sandhurst commissioned about ten Indians per year by the late 1920s, overstocking the Indianized units with junior officers.[64] When D.K. Palit joined his first battalion, there were thirty-eight Indian commissioned officers compared to an establishment of only fourteen commissioned officers in non-Indianized battalions.[65] The young Indian lieutenants were placed in command of platoons. Normally in the Indian Army, VCOs commanded platoons while relatively junior commissioned officers commanded companies.[66] The Kings Commissioned Indian Officers (KCIOs), as Indians commissioned at Sandhurst were known, greatly resented this "platoonism," which kept Indian officers at lower levels of command and meant that their status was not equal to that of British officers of similar rank serving elsewhere in the army.[67] This was one of the first of many contradictions between race and equality in the officer corps of the Indian Army. Later the number of Indianizing units would be expanded, to those comprising a full division. But it was not until the Second World War, when

---

[62] For overviews of Indianization, see Barua, *Gentlemen of the Raj*, Chapters. 1–2, pp. 1–43; Gupta, "The Debate on Indianization"; Omissi, *Sepoy and the Raj*, Chapter5, pp. 153–191; Sharma, *Nationalisation of the Indian Army*, Chapters. 3–8, pp. 35–172.

[63] Omissi, *Sepoy and the Raj*, p. 174; Sharma, *Nationalisation of the Indian Army*, pp. 72–74.

[64] Sharma, *Nationalisation of the Indian Army*, Appendix XIV.

[65] Palit, "Indianisation," p. 59.

[66] Indian Army practice in this regard differed from metropolitan armies, where lieutenants commanded platoons and captains or majors commanded companies.

[67] Kundu, *Militarism in India*, p. 21.

officers were desperately needed, that the army as a whole was opened to Indian officers.

Some of the discrimination Indian officers suffered was official, in that it was written into their commissions. KCIOs held the same commission as British officers, and were entitled to the same pay and terms of service, but this was not so for the Indian Commissioned Officers, or ICOs, graduated from Dehradun, which commissioned about sixty Indian officers a year from the early 1930s. They were paid less and allowed to command only those British troops serving with the Indian Army.[68] As a result, in any given battalion, an ICO doing the same work as a British officer received a lower wage and held a more restrictive commission. Lower pay was officially justified by the fact that Indian officers did not have to pay to travel home to see their families or to bring over their wives and children from the UK. Indian officers did find their pay sufficient but resented the lower pay scale because of its implied racial discrimination.[69]

Beyond official terms of service, the racism Indian officers encountered in the interwar period depended on the attitudes of the British officers they worked with. Some British would never accept the idea of native officers. Thimayya commented of them that "they sat on the club lawns, sipped *chota pegs*, viewed with alarm, damned the government, cursed the climate, and abominated the impudent young natives who had the effrontery to consider themselves *pukka* King's officers."[70] After the war, Field Marshal Auchinleck, reminded British officers that they

forget, if they ever knew, the great bitterness bred in the minds of many Indian officers in the early days of 'Indianization' by the discrimination, often very real, exercised against them, and the discourteous, contemptuous

---

[68] On the specifics of the various commissions, see Kundu, *Militarism in India*, p. 15; Sharma, *Nationalisation of the Indian Army*, Chapter 8, pp. 135–172.

[69] Note by EICO on measures to counter the Japanese sponsored attack on the loyalty of the Indian Army, INA and Free Burma Army, L/WS/1/1576, OIOC.

[70] Quoted in Evans, *Thimayya*, p. 174. The literal meaning of *chota peg* in Hindi is "small measure." For the British in India, a *chota peg* was a whiskey, or a whiskey soda or brandy soda, or more generally any alcoholic drink. The term was ironically associated with the heavy drinking habits of the colonial class. *Pukka* literally meant "cooked" or "ripe," and figuratively meant "fully formed" and "permanent" in Hindi and Urdu. A *pukka sahib* was a genuine, authentic, or first class gentleman. See Bolt, *Pseudo Sahib*, p. 6.

treatment meted out to them by many British officers who should have known better.[71]

Nearly every memoir by Indian officers commissioned in the interwar period provides more than one story of such treatment.[72]

For one ICO, S.P.P. Thorat, British officers confined their racism to off-duty socializing, where their attitudes "bordered on being hostile." They did not allow their wives to dance with Indian officers and in general ostracized them. "They made no secret that Indians were not wanted as officers." But "[w]hatever their social attitude toward us, the British officers were fair in their official dealings, and certainly took pains to train us in the various duties and responsibilities of young officers."[73] The behavior and professional standards of the Indian officers reflected on their British commanders and colleagues, and this motivated many British officers to hold the Indians to a high standard.[74] An Indian officer who established his professional competence was far more likely to be accepted. "Once you proved [to British superiors] you were good, you were good," one ICO remarked.[75]

Newly commissioned Indian Army officers spent their first year with a British unit stationed in India. This was a long-standing practice, and the idea was that the young officer (in the past, always British) would have the chance to acclimate to India while serving among his own countrymen. For young Indian officers, the experience was rather different. Some were seated at a separate table in the officers' messes of their British units. Others endured the free use of racial epithets.[76] A few British battalions ended up being more hospitable. S.D. Verma was sent to 1/Royal Welch Fusiliers. He learned later from one of its officers that they initially resented a "bloody wog being thrust upon us." But the Royal Welch acted professionally: "whatever the feeling, I was not made aware of it on arrival. Everything was done in a correct manner, as per regimental custom." Verma's performance on the

---

[71] Auchinleck, quoted in Connell, *Auchinleck*, p. 947.
[72] See Evans, *Thimayya*; Khan, *Friends not Masters*; Khan, *Memoirs*; Kaul, *Untold Story*; Narayan, *General J.N. Chaudhuri*; Singh, *Soldiers' Contribution*; Thorat, *Reveille to Retreat*; Verma, *Serve with Honour*.
[73] Thorat, *Reveille to Retreat*, p. 21.
[74] See e.g. Narayan, *General J.N. Chaudhuri*, pp. 49, 57, 65; Singh, *Soldiers' Contribution to Indian Independence*, pp. 35–36; Verma, *To Serve with Honour*, pp. 14–15.
[75] Quoted in Kundu, *Militarism in India*, p. 22.
[76] Barua, *Gentlemen of the Raj*, pp. 69–70.

battalion football team earned him acceptance. By the time he left, the commanding officer of 1/Royal Welch Fusiliers was impressed enough to use his influence to help Verma get a good posting, writing "[i]f I had the choice of keeping this young man in my regiment, I would be happy to do so."[77]

Typically for the Indian Army, diets caused tensions. For British officers in India, the mess had been an exclusively British environment. The menu consisted of "boiled, fried or roasted fish, chicken and scraggy mutton," that is, British cuisine, despite the fact that many British officers preferred curry.[78] The arrival of Indian officers in the mess caused considerable discomfort on both sides. In the 4/19th Hyderabad, British and Indian officers skirmished over whether the radio would be tuned to Western or Indian music.[79] B.M. Kaul found he was discouraged from speaking in his "own tongue" with other ICOs.[80] Many ICOs spent as little time in the mess as possible in the early years of Indianization. Some ate with their soldiers, while others arranged late-night meals with Indian food after going through the motions of dining in the mess.[81] One of the unforeseen consequences of limiting Indian officers to particular units, however, was that they were present in number and could both support one another and exercise more influence.[82] The Indian officers of the 16th Light Cavalry "after a long struggle managed to introduce into their own mess one mildly curried vegetable with every meal and were jubilant with this small success."[83] In the 1/14th Punjab, a battalion that later produced an unusual number of senior INA officers, they succeeded in getting curry served three nights a week.[84]

Military life did offer opportunities for integration. However divided by race and empire, Indian and British officers shared other social attributes. Many interwar Indian officers spent significant time in

---

[77] Verma, *To Serve with Honour*, pp. 14, 17.
[78] Narayan, *General J.N. Chaudhuri*, p. 72. "I am getting browned off with English meals . . . How I long for a curry," one British officer told Chaudhuri (p. 73).
[79] Evans, *Thimayya*, p. 98. See also Kaul, *Untold Story*, p. 41.
[80] Kaul, *The Untold Story*, p. 41.
[81] Evans *Thimayya*, p. 104; Narayan, *General J.N. Chaudhuri*, pp. 72–73.
[82] Evans, *Thimayya*, pp. 102–103; Kaul, *Untold Story*, p. 42; Narayan, *General J.N. Chaudhuri*, p. 54; Palit, "Indianisation," p. 60.
[83] Narayan, *General J.N. Chaudhuri*, p. 72.
[84] Khan, *Friends not Masters*, p. 13.

Britain and Europe, and socialized with Westerners. Culturally flexible, they adopted European dress and modes of comportment, as well as dietary habits, when appropriate.[85] The officer and upper classes had common interests in sports and other pursuits. When asked why he joined the army, one Indian officer replied, "It was a nice gentlemanly career...I am very fond of games and I liked the idea of an open air life."[86] Another Indian officer, who later became a senior commander in the INA, remarked that he "was brought up to see India through the eyes of a young British Officer, and all that I was interested in was soldiering and sport."[87] During his successful interview for admission to Sandhurst, in the middle of a disquisition about his home region and its economy, Thimayya was interrupted by the Viceroy. "What games do you play?" Thimayya replied, "Hockey, cricket, football, tennis, and squash."[88]

D.K. Palit remarked of his fellow Indian officers that "some had sold out to [the British] socially."[89] He thought the British were more class conscious than race conscious, and upper-class Indians got along more easily.[90] For Verma, "[m]uch depended on how one conducted oneself to be accepted or not. Those of us who were good at sports were accepted without any trouble."[91] Polo and polo ponies figure equally as prominently as military operations in J.N. Chaudhuri's memoir. In the "equine fraternity," he remarked of race relations among the upper classes, "there were no distinctions of any kind."[92] Even so, one of Chaudhuri's British commanding officers, an interwar regular, thought him "double-faced." The reason was that Chaudhuri, adaptable in his customs, ate beef with Muslim soldiers and pork in Hindu homes.[93] His hybridity had been read as duplicity. Prem Sahgal earned acceptance only when he demonstrated that he could hold his liquor and knew how to play polo.[94]

---

[85] Barua, *Gentemen of the Raj*, p. 80.
[86] Indian Sandhurst Committee, Vol. 10, Evidence, p. 174, L/MIL/17/5/1785/12, OIOC.
[87] Shah Nawaz Khan, quoted in Ram, *Two Historic Trials*, p. 103.
[88] Evans, *Thimayya of India*, p. 56; quoted in Barua, *Gentlemen of the Raj*, p. 50.
[89] D.K. Palit, Interviews commissioned by Trevor Royle and conducted by Gillian Wright for *Last Days of the Raj*, Mss Eur R 193, OIOC.
[90] D.K. Palit, Mss. Eur. T.51, OIOC.   [91] Verma, *To Serve with Honour*, p. 13.
[92] Narayan, *General J.N. Chaudhuri*, p. 92.
[93] Palit, *Major General A.A. Rudra*, p. 263.
[94] Fay, *Forgotten Army*, p. 29. See also Narayan, *General J.N. Chaudhuri*, p. 92. Palit comments, "It was always bad form if you couldn't hold your liquor. It

As more ICOs came into the service, and British officers adjusted to the realities of Indianization, "lower level professional relationships between British and Indian officers worked very smoothly."[95] Commenting on the improved relations after 1935, B.M. Kaul writes "[a]s the proportion of the Indian to the British officers increased in the battalion, the atmosphere steadily improved, from our point of view."[96] At the same time, in many units, off-duty relations remained strained and there was little social contact between British and Indian officers.[97]

The Color Line

Mutual respect among military professionals could go some distance in bridging the racial divide in the officer corps; in wartime, it would go even further. However, such respect did not extend to wider colonial society. When ICOs ventured out of their cantonments to socialize, they encountered the color bars of colonial clubs. Arriving at the Breach Candy Swimming Club in Bombay with two young British subalterns, Verma was told he could not go in as "natives were not allowed."[98] Thimayya found himself locked out of the Bangalore United Services Club and then the Basra Club when his unit was stationed in Iraq.[99] In Peshawar, although he was allowed in the club, Sahgal found that the wives of the British officers got out of the pool whenever an Indian officer went in. Sahgal was not deterred:

I collected my chaps, and we got beer and lashings of sandwiches and lay along the edge. When an English girl went in, we went in. And when she got out, we got out. So after a while she got tired of all this going in and getting out, and there was no more problem.[100]

Other Indian officers took a more sanguine view of the color bar at colonial clubs. They felt that the British who spent all day around Indians had a right to socialize with their "own kind" at the clubs.[101]

---

was considered a great asset if you could drink a lot, but hold it." Palit, "Indianisation," p. 60.

[95] Narayan, *General J.N. Chaudhuri*, p. 99.   [96] Kaul, *Untold Story*, p. 42.

[97] Interviews commissioned by Trevor Royle and conducted by Gillian Wright for *The Last Days of the Raj*, Mss Eur R 193, OIOC; Evans, *Thimayya*, pp. 158–161.

[98] Verma, *To Serve with Honour*, p. 13.   [99] Evans, *Thimayya*, pp. 88, 100.

[100] Quoted in Fay, *Forgotten Army*, p. 56.

[101] Interview with Rashid Ali Baig and his wife Tara, pp. 23, 45, Mss. Eur. T77–78, OIOC.

Some British officers sided with their Indian colleagues over admission to clubs. The officers of the Highland Light Infantry, the British unit Thimayya served with during his first year, offered to resign *en masse* from the Bangalore United Services Club when they discovered he was not permitted to join. "To my surprise," Thimayya remarked, "none of the H.L.I. officers knew that Indians were excluded. Moreover, they seemed genuinely indignant about it."[102] Stationed in Kelantan with the 2/10 Baluch, to protect Malaya from Japanese invasion, Sahgal found out he was not allowed in the local club. When the battalion band was invited to play at the club, Sahgal went to the CO. He reminded him that the three ICOs in the battalion, who paid toward the upkeep of the band, could not join the club. The colonel agreed, "quite right, it won't play."[103] Clubs in garrison towns in East Africa, where Indian Army units staged for operations against the Italians in Eritrea and Abyssinia in 1940–41, also prevented ICOs from entering. When Chaudhuri brought this to the attention of the British theater commander, he exclaimed "Who do these bloody people think they are? If Indian officers are good enough to fight for the King, they are good enough to be made members of any Club in the Sudan."[104] According to Chaudhuri, the commander rectified the situation by threatening to prevent all British officers from patronizing the clubs.

Once the war was underway, the expansion of the army changed matters for Indian officers in important respects. The wartime ECOs sent from Britain, many from middle class families without direct experience of the empire, had less overt racial prejudice than the old India hands. One remembered:

We junior officers were in our early twenties... and were pretty adaptable. Relations were civil and generally cordial considering that we were on active service and living in stressful conditions. Any strains which arose occurred among, as much as between British and Indians and there was no serious racial discord.[105]

Wartime commanders often frowned on expressions of racism by British officers. There was little trouble, one Indian officer claimed, except "when some British officers with colonial backgrounds started talking about how lucky the natives were who but for the white man's

---

[102] Quoted in Evans, *Thimayya*, p. 88.   [103] Fay, *Forgotten Army*, pp. 56–57.
[104] Quoted in Narayan, *General J.N. Chaudhuri*, p. 130.
[105] Major A.G. Bramwell, letter to the author, 18 May 2001.

presence would be at each other's throats."[106] Another Indian officer, drinking with four British ECOs in a club in Bombay, was asked to leave by the secretary of the club as Indians were not allowed: "My group would not stomach it, threw their glasses at the mirror behind the barman and we walked out!" In his view, "[t]here is no doubt that during the training and during war, there was excellent spirit of friendship between the officers."[107] Another Indian officer also distinguished between the "colonized Englishmen" of the regular Indian Army officer corps and the wartime British ECOs. The latter were not only friendly in his experience, but even mingled with Indian society. "I've seen ECOs eat with their fingers, wear Indian clothes, [and] learn about our music."[108]

During the war, higher command made explicit efforts to stop discrimination toward Indian officers. In one unit, British officers were instructed not to "speak in derogatory terms in the presence of Indian officers about their political leaders, customs, traditions or music."[109] The Infantry Committee, looking into the failures of the First Arakan campaign, identified voluntary segregation between Indian and British officers in the messes of the wartime officer training schools as a particular problem, recommending that commanders take a "personal interest" in integrating officers. "The Committee feels that the most strenuous efforts must be made from the moment the [Indian officer] joins his Training Centre . . . to ensure that no discrimination of any nature is permitted."[110]

War helped integrate the officer corps in other ways. Wartime battalions, when they were not on active service, frequently trained in remote areas where there were no clubs or colonial society to cause trouble. The intensity and close living of wartime service bred camaraderie which could overcome racial antagonisms and prejudices, in Indian as well as in other colonial formations. (See Figure 3.1) S.C. Singha, serving in 7/10th Baluch, "never had a complaint" about racism.[111] When units of 81 West African Division on their way to India were

---

[106] Col. S.C. Singha, letter to the author, 23 August 2001.
[107] Maj. Gen. Ranbir Bakhshi, letter to the author, 1 August 2001.
[108] D.K. Palit, Interviews commissioned by Trevor Royle and conducted by Gillian Wright for *The Last Days of the Raj*, Mss Eur R 193, OIOC.
[109] Col. S.C. Singha, letter to the author, 23 August 01.
[110] Report of Infantry Committee, p. 21, L/WS/1/1371, OIOC.
[111] Col. S.C. Singha, letter to the author, 23 August 01.

Figure 3.1 Brother officers: An ICO, Captain Kulip Singh, shows a captured Japanese sword to a British officer near Maungdaw in the Arakan, 1944.[112]

jeered by white South Africans during a stopover in Cape Town, one (white) officer had his men relieve themselves "and his feelings" in an orderly fashion on the pavement of a wealthy suburb.[113]

By late 1944, Thorat was commanding the 2/2nd Punjab, the first Indian commander of this battalion. His company commanders were all British: "I was doubtful how my coming would be received by the Britishers. But my misgivings were soon dispelled, for they gave me their fullest loyalty and later their affection."[114] After the war, Thimayya commanded a brigade sent to occupy Japan with British battalion commanders under him. He commented:

[T]imes had changed quickly. In most Indian Army units now, everyone was so accustomed to Indian officers that no one thought about it. I had ceased to think of my Staff in racial terms; the officers were either good, bad or indifferent.[115]

[112] IND 4002, Photo Archive, IWM.
[113] Hamilton, *War Bush*, p. 46. Pavements are sidewalks in US English.
[114] Thorat, *Reveille to Retreat*, p. 62.   [115] Quoted in Evans, *Thimayya*, p. 232.

At the beginning of the war there were only 577 Indian officers in an army of nearly 200,000, of whom approximately 140 were medical officers. By war's end, there were over 15,000 Indian officers, with 220 at the rank of lieutenant colonel and four temporary or acting brigadiers.[116] From a ratio of over ten British officers to one Indian officer in 1939, there were by September, 1945 only 4.1 British officers to each Indian officer.[117] As the Indian Army recovered from the defeats of 1941–43 in the Far East, it became an effective and integrated force, in which Indians played significant roles in staff and command positions in all but the most senior levels.[118] Indian officers could see a time coming when they would run the army of independent India.

Not all British officers gracefully accepted the end of empire. When handing over Gurkha regiments to India, many of their British officers stole or destroyed the regimental silver and furnishings. British Gurkha officers had been particularly chagrined by the choice of many serving Gurkha soldiers to opt for service in the Indian Army rather than in those Gurkha regiments that were to remain in British service after 1947.[119] The officers of the 2/9th Gurkhas held a last wild party and ruined much of the mess during it. When Palit arrived to take over the 3/9th Gurkhas, he and his officers had to dine off tin plates. He commented of the British: "I suppose you can't blame them. If some Chinese took my battalion over, I suppose I'd have felt the same." In the 1/5th Royal Gurkha Rifles, the British officers sunk so low as to take legal advice to the effect that they could dispose of the regimental silver and funds as they wished. They proceeded to strip the mess of furniture, silver, crockery, cutlery, paintings, the dining table, chairs, and even the billiard table. Much of it was sent back to England. This behavior appalled other British officers. When, back in the UK, the (ceremonial) Colonel of the 9th Gurkhas heard of the stolen silver, he tracked down every piece he could find and had it sent back to the regiment in India. The 5th Royal Gurkha Rifles regimental association also managed to repatriate some silver. A large trove of it was

---

[116] Figures from Kundu, *Militarism in India*, p. 50; Marston, *The Indian Army and the End of the Raj*, p. 89; Sharma, *Nationalisation of the Indian Army*, p. 174.

[117] Sharma, *Nationalisation of the Indian Army*, p. 184.

[118] Marston, *The Indian Army and the End of the Raj*, Chapter 2; Moreman, *The Jungle, the Japanese and the British Commonwealth Armies*.

[119] Gould, *Imperial Warriors*, pp. 308–316.

discovered in the attic of a retired officer when he died forty-seven years later. They sent it to India where, as the 5th Gorkha Rifles (Frontier Force), the regiment was still a going concern.[120]

In the interwar period, the Indian Army sought in fits and starts to racially integrate its officer corps, while retaining British control. The Second World War forced dramatic progress in race relations and brought opportunities for active service and professional advancement for Indian officers. But the war also brought nationalist politics to a head in India and unhinged the white empires in Asia.[121] Whatever discrimination they suffered in professional matters, Indian officers were also colonized subjects aware of the great political events of their times. What of their specifically political views and activities? Broadly nationalist, how did they reconcile their politics with service in the army of the British Raj?

Indian Officers and Nationalist Politics

Indian commissioned officers came from princely and, increasingly over time, middle class and professional backgrounds.[122] They were familiar with the issues of the day and differed among themselves on the path to independence and the eventual relationship with Britain. They were generally nationalist in their thinking.[123] As one of them put it: "I don't suppose there were many Indians who didn't want independence. At the same time, there were a large number [of officers] who wished to be well considered by the British."[124]

When he was a secondary school student, Verma was sufficiently inspired by Gandhi, whom he saw give a speech in Lahore, that he participated in the non-cooperation movement of 1921–22, boycotting school for a year as the Mahatma had called for.[125] In late 1931

---

[120] Farwell, *Gurkhas*, pp. 258–259; Gould, *Imperial Warriors*, pp. 316–318; D.K. Palit, Interviews commissioned by Trevor Royle and conducted by Gillian Wright for *The Last Days of the Raj*, Mss Eur R 193, OIOC.

[121] Bayly and Harper, *Forgotten Armies*.

[122] Barua, *Gentlemen of the Raj*, pp. 57–58.

[123] Kundu, *Militarism in India*, pp. 35–36. See also Subversive Attempts on Loyalty of Indian Army, Indian Army Morale and Possibly Reduction, L/WS/1/707, OIOC.

[124] Interviews commissioned by Trevor Royle and conducted by Gillian Wright for *The Last Days of the Raj*, Mss Eur R 193, OIOC.

[125] Verma, *Serve with Honour*, p. 2.

Thorat fell in love with and eventually married an "ardent admirer" of Gandhi.[126] Indian officers frequently socialized in the same circles as leading nationalist politicians.[127] As a young man in college in 1929, before he went off to Sandhurst, Kaul heard a speech by Jawaharlal Nehru. Soon after he was recruited by another student to carry out some clandestine leafleting.[128] He made no secret of his nationalist views to British officers but did not suffer any adverse consequences for his openness. He was once assigned during the war to work on Indian Army publicity because it was thought his nationalist views would be useful.[129] By contrast, other ICOs who openly voiced their opinions were drummed out of the service or encouraged to resign.[130]

Some ICOs covertly aided the nationalist movement. Thimayya claimed to have foiled a police plot to cut off the electricity where Gandhi was speaking on one occasion.[131] When his company was called out to suppress Quit India demonstrations in Agra, he ensured that his men did not have to fire through tacit agreements with the leaders of the demonstrations.[132] Kaul made a speech to a students' anti-British rally around the time of Quit India. He also arranged for an Indian Army mechanic to repair a wireless transmitter for unauthorized nationalist broadcasts and alludes to involvement in other underground escapades.[133]

Why join the army? For some, a sense of adventure attracted them to the service despite their nationalism.[134] Several justified their service by reference to the need an independent India would have for military professionals. Nationalist politicians encouraged this view. In Allahabad in the early 1930s, a civilian in a bar accosted Thimayya and asked how it felt to wear "the uniform of our British rulers?" "Hot" was his reply to the man who turned out to be Motilal Nehru, father of Jawaharlal Nehru.[135] Thimayya socialized with the upper-class nationalist community for a time but Nehru soon told him to stop as it would get Thimayya in trouble. He told Thimayya he would be of most use to an independent India if he concentrated on being the best officer he

---

[126] Thorat, *Reveille to Retreat*, p. 39.
[127] Narayan, *General J.N. Chaudhuri*, pp. 79–80; Palit, *Major General A.A. Rudra*, Chapter IV.
[128] Kaul, *Untold Story*, pp. 8–10.   [129] Kaul, *Untold Story*, p. 61.
[130] Kundu, *Militarism in India*, p. 37.   [131] Evans, *Thimayya*, p. 118.
[132] Ibid., pp. 179–180.   [133] Kaul, *Untold Story*, pp. 61–62.
[134] Ibid., p. 16.   [135] Quoted in Evans, *Thimayya*, p. 116.

could be and learned from the British.[136] Thorat reported a similar conversation with another prominent nationalist politician.[137] Chaudhuri came to the same view, which had the advantage of accommodating these officers' chosen careers with nationalist politics.[138] It was also convenient after 1947, for those who had served in the colonial military, to burnish in their personal accounts and memoirs any nationalist credentials available.

That the loyalty of Indian officers toward the Raj was conditional and ambivalent was evident in an exchange in 1925 between Lieutenant Rashid Ali Baig and Mohammed Ali Jinnah. Baig was giving evidence to a government committee looking into the possibility of an "Indian Sandhurst."

MR. JINNAH – You have lived in England for 15 years and been educated there; nevertheless you [sic] love for India is the same?
2ND LT.BAIG – Exactly.
MR. JINNAH – Your patriotic feelings have not abated?
2ND LT. BAIG – Not a bit.
        [. . . .]
MR. JINNAH – [. . .] Did you ever think that you would like to undertake the defence of your country?
2ND LT. BAIG – No. I am afraid I went in to the army entirely for selfish reasons.
MR. JINNAH – But now that you are in the army you got the spark?
2ND LT. BAIG – Yes, very much.
MR. JINNAH – You feel proud that you may be called on at any time to defend your country?
2ND LT. BAIG – Yes, I do.[139]

Baig's responses are compatible with a number of courses of action, depending upon how he chose to interpret "defending his country" at any given point. He resigned his commission in 1930, frustrated by the racism he encountered in the army. He felt that the British officers had denied him an appointment he deserved and that they made life difficult for him because of his friendships with nationalist politicians.[140] Had

[136] Evans, *Thimayya*, pp. 116–124.   [137] Thorat, *Reveille to Retreat*, p. 8.
[138] Narayan, *General J.N. Chaudhuri*, p. 80.
[139] Indian Sandhurst Committee, Vol. 10, Evidence, p. 174, L/MIL/17/5/1785/12, OIOC.
[140] See Baig, *In Different Saddles*, Chapter 5, pp. 52–75.

Baig stayed in the army and been captured in Singapore in 1942, he may well have joined the INA; had he not been captured, he may have gone on to serve the Raj loyally until 1947.

As one KCIO noted in the wake of the formation of the INA, "[l]oyalty is not quite as general as is believed by senior British Officers. A number of people are loyal but they will only remain so as long as it suits them." This was due to the fact that in his opinion "[e]very Indian (soldiers included) desires a higher political status for India. The difference is only in degrees."[141] Among the Indian officers Thimayya knew, "the consensus was that we should help the British defeat the Axis powers and deal with the British afterward." Even so, "[i]t was difficult for us ... to view [the INA] as anything but patriotic."[142] Thimayya's brother served in the INA. Kaul sums up his views and those of other ICOs he knew in similar terms. Of the period immediately following the fall of Singapore, he writes:

Although as Indians we were anxious to win the war against the Germans and the Japanese, we were equally anxious to have the British out of India so that we could be an Independent country. We, therefore, held the view that the weaker they grew politically and militarily, the sooner would they leave India.[143]

After the war, Indian military intelligence and the war department took the view that nearly all of the ICOs were sympathetic to the INA, with the exception of the most senior ones commissioned from Sandhurst.[144]

Yet, this ambivalence toward the British did not manifest itself in open rebellion during the war, quite the contrary, unless officers were caught up in situations of military defeat and organizational collapse. As the KCIO quoted above argued, the nationalist views of Indian officers only led to disloyalty under certain circumstances, in particular if the Japanese were to master the situation.[145] And mastery is precisely

---

[141] Letter from KCIO, 13 March, 1943, INA and Free Burma Army, L/WS/1/1576, OIOC.
[142] Quoted in Evans, *Thimayya*, pp. 180–181.   [143] Kaul, *Untold Story*, p. 61.
[144] Sympathies of Troops re: INA, 20 February 1946, Indian Political Situation, COS Papers, L/WS/1/1008, OIOC.
[145] Letter from KCIO, 13 March 1943, INA and Free Burma Army, L/WS/1/1576, OIOC.

what the Japanese achieved in Malaya, Singapore, and Burma at the outbreak of the Pacific War.

The Indian Army units garrisoning Malaya before the Japanese invasion had few seasoned troops, most of them had already been sent to the Middle East. Many of the battalions had been heavily "milked," sending back experienced officers and other ranks to India to raise new battalions. A high percentage of officers and men were inexperienced and of very short service.[146] All the interwar inequities in status and pay, as well as the racial strains within the battalions and between Indian officers and white colonial society, were keenly felt among the Indian officers in Malaya and Singapore. One ICO who was stationed in Singapore until just before it fell later reported that the ICOs in Malaya were quite discontented over the political situation, particularly the resignation of the Congress ministries at the outbreak of the war. ICOs were also angry at the disparity in salaries and incensed at the discrimination they encountered in the social clubs and when traveling on trains. He quoted one ICO, who later became a prominent INA officer, as stating before the war that "he'd be damned if he'd lift even his little finger to defend these Europeans."[147]

Before the Japanese invasion, there was a bizarre mutiny in the Ahir company of the 4/19th Hyderabad, sparked by the removal of its ICO commander who had fallen in love with a German agent and tried to suborn the company in league with her.[148] Relations were so bad in the battalion that "[t]he British and Indian officers were not even speaking to each other . . . the troops themselves . . . had become sullen and silent."[149] Thimayya kept the mutiny from becoming general in the battalion by telling one company they worked for him, not

---

[146] See Kirby, *War Against Japan*, Vol. 1, pp. 164–165.

[147] Note by EICO on measures to counter the Japanese sponsored attack on the loyalty of the Indian Army, INA and Free Burma Army, L/WS/1/1576, OIOC.

[148] See Discipline of Indian Troops in Singapore, L/WS/1/391, OIOC; Elphick, *The Pregnable Fortress*, pp. 98–100. The officer concerned, Lt. Zahir-ud-din, lived with the female agent while stationed up country in a remote location with his company. One of the soldiers later described to Thimayya a company parade in which Zahir asked if any of the troops ever had been allowed to touch the hand of a *memsahib*, or British woman. "Of course not," Zahir said, "We are filth to the British. But this German girl who follows Hitler wants to shake hands with each of you." Each of the Ahirs shook hands with her. Evans, *Thimayya*, pp. 167–171.

[149] Evans, *Thimayya*, p. 167.

the British.[150] The matter was eventually contained but, according to Thimayya,

[t]he sympathy of the Indian officers was with the mutineers . . . Our anti-British feelings were intense. The war in Europe and Africa was going badly for the Allies, and most of us greeted the news of a British defeat with delight.[151]

Another ICO, who was captured by the Japanese at Singapore and later tortured by them for subverting INA operations, for which he was awarded the George Cross, summed up the situation among Indian formations in Malaya this way: "The biased treatment of Indians by British officers and the general discontent of Indian troops of all ranks was universal in Malaya."[152]

Joining the INA

Singapore fell to the Japanese on 15 February 1942. Just over 60,000 Indian Army officers and other ranks surrendered.[153] The Japanese separated British officers from Indian soldiers, who were then collected in Farrar Park on 17 February. Although estimates vary, about 40,000 Indians were present. Most of the Indian soldiers who would join the INA were at Farrar Park on that day.[154] There, in a Japanese-directed ritual, they were handed over by a British staff officer to the Japanese and then to General Mohan Singh, formerly a captain in the 1/14th Punjab. He mustered them into something called the Indian National Army. Suddenly, the imperial army had become an anti-colonial, nationalist army.

Sitting in front of the Indian soldiers with the other 250 Indian officers and VCOs at Farrar Park, Shah Nawaz Khan later recalled that "I as well as most of the other officers had a feeling of being completely helpless at being handed over like cattle by the British to the Japs and by the Japs to Capt. Mohan Singh, whom they gave powers of life and

---

[150] Evans, *Thimayya*, p. 169.   [151] Quoted in Evans, *Thimayya*, p. 169.
[152] Quoted in Allen, *Burma*, p. 606. See also Menezes, *Fidelity and Honour*, pp. 388–389.
[153] Kirby, *War Against Japan*, Vol. I, p. 473. This total includes those captured earlier in the Malaya campaign.
[154] See Fay, *Forgotten Army*, Chapter 4, pp. 73–86; Ghosh, *Indian National Army*, p. 35.

death over us."[155] Another Indian officer present described the scene this way:

the British authority handed us over to the Japanese authorities and that authority handed us over to Mohan Singh, so many men felt that it was the British who handed us over, therefore they owed no loyalty to them, that they had no business to hand us over like this to Mohan Singh.[156]

Singh had surrendered to the Japanese in northern Malaya, shortly after the Japanese invasion in December, 1941. He began cooperating with a Japanese officer, Major Iwaichi Fujiwara, to raise a force of volunteers from Indian PoWs as the Japanese fought their way down the peninsula. Fujiwara was an intelligence officer who had been given the task of liaising with Indian and other anti-colonial nationalists in Southeast Asia before the war. In his appeals to the Indians, Singh emphasized the idea that they were "fighting troops," a face-saving theme for defeated, surrendered soldiers.[157] He expanded on this theme in his speech at Farrar Park, exonerating Indian soldiers for the loss of Malaya and Singapore, saying the British were to blame for the bungled defense. The days of the Raj were nearly over and India stood on the threshold of freedom: "it is incumbent on every Indian to fight and drive away those demons who have been for so many decades sucking the life-blood of Indians."[158]

Singh's speech elicited expressions of joy from his audience. One *subedar* present later recalled that the Indian soldiers "showed great pleasure."[159] For Singh this was due to patriotic and anti-British feeling among the soldiers. On Major Fujiwara's account, the Indian PoWs "rose for Mother India."[160] But Khan suggests another reason for the Indian PoWs' relief. "[W]e had been told numerous tales of Japanese barbarities and inhuman treatment that would be accorded to prisoners of war" and Indian soldiers now found out that the Japanese would

---

[155] Ram, *Two Historic Trials*, p. 105.
[156] Lt. Gen. Harbaksh Singh, p. 34, Mss. Eur. T95/2, OIOC. Minor grammatical alterations made to quote, which is from a transcript of a tape recorded interview.
[157] CSDIC Report on Capt. Mohan Singh, pp. 35–36, Mss. Eur. Photo. Eur 382, OIOC.
[158] Khan, *My Memories of I.N.A.*, pp. 19–20.
[159] Ram, *Two Historic Trials*, p. 51.   [160] Fujiwara, *F Kikan*, p. 186.

be treating them as comrades in arms rather than as PoWs. "Naturally there was a feeling of great relief and rejoicing."[161]

Commenting both on the speeches at Farrar Park and recruitment for the INA generally, another ICO captured in Singapore was of the view that the Indian soldiers had little grasp of the politics involved: "I don't think they understood the reality of the situation, because they had no way of knowing...they were uneducated people." His theory for why they joined the INA was straightforward. "They were promised easier times, happier times, and they had visions of dungeons that they might be thrown into if they remained as prisoners of war."[162]

The doubts many of the captured Indian officers initially had toward the INA in part arose from the fact Mohan Singh was regarded as "an efficient but a very average officer."[163] Captain Shah Nawaz Khan, who later became an INA Major General and division commander, was concerned that Singh would not be able to "cope with Japanese intrigue" and that the INA would "be exploited by the Japanese purely for their own personal ends."[164] Singh himself was concerned about Japanese efforts to limit the expansion of the INA. He eventually resigned and attempted to dissolve the INA in December 1942, in part because he realized that the Japanese had no intention of invading India at the time.[165]

In the months following the surrender in Singapore, Indian PoWs split into two groups, those who supported and those who resisted the INA. INA guards were put in charge of the PoW camps, and those who refused to volunteer for the INA were subjected to propaganda, punitive living conditions, and some violence.[166] Khan initially worked against the formation of the INA along with a clique of officers, telling others not to join. But when he saw that there were sufficient volunteers for the INA to be viable, he joined it in June 1942: "I decided in the interests of my men, to volunteer for the I.N.A. with full determination that I would do everything possible to break it or sabotage it from

[161] Khan, *My Memories of I.N.A.*, p. 20.
[162] Lt. Gen. Harbaksh Singh, pp. 34–35, Mss. Eur. T95/2, OIOC.
[163] Khan, *My Memories of I.N.A.*, p. 20.
[164] Khan, *My Memories of I.N.A.*, p. 21.
[165] See Ghosh, *Indian National Army*, Chapter 4, pp. 93–121; Singh, *Soldiers' Contribution*.
[166] See Ghosh, *Indian National Army*, Chapter 2, pp. 37–75; Khan, *My Memories of I.N.A.*; Ram, *Two Historic Trials*.

within the moment I felt it would submit to Japanese exploitation."[167]
Khan exercised some influence over the ICOs who were wavering over
joining the INA. When he joined, several others came with him.[168]
Initially, at least, many officers and soldiers who joined the INA had
the intention of defecting back to the British at first opportunity, and
quite a few did so.[169] As Khan remarks of some of the Indian PoWs,
they were "pro-British" and "insisted that they had taken an oath of
loyalty to the King of England."[170]

Aside from Indian independence, Khan and other officers had two
motives in mind in joining the INA. The INA was responsible for many
of the Indian PoWs in Singapore and Malaya. Joining the INA not only
meant better treatment for themselves but an opportunity to work for
improved conditions for their soldiers. Khan was placed in charge of
all Indian PoWs in Malaya and vigorously pursued their interests with
the Japanese, securing better conditions for them, the best of any PoWs
in the Far East, as he claimed at his postwar trial.[171] Another important motivation was the desire to protect Indian expatriates in Malaya,
Singapore, and Burma from the Japanese and, similarly, should the
Japanese actually enter India, to protect Indian civilians from their
depredations.[172] As Khan put it at his trial, "I had also seen with my
own eyes the indiscriminate looting and raping that the Japanese had
done in Malaya, and I did not wish it to happen in India."[173] Summing
up both these motivations, one ICO who joined the INA later said,
"[w]e decided to form I.N.A. to protect Indian soldiers from Jap treatment; and to protect Indian civilians and women from the Japs."[174]

Quit India also rallied many Indian PoWs to the INA.[175] The arrival
in Singapore of Subhas Chandra Bose transformed ambivalence into

---

[167] Quoted in Ram, *Two Historic Trials*, p. 105.
[168] Ghosh, *Indian National Army*, p. 74.
[169] Ghosh, *Indian National Army*, p. 60.
[170] Khan, *My Memories of I.N.A.*, p. 39.
[171] Ram, *Two Historic Trials*, p. 107. See also Ghosh, *Indian National Army*,
pp. 68–69; Khan, *My Memories of I.N.A.*, pp. 37–42. Khan writes with
evident pride of his accomplishments in securing better living conditions for
Indian PoWs and on a few occasions saving them from mistreatment and
execution at the hands of the Japanese.
[172] Ghosh, *Indian National Army*, pp. 70–71.
[173] Quoted in Ram, *Two Historic Trials*, p. 109.
[174] Quoted in Ghosh, *Indian National Army*, p. 69.
[175] Ghosh, *Indian National Army*, pp. 46, 56–57; Khan, *My Memories of I.N.A.*,
p. 40.

support. Bose was a former president of the Congress and leader of the Forward Bloc who had fallen out with Gandhi over the extent to which the Congress should participate in the institutions set up in the 1935 Government of India Act. Bose had pushed for an immediate mass struggle, a step Gandhi and Nehru declined to take until Quit India.[176] The British locked Bose up shortly after the war began because of his calls for rebellion. He was released after a hunger strike and escaped to Germany via Afghanistan and the Soviet Union in January, 1941.[177] From the very beginnings of the INA, Singh and others had asked for Bose to be brought over from Germany.[178]

In the eyes of many Indian officers, Bose's arrival in the Far East in May 1943 and his establishment of the Provisional Government of Free India gave the INA a legitimacy that it had lacked under Mohan Singh.[179] All told, there were around fifty Indian commissioned officers captured at Singapore. Around six of them were KCIOs, of whom two remained loyal to the British throughout their captivity. Four eventually joined the INA, for a variety of motives, although none did so immediately. About fifteen ICOs, or Dehradun products, remained loyal to the British throughout their captivity in very harsh conditions.[180] The rest of the officers and around one hundred VCOs eventually joined the INA and provided it with an essential core of experienced professionals.

British and Indian protagonists in the drama of the INA made a number of claims regarding how many of the 60,000 or so Indian Army soldiers captured in Malaya and Singapore ultimately volunteered for INA service. Philip Mason, a senior official in the Government of India and later an historian of the Indian Army, claimed that over half, "some thirty-five thousand, stood firm to their allegiance, facing continuous privation and hardship, sometimes torture and death, rather than be false to the salt they had eaten and the oaths they had taken when they enlisted."[181] For so many to choose Japanese captivity over the incomparably better conditions in the INA truly would be a feat of

---

[176] Chandra *et al*, *India's Struggle*, pp. 443–447.
[177] See Toye, *Springing Tiger*, Chapter 3.
[178] Ghosh, *Indian National Army*, pp. 127–129.
[179] Ghosh, *Indian National Army*, pp. 145–148.
[180] These figures are taken from Kundu, *Militarism in India*, pp. 54, 58, and should be considered approximations.
[181] From his Forward to Toye, *Springing Tiger*, p. v.

steadfast allegiance. For Lord Wavell, it was 45,000 who stood firm: "I say to you that amongst all the exploits of the last five or six years for which the world rightly extols the Indian soldier, the endurance of those men in captivity and hardship stands as high as any." He pointed out that over 11,000 Indian PoWs died in Japanese captivity while INA dead from all causes were less than 2,000.[182]

But on Mohan Singh's account, 42,000 of 55,000[183] Indian PoWs volunteered within a few months of the fall of Singapore.[184] Major Fujiwara agreed with this estimate.[185] One reason for the disparity in British and Indian estimates is that the Japanese initially armed only 16,000 of the volunteers. In the summer of 1942, the Japanese had no intention of invading India and the INA was a low priority. As a consequence, they began using Indian PoWs, ostensibly under Singh's command, for labor, with many being sent to the South Pacific and Thailand.[186] Even though they had volunteered for INA service, Indian PoWs still ended up in Japanese prison and labor camps, with their fearsome mortality rates.

Later, after Bose's arrival, the INA would eventually number around 45,000, but about 18,000 of these were recruited from Indian civilian communities in Southeast Asia.[187] According to Indian Army intelligence's wartime estimates, only around 5,000 Indian PoWs remained "staunch non-volunteers."[188] Gurkhas, Punjabi Muslims, and Pathans numbered heavily among the non-volunteers. Sikhs and the Hindu classes, Dogras and Jats, numbered heavily among the volunteers.[189] The INA reflected the divided political geography of the Raj, with those from the fringes or beyond – Nepal, Punjab, and Northwest Frontier Province – more likely to remain loyal to the British.

British insistence that large percentages of Indian PoWs "stood firm" when they had the chance to escape Japanese captivity reveals the

---

[182] Quoted in Menon, *Transfer of Power in India*, p. 225.
[183] Different authors on the INA use different figures of the number of Indian troops captured in Malaya and Singapore. Kirby's figures in the official history can be taken as definitive. 67,340 Indian Army personnel were lost from all causes in Malaya and Singapore. Less than 5,000 of these were KIA, the rest were captured by the Japanese. Kirby, *War Against Japan*, Vol. I, p. 473.
[184] Singh, *Soldiers' Contribution*, p. 112. See also Ghosh, *Indian National Army*, p. 59.
[185] Fujiwara, *F Kikan*, p. 186.
[186] See Ghosh, *Indian National Army*, Chapter 4.
[187] Connell, *Auchinleck*, p. 951; Fay, *Forgotten Army*, pp. 525–526.
[188] Fay, *Forgotten Army*, p. 525.   [189] Khan, *My Memories of I.N.A.*, p. 26.

shock the INA posed to martial race stereotypes. Indian soldiers were supposed to be not very intelligent, childlike men who were obedient and war-like.[190] That tens of thousands of Indian soldiers would "be untrue to their salt" shocked British officers and officials. The idea that "every Indian is a possible 5th columnist" was potentially debilitating. This explains in part the widespread official concern the INA caused, well in excess of its actual impact during the war.[191]

Notions of disloyal Indian soldiers becoming nationalist agents were as misplaced a view of the motivations of Indian PoWs as Fujiwara's reference to Mother India. Many soldiers were illiterate and had little education. They would have grasped their situation but not necessarily the higher politics of it. An Indian gunner who joined the INA claimed he did not know for what purpose it had been formed.[192] Francis Tuker tells of an Indian soldier from Mohan Singh's battalion who when asked why he joined the INA after the war said "that in the Army he was taught to obey, so when his officers ordered him to come with them he did so and so did his friends."[193] As the choice was between the INA and Japanese captivity, the outcome was overdetermined. One Indian officer said of his men "[a]ll my people preferred to be in the I.N.A. than to fall into the hands of the Japanese."[194] Mason tells of one *subedar*-major, whom he knew well, who joined the INA with his men. Their ICO told them "they had the choice between digging latrines for the Japanese and once more becoming soldiers – but this time in the service of an independent India. They chose to be soldiers."[195] Indian PoW camps were placed next to INA camps, so that the Indian prisoners could see the better conditions available to INA soldiers. "[T]he INA personnel will be eating their breakfast and doing the physical training, doing their drill and exercises where the prisoners of war will be taken as a group of labourers working in the streets, cleaning the streets, that sort of thing, to show the contrast."[196]

During the Second World War, the death rate among Allied prisoners held by the Japanese was over 27 percent, as compared to 4 percent for

---

[190] Nandy, *Intimate Enemy*, pp. 37–38; Omissi, *The Sepoy and the Raj*, p. 27.
[191] Letter from KCIO, 13 March, 1943, INA and Free Burma Army, L/WS/1/1576, OIOC.
[192] Ram, *Two Historic Trials*, p. 82.   [193] Tuker, *While Memory Serves*, p. 53.
[194] Major Rawat, quoted in Ghosh, *Indian National Army*, p. 69.
[195] Mason in Toye, *Springing Tiger*, p. vii.
[196] Lt. Gen. Harbaksh Singh, p. 35, Mss. Eur. T95/2, OIOC.

those interned by the Germans and Italians.[197] Indian PoWs in Singapore were treated somewhat better and, as one ICO noted, they knew they were being treated better because of the INA.[198] One *jemadar* who was not at that time in the INA described the poor conditions in his camp where the men were suffering from malaria and there were no medicines or proper shelter. An INA officer came by and told them "If you join the I.N.A. all these troubles will be solved."[199] While he did not join at that point, several months later when "our conditions were going from bad to worse" he and other men from his unit did.[200] Various folksy legitimations were offered to the captured troops as well. One INA officer tried to recruit Indian PoWs by telling them that "as Buddha [i.e. the Japanese god] was born in India, we should join hands with the Japanese."[201]

It is likely that many, as Shah Nawaz Khan who was supervising the Indian PoW camps put it, "signed up as volunteers in the I.N.A. in order to avoid hardship."[202] One Indian soldier captured in the Japanese conquest of Burma in 1942 described the rough treatment meted out to Indian PoWs by the Japanese. "The treatment of the Japanese soldiers with the Indian Prisoners was very rude and cruel."[203] There were beatings and a great deal of forced labor. After some time, INA officers visited the camp and encouraged them to join the INA and liberate India with the help of the Japanese. The Indian PoWs refused and were handed back to the Japanese, who beat them and locked them in barracks without food, supplying only water to the prisoners for fifteen days during which several died. The INA officers returned and this time the men volunteered, although the soldier who related the story re-defected at first opportunity.[204]

Unfortunately for the INA, the moment of maximum British weakness had already passed by the time Bose had re-energized it. The Japanese offensive in 1944, accompanied by the 1st INA Division,

---

[197] Tanaka, *Hidden Horrors*, pp. 2–3.   [198] Ghosh, *Indian National Army*, p. 69.
[199] Quoted in Ram, *Two Historic Trials*, p. 55.
[200] Quoted in Ram, *Two Historic Trials*, p. 55.
[201] Quoted in Ram, *Two Historic Trials*, p. 59.
[202] Khan, *My Memories of I.N.A.*, p. 48.
[203] Indian National Army – Counter Measures, Loose Archives 1/7 GR, G46, GM.
[204] Indian National Army – Counter Measures, Loose Archives 1/7 GR, G46, GM. This was a memo circulated in late 1942 to all C-in-C's of India Command. The appendix contains the statement of this Indian soldier.

failed to open the door to India. Had the INA and Japanese forces appeared in strength on the north-eastern border of India in late 1942, in the immediate wake of Quit India, Bose might have had a chance of raising India in revolt. But it was not to be and there were no further defections of significance from the British Indian Army to the INA after the fall of Singapore. Bose had to turn to recruiting Indian expatriates in Southeast Asia to fill the ranks of the INA. It was the INA which, in the face of the military debacle that befell it and the Japanese in 1944–45, suffered from mass desertion as its officers and men went back over to the British.[205]

Politics and Military Service

In colonial context, politics and military service did not come in the self-reinforcing packages of the nation state, where the enemy of the army was also the enemy of the national people. Even so, Indian soldiers, whatever their politics, mostly served the British obediently throughout the war, albeit with varying levels of vigor and effectiveness. The only time Indian Army soldiers joined Axis-sponsored independence forces in number was in the immediate aftermath of defeat and mass surrender, when the alternative was harsh and lengthy imprisonment. As army headquarters in India was to correctly note very soon after the formation of the INA, "[o]nce things are going well, troops are much less likely to be affected by Indian National Army propaganda."[206] For Indian soldiers, the conditions of service were more important than the politics of service. The army was able to generate discipline and loyalty of a kind without the "safety net" of a national polity.

In his account of US soldiers in World War II, Gerald Linderman remarks that many American soldiers certainly believed in the justice of their cause. But "[c]onsideration of principles and larger aims diminished drastically as soldiers realized they had no bearing on battle . . . [Such ideas] were extraneous to absorbing daily pursuits and

[205] See Ghosh, *Indian National Army*, pp. 188–189; Khan, *My Memories of I.N.A.*, p. 48; Menezes, *Fidelity and Honour*, pp. 394–397; Ram, *Two Historic Trials*, pp. 346–347; Sundaram, "A Paper Tiger."

[206] Indian National Army – Counter Measures, Loose Archives 1/7 GR, G46, GM.

consequently virtually disappeared from their thoughts."[207] Soldiers
faced circumstances in which the high politics of the war seemed irrel-
evant to what was immediately at hand and offered no clear guide
to action. Lord Wavell, with long experience of both the British and
Indian armies in two world wars, made a similar point: "[m]uch is
said nowadays of the necessity that the soldier should be convinced of
the justice of his cause; and he certainly cannot escape propaganda.
Yet many battles and campaigns have been won by men who had little idea of why they were fighting, and, perhaps cared less."[208] British
intelligence officers collating reports on the interrogation of Japanese
PoWs noted that even though some Japanese doubted their cause and
prospects for victory, such doubts "were never obvious in the way they
carried out their duties or went out to fight."[209] Meyers and Biderman's
volume on the Korean War noted that some Chinese People's Liberation Army officers and soldiers had severe political misgivings about
the communists, but were obedient and effective soldiers for them.
Some had switched sides between the nationalists and communists,
making accommodations with whichever side had the upper hand.[210]

Soldiers might be "disloyal," politically speaking, but still "loyal"
militarily. Such a description fits Indian officers in the Second World
War. They were not loyal to the Raj, but were willing to serve and fight
in its army. For soldiers and for officers, the conditions of service could
generate their own logic of obedience and discipline. The army's discipline is cosmopolitan. It can be adapted to various societies and situations. Yet, the army always has a local character. The social, cultural,
and political context of an army shapes its soldiers and their behavior, as it did for Indian soldiers who could avoid PoW camps precisely
because of the colonial character of their army.

With exception, and despite the tumultuous politics of the war in
India, the Indian Army's combat formations were militarily effective.
Indian soldiers were disciplined and willing to risk their lives. It was
one thing to structure the army so that it was disconnected from

[207] Linderman, *World Within War*, p. 24.
[208] Field Marshall Lord Wavell, The Good Soldier, GHQ (I) Infantry Liaison
Letters, No. 24, February, 1946, Appendix A, p. 18, L/WS/1/778, OIOC.
[209] Interrogation Report No. 8, Loose Archives 1/7 GR, G46, GM.
[210] William Bradbury and Jeane J. Kirkpatrick, "Determinants of Loyalty and
Disaffection in Chinese Communist Soldiers during the Korean Hostilities" in
Meyers and Biderman, *Mass Behavior in Battle and Captivity*, pp. 35–56.

anti-colonial, nationalist politics. But where did the army get its fighting spirit? Its willingness to kill and die? What was the source of its combat discipline? This is where national politics is supposed to underwrite modern military service, especially in mass armies in total war.[211] The Indian Army did not derive its fighting qualities form Victorian racial theory, or from orientalist incantations about the warrior qualities of Sikhs, Pathans, and the like. Having addressed the processural and co-constitutive character of army–society relations in this first part of the book, Part II takes up the question of the sources of discipline, solidarity, and sacrifice in battle.

In closing, it is worth foreshadowing a larger sense of disconnect between politics and war for soldiers. In its complexity, specificity, and, above all, contingency, war metes out fates in ways that lack ideological consistency. Many Indian soldiers who volunteered for the INA were still sent by the Japanese to labor camps. In one incident, a ship carrying Indian PoWs from Singapore was torpedoed and sunk by a US submarine. The submarine surfaced and machine-gunned the survivors, thinking they were Japanese crewmen.[212] Wartime outcomes are difficult to correlate with ideological expectations. All too often, war denies soldiers "meaningful" deaths. In its capriciousness, war enables no theodicy by which to make sense of soldiers' suffering. The actions and fates of soldiers resist a final political accounting or neat emplotment in nationalist narrative. This is one reason why a magical language of national sacrifice is so necessary in the many efforts to provide such narratives. To represent soldiers and their actions in the service of one or another nationalist cause is to reduce war to a political rationality. The problem is that war, and the fate of people caught up in it, exceeds politics.

[211] King, *Combat Soldier*, Chapter 4, pp. 62–97.
[212] Crasta, *Eaten by the Japanese*, p. 29.

Going to War

4 | *Defeat, Drill, and Discipline*

The more modern war becomes, the more essential appear the basic qualities that from the beginning of history have distinguished armies from mobs.

– Field Marshal Sir William Slim[1]

Part I of this book dealt with the character of army–society relations in British India, and their disruption and transformation by the Second World War. Part II concerns what happened when the Indian Army, along with other British and imperial forces, was sent to fight the Japanese in Burma. How were new soldiers made to replace those lost in the initial, shattering defeats? How did they react to the Imperial Japanese Army? Why did such intense fighting erupt and what sustained it? What can we learn about soldiers, armies, and war?

In answering these questions for national troops, many scholars have looked to culture, in the sense of the beliefs and ideas soldiers carry in their heads. Military sociology and history follow much of the "constructivist" turn in the social sciences and humanities in studying culture as analogous to textual interpretation. They examine soldiers' identities, political ideologies, religions, and views about military service, as evidenced in memoirs, letters, interviews, surveys, and other accounts.[2] But culture is not just what people think, it is also what they experience and do. The wartime Indian Army, and especially the 14th Army in Burma, was a multicultural agglomeration of young strangers thrown together for the war. The old regular Indian Army provided military backbone with its professional officers, VCOs, and long-serving soldiers. But emergency-commissioned officers and

---

[1] Slim, *Defeat into Victory*, p. 542.
[2] See e.g. Bartov, *Hitler's Army*; Cameron, *American Samurai*; Linderman, *Embattled Courage*; *World Within War*; Lynn, *Battle*; McPherson, *Cause and Comrades*; Merridale, *Ivan's War*; Watson, *Enduring the Great War*; "Culture and Combat in the Western World, 1900–1945."

wartime recruits filled out the units. What these soldiers from different backgrounds believed, what they identified with politically and culturally, what they thought about the war, was less significant than their common, collective experiences of military service, campaigning, and battle. These experiences transformed them and shaped their actions. Fighting drew in and remade participants. War surged into the circuits between army and society.[3]

The differing backgrounds of the British, Indian, African, and other imperial troops who fought in Burma mattered to who they were and how they fought. But the multiculturalism of British imperial forces underscores something else: the cosmopolitan character of military discipline and the experience of war. Common conditions generated comparable reactions among soldiers of different origins, even on different sides. Tough infantry training regimens, followed by campaigning and combat, put increasingly harsh demands and constraints on the people involved. At the front, action-reaction circuits settled in and governed the opposing forces, shaping and determining battlefield behavior. Soldiers and their units confronted a structure of battle with powers of life and death over them. In Burma, as elsewhere in the Asia-Pacific Wars, the Japanese and their opponents fought on stark and pitiless terms, but shared ones nonetheless. "It was a very cruel war," observed the Burma campaign's participant-historian, Louis Allen.[4]

When William Slim came to write his narrative of the re-conquest of Burma in 1944–45, primarily by the 14th Army under his command, he called it *Defeat into Victory*. Along with the military authorities in India, he built his army out of the remnants of British Indian forces shattered by the Japanese in Malaya and Burma in 1942–43. An army that recovers from a blow to emerge victorious is a useful optic to explore the sources of battlefield behavior. What made the army fail in the first place, and succeed later? My interest here is not so much in the strategic and operational contexts, although these are relevant, as it is in elementary questions of discipline, of the creation of effective soldiers. If Part I used the Indian Army as an example of how armies are articulated to particular social and historical contexts, Part II draws on British, Indian, and imperial forces in the Burma campaign to think about how the army produces a modicum of combat discipline. Most contributions to the combat motivation debates focus on fighting spirit

---

[3] Barkawi and Brighton, "Powers of War."   [4] Allen, *Burma*, p. xviii.

as a relative matter, on why some armies and units are better than others.[5] But what of the elementary sources of combat discipline? How do armies achieve a basic standard? What can the Burma campaign and the colonial Second World War teach us about these questions?

In order to fight effectively in regular warfare, soldiers have to take appropriate and correct actions (whatever they may be) in stressful and life-threatening conditions. Inculcating this ability in soldiers requires training and drill.[6] In modern armies, drill is not only for ceremonies and parade grounds. It remains the army's indispensable pedagogy, its correct execution necessary for combat effectiveness.[7] Just about any action soldiers or units need to take can be broken down into steps and taught as a drill. This produces a shared standard among trainees of differing abilities, and, with various teaching aids, provides effective instruction with a minimum of cultural and linguistic competence. Training teaches troops what to do at the appropriate shouts or prompts of command. How does drill achieve this? How should we think about and study drill?

Much writing about military discipline suspends drill between ritual and modernity. Obviously ritual, scholars emplot drill as a distinctive Western quality that originated in Greco-Roman antiquity.[8] Military drill appears modern and Occidental, while ritual is ordinarily associated with the pre-modern and non-West. Historically, in fact, peoples have invented and practiced forms of drill in widely disparate times and places.[9] The world histories of drill began in ancient Mesopotamia and Egypt and continued in China, Japan, India, and Africa as well as in Europe.[10] European forms of drill did become globally dominant, carried abroad with imperial expansion or imported by rising

---

[5] An important exception is King, *Combat Soldier*.

[6] King, *Combat Soldier*, Chapter 9, pp. 266–337; Lynn, *Bayonets of the Republic*; Strachan, "Training, Morale and Modern War."

[7] King, *Combat Soldier*, Chapter 8, pp. 208–265.

[8] See e.g. Hanson, *Carnage and Culture*, pp. 331–332 and *passim*; Parker, *Cambridge History of Warfare*, Introduction and Part One, pp. 1–58; Ralston, *Importing the European Army*, Chapter 1, pp. 1–12. Cf. McNeill, *Keeping Together in Time*, Chapter 5, pp. 101–150.

[9] Cooper, "Culture, Combat, and Colonialism," pp. 536–538. "As African and Asian archers had released arrows on command for thousands of years, the non-Western world did not have to wait to be told that firearms could be used in the same manner." Ibid., p. 537.

[10] Lorge, *Asian Military Revolution*; McNeill, *Keeping Together in Time*, Chapter 5, pp. 101–150.

powers.[11] But in conceiving drill as essentially Western and modern, its cosmopolitan character risks being overlooked. Mistakenly seen as underwriting distinctions between modernity/tradition and Occident/Orient, regular military discipline in fact destabilizes them. For infantry soldiers in particular, drill has an ancient heritage and ongoing histories that have always involved different peoples. Romans and Carthaginians drilled in their wars, as did British and Zulus in theirs.[12] Drill's reach across time and place best reveals its powers, rather than provincializing it in often triumphalist Western histories.[13] Drill does not work because of special Western properties, but because of its cosmopolitan powers, because it works for nearly anybody. Rethinking military drill as ritual helps critique and move beyond Eurocentrism in the study of military discipline; so, too, does focusing on a late imperial, multicultural army.

Fighting together in 14th Army's units, disciplined by military pedagogies, were farmers' sons from West Africa, the Punjab, and the north of England; volunteers from Madras, Wales, and Kenya; minor nobles from the English home counties and the princely states of the Raj; illiterates and the Oxbridge-educated; and many others. How could the army turn such diverse human material – Asian, African, and Western; colonized and modern; rich and poor – into a fighting machine, one ready to face the determined veterans of the IJA in the tangle of the Indo-Burmese border?

What follows in this chapter takes two steps toward answering these questions. The first looks at a moment when discipline failed: a campaign known as the First Arakan, fought in Burma in the winter and spring of 1942–43, around a year after the surrender at Singapore. In this shambolic and tragic affair, Indian soldiers panicked, ran away when fired upon, and shot themselves to escape the front. What went wrong? The Japanese were on India's doorstep, promising liberation; Quit India had swept the country; and both the INA and Congress

[11] Fahmy, *All the Pasha's Men*; McNeill, *Pursuit of Power*, Chapter 4, pp. 117–143; Parker, *Military Revolution*, Chapter 4, pp. 115–145; Ralston, *Importing the European Army*.

[12] Delbrück, *Warfare in Antiquity*, Book V, pp. 311–390; Laband, *Kingdom in Crisis*.

[13] See e.g. Gat, *War in Human Civilization*, Part 3, pp. 445–673; Hanson, *Western War of War*; Parker, *Military Revolution*, Chapter 4, pp. 115–145; "Introduction: The Western Way of War," in Parker, *Cambridge History of Warfare*, pp. 1–11.

activists were attempting to suborn Indian soldiers.[14] Had nationalist politics sapped Indian troops' fighting spirit, as the authorities feared? In fact, a lack of training and an effective system for replacing casualties proved to be the problem. Even when Indian soldiers sought to act directly on their political beliefs, the harsh antagonisms of the battlefield stymied them. If, as shown in Chapter 3, the PoW cage offered one set of harsh conditions and choices, the front was even more unforgiving. This was especially so for untrained soldiers on Burma's forested ridges; they did not know what the appropriate actions were or have the discipline to perform them. They encountered the front as something that had an external reality, one that dealt injury and death.

The chapter then turns from what was broken to how it was fixed. Drawing on a range of examples from the training of Indian and imperial troops, it outlines the application of the regular military's basic pedagogical techniques to local circumstances, and highlights how the military authorities in India dealt with some of the challenges they faced, from a polyglot imperial army and seething colony, to difficult jungle terrain and a determined opponent. In no small measure, they did so through drilling. The Indian Army, and General Slim and his officers, eventually managed to produce enough credible soldiers to win the infantry war in Burma. This shift from defeat to discipline exemplifies the application of the regular military's robust and sturdy ritual techniques to a particular social and historical context. In this movement, we begin to get a sense of how it is that the military reliably creates soldiers from diverse populations and circumstances.

Infantry soldiers have to do more than simply drill to be successful in combat. They must also be willing to kill and die. Chapter 5 takes up questions of solidarity and sacrifice, the meaningful dimensions of military ritual, as opposed to the merely disciplinary. Chapter 6 draws together the threads of discipline and spirit on the battlefield.

The First Arakan

In the summer of 1942, amid the Japanese high tide of the war and without the requisite ground, air, and naval forces, the chiefs of staff and the war cabinet in London planned the re-conquest of Burma.

---

[14] See Kamtekar, "The Shiver of 1942"; Khan, *Raj at War*, Chapters 8–9, pp. 93–121.

Winston Churchill was fighting World War II to preserve and, where necessary, regain the British Empire. The result in the winter and spring of 1942–43 – the dry campaign season in Burma – was a failed offensive fought under commanders giving off more than a whiff of Colonel Blimp.[15] What led the Indian Army units in the Arakan to behave the way they did? How did the wider crises in colonial society and the Allied war effort impact upon the army's infantry battalions?

As actually fought, the First Arakan was a remnant of grander schemes whittled away by reality. (See Map 4.1) Initially, the idea was to stage an amphibious operation into the Rangoon area via Akyab Island. It became a landward thrust down the Arakan's Mayu Peninsula with the object of taking Akyab Island. The Commander-in-Chief, India, General Sir Archibald Wavell, needed a victory to assuage London and to restore the badly shaken prestige of the Raj as well as the morale of the Indian Army. He gave the task to Eastern Army, under Lieutenant-General Noel Irwin. Irwin, in turn, ordered Major-General Wilfred Lloyd's 14th Indian Division to begin its advance from Cox's Bazaar in the Fall of 1942.

The Arakan was a formidable place, containing "some of the most difficult inhospitable, mountainous and malaria-ridden country in all of Burma" and consisting "of a mass of tangled, jungle-covered hills interspersed with paddy fields and mangrove swamps in the lower lying regions near the coast."[16] Down the middle of the Mayu Peninsula ran a jungle-covered mountain range with high crests and foothills thickly covered with tropical vegetation. The coastal strips on either side of the mountains, as wide as two miles in places, provided easier going. But they were broken up by paddy fields and swamps, and crossed by several deep streams and dry stream beds, called *chaungs*, which became rushing torrents in the monsoon. "The *chaungs* were tidal and many were several hundred feet wide. Not a few were fringed with mud banks and mangrove swamp."[17] To the east, the Mayu River valley

---

[15] For accounts of the First Arakan campaign see: Allen, *Burma*, pp. 91–116; Connell, *Wavell*, Chapter VIII, pp. 236–272; Kirby, *War Against Japan*, Vol. II, Chapters XV, XIX, and XX, pp. 253–268, 331–360; Latimer, *Burma*, Chapters 8 and 9, pp. 121–152; Madan, *The Arakan Operations*, Chapters I-VII, pp. 1–88; Moreman, *The Jungle, the Japanese and the British Commonwealth Armies*, pp. 64–76.

[16] Moreman, *The Jungle, the Japanese and the British Commonwealth Armies*, p. 64.

[17] Captain Rissik quoted in Thompson, *War in Burma 1942–45*, p. 44.

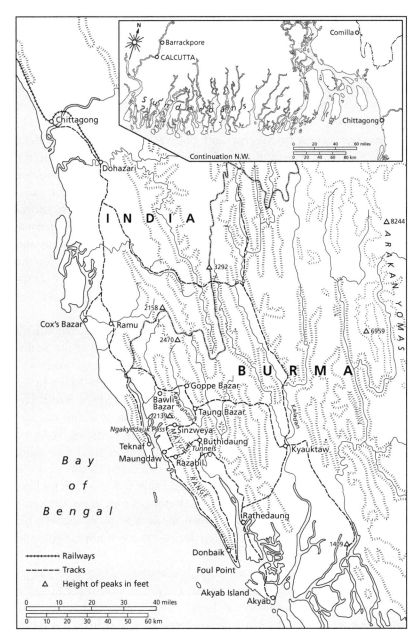

Map 4.1 Sketch map of the Arakan.[18]

[18] Ronald Lewin, *Slim: The Standardbearer* (London: Leo Cooper, 1976), p. 117.

consisted of more paddy and swamps, and more *chaungs*. Further east was the broken and difficult terrain of the Kaladan River valley and the Arakan Yomas, the open left flank of the British advance, upon which two regiments of the Japanese 55th division were descending to reinforce the two infantry battalions and ancillary elements which were the only forces the Japanese had in the Arakan until the end of January 1943.[19]

Japanese success in Malaya and Burma had come in part from their ability to navigate jungle terrain considered impassable by the British. The Japanese outflanked British Indian positions by moving around them in the jungle, showing up in their rear. British commanders failed to fully appreciate the dangers posed by Japanese movements and denied themselves opportunities to flank Japanese defensive positions. Once it completed its march across the Arakan Yomas and the Kaladan, the Japanese 55th Division would be able to sever the British line of communications in the Arakan by occupying the northern end of the Mayu peninsula, trapping British and Indian forces to the south.

By limiting their own operations to the coastal strips, the British made it easier for the Japanese to hold the southern end of the peninsula and tie up British and Indian units. The Japanese set up two blocking positions, one at Donbaik on the western side of the Mayu range and one at Rathedaung on the eastern bank of the Mayu River. The British obliged them by repeatedly attacking these positions on narrow fronts, rather than working around them. Of a briefing by Lloyd before one of his attacks on Donbaik, Slim commented: "I told him I thought he was making the error that most of us had made in 1942 in considering any jungle impenetrable and that it was worth making a great effort to get a brigade, or at least part of one, along the spine of the ridge," that is, to use the Mayu mountains to get behind the Japanese position.[20] In the end Lloyd decided this was not feasible and his brigadiers agreed.

By the end of February, the Japanese had assembled the better part of a division to strike back in the Arakan. They came across the Kaladan River valley and cleared the east bank of the Mayu River of British-Indian forces, just as the 6th Brigade prepared and delivered a futile,

---

[19] Latimer, *Burma*, p. 141; Kirby, *The War Against Japan*, pp. 255, 265. In the Japanese Army, a regiment was an operational unit with three infantry battalions, comparable to a British brigade.

[20] Slim, *Defeat into Victory*, pp. 153–154.

and failed, final attack at Donbaik on 18 March (of which more in Chapter 8). A week later the Japanese crossed the Mayu River and by the 29th they had cut off 47th Brigade on the eastern side of the peninsula. A few days later 6th Brigade, too, on the western side was cut off as the Japanese established a block at Indin. The 6th Brigade managed to fight its way out but 47th Brigade was forced to abandon heavy equipment and break out in small parties. On 14th April, Slim was given operational command: "I have rarely been so unhappy on a battlefield."[21] He counselled retreat. By May 1943, British Indian forces were back in Cox's Bazaar, where they had started in October, 1942. The First Arakan was over.

The events that had unfolded in the Arakan resulted as much from misguided British generalship as from the shaky state of many of 14th Indian Division's units. Raymond Callahan called the First Arakan perhaps the "worst managed British military effort of the war."[22] British commanders, in the style of the First World War, ordered assaults along narrow frontages in increasing depths against well-constructed Japanese defenses with interlocking fields of fire. They repeated mistakes made in Malaya and Burma in 1942, and the high command persisted in underestimating the Japanese right up until the end. Irwin was particularly concerned to blame his troops for the debacle, telling journalists that the Japanese are "frightening my soldiers from their positions" and urging Wavell to place responsibility on the "inability of troops to fight."[23]

What explains the poor performance of Indian battalions in the Arakan? On the one hand, their soldiers were unprepared for jungle warfare and they lacked trained replacements. On the other, anti-colonial nationalism in India peaked just as British and Allied fortunes were at their lowest ebb of the war. The discussion below considers each source of trouble in turn.

Jungle Warfare

The jungle was foreign to the Indian Army, which, by 1942, was experienced in mountain and desert operations. When the 7/10th Baluch was on its way to Rangoon before the Japanese invasion of Burma in

---

[21] Slim, *Defeat into Victory*, p. 157.   [22] Callahan, *Burma*, p. 59.
[23] Lt. Gen. N.M.S. Irwin, "Rough shorthand note of Army Commander's Press Conference," 9 May, 1943 and Irwin to Wavell, 8 May, 1943, 2/1, P139, IWM.

1942, its CO inquired about training areas his battalion might make use of. He was told that it was impossible to do any training as "it's all bloody jungle."[24] Once the Japanese invaded, and for the rest of the war, much of the fighting would occur in densely forested terrain.

Before the First Arakan, training establishments in India, overburdened with the pressures of expansion, struggled to incorporate jungle warfare into their syllabi. Tactics, doctrine, and courses for jungle fighting took time to develop and there were shortages of suitable equipment and experienced instructors. On their way to India, the officers of 2/Durham Light Infantry tried to school themselves using "out of date platitudinous pamphlets about fighting in the forests of the Ardennes and Finland."[25] Another problem was finding likely terrain for jungle training in much of India. At one officers' course, "Jungle Exercises Without Trees quickly replaced the more traditional Tactical Exercises Without Troops to give officers at least a theoretical idea of jungle conditions."[26]

The formations destined to fight in the Arakan had in any case little opportunity to train at all. They spent much of the spring and summer of 1942 constructing field defenses in Eastern India or heavily involved in internal security duties during the Quit India uprising. The unusually severe monsoon in the fall, just before the Arakan operations got underway, made matters worse. Living conditions deteriorated in the wet and mud and transport became difficult. Tropical diseases, including malaria, dysentery, scrub typhus, and assorted skin problems, increased massively. In some units, malaria struck between 70 and 100 percent of personnel.[27] Sustained and effective training could not take place under these conditions.

As a consequence, many soldiers were not psychologically acclimated to active service in the jungle: "They feared the eeriness, they dreaded the insects and snakes, they hated not being able to see the dangers. They imagined that death lurked behind every tree . . . they felt

---

[24] John Randle, interview with the author.

[25] Major D.C. Rissik, "Forgotten Front," p. 5, 91/8/1, IWM.

[26] Moreman, *Jungle, the Japanese and the British Commonwealth Armies*, p. 62. In staff college instruction, officers would practice operations in the field without using actual units of soldiers, hence "tactical exercises without troops," or TEWT.

[27] Moreman, *Jungle, the Japanese and the British Commonwealth Armies*, pp. 61–63.

Figure 4.1 Slit trench: Indian soldiers in a fighting position somewhere in the Arakan, 1943, armed with a Lee-Enfield rifle, a Thompson submachine gun, and a Bren light machine gun with a barrel magazine.[28]

glued to the spot, with threats all around them," recalled one general.[29] A brigade commander in the Arakan noted later that "[m]ost of our [troops] instinctively dislike the jungle – partly owing to the difficulty of movement in it and partly due to mistrust of the unknown."[30] One observer described Indian troops as "terribly afraid of walking through the jungles."[31]

Quite aside from anything the Japanese were doing, the jungle at night spooked soldiers waiting it out in their slit trenches. (See Figure 4.1) Whether or not they could hold their fire was a key indicator of training and discipline on active operations in Burma. A British officer described his first night in the Arakan later in the war:

The night was moonless and pitch dark; the 'tuck-too' lizards were starting their explosive and sudden calls, now from one tree and then from another.

---

[28] IND1973, IWM.
[29] Gordon Bennett quoted in Moreman, *The Jungle, the Japanese and the British Commonwealth Armies at War*, p. 23.
[30] Notes on lessons from the Operations in Arakan – 1943, Report by Comd 71 Indian Infantry Brigade, WO 203/1167, TNA.
[31] Lt. Gen. N.M.S. Irwin, "A Report from Mr. Zainuddin," 2/1, P139, IWM.

Jackals were howling from the coastal plain. Fireflies were winking in the bushes and beyond our wire. Were the lizards real? Were the flashes really fireflies? Were the Jackals really what they seemed to be?...Each sound, each movement by an animal, set our nerves on edge.[32]

If soldiers fired their weapons at these sounds, thinking they were under attack, they used ammunition difficult to supply in Burma and the muzzle flashes revealed their locations. This enabled the Japanese to map out British and Indian defenses, to register their artillery, mortars and other fires accordingly, and to launch raids to take out key positions before an attack.

To encourage unnecessary firing, and more generally to keep the enemy sleepless and on tenterhooks, the Japanese developed "jitter" tactics. They would move around British and Indian perimeters at night, occasionally firing a shot, imitating jungle noises, or even calling out, in order to induce firing. Well-trained, disciplined units resisted the temptation until they were under actual attack. On their first night in the line before Donbaik, 2/Durham Light Infantry fired not a single shot, noted the commander of a neighboring British battalion. But the Indian battalions "are very windy at night and the Japs succeed in drawing their fire very easily."[33] Around the same time, as the British 6th Brigade replaced the 55th Indian Brigade in front of Donbaik, Captain Rissik recalled how jumpy the 55th Brigade were: "on the nights before the hand over, they kept us [up with] almost continuous small arms fire during darkness, firing presumably at shadows or noises. It was almost unbelievable."[34] Two of its officers recalled of the MG Battalion/9th Jats, also at Donbaik, that "at nighttime, the slightest rustle in the twigs, they'd let off all their guns."[35]

One night in February near Rathedaung, the 1/15th Punjab thought it was under attack. They showered the imaginary Japanese with hand grenades. But they mostly forgot to remove the safety pins, although hand grenades were in fact one correct response to jittering as at night they did not reveal the location of the thrower.[36] When Slim came to the Arakan in early March on a fact finding mission, he discovered

---

[32] Leathart, *With the Gurkhas*, p. 69.
[33] Diary of Lt. Col. A.H. Williams, 10 March, 1943, 3722, RWF.
[34] Major D.C. Rissik, "Forgotten Front," p. 68, 91/8/1, IWM; quoted in Thompson, *War in Burma*, p. 49.
[35] Peter Francis and Tony Banks, interview with the author.
[36] Moreman, *Jungle, the Japanese and the British Commonwealth Armies*, p. 70.

that morale was low and that there was a lot of unnecessary firing after nightfall. In one unfortunate instance, this firing developed into a full-scale exchange between two of 14th Division's own units. "At least we won *that* battle!" remarked the Division's chief of staff the morning after.[37] The 8/13th Frontier Force Rifles holding Hill 551 was forced to withdraw after blazing off all its ammunition into the darkness and finding they had little left in the morning.[38]

Replacements

The standard of jungle and other training was particularly poor among replacements sent to the Arakan. Units on active service suffer "wastage" even in the best of conditions, as soldiers are killed, wounded, fall sick, and have accidents. In the Arakan, those infected by malaria beforehand rapidly became ill under the stress of campaigning. By the end of the First Arakan, the British 6th Brigade was sending back fifty men a day with malaria. In one six-day period 2,600 troops, a brigade's worth, most with malaria, were evacuated from all the units in the Arakan.[39] "In 1943 for every man admitted to hospital with wounds there had been one hundred and twenty from tropical diseases."[40]

For Indian units, the replacements for these losses were mostly raw recruits with only a few months basic training. "The complete breakdown of the machinery for providing trained British and Indian reinforcements was regarded as by far the most serious problem facing Indian high command."[41] The 1/7th Rajput, after suffering heavily in the fighting at Donbaik, particularly among its officers, junior commanders and trained soldiers, received in replacement "recruits of four months standing, totally untrained for jungle warfare."[42] The 2/1st Punjab, which also suffered severe casualties at Donbaik and elsewhere, including four company commanders killed, received after

---

[37] Quoted in Slim, *Defeat into Victory*, p. 153.
[38] Lt. Gen. N.M.S. Irwin, 2/1, "Report on a visit to Maungdaw front from 4/5/43 to 9/5/43," by a liaison officer from HQ 15 Corps, 2/1, P139, IWM.
[39] Moreman, *Jungle, the Japanese and the British Commonwealth Armies*, p. 74; Lt. Gen. N.M.S. Irwin, Slim to Irwin, 18 April, 1943, 2/1, P139, IWM.
[40] Mason, *Matter of Honour*, p. 496.
[41] Moreman, *Jungle, the Japanese and the British Commonwealth Armies*, p. 83.
[42] Sir Francis Tuker, Court of Inquiry – Operations in the Arakan, Opinion of the Court, 71/21/3, IWM.

these actions "a very large draft of reinforcements composed of young recruits averaging about six months service, many of whom had not even fired a Bren gun, and none had ever thrown a grenade."[43] British battalions complained similarly about receiving replacements of "dubious quality" from the "dregs of the reinforcement camps."[44] "The new men are quite the worst ill-disciplined troops the battalion has had in this war."[45] The poor quality of replacements only exacerbated the problem of incorporating them into units in the midst of active operations.

As discussed in Part I, in both world wars Indian Army regiments found that the villages and community networks from which they recruited ran out of suitable young men. They began to sign on men from communities from which they had not previously recruited. These recruits spoke different dialects and vernaculars, creating problems for those who had to train, command, and work with them. Because they had not previously served in the army, these new classes lacked their own junior leaders and experienced soldiers. They stood outside of the social ties that normally underpinned battalions composed of long service regulars. Whereas a peacetime recruit might encounter men from his village or extended family when he reached his battalion, soldiers from these new groups were strangers.

Chapter 2 showed that new classes of soldiers could be handled, but it took some time and sensible officering. The problem in the Arakan was that drafts of new classes were dumped on units in the midst of difficult operations. The draft sent to the 2/1st Punjab mentioned above was composed of a hundred Jat recruits, a class that had previously not served in the battalion. The draft did not include a single Jat NCO or VCO. How was a reduced battalion to find junior commanders of any class for these troops? Situations of this kind led one officer to describe the British Indian forces in the Arakan as a "rather unwilling raw band of levies."[46] Even so, raw recruits were only part of the problem.

---

[43] Sir Francis Tuker, Court of Inquiry – Operations in the Arakan, Statement of Major C.A.I. Suther, 71/21/3, IWM.

[44] Major D.C. Rissik, "Forgotten Fronts," pp. 99, 103, 91/8/1, IWM.

[45] Diary of Lt. Col. A.H. Williams, 13 May, 1943, 3722, RWF. See also entry for 6 April, 1943.

[46] Lt. Gen. N.M.S. Irwin, "Report on a visit to Maungdaw front from 4/5/43 to 9/5/43," by a liaison officer from HQ 15 Corps, 2/1, P139, IWM.

The INA Appears

The First Arakan happened at the moment of maximum British weakness in the East, from summer 1942 to spring 1943. The IJA reached the northeastern borders of the Raj as its cities erupted in revolt and its countryside seethed with discontent. The Bengal famine spread as the campaign was fought. To officialdom, the Indian Army seemed badly shaken. It had already supplied seven divisions for service in the Mediterranean and Malaya. Then, the Japanese shattered its remaining trained and formed forces. The disruption of expansion, casualties and repeated defeats, and continuing fears of Japanese military prowess, had taken a toll on the army.[47] In this context, the INA enticed Indian soldiers to defect in the Arakan, while Congress activists approached them in training establishments in India. Do anti-colonial politics explain why the Indian Army more or less ran away in the First Arakan, as many officials feared?

Indian Army intelligence discovered that INA infiltrators and escapees had returned to India across the Burma-India border. Other INA men dropped into India by parachute. The Japanese trained many of them as agents, with instructions to make contact with Congress, collect and transmit intelligence, engage in sabotage, and subvert serving soldiers. Some efforts were amateurish, such as an ex-*havildar* spotted "taking too obvious an interest in troop trains."[48] Others turned themselves in immediately on arrival in India, claiming they had volunteered for the INA to get out of PoW camps and back home to their regiments (which may just have been a more clever way to infiltrate).

For colonial rulers reliant on a colonial army, questions of loyalty remained indecipherable. Indian Army intelligence worried that many INA escapees slipped through their hands: "In a disquieting number of cases, individuals have managed to conceal from interrogators the fact that they have been in Japanese hands, have been coached in espionage and subversive propaganda and sent back with specific instructions. Cases are now coming to light of 'stragglers' who rejoined as long

---

[47] Marston, *Phoenix from the Ashes*, Chapters 2–4; Moreman, *The Jungle, the Japanese and the British Commonwealth Armies at War*, Chapters 1–2.

[48] Intelligence Summaries India-Internal, Weekly Intelligence Summary No. 76, 16 April, 1943, L/WS/1/1433, OIOC; quoted in Fay, *The Forgotten Army*, p. 411.

ago as August and September [1942] and have successfully concealed these facts."[49] In the battalions, the distance between British officers and their Indian soldiers contributed to the uncertainty. Unwittingly or otherwise, VCOs could allow troops who had become INA agents back onto the rolls without necessarily bringing it to the attention of British officers.

What most concerned British officials was the combination of efforts by the nationalist underground to subvert soldiers at home with the presence of INA contact parties at the front. In a widely circulated document prepared in March 1943, as the battle at Donbaik reached its climax, the chief of the general staff in India wrote: "It is now quite clear that a double attack is being made on the morale and loyalty of Indian troops – one directed from without India by the Japanese, assisted by renegade Indians, and the other directed from within India by Congress or congress inspired organizations."[50] Bose's radio broadcasts from Berlin called for an intensification of propaganda against the army and for nationalist sympathizers to join the army to spread dissent from within. Nationalist activists made contact with soldiers in battalions destined for the Arakan. A civil officer accompanying the 8/10th Baluch in the Arakan described it as "Congress-minded."[51]

In the 1/15th Punjab, these efforts bore fruit. Around one hundred soldiers from one of its two Sikh companies crossed the lines under command of a VCO and joined the INA during the First Arakan. How did this come to happen? There was a legacy of discontent in the battalion. Its Sikhs were involved peripherally in the disciplinary troubles early in the war. One of its ICOs was in a unit which had mutinied in May, 1940 in Singapore. Soldiers from the battalion were reported to have told Congress activists they would join the movement when the time was right. Before the campaign, the battalion suffered several desertions.[52]

Once the battalion was in the Arakan, eight escapees claiming to have deserted the INA came through its lines. The battalion's soldiers heard about the preferential treatment the Japanese bestowed on

---

[49] Subversive Activities Directed Against the Indian Army, INA, L/WS/1/1711, OIOC.

[50] Subversive Activities Directed Against the Indian Army, INA, L/WS/1/1711, OIOC.

[51] A Report from Mr. Zainuddin, Lt. Gen. N.M.S. Irwin, 2/1, P139, IWM.

[52] Extracts from Security History of 'X' Battalion, INA, L/WS/1/1711, OIOC.

Indian PoWs. They would have been keen to learn of the avenues open to them should they have to surrender. The INA escapees were interrogated at brigade headquarters, where concerns were raised about one *naik*, or corporal, in particular. As the fighting in the Arakan really got underway in January and February 1943, censors for the battalion reported a range of complaints in soldiers' letters about delays in pay and allotments for families, while earlier there had been a high incidence of sickness.[53]

In mid-February, the Japanese captured a soldier from 1/15th Punjab by the name of Peyarai. An INA contact party went to work. A few days later, one of the battalion's patrols discovered leaflets addressed to "Dear Army Brother" and invoking Peyarai by name:

most of his companions wish for independence and want to join our side. But they are frightened by untrue British propaganda that the Japs used to kill prisoners ... We soldiers of the Indian Army were all captured in Malaya and Burma, we have been given Independence and are forming an Independent Army to fight for the Independence of India.

The leaflet noted pointedly: "You are all come to sacrifice your lives for Rs.20/- or 25/- a month. For the cruel British you have left your dear parents, brothers, and relations." It closed with a practical if tricky route to joining the INA:

Any brother who gets this letter is requested to convey this message to all Hindu, Muslim and Sikh soldiers who come close to us. You can come straight away without fear after hiding your arms in the jungle... When you come to this side show a white flag and keep your hands up whenever and wherever you meet Jap soldiers. Tell them to take you to Capt. Mohan Singh, Indian National Army. The Japs will bring you straight away to me. Then you will be an independent soldier of the Independent Army under me.[54]

Carrying Mohan Singh's signature and the slogan "Get up and wake," the leaflet was effective. Later in the month, the hundred or so Sikhs went over to the Japanese with their arms. A few weeks later, Irwin

---

[53] Extracts from Security History of 'X' Battalion, INA, L/WS/1/1711, OIOC; Lt. Gen. N.M.S. Irwin, Irwin to Wavell, 29 October, 1943, 2/1, P139, IWM; Palit, *Major General A.A. Rudra*, pp. 257–260.

[54] Translation of manuscript letter in both Urdu and Gurmukhi script found in forward area in Arakan, INA, L/WS/1/1711, OIOC.

visited the 1/15th and described one of its companies as "somewhat shaken."[55]

Elsewhere in the Arakan, Japanese aircraft dropped leaflets exhorting Indian soldiers to join hands with their comrades from Malaya. At night in the jungle, INA contact parties would call out in the appropriate vernacular to Indian soldiers, inviting them to cross over. INA soldiers assisted the Japanese in interrogating Indian prisoners. Japanese intelligence, through INA interlocutors, communicated with disaffected Indian soldiers and officers in the Arakan.[56] In some cases, Indian soldiers recently captured by the Japanese were immediately sent back across the lines to encourage others to join the INA. "In this way it was hoped that they would rejoin their units so rapidly that they might appear merely to have got temporarily separated during action, and would not be suspected of having been in enemy hands."[57] One such man still carried a pass from the Japanese military liaison with the INA when he rejoined his unit.

The Accounting

India Command had been concerned about the "double attack" on the loyalty and morale of the Indian Army. But there were relatively few situations at the front in which Indian soldiers could defect to the Japanese. The hundred Sikhs of the 1/15th Punjab were the last sizable body of troops to go over to the INA for the entire war, and the only one to do so during the First Arakan. There had been no mass surrenders, and so no mass opportunities to join the INA, as at Singapore. Later, it would be the INA that surrendered to the Indian Army in large number as its formations crumpled in the campaigns of 1944–45.

Crossing the lines was dangerous. The enemy was likely to shoot first and investigate later. Coordinating surrenders, as the INA contact parties were trying to do, was fraught with fears of double cross.[58] Some Indian soldiers simply deserted, but the forbidding terrain of the

---

[55] Lt. Gen. N.M.S. Irwin, Irwin to Wavell, 9 March, 1943, 2/1, P139, IWM.

[56] See e.g. Nunneley and Tamayama, *Tales by Japanese Soldiers*, pp. 142–144. It is possible the incident described therein involves the 1/15th Punjab or it may refer to another, similar situation.

[57] "The survey report on the recent activities of the Indian National Army" in Sareen, *Select Documents on Indian National Army*, p. 182.

[58] See e.g. Allen, *Burma*, p. 227; Nunneley and Tamayama, *Tales by Japanese Soldiers*, pp. 142–144; Slim, *Defeat into Victory*, p. 327.

Mayu Peninsula and its distance from home made this an unattractive option.[59] Other campaigns and settings would offer different pressures and incentives for exits like desertion and surrender. The underlying point is that cumulatively such conditions – what will be called the "structure of battle" in Chapter 6 – shape the behavior of soldiers. In the Arakan, the ambivalent loyalties and nationalist politics of many Indian officers and soldiers did not particularly matter given available options.[60] The terrain, the character of the fighting and the opposing forces, and other factors mitigated against defection. Soldiers' sentiments and politics – their cultural beliefs – had less effect than their experiences and practical situation.

Like other Indian battalions in the Arakan, the 1/15th Punjab was a relatively effective fighting formation as long as it retained a large percentage of its initial complement of trained officers and men. But it had suffered from the Indian Army's rapid expansion. The commander of the company from which the Sikhs deserted was a former VCO, a *subedar* major, who had been given an emergency commission. He apparently played favorites among his soldiers, and ill-treated others, including a particularly able and popular *havildar*, while "shameless[ly] toadying to the British."[61] The British officers of the battalion lost authority because they tolerated this officer, perhaps unaware of his behavior. On top of this, the experienced and well-liked commander of the battalion was relieved early in the First Arakan. He had disagreed with the brigadier over the size of a reconnaissance. The commander wanted to send a larger force, fearing for the safety of his troops but the brigadier refused. The commander disobeyed sending the larger force anyway. Punished for trying to protect his soldiers from possibly ill-judged orders from higher command, his removal added to discontent in the battalion.

In January and early February the 1/15th Punjab was involved in heavy fighting in the hills north of Rathedaung, assaulting hill features and holding them against Japanese counterattacks.[62] In one such attack they were stopped with heavy casualties just in front of the main

---

[59] Moreman, *The Jungle, the Japanese and the British Commonwealth Armies at War*, p. 73.

[60] See INA Monographs, Monograph 5, "Front-line subversion of Indian Troops," L/WS/2/45, OIOC.

[61] Palit, *Major General A. A. Rudra*, p. 260.

[62] Kirby, *War Against Japan*, Vol. II, pp. 264–265, 267–268.

Japanese position. For weeks afterward, the decomposing bodies of their former comrades lay in view from the Punjabis' slit trenches, some hung on the Japanese wire.[63] Perhaps the corpses bloating and putrefying in the heat fertilized the agitation in the battalion. In the 1/15th Punjab, matters conspired to encourage defection to the INA, for a variety of motives, in risky circumstances. Nonetheless, such defections were limited, even in so compromised a unit as the 1/15th Punjab.

Rather than defecting to the INA, many battalions in the Arakan acted erratically, like the frightened, untrained, and sick soldiers they were composed of. The 8/10th Baluch was in an isolated position on the British left flank in the Kaladan, in the Kyauktaw area. This battalion was the one described as "Congress-minded" by a civil officer and was in a poor state of discipline, its soldiers abusing the local population, raping, appropriating houses and other goods, and drinking alcohol. According to the aggrieved civil officer, 90 percent nursed real or imaginary grievances against the British for unfair treatment. They were, he said, not prepared to fight under certain conditions, and lacked confidence in themselves "because they have the shameless belief that they are fighting not for their own cause but for the British and for grub." A withdrawal quickly turned into a rout when the "dismal and doleful" Indian troops were fired upon: "Our troops at once lost discipline and ran helter-skelter. Tommy guns, Bren guns, rifles, ammunition, steel helmets, water bottles, etc., were thrown away right and left."[64] The troops neither surrendered to the Japanese nor took up arms against the British. Instead, they fled for their lives.

The Sikh company of another battalion abandoned its officers during an attack, running away. In the 71st Indian Brigade, it was not uncommon for officers in charge of patrols to find themselves suddenly alone when there was threat of contact with the enemy. According to the brigade major of the 4th Brigade, a British officer had to lead every patrol, otherwise the patrols would just hide in the jungle. Fear may have kept troops alert in their slit trenches at night, but soldiers melted away in the face of the enemy when there was an option to do so.[65]

---

[63] Prendergast, *Prender's Progress*, pp. 173–174.

[64] A Report from Mr. Zainuddin, Lt. Gen. N.M.S. Irwin, 2/1, P139, IWM.

[65] Notes on Lessons the Operations in the Arakan, Report by Comd 71 Indian Brigade, WO 203/1167, TNA; Report on a visit to Maungdaw front from 4/5/43 to 9/5/43, by a liaison officer from HQ 15 Corps. 2/1, Lt. Gen. N.M.S. Irwin, P139, IWM.

Other soldiers sought a different exit from the Arakan: self-inflicted wounds. In a further sign of disarray, VCOs, NCOs, and other soldiers tolerated this behavior. "Many must know that a wound is premeditated and self inflicted, yet I know of no single case being voluntarily reported by either V.C.O. or I.O.R."[66] The 5/16th Punjab left wounded behind as it withdrew after an action. "[T]his was preying on everybody's minds," one of its officers noted at the end of the campaign.[67] The British battalions were not immune from disaffection either. In one, a corporal told a visiting officer, "Don't shoot, sir, they'll only shoot back."[68] A liaison officer who circulated among forward units toward the end of the First Arakan described their troops and commanders as "gutless." "That is the only word I can find for them," he said.[69]

Churchill would later refer to the operations in the Arakan as a "complete failure" and a "deep disgrace." He feared a "Frankenstein" had been created by putting modern weapons in the hands of "sepoys" who might rebel as they had in 1857.[70] Military and civilian officials with more experience of India were less concerned about the loyalty of Indian soldiers than they were about the use of green, half-trained troops with no instruction in jungle warfare. A senior Indian Civil Service official put it this way: "it would be hardly surprising if the young Indian soldiers fighting in Arakan, under very unpleasant conditions, think only of their own skin and think that if they desert, they will be better off." Given how poorly handled the operations were, it was not really the fault of the soldiers if they were captured. In such circumstances, a soldier would see "that the Japanese murder many of their prisoners; he naturally wishes to save his life and so he joins a [INA] 'contact party'. He is thus in my view more sinned against than sinning."[71] For this official, defection to the INA was less the result of

---

[66] Notes on Lessons the Operations in the Arakan, p. 3, Report by Comd 71 Indian Brigade, WO 203/1167, TNA. IOR is Indian Other Rank, an enlisted Indian soldier or NCO.

[67] Major Gebhard quoted in Thompson, *War in Burma*, pp. 60–61.

[68] Lt. Gen. N.M.S. Irwin, 2/1, "Report on a visit to Maungdaw front from 4/5/43 to 9/5/43," by a liaison officer from HQ 15 Corps, P139, IWM; quoted in Allen, *Burma*, pp. 115–116.

[69] Lt. Gen. N.M.S. Irwin, 2/1, "Report on a visit to Maungdaw front from 4/5/43 to 9/5/43," by a liaison officer from HQ 15 Corps, P139, IWM; quoted in Allen, *Burma*, pp. 115–116.

[70] Moon, *Wavell*, p. 3.

[71] Maurice Hallett to Lord Linlithgow, 18 May, 1943, INA, L/WS/1/1711, OIOC.

politics among the soldiers than the failure to properly train, prepare, and handle the troops.

High command realized it faced a crisis. After defeat in the First Arakan, it convened an Infantry Committee in May 1943 with the remit to make recommendations to improve the standard of British and Indian infantry battalions. In June, a widely respected and long serving Indian Army officer, General Sir Claude Auckinleck, was reappointed Commander-in-Chief of the Indian Army. He had previously served in the role in 1941, and at that time put an end to the system of restricting ICOs to Indianized units. His view was that officers should be treated equally "regardless of colour."[72] Now, he set about implementing the recommendations of the Infantry Committee. He raised standards for the selection of infantry recruits, lengthened training periods, developed jungle training facilities and doctrine, and found qualified instructors. Training staffs set up advanced infantry and jungle training programs for individual soldiers and for units destined for Burma.[73] Slim was appointed as commander of the 14th Army in October 1943, and he too put his ideas about infantry and jungle training to work throughout his command. As he saw it, troops needed both sound basic infantry training, and the specialized knowledge and procedures needed to live, move, and fight in jungle terrain.

Discipline

How did the Indian Army and other British and imperial forces make use of drill, training, exercising, and other military pedagogies to prepare soldiers for battle? What does this teach us about the general principles of military discipline and how they were applied to local circumstances? At its most basic, military discipline is the capacity to maintain order and take the correct actions under enemy fire. As historian John Lynn puts it, "The ability to perform with forbearance in the face of danger and chaos was far from natural; it had to be learned."[74] What military discipline required was not timeless, but changed with

---

[72] Quoted in Marston, *The Indian Army and the End of the Raj*, p. 86.

[73] See Report of Infantry Committee, L/WS/1/1371, OIOC; War Department History, Expansion of the Armed Forces, L/R/5/273, OIOC; Kirby, *War Against Japan*, Vol. II, pp. 385–387; Marston, *Phoenix from the Ashes*; Moreman, *The Jungle, the Japanese and the British Commonwealth Armies at War, 1941–45.*

[74] Lynn, *Battle*, p. 155.

historical transformations in warfare. In the eighteenth century, it largely was sufficient for soldiers to stand steady in the ranks and to load and fire their muskets when ordered, while receiving the enemy's fire. By the Second World War, infantry combat had become both more complex in technique and technology and more dispersed and "open" in its battle order. In open order, soldiers no longer fought shoulder to shoulder, but in small groups or pairs, often under cover and out of sight and hearing of their officers. As Slim commented, the infantry-man could no longer afford to be an "automaton" but rather "fights as a highly skilled individual."[75]

In the Indian Army, the syllabus that soldiers had to master was extensive and difficult, especially for peasant recruits, many of whom had to be taught how to tell time.[76] Their instructors were told that "Every private soldier must be made a tactician to survive on the modern battlefield."[77] Soldiers had to operate complicated machinery, including automatic weapons, grenades, mortars, vehicles, and radios; they had to master fieldcraft, the use of terrain for living, moving, and fighting; they had to be tactically competent, to know how to lay or react to an ambush, how to control their fire, what to do in various situations, and how to perform myriad tasks; and they had to be, especially in Burma, extremely physically fit, capable of enduring severe privation, and living in rough countryside without amenities. "War," one training handbook intoned, "demands toughness more than anything else in the world."[78]

Soldiers had to be trained to resist powerful and common inclinations. Those who come under fire for the first time often have a strong sensation that all the shooting is directed at them personally.[79] This is one reason behind a widespread problem, that insufficiently trained troops "go to ground" at the first sound of automatic fire.[80] Troops

---

[75] "Notes on Infantry by Commander Fourteenth Army," Director of Infantry's Report, Appendix F, L/WS/1/653, OIOC.

[76] "Experience of Indian Army Morale on Joining a Training Battalion," India Monthly Intelligence Summary No. 13, 5 January, 1943, L/WS/1/317, OIOC.

[77] Instructors' Handbook on Fieldcraft and Battle Drill (India), p. 4, L/MIL/17/5/2226, OIOC.

[78] Military Training Pamphlet No. 14 (India), Infantry Section Leading, p. 8, L/MIL/17/5/2256, OIOC.

[79] See Fire Effects Sub-Committee, Training – General Questions, L/WS/1/761, OIOC.

[80] See e.g. Demonstrations, Schools, Lectures, etc., L/WS/1/1283, OIOC; A Lecture to Infantry Officers on Man Management, L/MIL/17/5/2235, OIOC.

had to be made controllable, trained to follow orders in the face of danger and to take the correct actions in response to various tactical scenarios.

The jungle exacerbated some of the basic problems of modern infantry combat. An experienced division commander observed that for "most people first contact with the jungle is confusing if not actually frightening." Training had to familiarize troops with the jungle: "Our [troops] must... live and train in jungle as part of their training, so that movement and control in it becomes second nature."[81] In densely forested terrain, commanding or keeping track of even a section (a squad-sized unit of approximately 10) could be difficult. It was easy for individual soldiers to go to ground: "Nothing is easier in jungle or dispersed fighting than for a man to shirk. If he has no stomach for advancing, all he has to do is flop into the undergrowth... Only discipline – not punishment – can stop this sort of thing... "[82]

The jungle forced changes in basic procedures. Indian infantry, for example, had been taught that when they came under effective fire they should "Down – Crawl – Observe – Fire," or drop to the ground, crawl to a new position, observe the enemy, and return fire. However, in the jungle, such a drill was useless "as a man when once down can only crawl with difficulty and cannot observe at all."[83] Troops became disoriented in the jungle and lost contact with their comrades. The jungle heightened fears of darkness, insects, and reptiles.[84] Troops training in it for the first time were often afraid of leaving their positions at night even to urinate.[85]

The jungle posed novel tactical problems, but in its disciplinary system, the army possessed the pedagogical techniques necessary to train soldiers to fight in it. In early modern Europe, drill transformed the unemployed and impoverished at home, and the colonized abroad, all of whom were potential threats to property and its prerogatives, into soldiers – that is, into enforcers of the ruling order.[86] These powers of drill led Foucault to see in the army the prototype of modern

---

[81] Lessons of the Burma Campaign, April–May 1942, WO 203/5716, TNA.

[82] Slim, *Defeat into Victory*, p. 542.

[83] Battle Drill for Thick Jungle, p. 2, L/MIL/17/5/2236, OIOC.

[84] See Bergerud's discussion, *Touched with Fire*, Chapter 1, pp. 55–118.

[85] Battle Drill for Thick Jungle, L/MIL/17/5/2236, OIOC.

[86] McNeill, *Pursuit of Power*, pp. 132–139.

discipline, which produced human characters capable of effective and willing obedience within rationalized bureaucracies.[87] These were also the powers that the British military authorities sought to enlist in rapidly transforming illiterate peasants into soldiers capable of performing the myriad tasks required in modern armies. Why was the army so good at discipline?

Battle Drill

Drill is simultaneously training, practice, and ritual. It is pervasive in all regular armies, past and present. Along with other forms of military pedagogy, such as the step-by-step manual, it is widely adaptable to different military purposes and to recruits from different social and educational backgrounds. As Gwynne Dyer comments, one of the most "striking characteristics of armies" is their use of "rote learning and standardization."[88]

Battle drill is the modern incarnation of close order drill.[89] It offers a straightforward and practical pedagogy for tactical instruction. The basic idea is to identify the essentials of any given task, such as reacting to an ambush or a section (or squad) assault, and teach these essentials as a drill, or ideal plan of action.[90] In this way, the military's preference for "repeated practice of standard drills" could be applied to any tactical training task.[91] Battle drills were developed at different scales, from teaching a two-man fire team the principles of fire and movement (in which one soldier provides covering fire while the other moves) to section, platoon, and company maneuvers. Battle drills applied the classic principles of drill in ways that were tactically useful in modern combat. The various movements in parade ground drill, such as presenting arms or turning about, are taught in individual steps so that each detail can

[87] Foucault, *Discipline and Punish*, pp. 167–168 and *passim*. See also Dandeker, *Surveillance, Power & Modernity*; Drake, *Problematics of Military Power*; Weber, "The Origins of Discipline in War" in Gerth and Mills, *From Max Weber*, pp. 255–261.

[88] Dyer, *War*, p. 133.

[89] For a general account of the development of infantry battle drill in the British Army during World War II, see Place, *Military Training in the British Army, 1940–1944*, chaps. 4–5. See also King, *Combat Soldier*, Chapter 8.

[90] See Instructors' Handbook on Fieldcraft and Battle Drill (India), L/MIL/17/5/2226, OIOC.

[91] Keegan, *Face of Battle*, p. 18.

Figure 4.2 Mortar drill: General Auchinleck reviews Gurkhas demonstrating the drill to fire a three-inch mortar in Quetta, 1944.[92]

be mastered.[93] In time, a complex choreography consisting of many such movements can be assembled. Drill seeks to instill the habit of instinctive and automatic obedience to command. (See Figure 4.2)

The military authorities in India drew on these traditions of drill and adapted them to the challenges they faced, as Indian Army training materials show. Trainers broke battle drills down into their constituent elements. Drills were practiced repeatedly until done correctly. An instructor's manual noted, "If [a soldier] has no imagination he will just carry out the drill woodenly – and he still won't do it badly."[94] The army developed variations on drills to deal with different circumstances, giving trained soldiers a repertoire of actions. Drills were conducted in increasingly realistic conditions through the use of live ammunition, overhead machine gun fire, and explosions in an effort to "inoculate" men against the noise and confusion of battle.[95] By

[92] IND 2830, IWM.

[93] To "turn about" on the command "about turn" involves turning 180 degrees and is known as "about face" in the US armed forces.

[94] Instructors' Handbook on Fieldcraft and Battle Drill (India), p. 4, L/MIL/17/5/2226, OIOC.

[95] See Major-General A.C. Curtis, Report 14th Indian [Training] Division, July 1943-November 1945, P140, IWM; The Indian and Gurkha Infantry Recruit

"ensuring that every subaltern, sergeant, corporal and private soldier has a clear idea of an ideal plan photographed in this mind," battle drill helped to solve the problem of controlling men in jungle terrain.[96] Soldiers should know what to do without instructions, at least to some extent. Moreover, through repeated practice and rigid attention to detail, instructors hoped that battle drill generated a "military conscience" in soldiers, one that would help them perform the correct actions in conditions of stress and danger.[97] Battle drill sought to make battle discipline a habit. Repetitive training ideally leads to "automaticity" in behavior.[98]

In *Discipline and Punish*, Foucault observes that disciplinary systems seek to regulate everyday behaviors in detail. Normalizing judgments are employed in order to bring each individual into conformity with the expected standard. The "slightest departure from correct behaviour" becomes a disciplinary issue.[99] "[T]each *all* the details" an Indian army instructor's handbook insisted, while another manual reminded that "[f]aults due to slackness or neglect must be dealt with strictly."[100] Since the purpose of disciplinary training is to eliminate the gap between actual behavior and the standard required, punishing failure is insufficient on its own. Corrective techniques are required. Infantry section leaders were told to "never let a mistake or a fault pass unnoticed and uncorrected; the explanation and clearing-up of mistakes is one of the best methods of teaching."[101] If a man is a bad shot, more time and coaching on the rifle range is required, not some purely punitive punishment. "What matters first of all is the correctness of a man's action, nothing else."[102] Likewise, if a platoon is poor at

of the Indian Army, L/MIL/17/5/2232, OIOC; Military Training Pamphlet No. 19 (India), Notes on the Training of the Infantry Recruit, L/MIL/17/5/2261, OIOC.

[96] Instructors' Handbook on Fieldcraft and Battle Drill (India), p. 4, L/MIL/17/5/2226, OIOC. See also Place, *Military Training in the British Army, 1940–1944*, p. 64.

[97] Instructors' Handbook on Fieldcraft and Battle Drill (India), p. 69, L/MIL/17/5/2226, OIOC.

[98] Ben-Ari, *Mastering Soldiers*, p. 59.

[99] Foucault, *Discipline and Punish*, p. 178. See also pp. 177–184.

[100] Instructors' Handbook on Fieldcraft and Battle Drill (India), p. 69, L/MIL/17/5/2226; Military Training Pamphlet No. 14 (India), 1941, Infantry Section Leading, p. 6, L/MIL/17/5/2256, OIOC.

[101] Military Training Pamphlet No. 14 (India), 1941, Infantry Section Leading, pp. 4–5, L/MIL/17/5/2256, OIOC.

[102] Military Training Pamphlet No. 19 (India), 1941, Notes on the Training of the Infantry Recruit (India), p. 11, L/MIL/17/5/2261, OIOC.

close order drill, more close order drill is in order; "disciplinary systems favour punishments that are exercise – intensified, multiplied forms of training, several times repeated."[103]

John Masters offers a small but revealing example of what could be achieved in terms of finely grained self-control. Marching with a column of Gurkhas on the second Chindit operation, behind Japanese lines, Masters heard a flight of Japanese Zero fighters passing overhead:

I stopped and looked back. My heart leaped with delight, and pride. Every man and mule had stopped dead where he was. Not one face was turned up to see what the enemy aircraft, which could slaughter most of them in a single run, were doing. The Zeros droned on, and disappeared.[104]

Many of the troops were strung out in an open paddy field and move-ment or the flash of light on upturned faces might have given away their position. All had remembered the drill for enemy aircraft, auto-matically as it were. Even the mules, controlled by trained muleteers, were disciplined. In other circumstances, it was the tendency of soldiers to look at the ground while marching with heavy packs that had to be countered, lest columns stumble into ambushes: "It was necessary to detail a few men at a time to keep their eyes about them, relieving them every few minutes."[105] Elsewhere, officers eradicated coughing among Gurkhas training for Chindit operations. "Gargling parades and orders forbidding offenders to smoke did much to help and the training gained was to be of value later in the jungle."[106]

Military Pedagogy

Repetition and discipline were not always enough on their own, however. The Indian Army was a volunteer force, which placed outer limits on the harshness of the disciplinary regimes employed, something training manuals addressed and sought to remedy. They exhorted instructors to arouse with enthusiasm the troops' interest in

[103] Foucault, *Discipline and Punish*, p. 179.
[104] Masters, *Road Past Mandalay*, p. 212.
[105] Fergusson, *Wild Green Earth*, p. 164.
[106] 4/9 GR Battalion History, p. 19, G14, GM. Fergusson, too, waged disciplinary war on coughing among his Chindits: "I had a strict rule that anybody coughing within a quarter of an hour of getting up in the morning should have his cigarette ration docked, and only the stern enforcement of this order effected an improvement." Fergusson, *Wild Green Earth*, p. 183.

training.[107] Desertion was a constant problem during the war, especially in the early stages of training when recruits were first immersed in military life. Instructors were told to "work lightly" with trainees until they became more accustomed to the military.[108] The wartime officer Ralph Russell watched an instructor working with new recruits: "He would hold up his rifle and say, 'Yeh, kya hai? Rifle; yeh kya hai? Rifle.' (What is this? A rifle. What is this? A rifle) until the sepoys could themselves shout in unison 'Rifle' when he asked the question."[109]

The unfamiliarity of Indian and African peasants with modern machinery also posed problems. They had a great deal more to learn to reach the expected standard then their counterparts did in Britain. For example, the concept of motor transport and its elementary principles were often foreign. An elaborate system of "homely similes" was developed by one instructor involving a comparison between a truck and a horse-drawn cart, or *tonga*: "[t]o make a tonga pony move quickly you have to use a whip. The whip in the M.T. vehicle is the accelerator pedal. (Show pedal to recruits; start engine and rev. up for an instant)."[110] (See Figure 4.3)

The problem was not soldiers' native intelligence, but the imperial preference for recruiting peasants. Illiteracy and unfamiliarity with modern life did not imply a lack of critical judgment or other cognitive defect.[111] Major Gajendra Malla, a pre-war regular GO in the 9th Gurkha Rifles who was commissioned during the war, relates an anecdote from a platoon commanders' course that illustrates the savvy and the limitations of those who lacked formal education.[112] Malla found the course "extremely interesting" but in his view "for an Indian soldier, who generally comes from the agricultural class, and was not sufficiently educated, the subjects taught in the college were more than he could digest." The Chief Instructor paid a visit to the students and asked how the course was going.

---

[107] See e.g. Major-General A.C. Curtis, Report 14th Indian [Training] Division, July 1943-November 1945, P140, IWM.
[108] War Department History, Expansion of the Armed Forces, p. 28, L/R/5/273, OIOC.
[109] Russell, *Findings, Keepings*, p. 224.
[110] Army in India Training Memorandum, No. 13, Nov.–Dec., 1941, "Teaching Indian Recruits the Principles of M.T.," L/MIL/17/5/2240, OIOC.
[111] See Street, *Literacy in Theory and Practice*, Section 1.
[112] A Gurkha Officer, or GO, is the Gurkha equivalent of a VCO.

Figure 4.3 Rules of the road: Instructors teach Indian Army drivers with a "baby car," complete with "L" plate for learners (1944).[113]

One Pathan Havildar of the Frontier Force, stood up and gave his opinion, in the most interesting way and emphatically too. He said 'Sir...a water jug, which has the capacity to hold two seers of water...would certainly not be able to take any more. And if more water is put in it, the water will naturally overflow. Similarly to an Indian soldier, the subjects taught in this College, though quite interesting, are too many, so our heads cannot absorb them and they overflow through our nose, ears, so on and so forth.' In fact he was quite right too. This made the Chief Instructor think twice, with the result, that a few subjects were curtailed from the curriculum.[114]

As a consequence of the amount of material to be imparted, training manuals emphasized an ethic of care and motivation in disciplinary pedagogy than might have been the case otherwise.

[N]ever be hard on the backward man who is doing his best. He needs all your sympathy and patience...Critical of indifferent work you must be, but never fail to give praise for improvement or honest effort. Try to

[113] IND3372, IWM.
[114] "Rifleman to Colonel: The Memoirs of Major Gajendra Malla 9th Gurkha Rifles," compiled by Lt. Col. A.A. Mains and Elizabeth Talbot Rice, p. 26, GM.

avoid anything in the nature of sarcasm at a man's expense; few men forgive it.[115]

Another manual warned "the 'bright boys', who exist in every squad, must be kept reasonably in check. Otherwise they become favourites with the instructor, always in the limelight, while the slower members of the squad relapse into silent despair, recipients of little beyond occasional abuse."[116] In order to effectively instruct the men, a "drill complex" had to be avoided: "make instructional parades as informal as possible ... The aim should be to get men alert and interested."[117] Practical demonstrations were better than lectures. Instructors were told to let the men puzzle over the action of a Bren gun rather than lecturing them about it; "he's more likely to remember if he figures it out himself."[118]

Similar pedagogical sophistication marked efforts to introduce troops to the rigors of the battlefield. Training officers conceived infantry fighting as an art which required skilled craftsmen rather than automatons capable only of rigid tactics.[119] As one division commander put it, "The dominating asset [in Burma], more than anywhere else, is good junior leaders and skilful [infantry]."[120] They devised relatively elaborate scenarios and exercises to ensure soldiers remembered important lessons. Some of these were intended to teach recruits how concealment and surprise functioned. In one demonstration, a rifleman in a hidden position easily killed an attacker at a distance. Next, the defender was placed in an inadequately camouflaged position where the attacker could work around and shoot him in the back unseen. The recruits then acted out the lessons implied in a series of exercises

---

[115] Military Training Pamphlet No. 14 (India), 1941, Infantry Section Leading, p. 6, L/MIL/17/5/2256, OIOC.

[116] Military Training Pamphlet No. 19 (India), 1941, Notes on the Training of the Infantry Recruit (India), p. 12, L/MIL/17/5/2261, OIOC.

[117] Military Training Pamphlet No. 19 (India), 1941, Notes on the Training of the Infantry Recruit (India), p. 12, L/MIL/17/5/2261, OIOC.

[118] OIOC Training Liaison Letters, Appendix B, Methods of Instruction Teams, L/WS/1/766, OIOC.

[119] See e.g. Papers of Major-General A.C. Curtis, Report 14th Indian [Training] Division, July 1943–November 1945, P 140, IWM; Military Training Pamphlet No. 19 (India), 1941, Notes on the Training of the Infantry Recruit (India), p. 12, L/MIL/17/5/2261, OIOC.

[120] Maj. Gen. Frank Messervy quoted in Moreman, *The Jungle, the Japanese and the British Commonwealth Armies at War*, p. 114.

referred to as "tiger hunting," "dog shooting," and "the poacher," each of which taught skills of stalking and fieldcraft in different contexts.[121]

To teach soldiers to deal with their fears, battle inoculation courses deliberately avoided overly frightening trainees. These courses worked on the idea that fear was a normal and expected part of combat, and sought to help soldiers overcome it. They induced anxiety, and then tried to inure soldiers to it. When the trainees discovered that they could cope, they gained extra confidence. Similarly, on assault courses in which troops performed battle drills under overhead machine gun fire, instructors exaggerated the danger of any mistakes beforehand. When trainees came through without injury they became more confident of facing danger, learned that noise can be harmless, and that one can get used to it. They were more likely to discipline themselves and take the appropriate actions in combat.[122]

Fire Control

As the wild firing at night in the First Arakan indicated, fire discipline posed a major problem for the 14th Army in Burma and a challenge for Indian Army instructors. They drew on battle drill technique to resolve it. Fire discipline refers to holding fire until the appropriate moment, the careful marking of targets, and restraint in using ammunition. Raw troops fire too soon and use up their ammunition too quickly, tendencies exacerbated by Japanese jittering tactics.

While always important, fire discipline was of particular significance in Burma.[123] One reason was the difficulty of supply, which was often by air drop, coupled with the ease with which extraordinary amounts of ammunition could be used up by modern rapid fire weapons. But the main reason had to do with Japanese tactics and jungle terrain. The force to space ratio in Burma was very low; there was no continuous front. Rather, units operating in the jungle had to protect themselves from possible attack from any direction. On defense, circular

[121] Military Training Pamphlet No. 19 (India), 1941, Notes on the Training of the Infantry Recruit (India), p. 12, L/MIL/17/5/2261, OIOC.

[122] Report 14th Indian [Training] Division, July 1943–November 1945, Major-General A.C. Curtis, P140, IWM; The Indian and Gurkha Infantry Recruit of the Indian Army, L/MIL/17/5/2232, OIOC; Strachan, "Training, Morale, and Modern War," pp. 216, 223.

[123] Sir Douglas Gracey, "Note on Jap Tactics," 2/8, LH; Lt. Gen. Sir Frank Messervy, 5/4, 7 Ind Div Comd's Operation Notes No. 4, 5/4, LH; GHQ(I) Infantry Liaison Letters, No. 26, May 1946, Appendix C, L/WS1/778, OIOC.

Figure 4.4 Positions were hard to spot in the jungle: A Punjabi soldier peering out of the firing slit of a camouflaged bunker somewhere in Burma, 1943.[124]

perimeters were set up which relied upon interlocking fields of fire from concealed positions. In order to effectively attack such a defended locality, the defenders' positions first had to be identified, a difficult task in the jungle. (See Figure 4.4) The easiest way to do so was to induce a defending position to open fire. This was the reason why the Japanese tried to "jitter" the defenders, along with inspiring fear and preventing sleep. Yet, for the anxious and frightened defenders, "[j]ust to blaze off a weapon gave a sense of well-being, which overcame the fear of the darkness and the bamboo rustling in the breeze."[125]

Their inclination to fire was increased by the fear that every sound was that of a Japanese soldier sneaking up on them.[126] "During the long string of nights," recalled one officer present at the siege of the Admin Box,

I would hear sounds out there. Was it the wind rustling the bamboo? Was it bodies moving? How close? The Japs would fire a few shots, hoping to draw a response. They would call out in carefully rehearsed English or Urdu: "Give

---

[124] IND2696, IWM.
[125] Major P.H. Gadsdon, untitled account of his war service, p. 89, 78/6/1, IWM.
[126] Peter Francis and Tony Banks, interview by the author.

up, Limey, or you will die." "Johnny Gurkha, we are your friends." These voices from the dark were both absurd and unsettling.[127]

The correct way to deal with "jittering" was to wait silently until the Japanese party withdrew or could be dispatched by grenade or bayonet in ways which did not reveal the defenders' positions. But it required nerve to sit and do nothing until the Japanese were close enough. Veteran soldiers learned that such nerve aided survival. Japanese units unable to jitter a particular company could shift their efforts, and any forthcoming attack, to another, less disciplined unit.

Instructors had to teach recruits forms of self-control and mastery over their emotions in these excruciating situations.[128] To do so, they made use of the masculine analogies latent in fire discipline, the self-control involved in holding fire until the right moment. In one exercise, trainees were placed in a defensive position, given a limited supply of ammunition and told the exercise would last several hours. They were then subjected to a series of mock assaults and almost invariably they used up their ammunition far too quickly.[129] At this point, the instructors came out to harangue the trainees for being weak, childish, feminine, and unable to control themselves. Sometimes the trainees would be made to put on *saris*, i.e. women's clothes, to emphasize the point. In another variation, the instructor appeared dressed as a Japanese officer and told the trainees: "you behave like a lot of raw recruits. Trained soldiers keep cool in action. They do not get excited and lose their nerve . . . You are just a bunch of schoolboys. Instead of trying to fight soldiers like us you ought to be back in your homes with your mothers to look after you."[130] Particularly notable about this exercise is the way it sought to articulate warrior masculinity with the requirements of modern infantry tactics, which involved individual discipline and self-regulation. Any heroic displays of fighting prowess or use of weapons had to occur at the appropriate moment.

[127] Gilmore, *Connecticut Yankee*, p. 139.
[128] Such "emotional control" is a major theme of Ben-Ari's *Mastering Soldiers*.
[129] Report 14th Indian [Training] Division, July 1943–November 1945, Major-General A.C. Curtis, P140, IWM.
[130] Report 14th Indian [Training] Division, July 1943–November 1945, Major-General A.C. Curtis, P140, IWM. Ben-Ari notes that the Israeli army favors the man/child binary in similar circumstances ("not to act spoilt" or "not to behave like babies"), while the US Marines favor the man/woman distinction. See Ben-Ari, *Mastering Soldiers*, pp. 55–56, 114–115; Eisenhart, "You Can't Hack It Little Girl."

As can be seen, some effort was made to translate exercises into the cultural idiom and educational level of Indian soldiers. But this required less expert cultural knowledge than might be thought. A field-craft exercise for British troops could be called "cops and robbers." The same exercise for Indians would be "tiger hunt." The fire discipline exercise made use of *saris* as the culturally appropriate sign for femininity. Haranguing the soldiers as children, or forcing them to wear women's clothes, drew on cultural resources of misogyny and patriarchy available to Indians and British alike.

But the effectiveness of the exercise, in any cultural idiom, resides in the way it simulates a situation recruits would later experience in Burma. Trainees did not need much imagination to figure out what would happen if they used up all their ammunition in actual combat. Taking the correct actions enabled their survival. The instructors, many of whom could enliven the training with tales from their own experience, worked hard and creatively to impart the lessons. Perhaps the ham-fisted deployment of the *saris* did the trick. As likely, the point was driven home when the trainees realized their magazines were empty and the mock Japanese kept on coming. A minimum of ethnographic knowledge was required to adapt exercises like this to new contexts. Such modes of training are one reason why the regular military can produce similar standards of discipline and teach similar lessons to recruits around the world.

From Discipline to Spirit

As part of the reorganization of 14th Army's training, army headquarters in India established two training divisions that provided advanced battle courses, including the fire control exercise discussed above. Slim wrote that, "Within a few months the quality of reinforcements reaching us from these divisions . . . had completely changed, not only in skill but, above all, in morale."[131] Soldiers gained familiarity with confusion and noise; they learned to endure operations that lasted days and weeks, in bad weather and rough terrain.[132] Auchinleck remarked at the war's end, "training has been very hard . . . and

---

[131] Slim, *Defeat into Victory*, p. 191; quoted in Strachan, "Training, Morale, and Modern War," p 224.
[132] Strachan, "Training, Morale, and Modern War," pp. 216, 223.

sometimes extremely unpleasant for those undergoing it. Conditions at some of the camps are not too good and this has been done on purpose."[133] Training took the form of challenges that groups of soldiers had to overcome.

As Hew Strachan notes, Slim emphasizes not only the discipline inculcated by training but also something more ineffable, confidence and morale. If Indian troops in the First Arakan lacked discipline and spirit, by the time of the great campaigns of 1944 and 1945 that was no longer the case. In January, 1945 after enduring a night of Japanese assaults, mortar, and shell fire, as well as fire from two medium machine guns, dawn found a company of the 7/16th Punjab standing in "their trenches half filled by the sand thrown up from the enemy's mortaring, shelling and grenading" but still "in excellent fighting trim."[134] The intensified training instilled both the ability to take the correct actions and group solidarity. How drill helped instill this last quality is the subject of Chapter 5.

[133] Army Commanders' Conferences, C-in-C's Opening Address, August, 1945, L/WS/1/1523, OIOC.
[134] "The Kyeyebyin Battle," Reports on Operations: General, WO 203/2607, TNA.

5 | *Ritual, Solidarity, and Sacrifice*

Men are more confident because they feel themselves stronger; and they really are stronger, because forces which were languishing [are] now reawakened in their consciousness.

> – Emile Durkheim, on participating in rituals[1]

For many scholars who do not study military subjects, Foucault is an important source of knowledge about the army. There is a curious absence in Foucault's use of the army as the model for modern discipline. Soldiers appear as disciplinary automatons. Their bodies are correctly trained, docile, examined.[2] But meaning is missing, and with it, any basis for the group solidarity that underwrites combat.[3] Battles are conducted under warrior totems, doused in myth, and marked by ritual. Soldiers seek meaning, like other human beings, and pursue relations of estrangement and identification with others. Their group identities have a historically specific cultural and social character. Military sociologists and historians disagree on the basis of solidarity, but not on its significance. Fighting in regular warfare requires group spirit.

In military history and sociology, analyses of the meaningful dimension of group solidarity take two broad approaches. For many scholars and officers it is near dogma that soldiers fight for their buddies, for their "primary group" in the cognitive psychological language of Edward Shils and Morris Janowitz's classic article.[4] Other scholars turn to the nation, political ideology, and culture – to the ideal groups of political imagination – to explain why soldiers fought, especially

---

[1] Durkheim, *Elementary Forms*, p. 387. The bracketed "are" replaces an "and" in the text.
[2] Foucault, *Discipline and Punish.*   [3] Smith, "Meaning and Military Power."
[4] Shils and Janowitz, "Cohesion and Disintegration."

for particularly intense combat involving savagery and atrocity.[5] The
debate can be caricatured as one over which group soldiers sacrifice
for, their buddies or their nation, although the two are by no means
exclusive.[6]

Collectively, three presuppositions have shaped the debate over
"combat motivation." First, casualties corrode fighting spirit and
group solidarity. Casualties and cohesion correlate inversely. Second,
because industrialized war was deadlier, soldiers required additional
sources of motivation to prevail in battle.[7] In modernity, the meaningful dimension became more significant for fighting spirit than for pre-
modern soldiers. Third, army–society relations took nation-state form.
National histories and politics provided the relevant cultural context.
The first sections below elaborate and critique these presuppositions.

In Burma, the fighting took on an intense, no-quarter character, as it
did nearly everywhere the Imperial Japanese Army (IJA) was encountered. For the multicultural, colonized Indian and imperial forces,
national causes did not motivate them to fight. Most Indian and
African soldiers knew very little about the war until they were in the
army and subjected to propaganda. There was little historic animosity, racial or otherwise, between Punjabi peasants and imperial Japan.
Neither the nation nor national racisms can serve as explanatory fall-
backs for the motivations of Indian soldiers, the basis for their solidarity, or the reasons for any savagery they participated in. This did not
mean that meaning was any less important or significant for Indian
and imperial soldiers than it was for other soldiers, ancient, modern
or otherwise. It just means that it cannot perform the functions it does
in Eurocentric accounts of cohesion and fighting spirit, underwriting
groups and motivating combat.

How might we think differently about the meaningful dimensions
of soldiering, about solidarity and sacrifice, in ways that essentialize
neither buddies nor nations? What other account of groups in the

---

[5] See e.g. Bartov, *Hitler's Army*; Cameron, *American Samurai*; Dower, *War
Without Mercy*; Fritz, *Frontsoldaten*; Janowitz and Wesbrook, *Political
Education of Soldiers*; Wesbrook, "The Potential for Military Disintegration."

[6] In *Combat Soldier*, King argues that politics and ethnicity were important in the
large conscript armies of the World Wars, while military professional identities
and sources of cohesion predominate in contemporary Western armies. King,
Combat Soldier, Chapter 4. See also Chodoff, "Ideology and Primary Groups";
Moskos, *American Enlisted Man*.

[7] Batov, *Hitler's Army*; Du Picq, *Battle Studies*; McPherson, *Cause and Comrades*.

army might we come up with that allows for the British Indian Army and other foreign and imperial armed forces? This chapter provides such an account in paradigmatic form, centered on the notion of ritual and its powers of group formation. It makes use of Emile Durkheim and the imagined Australians that populate his *The Elementary Forms of the Religious Life*, a text rich in interpretive possibilities, however Eurocentric Durkheim's construction of aboriginal peoples.[8] The last chapter focused on ritual as training, on how military rituals like drill inculcated the ability to take correct actions in stressful conditions. This chapter turns to ritual as group formation and hierarchy, more traditional uses of the concept. For present purposes, Durkheim's central insight can be characterized this way: groups do not have rituals; rituals have groups. Living and acting like a group, in daily and periodic rituals, creates group feeling. Groups do not require an "outside" social basis or essentialized identity like nation, religion, or caste to account for their solidarity or common behavior. Rituals produce groups. This makes possible the replicability of the army upon varied political, social, and historical terrain.

Culture matters, but the approach taken here requires thinking about, and studying, culture in a different way, as about ritual practices and the sentiments they evoke.[9] This chapter is more self-consciously theoretic in intent and execution. Theory is useful for that which leaves little archival or other trace, and to challenge the effects of the "evidence of experience" in Joan Scott's phrase.[10] As Scott warns, relying upon veterans' accounts of their experiences threatens to reproduce ideological systems and preclude inquiry (by trumping other evidence with authenticity). Here are found the many soldiers and veterans who write about the importance of their buddies, patriotism, regimental spirit, ideology, nationalism, racial animus, and so on, and whose representations of their experiences are effectively understood by scholars as accounts of motivations. In colonial context, given the way many Indian soldiers framed their experience by reference to caste and religion, such an approach leads to the Hindu *varnas* and the

---

[8] See e.g. Allen, Pickering and Miller, eds., *On Durkheim's Elementary Forms*. See also King, *Combat Soldier*, pp. 15–16.

[9] Lincoln, *Discourse and the Construction of Society*. Cf. Wedeen, "Conceptualizing Culture."

[10] Scott, "Evidence of Experience"; Zimmerman, "Africa in Imperial and Transnational History," pp. 337–340.

Bhagavad Gita as explanations for Indian soldiers' fighting spirit and battlefield behavior.[11]

Scholars have long sought to recover the thoughts and experiences of soldiers, and the discourses of subaltern agents like colonial soldiers.[12] Within the constraints and demands of interdisciplinary work, I draw on and contribute to this scholarship. But the point here is to understand the army and why it works, not South Asia and the cultural constructs of Indian soldiers. As we saw in Part I, even at the height of the martial races army, British officers did not "understand" Indian culture. What they understood more or less poorly was some orientalist caricature. Those that managed the army did not "know" their soldiers, but the army worked anyway. British officers, or enough of them, knew their soldiers in another sense, via the practical judgments of military leaders. Colonial officers were hobbyists in matters of colonial ethnography; they were experts, more or less, in military rituals like battle drill. This chapter theorizes the army from the point of view of these practitioner-officers, and their historical counterparts in different times and places, tasked with raising troops from populations of which they had little real understanding or affinity. How do officers structure military life such that it generates discipline, belonging, and hierarchy? They do so with a package of ritual practices, articulated to local conditions. Merely participating in these practices generates group feeling, while also instantiating hierarchy.

The final way in which this chapter deals in ritual is in terms of sacrifice, as understood in some classic statements in sociology and anthropology.[13] There, sacrifice generates solidarity. In the combat motivation debates, by contrast, "casualties" undermine cohesion. Of course, losses may demoralize military units, and destroy their capability. But sacrifice among members of solidary groups evokes fellow feeling in those remaining. Casualties do not pose in principle a problem for the army in creating the will to combat. If sacrifice feeds solidarity, high causalities may intensify rather than undermine an army's powers of group formation, other things being equal.

---

[11] As John Lynn aruges in *Battle*, pp. 51–72, 164–174. See Cooper's critique in "Culture, Combat, and Colonialism," pp. 545, 548.

[12] See e.g. Morris, ed., *Can the Subaltern Speak?*; Omissi, *Indian Voices*; Scott, *Weapons of the Weak*; Singh, *Testimonies of Indian Soldiers*.

[13] Bell, *Ritual Theory, Ritual Practice*; Bloch and Parry, *Death and the Regeneration of Life*; Durkheim, *Elementary Forms*; Girard, *Violence and the Sacred*; Kertzer, *Ritual, Politics, and Power*; Turner, *Ritual Process*.

Ancient and Modern Battle

In the Franco-Prussian War, artillery fire mortally wounded Colonel Ardant du Picq while he was practically demonstrating the very spirit he theorized modern war required. He had exposed himself to artillery fire in order to "put heart into his troops by his attitude," in the words of the regimental history.[14] His writings were posthumously collected under the title "Studies in Combat" in 1880. Du Picq wrote about a development obvious to any professional officer of his time: battle was becoming much deadlier for soldiers, even as modern sanitation and medical care improved conditions dramatically in other respects. Rifling, breech loading, modern cartridges and shells, among other developments like mass and precision production, vastly increased the range and effectiveness of weapons over the course of the nineteenth century.[15]

Du Picq drew with remarkable clarity an implication that has, in one way or another, framed writing on combat motivation ever since. If greater "perfection of weapons" made battle more terrifying and deadly for soldiers, then "discipline becomes more difficult to maintain."[16] Du Picq observed of French troops in the Crimean War that a "considerable number conceal themselves" by lying in tall grass.[17] He surmised that soldiers now required a greater degree of "moral cohesion" to prevail, to advance in the face of withering fire or stand their ground under artillery barrages while taking casualties.[18] For Du Picq, because of battle's new deadliness, modern infantry required additional spirit to fight effectively.

His analysis rested on a distinction between ancient and modern battle, and on their respective implications for discipline. In a close order formation like an ancient phalanx, each hoplite's shield protected the man to his left from missiles and blows. As long as the phalanx stayed together, it generally suffered very few casualties. Paradoxically, it might seem, fear of death motivated hoplites to keep order during the fight, to resist the urge to flee, and continue to participate in battle. The phalanx struck a bargain between mutual cooperation and the

---

[14] "Extract from the History of the 10th Infantry Regiment" in du Picq, *Battle Studies*, p. 35.
[15] McNeill, *Pursuit of Power*, Chapters 7–8.
[16] Du Picq, *Battle Studies*, p. 114.   [17] Du Picq, *Battle Studies*, pp. 98, 271.
[18] Du Picq, *Battle Studies*, p. 102.

instinct for self-preservation: fight together and live. It did not require heroes. "The fixed framework of the phalanx carries along with it even the moderately trained man and the moderately brave man."[19] Battles were lost and soldiers slaughtered when panic set in and rout began. "Man in battle," Du Picq wrote, "is a being in whom the instinct of self-preservation dominates, at certain moments, all other sentiments."[20]

The phalanx's bargain required coolness, determination, and mutual confidence in each other's abilities to sustain, but it paid off. In ancient times, victorious armies suffered relatively few losses. But in the American Civil War, for example, both victorious and defeated armies sustained large and broadly equivalent numbers of casualties in the major engagements. With the musket, rifle and cannon, and later the machine gun and the air strike, soldiers could no longer protect one another against the "fate" of flying lead and steel. "Death is in the air, invisible and blind, whispering, whistling. As brave, good, trustworthy and devoted as my companions may be, they do not shield me," wrote Du Picq.[21] Hoplites were more likely to survive a battle by continuing to fight together, but a modern soldier often had a better chance if he fled, cowered in a hole, or found some other place to hide. Fear of death no longer compelled cohesion among soldiers; a lot of them were going to die no matter how good their discipline.

The problem became even more severe than du Picq could know. In his day, troops still mostly trained and fought in closely packed lines and "columns."[22] In the twentieth century, armies made a fraught transition from such "close order" formations to the "open order" characteristic of modern infantry combat. In a close order formation, officers and NCOs can observe directly their soldiers in a single body, and command them by voice. In open order, troops are dispersed. A defensive line consists of separate fighting positions, while troops spread out for attacks or to maneuver in order to reduce casualties from automatic and artillery fire. Note how in du Picq's Crimean example, close order formation made it possible for him to identify and record the

---

[19] Delbrück, *Warfare in Antiquity*, p. 151.
[20] Du Picq, *Battle Studies*, p. 51.   [21] Du Picq, *Battle Studies*, p. 99.
[22] In plain English, "column" is misleading. A line was a linear formation that was two or three ranks deep. Columns varied in composition but can be thought of as a rectangle, similar to a phalanx, with one of the long sides facing the enemy and on the order of 10–20 ranks deep. Columns were used for attack, their depth intended to absorb casualties on the approach and provide mass to break the enemy's line.

disciplinary infraction. A body of infantry in Napoleonic garb trying to hide in tall grass is not that difficult to spot. It would be less easy to catch more modern shirkers such as a patrol which lies up and returns with false reports, or the occupants of a foxhole who choose to curl up in the bottom.

Modern battle kills a lot of soldiers, and it spreads them out. The solution seemed to be more self-discipline on the part of soldiers themselves, more spirited willingness to go forward anyway, despite the increased chance of death. The questions became how this discipline could be instilled, and what was to be the basis of this new spirit?

Morale, Primary Groups, and National Society

Du Picq's analysis foreshadowed nearly every aspect of the twentieth century debate. R.E. Dupuy remarked in a review of one of military sociology's founding research projects, Samuel Stouffer's *The American Soldier*, "Actually, nothing in this work has not been set forth in one fashion or another by Col. Ardant du Picq."[23] Many of Stouffer's studies, and in a different way Shils and Janowitz's, were about "morale," another word used for the character and degree of military group spirit. The spirit held necessary to prevail on the modern battlefield is, in many respects, a central concern of military sociology, and the principal preoccupation of many military writers.[24] The increasingly mass and citizen character of Western armies in the total war era gave further impetus to the focus on morale. Citizen soldiers were especially in need of additional sources of discipline, it was thought.[25] Du Picq wanted troops to have a "passion": "a violent desire for independence, a religious fanaticism, national pride, a love of glory, a madness for possession."[26]

---

[23] R. Ernest Dupuy, "Review of S.A. Stouffer *et al.*, *The American Soldier*, Vols. 1 and 2," *Christian Science Monitor*, 2 June 1949, p. 18; quoted in Smith, *For a Significant Social Psychology*, p. 43.

[24] See e.g. Hanson, *Carnage and Culture*; Henderson, *Cohesion*; Moran, *Anatomy of Courage*; Richardson, *Fighting Spirit*.

[25] See King's discussion in *Combat Soldier*, Chapter 7, pp. 164–207.

[26] Du Picq, *Battle Studies*, p. 95.

More significant for du Picq, however, in a precursor of primary group theory, was his insight that small teams could intensify fellow feeling. He located discipline at the level of the squad or section, units of approximately ten soldiers. This entailed masculine acquaintance-ship and reciprocal surveillance, which grew out of long hours of train-ing and entailed mutual confidence in success and fear of reproach for failure. "From living together, and obeying the same chiefs, from commanding the same men, from sharing fatigue and rest, from coop-eration among men who quickly understand each other in the execution of warlike movements, may be bred brotherhood, professional knowledge, sentiment, above all unity."[27] For du Picq, armies should be organized and managed so as to develop and maintain this kind of cohesion among troops. Many officers and analysts came to share and develop his views. They emphasized not only the disintegrative effects of modern firepower and the dispersed battlefield, but also how appar-ently "rational" bureaucratic procedures, especially those concerning personnel and replacements, could undermine cohesion in armies.[28]

This thinking, and the military experience that informed it, took place against the implicit backdrop of the national armies of the leading Western states. For du Picq, modern warfare ultimately favored France: "French sociability creates cohesion in French troops more quickly than could be secured in troops in other nations."[29] Du Picq partic-ipated here in a whole genre of military writing whereby the local cul-tural attributes of recruits shape their character as soldiers. "The vary-ing effectiveness of different national armies has often been popularly ascribed to the putative martial spirit of their respective citizenries."[30] His combination of an army's shared, animating purpose with inten-sified cohesion at the primary group level anticipates the common sense of military sociology, which focuses on military organization but makes room for important elements drawn from national society and politics.[31]

---

[27] Ibid., p. 96.
[28] See e.g. Creveld, *Fighting Power*; Griffith, "The Army's New Unit Personnel Replacement and Its Relationship to Unit Cohesion and Social Support." A recent version of this argument is Wong *et al.*, *Why They Fight*.
[29] Du Picq, *Battle Studies*, p. 225.
[30] Moskos, *American Enlisted Man*, p. 134.
[31] In 1981, among an interdisciplinary group of thirty-five social scientists who studied the military profession and military organization, "there was

Other scholars made a more decisive turn toward national politics, and toward social and cultural context.[32] Primary group theory, it turns out, has a fatal ambiguity.[33] If soldiers fight for their buddies, in order to protect one another in conditions of mortal danger, why would they vigorously follow orders placing comrades in harm's way in the first place? To be sure, once in combat, fighting effectively together can secure mutual protection. But it is safer to avoid danger as a group. Many forms of combat indiscipline, like the fake patrol mentioned above, require collusion among soldiers to carry out. "Fragging," the murder or attempted murder of officers considered dangerous either for their offensive spirit or incompetence, is also often collective in nature. Indeed, few undertakings require as much cohesion as mutiny, the willingness of a group to defy orders. The group solidarity championed by primary group theory cuts both ways. It can be the basis of discipline or indiscipline.

In this situation, national identity offers a way out of the dilemma, "pointing" primary groups in the right direction, toward the enemy. The nation, its politics, society, or culture, provided the element of additional spirit the army could not itself create. In mostly studying Western national armies, military history and sociology left themselves an explanatory fallback. National society was the obvious place to turn when scholars exposed the problems with primary group theory. Indeed, the national "case study" is a basic approach to inquiry in both disciplines. As one scholar notes, "the predominance of studies focusing on only one army and society has sometimes led historians to overestimate the distinctiveness of their subjects."[34]

The bias toward the nation and national armies had other sources too. The nation-state, and in particular the United States, stood at the origins of military sociology. During World War II, Samuel Stouffer was the director of the research branch of the US Army's Morale Division, later renamed the Information and Education Division, and his studies facilitated recruitment and personnel policy.[35] Edward Shils

---

widespread agreement that military morale and combat effectiveness rested on primary group and small group solidarity and cohesion." Janowitz, "Preface" in Janowitz and Wesbrook, *Political Education of Soldiers*, p. 10. See also, Moskos, *American Enlisted Man*, Chapter 6.

[32] Bartov, *Hitler's Army*; Cameron, *American Samurai*; Lynn, *Battle*.

[33] See King, *Combat Soldier*, pp. 30–39; Shibutani, *Derelicts of Company K*.

[34] Watson, "Culture and Combat," p. 545.

[35] Herman, *Romance of American Psychology*, p. 67.

and Morris Janowitz worked for the Psychological Warfare Division of Allied headquarters in Europe. They were trying to figure out why German soldiers continued to fight, and how to get them to surrender. After 1945, states continued to commission and control research in military sociology, especially in the United States, even as many researchers came to be based in universities.[36] Survey and interview methods required access to serving soldiers. Researchers focused on contemporary problems occupying the attention of policy makers, defense staffs, and research funding agencies. Key postwar publications, such as Janowitz's *The Professional Soldier* or Samuel Huntington's *The Soldier and the State* were concerned almost entirely with the US armed forces. As military sociology became institutionalized in other Western academies, cross-national comparisons became a standard way of organizing research.[37] Inquiry focused on similarity and difference between the armed forces of various countries. In these accounts, the military appeared always already as a national institution. Scholarly debate tracked matters of national interest in the leading Western states, such as ending conscription or racial and sexual integration.[38] In various ways, armies were reified in national terms, conceived within separate national containers.

[36] See Giuseppe Caforio and Marina Nuciari, "Social Research and the Military: A Cross-National Expert Survey" in Caforio, ed., *Handbook of Military Sociology*, pp. 27–58. One American respondent to Caforio and Nuciari's survey wrote in: "The United States' military does much more social science than any other country I can think of. I would like to see government social scientists, like me, get more freedom to determine what we will work on." (p. 34). Caforio and Nuciari rank the United States in their highest category of government control over research on the military, along with Russia and Argentina among others (p. 41). Overall, in their survey of military sociology in twenty countries, the main commissioner of research was the state (p. 32). Notably, of the twenty countries, fifteen are European, the others being the United States, Argentina, Israel, India, and South Africa (p. 27). As these researchers mainly study their own militaries, not only does military sociology remain firmly in the grip of the nation-state, but it exhibits a heavy Western bias in its research topics.

[37] See e.g. Creveld, *Fighting Power*; Hauser, *America's Army in Crisis*; Henderson, *Cohesion*; Moskos, Williams and Segal, eds., *Postmodern Military*. Tellingly, even reflections on military sociology itself took national-comparative form. See the special issue on "Sociology at Military Academies around the Globe," *Armed Forces and Society*, Vol. 35 (1), 2008.

[38] See e.g. Mershon and Schlossman, *Foxholes and Color Lines*; Kier, "Homosexuals in the U.S. Military."

Given the predominance of the United States, the Vietnam War became a milestone in the critique and development of primary group theory. Morale problems in the US military and the contrasting performance of the opposing Vietnamese forces turned researchers' attentions to the social and political contexts of the war.[39] Ideology, nationalism, and cultural homogeneity seemed to play an important role in the success of Vietnamese communist forces.[40] At the same time, societal factors such as racial tension, drug use, and the political unpopularity of the war at home eventually undermined discipline in the US military.[41] Military sociologists supplemented primary group theory with social factors, particularly beliefs and attitudes conducive, or not, to military service and obedience. In a study of American enlisted soldiers in Vietnam published in 1970, Charles Moskos, a leading military sociologist, wrote: "I argue that combat motivation arises out of the linkages between individual self-concern, primary-group processes, and the shared beliefs of soldiers. The ideological and primary-group explanations are not contradictory."[42] With allowances for the language of social science, essentially this had been du Picq's position.

A version of du Picq's distinction between ancient and modern battle also reappeared, in the form of the "coercive" discipline of pre-twentieth century armies and the "normative" discipline of twentieth century armies. As Janowitz put it, "the integration of small groups into the larger military organization in the contemporary period required more explicit symbolic rationalization."[43] Another scholar spoke of the necessity of soldiers' "moral involvement with a larger collectivity." This depended on a soldier's "sense of national identity, his belief that the sociopolitical system is meeting the basic needs of most members of society, and his acceptance of national ideology."[44] Moderns were motivated by ideas, even amid the intense stress and fear of battle.

---

[39] Balkind, "A Critique of Military Sociology"; Helmer, *Bringing the War Home*; cf. Savage and Gabriel, "Cohesion and Disintegration in the American Army."
[40] Henderson, *Why the Viet Cong Fought*; *Cohesion*.
[41] Hauser, *America's Army in Crisis*.
[42] Moskos, *American Enlisted Man*, p. 135.
[43] Janowitz, "Preface" in Janowitz and Wesbrook, *Political Education of Soldiers*, p. 11. See also Chodoff, "Ideology and Primary Groups."
[44] Wesbrook, "Sociopolitical Training in the Military" in Janowitz and Wesbrook, *Political Education of Soldiers*, pp. 36, 44. See also Kindsvatter, *American Soldiers*, p. xxi.

National society seemed to account for other significant features of modern warfare as well, such as its barbarism and atrocity and its cycles of intense fighting. Racialized ideologies of national friends and enemies play an especially significant role. Omer Bartov's Nazi soldiers on the Eastern front were murderous believers who fought in a titanic struggle against the Judeo-Bolshevik menace.[45] The Pacific War was a "war without mercy" in John Dower's title phrase, where no quarter was given and mutual racism contributed to "an orgy of bloodletting." Racial prejudice led to atrocities on both sides, which in turn fed mutual hate. Dehumanizing the enemy "contributed immensely to the psychological distancing that facilitates killing."[46] American, British, and Japanese combatants were products of the cultures and societies of their day, embodying prevailing racial attitudes and stereotypes that shaped the character of the fighting. Another scholar in this vein, Craig Cameron, remarked of the US Marines that, "[t]he precise images that influenced the nature of Marine ground combat in the Pacific War were products peculiar to American society, culture and this particular military institution at that moment in time."[47] Drawing on letters, diaries, and other writings, he portrays the mentality of the marines and Japanese soldiers fighting on Guadalcanal as "a spiritual clash between warrior representatives of the two cultures."[48] Each side was determined to fight to the death. Here is the evidence from experience of which Joan Scott warned, reproducing ideal self-images.[49]

Participation in intense fighting and savagery indicated, it was thought, some extraordinary social characteristic among those involved, such as extreme ideology, virulent racism, or militant nationalism. Dower, for example, assumed psychological distancing was needed to facilitate such killing, and found it in racism. Bartov searched for what blunted soldiers' "sensitivity to moral and ethical issues," and found it in Nazi ideology.[50] Cameron, too, assumed his subject was distinctive, and had to be explained with phenomena specific to the United States and the US Marines, such as traditions of American Indian hating. Intense fighting and atrocity appear less as a common human capacity, and more as attributes of particular groups in specific

---

[45] Bartov, *Hitler's Army*.   [46] Dower, *War without Mercy*, pp. 10, 11.
[47] Cameron, *American Samurai*, p. 20.   [48] Cameron, *American Samurai*, p. 104.
[49] Scott, "Evidence of Experience."   [50] Bartov, *Eastern Front*, pp. 35–36.

historical circumstances. Evidence for these arguments is drawn from the cultural constructs of participants.

From Nations to Rituals

Dipesh Chakrabarty remarks that "'History' as a knowledge system is firmly embedded in institutional practices that invoke the nation-state at every step."[51] Certainly the combat motivation debates did so Knowledge about armies and war is produced within national histories of martial antagonism.[52] Eurocentric visions of the world wars provided a common historical frame. Scholarship and popular writing tracked over and over the same armies and campaigns – the western front in the First World War, the eastern front in the Second, the Anglo-American war against Nazi Germany, the US war against Japan. A few other wars and armies, the American Civil War, Korea, Vietnam, the Russians, the Chinese, and the Vietnamese, play supporting roles. Bartov's Nazi fanatics, the phlegmatic Tommies, the citizen-soldiers celebrated by American authors, the culturally cohesive Vietnamese communists, and the emperor-worshipping Japanese, are all figures caught up in the national and civilizational politics of wars. Thinking about soldiers and armies has been enveloped in national – and Western – war stories, especially those of the United States.[53] It becomes hard to imagine that colonized Indian and African soldiers fought the Japanese in a way akin to that of the US Marines.

Scholars have many good reasons to situate the mass and citizen armies of the nineteenth and twentieth centuries in national context. National conscript and professional armies in Europe reflected their societies. The particular histories and sociologies of Western states, societies, and their armed forces were important and distinctive objects of inquiry in their own right. Nationalisms and national racisms shaped soldiers' mentalities and experiences. Military sociology's combination of primary groups and nationalism as the two sources of fighting spirit

---

[51] Chakrabarty, *Provincializing Europe*, p. 41.
[52] See the discussion of "war/truth" in Barkawi and Brighton, "Powers of War," pp. 139–141.
[53] See e.g. Ambrose, *Citizen Soldiers*; Bartov, *Hitler's Army*; Dower, *War Without Mercy*; Hanson, *Soul of Battle*; McPherson, *Cause and Comrades*. Cf. Fujitani, *Race for Empire*, pp. 14–17.

reflected this connection between army and society in national context. Eurocentric inquiry is not necessarily or entirely misguided by any means.

But what if the original thrust of du Picq's distinction between ancient and modern battle misled? What if the army's old techniques for creating solidarity and discipline were not so easily outmaneuvered as he feared, so compromised by modern firepower? In collapsing army into national society, we lose sight of the army's – and war's – powers. Armies generate their own sources of discipline and group solidarity, even as they do so through articulation with social context. What theories of national society and of the primary group have tried to provide is an essentialized group for which soldiers can be said to kill and die. If soldiers identify with a group, then their individual sacrifices for the group can be rationally explained. This is why military sociologists and historians agree on the significance of group solidarity even as they disagree on its social basis; they need a group for soldiers to sacrifice for.

Such thinking conceives of the nation and the primary group as horizontal communities and the objects of a kind of rational, willing sacrifice on the part of soldiers. But the army is a hierarchy. Armies exhibit in particularly concentrated fashion a dilemma which has long puzzled social and political theorists: how is solidarity achieved amid hierarchy? Soldiers are both disciplined subjects and members of solidary groups; they are ranked in relations of super- and subordination and they experience powerful sentiments of fellow feeling. They fight and die together, but when ordered to do so. Solidarity in the army cannot be thought separately from hierarchy.

Ritual has long been used to think about group formation and authority together.[54] Rituals instantiate hierarchy while evoking sentiments of belonging (and of differentiation). As noted, they do so in ways that dispense with the need for an "outside" social basis: rituals generate groups, not the other way around. Rituals exercise their powers simply through participation in them. They do not depend upon shared beliefs or even on agreement on the meaning of the rites people are participating in. At the same time, rituals are not disconnected from their social context. Ritual repertoires reflect and adapt to social contexts. Taken together, these general features of ritual comprise the

[54] Bell, *Ritual Theory, Ritual Practice*; Kertzer, *Ritual, Politics, and Power*.

makings of an alternative paradigm of group formation in the army. The place to begin is on the parade ground, where recruits in regular armies begin their training with the most pervasive ritual of military life.

Close Order Drill

The first thing most regular armies do with recruits is to subject them to large doses of close order drill. Drill arouses sentiments of affinity with one another and the sense of immersion in a larger collectivity. "At the beginning of their training the recruits must be taught the military pace," noted Vegetius of the Roman imperial army.[55] As one Indian Army training pamphlet put it, drill stimulates "by means of combined and orderly movement, the man's pride in himself and his unit" and involves not "tedious parade ground movements carried out in perfunctory manner, but rather the physical satisfaction to be derived from sinking one's own individuality in the perfect timing of a mass movement in which every individual is keyed up to the maximum personal tension."[56] John Keegan remarked of drill that its function was "choreographic, ritualistic, perhaps even aesthetic, certainly much more than tactical."[57] Drill socializes participants by disposing them to act in certain ways.[58]

As with the training techniques discussed in the last chapter, drill worked its effects in widely different cultural contexts. The historian William McNeill used his experience of drill in the US Army as the basis for a book on how "keeping together in time" produces social solidarity across historical eras and cultural spaces. He argued that moving together rhythmically as a group while giving voice can induce "euphoric fellow feeling" and wrote of drill that "[w]ords are inadequate to describe the emotion aroused by the prolonged movement in unison that drilling involved."[59] What drill could do in India and the United States, it could also achieve in Africa. Charles Carfrae describes

---

[55] Vegetius quoted in Watson, *Roman Soldier*, p. 54.
[56] Infantry Section Leading, Military Training Pamphlet No. 14 (India), 1941, p. 61, L/MIL/17/5/2256, OIOC.
[57] Keegan, *Face of Battle*, p. 33.   [58] Bell, *Ritual Theory, Ritual Practice*, p. 98.
[59] McNeill, *Keeping Together in Time*, pp. 2–3.

how his company of Nigerians enjoyed, and was exceptionally proficient at, the drill they practiced every morning:

Since Sandhurst days six years before I had had a weakness for drill done really well and my heart would fill with foolish pride as I shouted my words of command, felt the soldiers' emotional response and watched the flash and glitter of a hundred bayonets moving as one. The men called drill 'dancing' in Hausa and it was as gratifying to them as to me that they performed better than any other company.[60]

Whistle commands often punctuated the battle drills described in the last chapter, which exhibited many of the same ritual characteristics as their parade ground counterpart.

Soldiers participate in close order drill throughout their military careers. It plays a prominent role in the numerous daily and periodic ceremonies performed by units in garrison. Indian Army officers were aware of how drill could revivify a collective sense of pride even in veteran units, especially those that had suffered heavily in combat or had not performed as expected.[61] Commanders would often insist on a "smart turn out" for parades shortly after a unit was pulled out of the line. After battle, the Indian Army taught its infantry officers, "[t]here must be no relaxation of...saluting and turn out."[62] One Indian battalion drilled all its companies together after a period in which they had been dispersed for training in order to build the cohesion of the battalion as a "fighting entity." As one of its officers explained, "[i]t was considered that a very short, periodical spasm of close order ceremonial drill, with all [the companies] massed together, acting together with the utmost smartness under the orders of their C.O. would do a good deal to counteract the centrifugal tendencies of modern training."[63] A British battalion in Burma, which broke and

[60] Charles Carfrae, "Dark Company," second version, p. 54, 80/49/1, IWM.
[61] A training instruction for 28 (EA) Brigade on ceremonial drill and parades stated: "There is no need to stress the necessity for smartness in turnout as a means to discipline and unit efficiency. Commanders from all theatres draw attention to the corollary that the smart and clean soldier is usually the best fighting soldier." 28 (EA) Infantry Brigade Training Instruction No. 9, 24 August 1944, Dimoline Papers, IX/2, LH. See also 7th Indian Division Training Instruction No. 1, 4 June 1945, Messervy Papers, V/19, LH.
[62] A Lecture to Infantry Officers on Man Management, L/MIL/17/5/2235, OIOC.
[63] 8/6th Rajputana Rifles, Digest of Services, p. 5, 7512-5-2, NAM.

ran after receiving enfilading fire during an advance, was put through hours of drill and ceremony shortly afterward as a means of rebuilding unit pride.[64] Some version of McNeill's views about social solidarity and "keeping together in time" circulated among the officers of British, Indian, and imperial forces.

That said, Durkheim and other analysts of ritual often overemphasize generating solidarity to the neglect of other properties of ritual.[65] Rituals not only evoke sentiments of belonging, but they also can differentiate the group from other groups, invest the hierarchy of the group with sacred properties, and articulate emotions to a world view or mythology, however imperfectly and diversely understood by participants.[66] Drilling brings forth sentiments of unity to be sure. But consider other aspects of the organization of the parade ground as a ritual space, principally the fact that it mirrors the hierarchic relations of military society.[67] Soldiers are arranged in ranks and files as a single body, under the immediate command of a non-commissioned officer or subaltern who marches or stands just to the side or in front of each body of troops. Officers, sometimes on an elevated platform (or in times past, a horse), exercise command over several such bodies of troops. The sentiments drilling generates are situated within, and articulated to, the hierarchical order of the military. Equally, the separation between the various bodies of troops, between the platoons of a company or the companies of a battalion, serves to instantiate relations of affiliation but also of estrangement between groups. In this way, platoons, companies, etc., are constructed for soldiers both as separate groups and as affiliated with one another in ways which parallel the organization of higher formations. "The group is simultaneously both highly differentiated and exalted as a corporate unity above the interests of the self."[68] The ritual system and military organization are as one in close order drill.

---

[64] Demetriadi interview. This was the 1/Royal Welch Fusiliers and the commander in question had replaced Lt. Col. Williams. See Chapter 8 pp. 274–275.
[65] That ritual has other effects besides the generation of solidarity is one of the principal arguments of Bell's *Ritual Theory, Ritual Practice*.
[66] Kertzer, *Ritual, Politics, and Power*; Turner, *Ritual Process*, pp. 42, 93.
[67] For a similar point made with reference to ceremonial meals, see Lincoln, *Construction of Society*, p. 79. See also Kertzer, *Ritual, Politics and Power*, p. 30.
[68] Bell, *Ritual Theory, Ritual Practice*, p. 178.

Worldly Religion

Close order drill suggests how we might begin to re-describe pervasive features of military life as ritual practices, and in so doing reveal some of their effects. The turn to ritual suggests that the army can be conceived as a religious institution of some kind. Religion, for Durkheim, is about the forces that bind together groups. Rites and representations concerning the gods mediate group feeling. Ritual practices do the binding; they are the mechanisms for religion's effects. In studying what he thought were the "elementary forms" of religion among Australian aboriginal peoples, Durkheim hoped to understand religion in the national-scale societies of his day. Despite these intentions, his text is most useful for thinking about the generation and regeneration of solidarity among small groups.[69] The aboriginal clans are eerily appropriate for thinking about armies, with their tightly knit, closed, yet internally differentiated and hierarchically ordered units. Much like clan totems, the emblems and designations of units both distinguish each unit from others while also marking out relations of affinity between units, as in the manner of the battalions of a regiment. Moreover, just as in Durkheim's account of the clans, the members of each unit are thrown together more or less arbitrarily, united by the fact of having been placed together in the same unit.[70]

With his concept of religion Durkheim sought to understand the nature of group spirit, how it was possible. What enables members of a group to cooperate in situations that require them to forego their individual interests, inclinations, and desires? "[Society] requires that, forgetful of our own interest, we make ourselves its servitors, and it submits us to every sort of inconvenience, privation and sacrifice,

---

[69] See Collins, *Interaction Ritual Chains*, esp. pp. xi, 14–15. Durkheim hoped that by studying "the most primitive and simple religion" religion in general could be understood, including its role in advanced societies. *Elementary Forms*, p. 13*ff.*

[70] According to Durkheim, clan members were not necessarily united by kinship bonds or common descent, and often lived in geographically dispersed spaces coming together only for specific rituals. The unity of a clan "comes solely from their having the same name and the same emblem, their believing that they have the same relations with the same categories of things, their practising of the same rites, or, in a word, from their participating in the same totemic cult." Durkheim, *Elementary Forms*, p. 194.

without which social life would be impossible."[71] He wanted to know how people came to identify with social groupings, why they felt obliged toward them, to the point of acting in self-denying ways.

Durkheim's basic insight is that to act like a group is to be a group. In rituals, people behave like members of groups, under signs that represent the group. Their performance of common actions under common emblems were part of the always on-going construction of the group.

> It is by uttering the same cry, pronouncing the same word, or performing the same gesture in regard to the same object that they become and feel themselves to be in unison … it is the homogeneity of these movements that gives the group consciousness of itself and consequently makes it exist.[72]

Durkheim's language is redolent of the parade ground. A platoon of recruits, falling in for the first time under some arbitrary numerical designation, and subjected to commands as a single body, has already all the elements necessary for group formation. The basis for solidarity is created by collecting people together, placing them in common conditions, and designating them by a common symbol. Military life offers many situations in which members of a unit, under the command of a ritual expert (the officer or NCO), might "utter the same cry" or perform the same action, on and off the parade ground.

In developing ritual as a paradigm for military discipline, the chief focus is not on formal ceremonies, or "obvious" rituals, but on ritual practices as generic forms of social interaction. Rituals distinguish themselves from ordinary interaction in more or less subtle ways. The salute of a senior officer is one example. It can be done casually in daily working life, or crisply and formally in a ceremony, or in a variety of other ways. However done, and despite its frequency, the salute appears as a distinct and privileged happening compared to the ordinary or quotidian.[73] One scholar of ritual, Catherine Bell, notes that "what counts as ritual can rarely be pinned down in general since ritualized practices constantly play off the field of action in which they emerge, whether that field involves other ritualized activities, ordinary action deemed by the contrast to be spontaneous and practical, or both

---

[71] Durkheim, *Elementary Forms*, p. 237.
[72] Durkheim, *Elementary Forms*, pp. 262–263.
[73] Bell, *Ritual Theory, Ritual Practice*, p. 74.

at the same time."[74] Among other effects, a salute performs respect for
authority and tradition, shows willingness to obey, and evokes joint
belonging in a military organization among those of different rank.

Ritual is a pervasive feature of social life. Randall Collins identifies
four elements of ritual and four outcomes or effects:

Elements	Effects
Physical assembly of the group	Group solidarity
Barriers to outsiders	Emotional energy
Mutual focus of attention	Symbols representing the group
Shared mood	Sentiments regarding the group's good character[75]

Many ordinary social situations (e.g. a queue waiting for a bus) contain
all four of Collin's elements, which he suggests are chained together in
patterns of interaction. Military life, especially of regular infantry in
training and on active service, consists of chains of rituals formally
drawn up in unit schedules by commanders and their staffs. Sleeping,
eating, training, working, preparing, washing, recreating, and so on,
are all ordinarily done in groups and at set times. (See Figure 5.1)

A primary characteristic of ritual is the physical assembly of the people involved.[76] The army groups soldiers together, gives them a designation as a group, and tasks them with various purposes, such as
training or fighting or passing signals. A unit's soldiers live and work
together in close quarters. They are subject to the same commanders,
wear the same uniform, and are marked by the same insignia. Frequently units are isolated from contact with civilian populations or
even other units. Battalions preparing for service in Burma were often
broken down into companies in remote jungle areas, marching, training, and living together under canvas for weeks at a time. "Intimacy
was forced upon us; we could not escape our companions; yet we

---

[74] Bell, *Ritual Theory, Ritual Practice*, p. 141.
[75] Adapted from Collins, *Interaction Ritual Chains*, pp. 48–49.
[76] As Durkheim puts it, "The very fact of the concentration [of the clan] acts as
an exceptionally powerful stimulant." *Elementary Forms*, pp. 246–247. See
also Collins, *Interaction Ritual Chains*, pp. 33–34.

Figure 5.1 Ritual and recreation: Soldiers of an Indian motor transport unit watch a wrestling match.[77]

valued and trusted each other," remarked Carfrae of training Nigerian soldiers in preparation for Chindit operations.[78]

Ritual and ritual practices here threaten to become synonymous with the military. In a sense, that is the point. Training, which occupies a great deal of time in military calendars, doubles as both ritualized solidarity-building and disciplinary instruction in taking the correct actions. Durkheim means to turn religion and ritual into categories appropriate for understanding important dimensions of everyday life. But, analytically speaking, how do we distinguish between the ritualized and the "profane" aspect of social activities? Durkheim defines ritual as the rules of conduct in the presence of sacred objects.[79] As religion is that social force that binds people into groups, the "sacred" are those activities and symbols which evoke sentiments of unity and fellow feeling.

Armies set out to build cohesion, and design training and other activities to do so. They develop elaborate, overlapping systems of unit

[77] IND 2265, IWM.
[78] Charles Carfrae, "Dark Company," p. 96, 80/49/1, IWM.
[79] Durkheim, *Elementary Forms*, p. 56.

names and identities under which to group their soldiers: that is, armies have totems. A clan totem, on Durkheim's account, refers to a god, but it also designates the group. Totems, like many military emblems, were often representations of warlike animals.[80] When a group of people worshiped their god, performed rituals, and offered sacrifices under the sign of their totem, they were worshipping a representation of their own collective identity. In doing so, the bonds of solidarity uniting the group were revivified. "[T]he sacred ultimately refers not to a supernatural entity, but rather to people's emotionally charged interdependence, their societal arrangements."[81] The symbols and signs mediate the sense of the sacred. For Durkheim, people are correct in believing that their god is "a force upon which [their] strength relies."[82] It is belief in a god, and the rituals performed under the signs of this belief, which evokes the sentiment of belonging in individuals, and enables their cooperation. "[W]e are able to say that men make their gods, or, at least, make them live; but at the same time, it is from [the gods] that [men] live themselves."[83] In place of gods, the army has *esprit de corps*, organized around systems of unit identities and insignias.

In Durkheim's set-up, to participate in rituals in the name of a military unit, under its symbols, is to participate in activities which are about one's own identity and sense of belonging. Soldiers' self-images (as a martial race for example) can be formed through symbolic identification with their units. To praise the unit in various ways is to praise one's self and one's comrades, as warriors, as honorable, as steadfast,

---

[80] Wingate chose a *chinthe* for the emblem of his Long Range Penetration Force, which was popularized as 'chindit' and refers to a lion-headed dragon in Burmese mythology. The 11 (EA) Division had a rhinoceros for its divisional sign and the 17th Indian had a black cat. The 19th Indian Division had a gold device of a hand thrusting a dagger against a scarlet field. Of the menacing spider for 81 (WA) Division, John Hamilton tells us: "As the Division's badge General Woolner chose a black spider, head down, on a yellow ground. This spider represented Ananse, a well-known figure in Ashanti mythology, who can change into many guises and perform seemingly impossible feats, overcoming his enemies by guile rather than by force. He was depicted head down because thus he would appear to be going forward when a soldier wearing the badge on his shoulders was about to fire his weapon. Although publicists identified him as a Tarantula that species is not found in West Africa and is not black." *War Bush*, p. 5.

[81] Kertzer, *Ritual, Politics, and Power*, p. 9.

[82] Durkheim, *Elementary Forms of the Religious Life*, p. 240.

[83] Ibid., p. 383.

as aggressive, masculine, and so on.[84] When officers toast the regiment, they are toasting themselves. Soldiers and officers express sentiments of attachment to, and belief in, their formations. "'Fourth' – an honourable number. I soon came to believe with a passion worthy of a religion that there was no regiment on earth like it," remarked John Masters on joining his Gurkha regiment.[85] On his posting to the 5/14th Punjab, one officer wrote home "[t]hey are far and away the best regiment in the Indian Army."[86] "[A] soldier always believes that his own mob is best," noted a British ECO in the Indian Army.[87] "The talk of belonging to the best Platoon, of the finest Company, of the crack Battalion, of THE Regiment, means something much more real to the soldier than the fact that he is enlisted in the British Army," remarked one British soldier who fought in Burma.[88] "[E]ven the most cynical, reluctant conscript was conscious of belonging to something special," said another.[89]

Officers, and in particular commanders, play a crucial role as personified symbols of the collective. Commanders can symbolize the identity and spirit of military formations. The association between the 14th Army and Slim is one example of this phenomenon. Laudatory accounts of Slim are found throughout the memoir literature.[90] Slim was an exceptionally capable general and one of the great commanders of the Second World War. His humanity and concern for his soldiers and their welfare were evident in numerous ways.[91] However, these facts do not exhaust the reasons for the praise of Slim, which often mention his many impromptu talks to troops delivered from the bonnet of his jeep. As with toasting the regiment or otherwise praising one's unit, to laud one's commander is also to laud oneself and the collective of which you and the commander are members. During the retreat through Burma in 1942, one Indian battalion history notes the significance of "absolute faith" in Slim in preventing the retreat from

---

[84] See Kertzer, *Ritual, Politics and Power*, p. 16.
[85] Masters, *Bugles and a Tiger*, p. 103.   [86] Lt. Col. S.P. Fearon, LH.
[87] Schlaelfli, *Emergency Sahib*, p. 137.   [88] Cooper, *'B' Company*, p. 46.
[89] Fraser, *Quartered Safe Out Here*, p. 11.
[90] Masters, *Road Past Mandalay*, pp. 44–45; Gilmore, *Connecticut Yankee*, pp. 186–187; Leyin, *Tell Them of Us*, pp. 123–124; Khan, *Memoirs*, pp. 38ff; Shipster, *Mist Over the Rice-Fields*, pp. 31–32.
[91] An important example, which dovetailed with practical military necessity, is the amount of time and effort he put into the medical arrangements for his troops. See Harrison, *Medicine and Victory*, Chapter 5, pp. 185–231.

becoming a rout. Indian soldiers remarked "Slim Sahib saved me."[92]
Slim is a symbolic place marker for the qualities of the unit and its
soldiers which enabled it to persevere.

Hierarchy

What about the problem of solidarity amid hierarchy? Scholars often
address this question in terms of the ways in which power and hierarchy are mystified, obfuscated, and/or legitimated to the lower orders.[93]
Durkheim develops a novel response. Rather than focusing on how the
disempowered become confused as to their situation (false conscious-
ness/happy slaves), or on the ways in which they are controlled despite
their beliefs (constrained choices/coercion), Durkheim attends to how
individuals feel empowered through their incorporation in collectivi-
ties, even in subordinate positions.[94] To be a soldier, even a private, is to
partake in the collective power of a military organization. For McNeill,
drill created "[a] sense of pervasive well-being . . . a strange sense of personal enlargement; a sort of swelling out, becoming bigger than life,
thanks to participation in collective ritual."[95] On his promotion to the
very lowest rank above private soldier in the Indian Army (one stripe),
the future leader of the INA, Mohan Singh, recalled "I must admit
that this petty promotion to the rank of a Lance Naik gave me an
immense pleasure and satisfaction," more satisfaction than later earning his commission.[96] As Bell comments, ritualized activities express-
ing a social hierarchy offer participants the sense of "a state of prestige within [an] ordering of power" and "a vision of empowerment."[97]
Everyone has their role to play in the unit.

One of the common ways in which a hierarchy is instantiated in
a group is, paradoxically, through rituals which reverse the official
hierarchy.[98] These rituals represent superiors as members of the group

---

[92] Brigadier A.B. Gibson, Unofficial War History, 2/13th Frontier Force Rifles,
p. 29, I/4, LH.
[93] See Beetham, *Legitimation of Power*.
[94] See Bell, *Ritual Theory, Ritual Practice*, Chapter 9.
[95] McNeill, *Keeping Together in Time*, p. 2.
[96] Singh, *Soldiers' Contribution*, p. 28. A lance naik is roughly equivalent to a
private first class in the US Army. A naik is equivalent to a corporal.
[97] Bell, *Ritual Theory, Ritual Practice*, p. 84.
[98] Turner, *Ritual Process*, Chapter 5, pp. 166–203.

in ways which erase or invert their official rank. They serve to exalt the corporate unity of the group in order to more effectively establish its internal hierarchic differentiation. As Victor Turner shows, to maintain solidarity amidst hierarchy and continually re-incorporate subordinates into the group, rituals which evoke strong sensations of community, rather than hierarchy, are of particular importance.[99] One of the most common forms of military "reversal of hierarchy" rituals involves mocking and impersonating officers. Typically, private soldiers impersonate officers and NCOs among themselves, with individuals becoming accomplished in the comic representation of particular superiors' gesticulations or speech patterns. One British officer of West African troops said of such characters that "[t]hey were clever mimics, gave disgraceful nicknames to their white officers and NCOS, and would slyly take the micky if they thought they could get away with it."[100] Of his Gurkhas, Scott Gilmore wrote "[a]t company and battalion entertainments, we Westerners could count on watching ourselves on stage, with sharp caricatures of mannerisms and idiosyncrasies."[101] John Masters, too, remarked on the "horrifyingly accurate caricatures of English tribal customs" put on by his Gurkhas in evening entertainments.[102] One British Army tradition is the "sod's opera" in which a unit's jesters do their best impersonations of the quirks of sergeants and officers.[103] Such practices can be seen as "weapons of the weak" which, through ridicule, seek to corrode the authority of officers.[104] However, safely contained, such events create the sense that superiors are part of the group, subject to ridicule and jokes like everyone else. The effectiveness of reversal of hierarchy rituals is due in part to the direct contrast between the apparent powerlessness of superiors in the ritual space with their institutional power outside that space. The contrast makes

---

[99] Turner, *Ritual Process*, Chapters 3–5, pp. 94–203.

[100] Jack St. Aubyn, address given at Puddletown and Milton Abbas Parish Churches during Services of Remembrance to mark the 50th Anniversary of the Second World War. 20 August 1995. Mr. St. Aubyn provided a copy to the author.

[101] Gilmore, *Connecticut Yankee*, p. 93.

[102] Masters, *Bugles and a Tiger*, p. 152.

[103] Author's correspondence with Shane Brighton, 26 January 2001. A "sod's opera" refers to a performance in which, among other things, male soldiers impersonate women.

[104] Scott, *Weapons of the Weak*; Lincoln, *Authority*.

the hierarchy visible and evident, while the ritual itself evokes sentiments of common feeling among subordinates and superiors alike. Rituals of this kind help establish the authority of officers.

Many rituals and practices with ritualized effects in military life evoke sentiments of solidarity while also incorporating the military hierarchy and worldview, much in the way close order drill does. For example, a common tactical procedure for units in the field, in Burma and elsewhere, was the "stand-to." At likely times of enemy attack, typically dawn and dusk, units in a defensive perimeter stood prepared to repel an enemy assault. Every soldier was alert in their foxhole covering an assigned field of fire with weapons and extra ammunition at the ready; sergeants went around checking each position; the commander stood by the radio, ready to call in artillery fire or reinforcements; a reserve platoon or section was placed in the center of the position, ready with bayonets fixed to evict any attackers who broke through the perimeter. Obviously "stand-to" had a clear tactical function, to ensure maximum readiness at times of maximum risk. Equally, there were ritual dimensions. It involved the common participation of all members of the unit at fixed times, evoking sentiments of affinity with one another and of estrangement from the world outside the perimeter; it inscribed in various ways the gradations of rank among members of the unit; and it symbolized collective preparedness to face danger, an essential component of the military worldview. Indeed, the image of "stand-to" is a common representation of military preparedness, and veterans of service in Burma mention "stand-to" in the context of unity in the face of fear.[105] "Stand-to" generated sentiments of solidarity and articulated those sentiments to military organization, its hierarchy and worldview, and did so in the context of an everyday tactical practice. As Clifford Geertz has commented, "[i]n a ritual, the world as lived and the world as imagined . . . turn out to be the same world."[106]

Many of the formal, periodic ceremonies of military formations seek to instantiate a worldview or mythology. Such ceremonies often involve the annual celebration of a unit's past exploits, sometimes involving stylized re-enactments. A British tank squadron, for example, paraded annually without its officers to commemorate a battle in Burma in

---

[105] Gilmore, *Connecticut Yankee*, p. 142; Griffiths, "The Railway Corridor and Before," p. 57.

[106] Geertz, *Interpretation of Cultures*, p. 112.

which all the officers became casualties. The ritual conveyed the notion that the unit was to carry on with its mission even if its commanders were killed. The ritual also invested the present officers, through their absence, with a sacred aura derived from the sacrifices of their predecessors.[107] One war-raised Indian battalion captured a Japanese infantry gun in one of its first actions. This gun was then used regularly in battalion ceremonies, a symbol of the unit's prowess on the battlefield.[108] Officers could rapidly invent a set of traditions for a unit that had no history prior to its formation during the war.[109]

Participation not Belief

One of the least convincing aspects of military sociology's turn to national society and politics is the notion that solidarity and discipline depend on the shared beliefs of soldiers, on a common ideology of some kind. Soldiers in mass armies were too varied in origin, education, and ability, and battle too stressful an environment for this to obtain. Ritual practices, by contrast, exercise their effects simply through participation in them. What rituals evoke and organize are sentiments and not, in the first instance, ideas.[110] Sentiments do the primary work of rituals, which can be thought of as instruments of sentiment evocation.[111] The point of ritual systems is to not to change belief, but to dispose people toward acting in particular kinds of ways, those intended by ritual experts.

Drill, for example, varies by national style, branch of service, regimental tradition, and so on. It involves symbolic codes, specific histories, and explicit associations with past events. But its powers of group formation arise from participation in it, not decoding it. Drilling generates sentiments among those doing the drilling. Groups do not have drills; drills generate groups. As Bell puts it, "ritual systems do not function to regulate or control" some prior social order, "they *are* the

---

[107] Allen, *Burma*, p. 258, n. 2.
[108] The 14/13th Frontier Force Rifles. See Col. E.C. Pickard, private diary, 96/8/1, IWM.
[109] Hobsbawm and Ranger, *Invention of Tradition*.
[110] See Asad, "Toward a Genealogy of the Concept of Ritual" in his *Genealogies of Religion*; Bell, *Ritual Theory, Ritual Practice*; Kertzer, *Ritual, Politics and Power*.
[111] Lincoln, *Construction of Society*.

system."[112] Training and drilling under military totems creates *esprit de corps* in serving soldiers through participation in training and drilling, not necessarily because their flags and unit insignia reflect an outside political order, a national or ethnic group, or regimental lore (although they may also do these things).

One of the properties of ritual is that people can participate with varying levels of commitment, and yet still participate. As Durkheim puts it, "the real function of religion is not to make us think . . . but . . . to make us act, to aid us to live."[113] Recall the battle drill manual from the last chapter: "If [a soldier] has no imagination he will just carry out the drill woodenly – and he still won't do it badly."[114] Individuals can even read different meanings into the same ritual. Ritual symbols and practices "condense" meaning or "unify a rich diversity of meanings," making them "multivocal."[115] At a ceremony for the award of medals of valor, for example, soldiers may experience different sentiments, such as grief or pride or boredom. There may even be anger at higher command that the unit was placed in a situation where costly heroism was necessary. There is no necessity for a common interpretation of the rites in order for sentiments of belonging to be evoked.[116] By requiring neither consensus nor explicit beliefs, ritual practices avoid drawing attention to potential conflicts within the group. The perception and experience of solidarity is maximized while at the same time allowing for degrees of commitment and emotional participation among individuals, some of whom may merely comply with or quietly evade the rites.[117] As Maurice Bloch observes, "[y]ou cannot argue with a song."[118] (See Figure 5.2) The same can be said about a bugler blowing the retreat, or about the many moments when soldiers sing together, as on route marches.[119] Significantly, not only are ritualized activities pervasive in military life, soldiers are not generally given

---

[112] Bell, *Ritual Theory, Ritual Practice*, p. 130.

[113] Durkheim, *Elementary Forms*, pp. 463–464.

[114] Instructors' Handbook on Fieldcraft and Battle Drill (India), p. 4, L/MIL/17/5/2226, OIOC.

[115] Kertzer, *Ritual, Politics, and Power*, p. 11.

[116] See Fernandez, "Symbolic Consensus in a Fang Reformative Cult."

[117] Bell, *Ritual Theory, Ritual Practice*, pp. 122–123.

[118] Bloch, "Symbols, Song, Dance and Features of Articulation," p. 71; quoted in Bell, *Ritual Theory, Ritual Practice*, pp. 214–215.

[119] "Retreat" refers both to the ceremony and bugle call involved in lowering the flag of a military station at sunset. John Nunneley describes "retreat" at a KAR outpost in Ethiopia: "[t]he company paraded for 'Retreat' a few minutes

Figure 5.2 "Cannot argue with a song": A Frontier Force Rifles ceremony somewhere in Burma.[120]

a choice about participating in them. Ritualized activities and their effects are inescapable. They are a "strategic form of socialization."[121]

For the soldiers of a unit to come together and utter the same sounds, in the performance of ritualized activities and in the presence of the appropriate insignia, is to renew what Durkheim's Australians called *mana*. *Mana* is a "vague power" or "force" that seems to flow through and among participants in ritual, conjoining group members, their totems, and their god, and inspiring sentiments of unity, cooperation,

after my arrival and as a visitor I stood and watched a ceremony which, for me, never lost its impressive solemnity, especially when performed in a lonely desert outpost." *Tales from the King's African Rifles*, p. 89.
[120] SE 4088, IWM.   [121] Bell, *Ritual Theory, Ritual Practice*, p. 98.

and sacrifice.[122] When the group acts collectively under its totemic symbols (which may also be informal and local), it revivifies the *mana* flowing through members. For participants, *mana* seems to circulate through the mediation of the totem, the visible sign of god and of the group, which is why totems such as military insignia are invested with emotional power.[123] Of such moments, Durkheim writes: "[m]en are more confident because they feel themselves stronger; and they really are stronger, because forces which were languishing [are] now reawakened in their consciousness."[124] Fed by daily and periodic ritual activities performed under common symbols and identities, formal and informal, *mana* is what military professionals call e*sprit de corps*.

Group solidarity in the army enables soldiers to sacrifice, in small and large ways, for the good of the unit. Ritualized training disposes soldiers toward working together and sacrificing individual interests. But does sacrifice draw down the bank of group solidarity? Do soldiers "use up" their group spirit when they act in self-denying ways? In the combat motivation debate, casualties corrode and ultimately undermine cohesion.

Sacrifice

A different line of thought is offered by Durkheimian and neo-Durkheimian approaches to ritual and sacrifice. Sacrifice makes the group exist, calls it into being, and revivifies its energies. Sacrifice regenerates the solidary bonds of the group.[125] It makes the group take on greater reality in the minds of those remaining.

The logic of these insights leads to the apparently paradoxical proposition that the more members of the group sacrificed, the greater the solidary bonds uniting the living and the dead. Each drop of blood spilled can regenerate the forces which bind them together, a dynamic registered in funeral rites. Notably, symbols of fertility and rebirth are ubiquitous in such rites.[126] In assembling for a funeral, the group reaffirms its solidarity and seeks to compensate for the loss. Durkheim's

---

[122] Durkheim, *Elementary Forms*, pp. 217, 228.   [123] Ibid., p. 251.
[124] Ibid., p. 387. The bracketed "are" replaces a misprinted "and" in the text.
[125] See e.g. Durkheim, *Elementary Forms*, pp. 383, 387; Hubert and Mauss, *Sacrifice*, pp. 62–64; Lincoln, *Death, War, and Sacrifice*, Chapter 3.
[126] Bloch and Parry, *Death and the Regeneration of Life*.

Australians had violent mourning rituals. "The shedding of blood which is practised so freely during mourning is a veritable sacrifice offered to the dead man."[127] The violence of the mourners, their "weeping, groaning, or inflicting wounds upon themselves or others," is testimony "to the fact that at this moment, the society is more alive and active than ever." Their "collective manifestations" are evidence of a "moral communion," which strengthens and restores energy to the group.[128]

That death should have regenerative properties is of course an irony, not least for those who have lost their lives. But these properties help sketch out how combat and military group solidarity feed one another; how through sacrifice battle can spark the motive forces for more battle. The potential of violence between groups to generate an "interminable escalation" is a central theme of Rene Girard's influential account of sacrifice. "Vengeance professes to be an act of reprisal, and every reprisal calls for another reprisal," he wrote, setting in train "an interminable, infinitely repetitive process."[129] Death inflicts a loss on a group of soldiers, a blood debt which they compensate through further combat, revivifying the group either through further loss of their own or through inflicting loss on the enemy, or both. The act of sacrifice/combat provides energies which increase the solidarity of the group and enable it to engage in further combat. Theoretically, this is a series which can continue to the point of annihilation. Combat is a potentially interminable discharging of blood debts between groups of soldiers. Soldiers' solidary bonds are revivified by violent loss, which energizes both sentiments of vengeance and increased solidarity, providing further impetus to combat, where further losses are suffered and the cycle repeats. As Barbara Ehrenreich commented, "[w]arriors make wars, but it is also true that, in what has so far been an endless reproductive cycle, war makes warriors."[130] Fighting produces more fighting.

---

[127] Durkheim, *Elementary Forms*, p. 448. Durkheim suggests that it is from such sacrifices at funerals that the idea of immortality for the deceased arises and takes on reality for mourners.

[128] Durkheim, *Elementary Forms*, p. 448, 459.

[129] Girard, *Violence and the Sacred*, pp. 14, 17.

[130] Ehrenreich, *Blood Rites*, p. 158.

Primary Groups Revisited

In the late afternoon of 22 October 1944, "C" Company of the 22 (Nyasaland) Battalion of the King's African Rifles launched an attack on Brown Hill in the Kabaw Valley shouting their battle cry "sokolai, sokolai, yao-oo-oo."[131] Climbing the hill on the left flank, No. 15 Platoon came under grenade discharger fire from a bunker with four Japanese soldiers in it. They suffered several casualties, among them the British officer commanding the platoon, killed as he crossed the start line.[132] Two soldiers sought to "avenge" their dead platoon commander, crawling up to the bunker to throw grenades into the aperture.[133] Both were killed. Following in the tracks of their dead comrades, who lay before the bunker, two more soldiers finally succeeded in killing all four Japanese with grenades. One of them was seriously wounded. After the hill had been taken, the platoon buried its officer between the two men who had died following after him, an ordering of space which reflected the military hierarchy in which they had lived and fought. The padre read out the names of the dead in an impromptu ceremony, versions of which often follow battles. Afterward, the battalion commander wrote to his wife that his "heart ached."

The four soldiers – or *askaris*, as they were known in the KAR – who assaulted the bunker were already a remnant of their section when they did so. They were all private soldiers. Their section commander as well as the next most senior soldier had been killed or wounded along with the platoon commander. Only one soldier from this section survived the action unscathed. The primary group had started dying on the start line and the soldiers carried out their exemplary if costly act of fighting spirit in the absence of junior leadership. They fought

---

[131] This account is based on Brigadier K.H. Collen, "A Story of the Gallant 22nd Battalion King's African Rifles based on extracts from Ken's letters," 28 October 1944 and 3 November 1944 and History of the 22nd Battalion, King's African Rifles, Appendix C: Report on Operation by 'C' Coy 22 (NY) K.A.R. on 27th October 1944, 79/21/1, IWM.

[132] In British East and West African forces, British officers commanded platoons, which in the Indian Army were commanded by VCOs. The battalion commander wrote of this officer, "I knew he would be killed, he was so keen – almost to the point of foolhardiness." Brigadier K.H. Collen, "A Story of the Gallant 22nd Battalion King's African Rifles based on extracts from Ken's letters," 28 October 1944, 79/21/1, IWM.

[133] Brigadier K.H. Collen, "A Story of the Gallant 22nd Battalion King's African Rifles based on extracts from Ken's letters," 3 November 1944, 79/21/1, IWM.

until one remained standing, victorious. That soldiers fight for their comrades, the core idea of primary group theory, lacks purchase if literally interpreted. The *askaris'* buddies were dead and wounded, and further attempts on the bunker only made the survivors casualties as well. But the destruction of their leader and comrades did not prevent the remainder from fighting on. Death was not destructive for the solidarity of the unit. Death was fertile and sentiments of fellow feeling attained their highest pitch in its wake, as soldiers sought revenge for their dead and hearts ached.

In this chapter, I have re-described the army and combat in an anthropological language of ritual and sacrifice, in order to illuminate aspects of group solidarity and fighting spirit in the army. I do not argue that every unit achieves the ideal typical capacity to sacrifice to the point of annihilation. Most combat formations do not fight to the last, but break and run well before. Shils and Janowitz's view that cohesion collapses after some number of casualties has been suffered is well-grounded in empirical observation of the behavior of combat units. As Max Weber remarks of ideal types, they are utopias not found in their "conceptual purity" in reality.[134] Solidarity and sacrifice are not the only factors at work among soldiers in battle. For many, the experience of mortal fear produces immobility or flight, overcoming all other sentiments and desires.[135] Other soldiers may have resisted significant integration into the group, and feel no compunction about shirking their responsibilities on the battlefield or elsewhere.

For many soldiers, however, drill and ritual imprinted powerfully on their consciousnesses. Analytic constructs and language cannot capture what it is like to experience solidarity and sacrifice, or even just to drill on the parade ground. "It was something felt, not talked about," McNeill remembered.[136] Army life, in a rough and ready way, regularly generates sentiments of solidarity amid hierarchy. Scholars cannot recreate these sentiments, but to understand soldiers, we must try to apprehend them.

---

[134] Weber, *Methodology of the Social Sciences*, p. 90.
[135] Ehrenreich, *Blood Rites*, Chapter 5, pp. 77–96.
[136] McNeill, *Keeping Together in Time*, p. 2. "[V]isceral" is another word McNeill uses in the same passage.

6 | Battle

It is the war that forces us to do the killing.

– Captain Shosaku Kameyama[1]

Of German soldiers on the eastern front in World War II, Omer Bartov asks, was it "possible to fight for years on end in a foreign and hostile land, with the imminent danger of death lurking behind every tree and hill and to endure the most terrible physical and mental hardship, without believing that all this was necessary for the achievement of some 'higher cause'"?[2] He concludes these soldiers were "devoted believers in a murderous ideology."[3] Scholars have qualified and developed Bartov's argument.[4] But his general notion is surprisingly common and persistent: ideology, political myths and ideals, and, above all, nationalism and ethnic chauvinism supply an additional spirit needed for sacrifice in wartime. For Benedict Anderson, for example, the nation has made it possible "over the past two centuries, for so many millions of people, not so much to kill, as willingly to die."[5] A kind of spirit-over-body psychology underwrites these arguments. It provides

---

[1] Quoted in Nunneley and Tamayama, *Tales by Japanese Soldiers*, p. 160.

[2] Bartov, *Eastern Front*, p. 38.

[3] Bartov, *Hitler's Army*, p. viii. Like du Picq, Bartov thought that a high rate of casualties meant that an additional source of motivation was required. He argued that from the winter of 1941 onwards, primary groups did not have time to form in the *Wehrmacht*; soldiers were killed off too quickly. Rüdiger Overmans' analysis of casualty statistics in his *Deutsche Militärische Verluste im Zweiten Weltkrieg* shows that it was the losses of 1944 that fundamentally disrupted the *Wehrmacht's* ability to replace casualties. Nonetheless, Bartov raises an important conceptual issue for primary group theory. How do primary groups account for fighting spirit amid high losses, when the groups that supposedly sustain soldiers and give them a reason to fight are being rapidly killed off?

[4] See e.g. Fritz, *Frontsoldaten*; Rutherford, *Combat and Genocide*.

[5] Anderson, *Imagined Communities*, p. 16. See also Koenigsberg, *Nations Have the Right to Kill*. Cf. Collins, "Does Nationalist Sentiment Increase Fighting Efficacy?"; Farrar, "Nationalism in Wartime."

an unconvincing basis for obedience in a mass army or for discipline in combat.

The notion of fighting spirit, whether derived from ideology, nationalism, *esprit de corps*, or their combination, portrays the battlefield as a domain of agency, expressive of the individual and collective character of soldiers and their units. They kill and die in accordance with their national styles. But battlefields are also sites of extreme constraint. They thrust harsh choices upon combatants. Combat is reciprocal, tit for tat. Variable patterns evolve which ensnare both sides and govern their behavior. Ideology may initiate the intense fighting of "race war," but once in motion it requires neither racist nor heroic soldiers to sustain it. The interaction of opposing sides forms a structure of battle that confronts soldiers and their units as an external reality, the rules of a game already underway. For those involved, apparently extreme reactions like combat suicide or fighting to the "last man, last round" can be reasonable responses to the situation. Indeed, such responses were often shared across the lines. From different nations, in different armies, soldiers acted in comparable ways when caught in similar straits during the Burma campaign.

The discourse of "race war" provided to officers and soldiers a language to make the fighting intelligible, representable.[6] The fighting pressurized those involved, motivating them to fight in particular ways. This chapter draws out these battlefield sources of soldiers' behavior in Burma, sources easily overlooked in assimilating and reducing war experience to national histories. It begins with an extraordinary example of an ordinary type of engagement in Burma, the defense of an all-round perimeter. "C" Company's stand at Kanlan Ywathit demonstrates how a version of the phalanx's bargain between unity and self-preservation functioned in modern conditions, even at a higher rate of casualties. Conducted in remote, inhospitable, and often forested terrain, the fighting in Burma had a way of locking participants into intensifying, no-quarter spirals.

The Japanese had initiated this kind of war, refusing to accept surrender and abusing those they did capture. Once underway, this form of fighting reproduced itself. Allied soldiers reciprocated the Japanese refusal to accept surrender, shutting tight combat's exit valve. Below, a look at the problem of surrender in Burma, and how soldiers thought

[6] Wedeen, "Conceptualizing Culture."

about it at the time, helps show how no-quarter fighting gets going and sustains itself, irrespective of individual belief or level of motivation.

Contingency and agency, however, played their role. Chance happenings, the decisions of commanders, and the actions of soldiers, conspired to shift patterns of fighting and march them down different paths. The chapter closes with a look at the Battle of Sangshak and some other engagements in the initial stages of the Japanese U-Go offensive at Kohima and Imphal. Different responses to similar situations set in train alternate action–reaction cycles, even in respect of the treatment of prisoners.

Although Du Picq thought modern battle required additional spirit, he emphasized the centrality of fear. Combat discipline did not, and could not, depend primarily on individual bravery or national qualities. It was about getting groups of frightened soldiers to fight together.[7] Of course there are heroic individuals, just as there are ideologically-motivated people who can overcome their instincts or commit awful acts. The ubiquity of reciprocal, organized violence in human histories, however, suggests there are sturdy and robust mechanisms for impelling it, even in its more merciless, intense forms. In strategic scale, Burma was a sideshow, involving forces in the low hundreds of thousands over three and a half years. But in the intensity of its combats it resembles other Pacific War battlefields, despite the colonial and multicultural character of many of the Allied troops involved. In Burma, soldiers from many different places fought the Japanese in similar ways. Supposedly national styles of fighting were revealed as situational.

The Fight at Kanlan Ywathit

To break back into central Burma in early 1945, General William Slim had to get the 14th Army across the Irrawaddy River and take Mandalay. He did so with a series of well-timed feints and crossings. One bridgehead across the river at Satpangon, meant to draw out the Japanese, succeeded all too well in its purpose. Near a village called

---

[7] "I have heard philosophers reproached for studying too exclusively man in general and neglecting the race, the country, the era . . . The opposite criticism can be made of military men of all countries. They are always eager to expound traditional tactics and organization suitable to the particular character of their race, always the bravest of all races. They fail to consider as a factor in the problem, man confronted by danger." Du Picq, *Battle Studies*, p. 109.

Kanlan Ywathit, two companies of the 14/13th Frontier Force Rifles held the center-right of the bridgehead, "B" Company under Major Akbar Khan, and "C" Company under Major George Coppen. Over the night of 16–17 February, one of Coppen's platoon commanders, Jemadar Parkash Sing, earned the Victoria Cross for his role in the defense of the "box" – or all-round perimeter – made up of the two companies, with "C" company forward. Kanlan Ywathit offers a window on a common type of combat in Burma, the nighttime defense of a perimeter, and also on how even acts of great individual bravery and sacrifice – the epitome of fighting spirit – were structured by the nature of that combat, by its rules and patterns.[8]

From the morning of the 16th, elements of the Japanese 33rd Division prepared their attack on the bridgehead, shelling it and sending forward advance parties. "C" Company soldiers heard them moving through the elephant grass covering much of the area: "It crackles as you walk through it."[9] That evening, "C" Company dug positions in the sandy ground and pre-registered artillery to bring fire down on likely routes of attack. After 9 p.m. on a very dark night, a patrol reported enemy advancing in some strength. The forward observer called in an artillery barrage on suspected Japanese staging areas.[10] At 10:30 p.m., a Japanese soldier was shot dead on "C" Company's perimeter, the first of many. The Japanese began digging nearby and sniped at "C" Company's positions. From 11 p.m., the Japanese launched a series of determined infantry attacks supported by artillery, heavy mortar, grenade, and machine gun fire as well as flamethrowers. The main weight fell on the sector held by Sing's platoon. During the first half hour's fighting, Sing was wounded in both ankles by machine gun fire. Coppen ordered him back to the company command post and sent another officer, Lieutenant Hamid Khan, to take over his platoon.

---

[8] The process of recommending and approving awards of valor produces unusually good records of the engagements concerned, including testimony taken at the time. The following account is based on: Allen, *Burma*, pp. 409–415; Condon, *Frontier Force Rifles*, pp. 412–414; Latimer, *Burma*, Chapter 23; George Coppen, interview by the author; "Statement made by Major G.C. Coppen in respect of Jemadar Parkash Sing," copy provided to author by Major Coppen; "Statement of Havildar Sandhia Dass in respect of Jemadar Parkash Sing," copy provided to author by Major Coppen; Colonel E.C. Pickard, Victoria Cross citation for Jemadar Parkash Sing, 96/8/2, IWM.

[9] Lieutenant P. Noakes, quoted in Thompson, *War in Burma*, p. 295.

[10] A forward observer is an artillery officer, or gunner in Commonwealth parlance, attached to forward units in order to direct artillery fire.

At the command post, Sing loaded Bren magazines, collected grenades, and sent ammunition forward to the soldiers fighting.[11]

By 1 a.m., charging Japanese had twice penetrated "C" Company's perimeter, only to be beaten back in close quarter fighting atop "C" Company's positions. Explosions sent sand into the slit trenches, filling them up, exposing the occupants above ground. The Japanese jammed the wireless preventing close supporting artillery fire from being called in. In any case, the forward observer, his wireless set and men had all been destroyed. "They were dead, in bits," recalled Coppen.[12] A half hour later, the Japanese had established a foothold, digging in a medium machine gun within twenty yards of "C" Company's perimeter. A bayonet thrust in the chest wounded the officer sent to replace Sing. The Japanese were now "everywhere" and a "hand to hand filthy fight" developed, a matter of "brute force and ignorance" in darkness lit only with explosions and muzzle flashes. Coppen could only influence events immediately around him: "There was no control. I had to rely on the individual training and discipline of my soldiers. You fall back on the ultimate: the man."[13]

Sing now went forward again, crawling on his hands and knees. Taking over his platoon once more, he encouraged his soldiers and directed their fire. Checking on positions sometime later, Coppen found Sing propped up by his wounded batman, firing the platoon's two inch mortar "with great effect."[14] After exhausting the supply of mortar rounds, Sing dragged himself around his platoon area, picking up ammunition from the dead and wounded, telling his soldiers to hold their fire until they were certain of killing Japanese. By now, most of the leaders in the company were injured or dead. Sing extended his rounds to the positions of the neighboring platoons, motivating their hard-pressed soldiers. He gave voice to the Dogra war cry, a shout heard above the din of battle and taken up by "C" Company's troops amid the swirling brawl in the dark.[15] It was, Coppen remembered, "noise and dirt and fear and a peculiar form of ecstasy."[16]

---

[11] A Bren gun is a magazine-fed light machine gun.
[12] George Coppen, interview by the author.   [13] Ibid.
[14] "Statement made by Major G.C. Coppen in respect of Jemadar Parkash Sing." A batman is a soldier who serves as an officer's personal assistant, looking after his kit, food and sleeping arrangements among other duties.
[15] "Statement of Havildar Sandhia Dass in respect of Jemadar Parkash Sing."
[16] George Coppen, interview by the author.

Back in his own platoon area, Sing discovered that the soldiers of one section were all casualties just as a Japanese attack was coming in. Unable to stand in a trench, he sat beside one, cradling the section's Bren, managing to hold off the rush until Coppen could get reinforcements to him. During this fighting, Sing was again severely wounded in both legs above the knees. Weak from multiple wounds and loss of blood, he lay on his side, facing the enemy, continuing to shout to his men. Clearly dying, he was carried back to the company command post where he announced, "Don't worry about me...I will be alright."[17] More fire came in. As he laid the wounded VCO down in his own trench, Coppen felt a heavy thump on his back. At that very moment, Sing was hit for the last time and died. "I could hear him, he was killed instantly, finished off, wound in the body."[18]

Around 2:30 a.m. came yet another fierce attack. With Japanese streaming through the position and ammunition nearly exhausted, Coppen reported that he could no longer hold. "C" Company, and Major Khan's "B" Company positioned behind it, now withdrew as best they could, retiring off to their right toward units of another battalion. Pausing after their enemies' unexpected line of withdrawal, the Japanese remained on the positions they had captured just long enough for the corps artillery to bring down a concentration upon them. "You could see those guns open up in a half arc and hit the ground we had just left," Coppen said, "[i]t was like an earthquake."[19]

By the morning of the 17th, the Japanese too had withdrawn. They left behind nearly a hundred dead including a battalion commander, later buried by bulldozer along with hundreds of other Japanese soldiers killed in succeeding days. "C" Company counted only twenty soldiers that morning, out of around a hundred, with more survivors scattered by the fight coming in during the day. In all, the two companies suffered nearly forty dead and forty wounded overnight.[20] As the light brightened, another soldier yelled at Coppen not to move. Grenades in his ammunition pouch had been smashed by Japanese rifle fire during

---

[17] "Statement made by Major G.C. Coppen in respect of Jemadar Parkash Sing."

[18] George Coppen, interview by the author.

[19] Ibid. In plain language, "corps artillery" are batteries of large-caliber cannon attached to the corps headquarters. In this instance, they were used to fire on the Japanese just after they captured "C" company's positions. Those positions would have been pre-registered with the artillery units in case of such an eventuality.

[20] Condon, *Frontier Force Rifles*, p. 414.

the night. The soldier carefully plucked out the fuses. Coppen realized that fragments from these grenades, which had stopped bullets entering his back, delivered the *coup de grace* to Sing. "It just shows you, luck's a great thing. A wonderful thing."[21]

Perimeter Defense

Jemadar Sing gave his life trying to plug a gap in the defense of "C" Company's perimeter. Commanders site positions along a perimeter for mutual support, with interlocking and overlapping fields of fire. (See Figure 6.1) When a position ceases fire, it opens up avenues through which attackers can approach unmolested. The Japanese would suppress the fire of neighboring positions with heavy weapons, while rushing another position in short charges out of the darkness, delivered with their characteristic "banshee shouting business," that could really "upset people."[22] Once they broke into the perimeter, they could approach the defenders' positions along uncovered lines, or force the defenders to fire in the direction of their own troops. For this reason, commanders defending a box, of whatever size, kept a reserve to evict any enemy that did get in. The art of the defense consisted of plugging the gaps and keeping the ammunition going forward. "C" and "B" companies retreated in part because they started to run out of ammunition. A notable feature of the Japanese attack was the quality of its reconnaissance. Taking out the forward observer's position early on with mortar or gun fire exemplified the often professional and deliberate quality of Japanese infantry tactics in Burma. These included quick rushes – "banzai charges," so to speak – delivered in tactically rational ways. Any infantry attack ultimately involves a final rush to overcome the enemy's positions and panic or kill their defenders.

As can be seen, perimeter defense has a grim logic: the line was only as strong as the weakest link. Each position had to be defended vigorously. Soldiers failing to do so faced the prospect of being overrun, bayoneted, or grenaded in their holes, or falling into the hands of an enemy known to mistreat prisoners. (See Figure 6.2) Once in the situation, dug in around Kanlan Ywathit, everyone's best chance of coming out alive was keeping cool and fighting together, a phalanx's bargain at

---

[21] George Coppen, interview by the author.
[22] Michael Demetriadi, interview by the author.

Figure 6.1 Infantry fighting position: British soldiers of 1/RWF wait for a Japanese counter-attack on the Shewbo plain in central Burma, January 1945. From front to back, they are armed with a sten submachine gun, a Lee-Enfield rifle, and a Bren light machine gun. Note the stacked magazines next to the Bren's barrel, ready for rapid reloading.[23]

a higher rate of casualties. Training and then experience taught soldiers this lesson, and gave them some wherewithal to act on it.[24]

Sing's actions reflected this logic. He exposed himself most egregiously – sitting above ground firing the Bren– when he had to hold a section of the line on his own. His sacrifice was tactical. It is not in

---

[23] SE2374, IWM.
[24] The significance of holding a perimeter under assault was common sense among trained soldiers and officers. See e.g. Croft, "A Company Commander," p. 20.

Figure 6.2 Sikh troops clear a Japanese foxhole, after throwing a phosphorous grenade. Mandalay, February–March 1945.[25]

any way to detract from Sing's qualities as a combat leader to say that he did what he had to do. Either he stayed back, the positions fall, and he would likely die in the Japanese overrun; or he risked his life holding off the attack so the rest of the unit could survive that much longer. One of the telltale signs of social structures in operation is that they take on an external reality from the point of view of the agents involved, falling on them like a ton of bricks. Combat put soldiers in "damned if you do, damned more if you do not" situations. Stand up in the slit trench and fire to help defend the perimeter and risk getting hit; or fail to do so and contribute to the whole position being overrun with everyone dead or in Japanese captivity. Beyond vigorous defense, options were limited. The logic of the perimeter constrained the agency of its defenders.

Perimeter defense, like other typical types of engagement, had its own dynamics shaped by the interaction of the opposing sides. Night-fighting and dense terrain brought the forces very close together – the

[25] IND4550, IWM.

Japanese at one point digging in a medium machine gun to rake "C" Company positions at point-blank range. As attackers, the Japanese would have more success, and ultimately suffer fewer casualties, if they followed up on any gains with alacrity. The defenders knew this too, and this is how hand-to-hand and other close quarter fighting occurred atop the defenders' positions, as the Japanese attacks met counter-attacks from "C" Company's reserve. The fight took on an ebb and flow quality as soldiers and commanders regrouped and reorganized. "C" Company's soldiers knew that their comrades in the holes near them were still fighting by the sounds of their weapons and the flashes of their muzzles. The war cry – mentioned in several accounts of the battle – reminded everyone the unit was still alive, fighting for its life. Not all fighting was as unforgiving as that at Kanlan Ywathit. Fighting is historical, context-dependent. But however so, it takes on a life of its own. In Burma, it formed an iron cage around its immediate inmates.

Here is the climax of another perimeter defense in Burma, this time by "A" Company of the 3/1 Gurkha Rifles in the early morning hours of 27 April 1944, on a position known as Crete West. Assaulting Japanese infantry had forced back their perimeter and the Japanese were consolidating their gains ten paces from the company command post. The company commander ordered a platoon to counter-attack at 5:45 a.m. and they went forward with *kukris* (Gurkha machetes) and grenades. "The tempo of the fighting increased and the [y]elling of [k]ukried Japs, the g[r]oans of bayonetted Gurkhas with the shouts and laughter of the unwounded Gurkhas all combined to make the area like a nightmare."[26] A Japanese artillery concentration halted the Gurkha platoon attack, killing the whole of the forward section. Rallied by the platoon commander who was a Gurkha Officer, and a company officer, they put in

another wild charge. This time the Japs could bear it no longer and turned and fled. Maddened with blood after their kukri massacre this was the signal for all able bodied men to rush forward and urge them on their way with yells and screams and a crescendo of fire from their LMGs and Tommy guns. When daylight came it was impossible to tell between Gurkhas and Japs. Due to the [artillery fire] the forward bunkers were like a hellish butchers shop[.] 20 bodies were counted but no one could stand any more and the remainder

---

[26] General Sir Douglas Gracey, History of the 3/1 KGVO GR, chap. 2, p. 4, 2/6, LH.

were buried in situ. Two outside observers afterwards estimated the Jap killed as over 60. Our own casualties were 20 killed and 34 wounded.[27]

Desperate defense of the perimeter inspired greater efforts to breach it. Each move evoked a reciprocal one from the other side in an intensifying dynamic, ebbing and flowing over the same ground until the collapse of one of the players.

We do not usually think of conflict, much less battle, as a social structure, as patterned and rule-governed. In his essays on *Conflict and the Web of Group-Affiliations*, Georg Simmel approached conflict as a kind of "sociation" which worked to shape the parties to the conflict in common ways.[28] Conflict, for example, integrated, tending to concentrate and centralize the opposing groups, and enabling their members to endure sacrifice and privation. Parallel pressures operated on both sides. The parties co-constituted the conflict, forming it through action/reaction cycles, and it in turn constrained and shaped their behavior. Battle, or more precisely battles – iterations of engagements, are structured and structuring.

From the perspective of the study of combat, a notable premise of Simmel's is the sociological one of human commonality. In contrast to much of the writing on fighting spirit and the experience of war, Simmel does not begin from the point of view of human difference, whether ethnic, racial, national, or otherwise. For Simmel, the people involved on either side have similar capacities. Attributes and actions emerge conjuncturally in the conflict situation itself, and are not necessarily indicative of pre-existing social or cultural characteristics of the parties involved. The Gurkhas on Crete West managed pretty good "banzai charges"; these were not just a special Japanese trait. Deadly opponents, soldiers inhabited a common battlefield environment and interacted with one another in more or less regularized ways, creating a shared context which channeled and reproduced patterns of behavior. Some convergence in the thought and actions of soldiers on both sides resulted. As Cameron observed of US Marines on Guadalcanal, "the way in which the cultural values of the enemy, so often portrayed as alien to the West, were matched among the marines is striking."[29] In

---

[27] General Sir Douglas Gracey, History of the 3/1 KGVO GR, Chapter 2, p. 4, 2/6, LH. A Gurkha Officer was the equivalent of a VCO in Gurkha regiments.

[28] Simmel, *Conflict and the Web of Group-Affiliations*, p. 13.

[29] Cameron, *American Samurai*, p. 104.

the face of the antagonisms of war, Simmel's structural approach offers purchase on shared humanity.

Thinking about combat as a structure should not distract from the large role played by brute, violent contingency. The main weight of the Japanese attack just happened to fall on Sing's platoon. The forward observer at Kanlan Ywathit, and the forward section of the counter-attacking Gurkhas at Crete West, fell victim to quick thinking and accurate Japanese gunners; they might not have. Coppen's life was saved, and Sing's ended, because of the position of some grenades on Coppen's webbing. Chance shapes battle.[30]

One of the most prominent dimensions of the fighting in Burma was the difficulty and relative rarity of surrender. Investigating why this was so shows how values and behavior which seem specific to one side came to be shared by both. Soldiers can believe they are different from their enemy, yet act in remarkably similar ways.

Sameness and Difference

In his history of the land war in the South Pacific, Eric Bergerud tells the story of two Japanese officers found by Australian soldiers wandering in a creek near Buna, Papua New Guinea. The officers were survivors of the crack South Sea Detachment which the Australians had defeated in detail in late 1942. The Australian battalion commander, A.S. Arnold, had "no stomach left for useless killing." Arnold wanted to give the Japanese every chance to surrender. He called out to them, but they ignored him. One moved leisurely off into the jungle, and was later found hanging by his neck, a suicide. The other splashed himself with water and bowed three times into the sun. "I'll give you until I count to ten to surrender" yelled Arnold. The Japanese officer brandished the flag of the rising sun. Drawing his sword and facing the Australians, he held one end of the flag by his sword hand and the other in his left hand so that the flag covered his breast. When Arnold reached nine, the Japanese officer completed the count for him, shouting a loud and clear "Out!" The Australians riddled him with bullets.[31]

---

[30] "War is the realm of chance. No other human activity gives it greater scope: no other has such incessant and varied dealings with this intruder." Clausewitz, *On War*, p. 101.

[31] Bergerud, *Touched with Fire*, pp. 144–145.

Working a theme central to Pacific War historiography, Bergerud wants to impress on the reader just how different the Japanese were from Western soldiers. Among Japanese soldiers was an "extreme veneration of death," a "cult of oblivion" in which to die in battle was an "honor to the family and a transcendent act on the part of the individual."[32] Every Japanese soldier carried a copy of the Emperor Meiji's Imperial Precepts to Soldiers and Sailors of 1882, a kind of bushido code for ordinary soldiers in which loyalty outweighed death. By contrast, "[t]here was certainly no cult of honorable death in the U.S. military."[33] Bergerud intends to account for a remarkable feature of Japanese battlefield behavior in World War II: a very high percentage of Japanese soldiers refused to surrender and fought to the death, regardless of the tactical situation and whether any military purpose was fulfilled by continuing to fight. This phenomenon astounded participants and observers alike. A US marine on Guadalcanal exclaimed "[t]hose [expletives] Japs, they're crazy. They don't think anything of human life. Plain crazy, sick in the head, that's all."[34] For Bernard Fergusson, the Chindit brigadier, what was most extraordinary was that Japanese soldiers regularly fought to the death even when no one was present to observe their heroism but the enemy: "Few soldiers can be found in other races who are prepared to fight alone and unsupported, to die anonymously and unseen by their comrades, to spit out their last breath without an eyewitness to carry back the news of how they died."[35]

In analyses of battle which emphasize the respective "otherness" of opponents, distinctive social and cultural differences manifest in battlefield behavior. It is national style all the way down. The pre-formed

---

[32] Bergerud, *Touched with Fire*, pp. 130–131. But for Captain Kameyama, speaking of those he served with, "Nobody wants to die . . . Nobody dies smiling." Quoted in Nunneley and Tamayama, *Tales by Japanese Soldiers*, p. 156.

[33] Bergerud, *Touched with Fire*, p. 161. Cf. Cameron, *American Samurai*.

[34] Quoted in Linderman, *World within War*, p. 163. Expletives excised in original.

[35] Fergusson, *Wild Green Earth*, p. 205. He goes on: "Most fighting men have a secret dread of being 'missing'. They will die almost willingly at the head of their men, or among their comrades, so long as somebody is there who will know what has happened, or what has probably happened . . . But your jungle fighter who is overrun in his foxhole, or who gets a chance to sell his life profitably but dearly while on a lone patrol, minds most of all the knowledge that he will be missing, and that vain hopes for his return will linger on for maybe years to come."

characteristics of each side collectively shape battle, which becomes a clash between the armed representatives of essentially different societies. The savagery of the Pacific War, according to many veterans and commentators, was due to Japanese determination to fight to the death even when defeated, and their violations of the laws and norms of civilized warfare, especially as regards PoWs. Battle was the way it was because of Japanese characteristics. "I believe that the unique ferocity of the war in the Pacific stemmed from Japanese policy," comments Bergerud; for Slim, the Japanese were "apart from the rest of humanity."[36]

For British observers, the characteristic difference between "rational" soldiers and the "fanatical" Japanese was that the latter did not surrender when the situation warranted, choosing instead to fight to the death or take their own lives.[37] "Never known a nation that wanted to die, except the Japs," said one British infantryman. "We retreated, they don't."[38] British surprise at this puzzling battlefield behavior is registered in any number of places, from official documents to memoirs. Slim wrote of a party of fifteen Japanese, the last survivors of a unit which had stubbornly resisted almost to the point of annihilation the 20th Indian Division's drive on the Irrawaddy in early 1945. They were caught on the wrong side of the river. In full kit and with closed ranks the Japanese, "under the astonished eyes of our men," marched parade-ground style down to the river to be gunned down by Indian troops.[39] Peter Gadsdon describes a shocking discovery after a Japanese attack on the Letse Box over the night of 19–20 March 1945. The Japanese assaulting force had been unable to penetrate three coils of wire along the perimeter of the box, apparently lacking wire cutters or explosives. Those Japanese who reached the wire were trapped, prevented from retreating by enfilading machine guns firing along fixed

---

[36] Bergerud, *Touched with Fire*, p. xv; Slim, *Defeat into Victory*, p. 534.

[37] Charles Carfrae, "Dark Company," p. 128, 80/49/1, IWM.

[38] Private Ivan Daunt quoted in Thompson, *Forgotten Voices of Burma*, p. 121.

[39] Minutes of the Meeting at Chatham House on the Mentality of Japanese Troops, 8 September 1948, AL5304, IWM; Slim, *Defeat into Victory*, p. 418. In *Defeat into Victory* Slim writes that the Japanese drowned themselves, which would have been quite an act of will on their part, but at Chatham House he stated that they were gunned down. He may have sought to sanitize the account for publication in *Defeat into Victory*. In any case, I give credence to the statement at Chatham House because it is more plausible and it was made closer in time to the events concerned.

lines just behind them. A patrol led by Gadsdon the following morning found forty-nine Japanese bodies on the wire, many with the same
wound, that which comes from clutching one of the small Japanese
grenades to the abdomen and detonating it. Gadsdon offers the stock
British explanation for this collective suicide: "Since all Japanese prisoners were considered dead by their families, this form of 'hari kiri'
was a quick way out and a passport to Heaven."[40]

Such views about the Japanese circulated widely during the war,
and were invoked to explain just such perplexing events.[41] British and
Indian soldiers passing through the Jungle Warfare School at Shimoga
were told in a lecture:

The Jap is not permitted to become a POW. If he should, by chance, fall
into our hands, he is immediately writeen [*sic*] off by the Japs as <u>dead</u>...HE
CAN NEVER GO BACK TO JAPAN AGAIN, AND HE CAN NEVER SEE
HIS FAMILY. It is for these reasons that he will fight to the bitter end, rather
than surrender.

The lecture goes on to root this Japanese characteristic in religious
fanaticism:

Jap religion is Shinto, which means "Way of the Gods". If the Jap dies for
his Emperor and Country, he immediately becomes an Ancestor, and he is
worshipped in the Shinto Shrine...he will not surrender, and prefers death
to that. Has been known to kill himself if he thinks there is a chance of being
captured. On being taken prisoner, his first request is for a weapon to kill
himself with. Owing to Shintoism, [he] will hold the [position] to the bitter
end, and will die at his post.[42]

The lecture both described and tried to explain elements of Japanese
battlefield behavior. The psychology it offers is unconvincing, but the
Imperial Japanese Army's ideology, organizational qualities, and historical trajectory did inform its way of battle. There were important

[40] Gadsdon, *An Amateur at War*, unpublished MS, pp. 75–76; Peter Gadsdon,
      interview by the author. Calvert describes another example when his troops
      overran a Japanese field hospital: "Five Japs had crept off their wooden bunks
      and put their heads together round their one and only grenade, and pulled the
      string. This had been effective." *Prisoners of Hope*, p. 195.
[41] Dower, *War without Mercy*, Parts I and II, pp. 3–200; Linderman, *World
      Within War*, Chapter 4, pp. 143–184.
[42] "The Jap," Lecture, Jungle Warfare School, Shimoga, 7304-1-2, NAM.

differences between armies. But how else might we account for Japanese refusal to surrender? A thought to hold in mind is that it takes two antagonists to sustain the kind of fighting to which the lecture at Shimoga refers.

Indecisive trench warfare in the First World War had shaped Western armies' thinking. The combination of high casualties and prolonged stalemate had inspired a search for alternatives to close order infantry assaults against fortified positions defended by artillery and automatic weapons. By contrast, the IJA had not experienced trench warfare on the same scale and duration. Japanese doctrine still emphasized overcoming weight of firepower and material through vigorous and spirited offensive action, with massed infantry instructed to press the attack at all costs.[43] This Japanese approach was one of the sources of the intensity of the fighting wherever they were encountered on the offensive. One British division commander in Burma reported of his experiences: "The Jap is a 'killer' and he does not mind being killed . . . The fighting therefore is always at a remarkably 'intense' tempo."[44] In a note on Japanese tactics, a brigade commander observed that: "The Jap is not deterred by losses. If the first wave of attackers are killed, he keeps on attacking. If each successive wave inflicts only a few casualties on the defenders, the time eventually arises when by sheer weight of numbers he overwhelms the defence."[45]

A similar emphasis on offensive "spirit" combined with numbers had characterized Western doctrine before and during much of World War I. Back then, the prevailing view had been that "[v]ictory would go to the army that had been trained to die rather than to avoid dying."[46] Such views were still held in the *Waffen SS* and the US Marine Corps in World War II.[47] What distinguished the Japanese was their ability to instill this spirit of determination in nearly all of their infantry and maintain it until very late in the war, when cracks did begin to show and relatively more Japanese prisoners were taken. On the eve

---

[43] Allen, *Burma*, p. 616; Bergerud, *Touched with Fire*, pp. 124–145; Edgerton, *Warriors of the Rising Sun*.
[44] Lessons of the Burma Campaign, 1942, April–May, preamble, para F, WO 203/5716, TNA.
[45] General Sir Douglas Gracey, HQ 80 Ind Inf Bde to HQ 20 Ind Div, 11 May 1944, 2/8, LH.
[46] Bond, *War and Society*, p. 93.
[47] Cameron, *American Samurai*; Stein, *Waffen SS*.

of the U-Go offensive, the commander of the Japanese 33rd Division told his troops that they should regard "death as something lighter than a feather" and that they should expect the division to be "annihilated" in the course of achieving victory.[48] The division lived up to its commander's expectations, at least as regards annihilation, suffering 70 percent casualties before turning and trying to fight its way back to the Chindwin River.[49] To achieve such results, as in the *Waffen SS*, the Japanese made use of a very harsh training regime, brutal discipline, and extensive indoctrination of junior officers.[50] Also, Japanese troops were repeatedly told that the Allies would mistreat and kill them if they surrendered.[51]

The Problem of Surrender

An Indian officer reported of a Japanese signals officer captured near the end of the war that "I had the impression he was prepared for brutality. He was taken aback at my civil treatment."[52] The Japanese fear of abuse if they tried to surrender was not wholly misplaced. Evidence suggests that many Japanese and INA prisoners were killed out of hand by British, Indian, and imperial troops. This often happened immediately after capture while the PoWs were with front-line infantry troops being escorted rearwards, or when Japanese soldiers were attempting surrender.[53] When a party of Japanese tried to

[48] Quoted in Slim, *Defeat into Victory*, p. 337.
[49] Allen, *Burma*, p. 284. Slim writes: "There can have been few examples in history of a force as reduced, battered and exhausted as the 33rd Japanese Division delivering such furious assaults, not with the object of extricating itself, but to achieve its original offensive intention." *Defeat into Victory*, p. 336.
[50] Bergerud, *Touched with Fire*, pp. 124–145; Edgerton, *Warriors of the Rising Sun*.
[51] See The Warrior Tradition as a Present Factor in Japanese Military Psychology, p. 12, para (d), Wartime Translations Seized Japanese Documents, 10-RR-76.3, MFF6, LH; No. 1 General Characteristics, Morale and Training, Periodical Notes on the Japanese Army 1942–44, L/MIL/17/20/25, OIOC.
[52] Col. S.C. Singha, correspondence with author, 24 September 2001.
[53] For examples see below and Edwards, *Kohima*, p. 292–293; Slim, *Defeat into Victory*, p. 327. Gwylm Davies, Ron Thomas, and Gian Singh, interviews by the author. All three witnessed incidents of this kind, involving British, Gurkha, and Indian troops. Professional military writers in the post-1945 era are increasingly careful about not including evidence of war crimes or atrocities in publications. There are no systematic studies of Allied war crimes in World

surrender to some British troops in Calvert's Chindit brigade, they were "automatically shot," apparently on the grounds that it was so unexpected for Japanese to surrender.[54] The historian of the 81 (WA) Division, who served with the division, reports that West African troops generally refused to take Japanese prisoners, a fact apparently known to the Japanese. Two Japanese soldiers trying to surrender to a unit of the division sought out a company headquarters where there were several Europeans before coming out of the bush, and even then approached very cautiously until they were reassured they "would not be summarily disposed of."[55] Gold Coast regiment soldiers shot any Japanese who fell into their hands alive.[56]

Captured wounded Japanese were also killed. After flagging down a passing vehicle to assist a badly wounded Japanese he had found, Gwylm Davies watched in horror as the British driver poured petrol over the conscious soldier and lit him afire.[57] On at least two separate occasions, Indian soldiers mass murdered wounded Japanese, immolating 120 in one incident and burying alive between twenty and fifty in another.[58] The scale of these killings makes it very likely that officers knew of them, indicating at least tacit acceptance on the part of immediate commanders. British and imperial soldiers who carried out such acts likely justified them by reference to the well-known Japanese mistreatment of Allied prisoners.[59] Nonetheless, the Japanese expectation of brutality was not simply a product of IJA propaganda. Certainly the Japanese sergeant-major who watched from a nearby hilltop over a hundred of his wounded comrades being burned alive by Indian soldiers – "[s]houts of wild anger rolled up the hillside, frightened moans, shrieking yelling voices" – could be expected to avoid Allied captivity at all costs, and to encourage his men to do likewise.[60]

Of course, there were relatively few Japanese prisoners for British and Imperial troops to mistreat or murder. Aside from Japanese unwillingness to surrender, one reason for this was that it was Allied practice

War II with which I am familiar, although there is much anecdotal evidence of refusing to take, mistreating, and murdering prisoners (see e.g. Beevor, *Ardennes 1944*, p. 235). For a discussion and examples of similar behavior in that and other conflicts, see Keegan, *Face of Battle*, pp. 47–49.

[54] Calvert, *Prisoners of Hope*, p. 235.   [55] Hamilton, *War Bush*, pp. 64–65.
[56] Phillips, *Another Man's War*, p. 85.
[57] Gwylm Davies, interview by the author.
[58] Allen, *Burma*, pp. 295–296; Fraser, *Quartered Safe*, p. 190.
[59] See e.g. Fraser, *Quartered Safe*, p. 191.   [60] Allen, *Burma*, p. 296.

to kill every Japanese soldier they encountered no matter what, often several times over. As Gian Singh wrote in his poem on Kohima, where he fought,

> No prisoners we took, no mercy we gave
> Their crimes against comrades we never forgave.[61]

Offering no quarter was justified by the notion that all Japanese were dangerous until dead.[62] "Many a casualty has been caused by a 'dead' Jap."[63] For General Sir Douglas Gracey, commander of the 20th Indian Division in Burma, "every Japanese in a defensive position must be dealt with. At present, he will fight to the death even when severely wounded."[64] An operations research report from the first Chindit operation described how in an initial engagement some apparently dead Japanese sprang back to life and shot British troops in the back. From then on it became "universal practice to put a round or a bayonet into any Jap not obviously dead... This undoubtedly resulted in many potential prisoners being killed, but it was a very necessary practice."[65] The report notes that the Japanese did the same to Allied dead and wounded. After a British officer was killed by a Japanese soldier feigning death, his friend wrote "[w]e found out then what we were never afterwards to forget – it doesn't pay to leave wounded Japs breathing."[66] Other Allied soldiers retaliated by playing dead themselves in order to kill unsuspecting Japanese.[67] Such stories of initial

---

[61] Singh, *Memories of Friends and Foes*, p. 2.

[62] See e.g. Masters, *The Road Past Mandalay*, pp. 162–163; Slim, *Defeat into Victory*, pp. 325, 336, 366–367; Major H.C. Gay, extracts from his memoirs, p. 122, 88/48/1, IWM; General Sir Douglas Gracey, Appreciation of the Situation on 4 Corps Front, 20 September 1943, points 2 and 3, 1/5, and 2/24, Suggestions for training for and conducting war against the Japanese for troops who have been fighting in European theatres of War, para 1 (b) and 6 (d), 2/24, LH; Lt. Col. Donald P. Bryce, Operational Memos on Use and Employment of LRP Forces, Chapter IX, para 3 (a), 2/3, LH; "The Jap," Lecture, Jungle Warfare School Shimoga, para 9, 7304-1-2, NAM.

[63] Ferguson, *Wild Green Earth*, p. 206.

[64] General Sir Douglas Gracey, Suggestions for training for and conducting war against the Japanese for troops who have been fighting in European theatres of war, in the form of answers to a questionnaire submitted by an officer of the Canadian Army, p. 2, 2/24, LH.

[65] Operation No. 5, No. 10 Indian Operational Research Section, pp. 50–51, WO 203/1833, TNA.

[66] Captain N. Durant, account of the second "Wingate show," p. 10, 80/49/1, IWM.

[67] Ferguson, *Wild Green Earth*, p. 206.

Japanese treachery followed by Allied retaliation have their counter-parts on other Pacific War battlefields.[68]

Sometimes even when disarmed, Japanese soldiers were not given the chance to surrender. After espying a Japanese squad undress "by the numbers" and march down to the riverside to bathe, D.M. Cookson's Gambians gunned them down with their Brens.[69] When Calvert's Chindits surprised some Japanese troops bathing in a *chaung*, they immediately went at them with their bayonets, having been instructed not to fire unless necessary. Not long after, Calvert was "astonished to see a stark naked Jap running gingerly through the jungle chased by a heavily bearded and accoutred Devonshire man trying to prod him with his bayonet."[70] One of Calvert's staff officers could not figure out why so many of the Japanese killed by the Brigade had bayonet wounds in them. "He found the reason was that few men would pass a Jap lying on the ground without sticking a bayonet in him to ensure that he was really and truly dead and would not shoot them in the back."[71] For Ferguson, too, "The Jap takes as much killing as a conger-eel, and is every bit as slippery."[72]

In a memo, a British brigade commander reflected on the fact that Japanese casualties were composed almost entirely of soldiers killed in action. He concluded that the reason was that wounded Japanese soldiers who were capable of fighting carried on doing so until they were killed. He put this down to Japanese "determination" and "complete disregard of life." It did not occur to him that, whatever the differences in "outlook on life" with the Japanese, the actions of his own British and Indian troops might have had something to do with the absence of Japanese wounded and prisoners.[73] Calvert, also a brigade commander, offered a more straightforward explanation than Japanese philosophy of life. He put the lack of Japanese wounded and prisoners down to the tendency of his troops to make certain that Japanese soldiers were dead before closing with them, "as with a wild beast." His troops did this, he believed, because so many of them had been killed or wounded by

---

[68] See e.g. Cameron, *American Samurai*, pp. 110–112; Linderman, *World Within War*, Chapter 4; Hamilton Simonds-Golding, Bamboos and Partisans, Chapter vi, pp. 1–3, Mss Eur B386, OIOC.

[69] Capt. D.M. Cookson, "With Africans in Arakan," p. 73, 82/37/1, IWM.

[70] Calvert, *Prisoners of Hope*, p. 128.   [71] Calvert, *Prisoners of Hope*, p. 237.

[72] Ferguson, *Wild Green Earth*, p. 206.

[73] General Sir Douglas Gracey, HQ 80 Ind Inf Bde to HQ 20 Ind Div, 11 May 1944, 2/8, LH.

wounded Japanese feigning death.[74] One company commander told his Indian soldiers going on patrol to "shoot first and ask questions afterward," signaling that any potential prisoners were not worth the risk.[75] Explaining why he and his comrades immediately killed any Japanese they found alive, a Nigerian soldier remarked "they didn't spare our people, we didn't spare them."[76]

That British and imperial troops generally left no Japanese alive on ground they occupied goes some way toward accounting for a feature of Japanese battlefield behavior that did not square with their legendary "fanaticism." It was not at all unknown for the Japanese to flee when their positions were being overrun.[77] "[T]he Jap...can show a good turn of speed when driven out of a position."[78] In one action in which twenty-four Japanese were bayoneted and grenaded in their holes by attacking East African troops, a British officer commented in a letter home "[t]he odd thing is, after all one has heard [about Japanese fanaticism], that the Japs were absolutely scared stiff and took every possible opportunity of beating it."[79] On other occasions Japanese about to be overrun would simply stop fighting and wait to be killed by the assaulting British or imperial troops. As one report on fighting the Japanese noted, they "will often stop fighting and wait for death if our troops use the bayonet and get within fifteen to twenty yards of their positions."[80] The lecture at Shimoga also noted this phenomenon, saying that Japanese held their positions with determination "until attacking [troops] are very close, and then appear to crack up, cowering at the bottom of the trench, waiting to be bayoneted. If he wants the bayonet, so let it be."[81]

This rarity of Japanese surrender reflected more than cultural, ideological, and doctrinal reluctance to become prisoners. Practically

---

[74] Calvert, *Prisoners of Hope*, p. 237.

[75] Croft, "A Company Commander," p. 32.

[76] Marshall Kebby quoted in Phillips, *Another Man's War*, p. 85.

[77] See e.g. Allen, *Burma*, p. 408; Calvert, *Prisoners of Hope*, p. 189; Masters, *Road Past Mandalay*, p. 217; Brig. Arthur Blair Gibson, Unofficial War History, 2/13 Frontier Force Rifles, p. 46, 1/4, LH; Annexure to R.C. Part I Order No 1924 Dated 9 October 1944, Awards – Victoria Cross, 5 RGR, Loose Archives, GM; John Hamilton and John Nunneley, interviews by the author.

[78] Lessons Learnt from Operations in Chin Hills, Chin Hills Operation Notes and Imphal Operations, 24 May–May28/43, G23, GM.

[79] Brig. K.H. Collen, letter of 30 September 1944, 79/21/1, IWM.

[80] Lt. Col. Donald P. Bryce, Operational Memos on Use and Employment of LRP Forces, p. 38, 2/3, LH.

[81] "The Jap," Lecture, Jungle Warfare School Shimoga, 7304-1-2, NAM.

speaking, it was very difficult to surrender on Burmese battlefields. Wounded, or even cowering, enemy troops were killed from a distance rather than tended. Playing dead, even with the intent to surrender rather than trick, generated bayonet thrusts. Suspicions of double-cross led to light trigger fingers, even when other obstacles to surrender were overcome. In the initial invasion of Burma, a Japanese officer approached to take the surrender of a Gurkha company from its British commander. Some Gurkhas fired at the Japanese officer. The Japanese shot down the British officer in retaliation and a melee ensued.[82] The actions of British and Indian soldiers help account for Japanese behavior attributed to Japanese national character.

Action/Reaction

For their part, the Japanese carried on with the no-holds barred warfare they had initiated. They refused to take prisoners and dispatched enemy wounded on the battlefield. A harsh code of military rationality sanctioned suicide or the killing of their own wounded when necessary.[83] Japanese officers sometimes "blooded" their raw troops by having them bayonet or otherwise brutalize Allied prisoners.[84] On the hurry in an attack, in one notorious example, they massacred the doctors and patients of an Indian field hospital.[85] As occupiers, the Japanese publically executed Allied PoWs and other prisoners to overawe civilian populations. To conduct war in this way is to invite reply in kind. Such atrocities provided material for stories about the Japanese circulating among Allied soldiers, stories which inspired revenge such as the tit-for-tat mass immolations of wounded prisoners.[86] When they discovered the beheaded body of one of their comrades who had been captured by the Japanese a few days previously, an Indian company went "berserk" during an attack "rushing the position and killing any Japanese in sight."[87]

[82] "A Subedar Remembers and Thirty Pieces of Silver," pamphlet, GM.
[83] See Edwards, *Kohima*, p. 415; Slim, *Defeat into Victory*, p. 351.
[84] Mentality of Japanese Soldiers, Minutes of the meeting at Chatham House, 8 Sept 1948, AL 5304, IWM.
[85] Allen, *Burma*, p. 183; Slim, *Defeat into Victory*, p. 240.
[86] See e.g. ALFSEA Morale Reports, February, March, and April 1945, p. 3, WO 203/2355, TNA.
[87] Major P.H. Gadsdon, untitled memoir of his wartime service, p. 82, 78/6/1, IWM.

Noting and studying the Japanese way of war, British commanders insisted that their men, too, refuse to surrender. They told their soldiers to hold their positions to the "last man, last round," and even to adopt non-European attitudes toward warfare (or at least "Prussianism" in the words of one senior British general).[88] Part of the secret of Japanese success, it was believed, was that they combined modern military organization with the "unorthodox tactics of the savage in thick jungle."[89] After the First Arakan, Irwin had bemoaned in his own troops the "absence of the fanatical quality possessed by the Jap."[90] Training documents for the 20th Indian Division sought to instill this "fanaticism," urging "no surrender under any circumstances whatsoever." The document quoted a Zulu chief's exhortation to his surrounded men: "If we go forward, we die, if we go back, we die, let us go forward my brothers." In 1942, the division commander exhorted his division to "be imbued with the absolute determination to achieve . . . the ruthless spirit to knock hell out of the Japanese and their traitor followers."[91] Such injunctions differed little from those issued by Japanese officers. A captured Japanese operations order stated "[i]f there are no orders, each defence area must be defended until death by the last soldier."[92] Both sides began to define their overall aims in terms of killing each other. Slim referred proudly to his units' increasing proficiency "in the art of killing Japanese."[93] One of his officers wrote home in March of 1944: "The morale of our troops is first class and not many prisoners are being taken. Kill them all is the byword."[94] The Japanese order stated simply "[t]o win a battle, the enemy must be killed . . . KILL, KILL and KILL."[95]

British commanders were less effective than the Japanese at actually generating the desired behavior from their troops. Nonetheless

---

[88] Lt. Gen. Thomas J. Hutton, "Operations in Burma," p. 56, 3/6, LH.

[89] Wavell quoted in Moreman, *Jungle, the Japanese, and the British Commonwealth Armies*, p. 53.

[90] Lt. Gen. N.M.S. Irwin, Letter to all officers of Eastern Army, 15 May 1943, P139, IWM.

[91] Gen. Sir Douglas Gracey, Policy for Training and Operations – 20th Indian Division, 13 April 1942, 1/1, LH.

[92] Lt. Gen. Sir Frank Messervy, XV Indian Corps History of the Arakan Campaign 1944–45, p. 101, 10, LH.

[93] Slim, *Defeat into Victory*, p. 363.

[94] Major H.C. Gay, Extract from his memoirs, p. 122, 88/48/1, IWM.

[95] Lt. Gen. Sir Frank Messervy, XV Indian Corps History of the Arakan Campaign 1944–45, p. 101, 10, LH.

the influence of such ideas on training and operations, and the stories and experiences circulating in British, Indian and imperial units, contributed to the feedback loops of merciless fighting. It became difficult to escape the cycle set in train. In 1942, the Japanese overran most of John Randle's battalion, the 7/10 Baluch, and then later probably killed the wounded survivors. Randle and some others fought their way out and served with the reconstituted battalion. He reported: "News of [the massacre of the wounded] got back to us and this conditioned my, and the whole battalion's, attitude towards the Japs. We were not merciful to them for the rest of the war. We didn't take any prisoners."[96]

Surrender for troops on both sides became very dangerous if not impossible to attempt. Soldiers on both sides chose to go out fighting or to take their own lives. When a wounded West African soldier was recovered by his unit after two days hiding in the bush, "[h]e explained to his rescuers he had not worried because if his own people found him everything would be all right and if the Japs found him – he startled the doctor by producing a grenade from inside his tunic – he had only to pull the pin and everything would still be all right."[97] His willingness to blow himself up probably seemed reasonable to those who found him, given the stories of Japanese mistreatment of prisoners.[98] The remark of a lone Japanese soldier captured hiding in a village with no ammunition by a Nigerian Chindit patrol perhaps reflected the wishes of many soldiers in Burma for escape from such dire and limited choices. He told his captors "I want to resign."[99]

Combats in Burma became unforgiving affairs for everyone involved, and even successful surrender did not guarantee survival. Over the night of 10 and 11 June 1944, the Japanese attacked a hilltop known as "Bastion." Speaking Urdu as they came on to trick the Indian troops into not firing, and making use of Bangalore torpedoes, the Japanese captured Bastion and took a number of Indians prisoner. The 152nd Indian Parachute Battalion retook the hill with an immediate counter-attack, supported by heavy covering fire from tanks,

---

[96] John Randle quoted in Thompson, *Forgotten Voices*, p. 14. See also Grant and Tamayama, *Burma 1942*, pp. 90–91.

[97] Quoted in Hamilton, *War Bush*, p. 71.

[98] Japanese mistreatment of prisoners was a common theme both of propaganda and instruction for British and imperial forces. See e.g. "The Jap." Lecture, Jungle Warfare School Shimoga, 7304–1-2, NAM; J.A.H. Heard, copies of "Josh" weekly newsheets, LH; Fraser, *Quartered Safe*, pp. 44–45.

[99] Quoted in Hamilton, *War Bush*, p. 300.

machine guns and artillery. Low on ammunition, the Japanese fought back as best they could while the Indian paratroopers methodically reduced each Japanese position. One Japanese soldier sought a quicker exit. According to the British brigade major's report of the action, "[a] solitary Jap climbed out of his trench and took up a standing [position] on the parapet facing our infantry. He was cut down by our fire." Knowing they would be driven off, the Japanese murdered many of the Indian prisoners they held on the hill, bayoneting and grenading them. An Indian cook was found dead with his arms tied behind his back and his eyes gouged out. "Such facts," the brigade major concludes, "should surprise no one. The feeling of revulsion [amongst the Indian paratroops] completely out weighed any respect they might have felt by witnessing the Japs ferocious defense in the face of overwhelming fire. But they were animals and as such they were treated."[100] This last comment indicates the likely fate of any Japanese who survived their initial wounds.

Surrendering can act as a "relief valve" for battlefield violence. A defending force which gives up in timely fashion, before inflicting heavy casualties on the attacker, might be allowed to do so without severe mistreatment.[101] However, the more casualties inflicted on the attacking troops, the less likely they will offer quarter.[102] In foreclosing exits, prohibitions against surrender help the fighting take on a last-ditch character. Soldiers on both sides figured that the best way to survive was to try and win the battle, and that, if one had to, the best way to die was while fighting. Jungle terrain also helped intensify combat in Burma. Engagements occurred at extremely short ranges and in conditions of surprise, making retirement difficult; consequently, fights were often to the finish. Wherever fighting takes on a no-quarter character, the energies built up in suffering casualties can find release in battlefield atrocities ranging from refusal to take prisoners to the massacre, immediately afterward, of any enemy who do survive. One Japanese officer in Burma described such situations in this way: "After fierce battles when many comrades were killed, men were excited and felt strong

---

[100] General Sir Douglas Gracey, 2/8, "A Survey of Enemy Ops to Capture Bastion on the Night of 10/11 June," HQ 100 Ind Inf Bde to HQ 20 Div, 17 June 1944, 2/8 and "Fitness for War of 152 and 153 Para Bns," HQ 20 Ind Div to 4 Corps, 17 June 1944, 2/10, LH

[101] See e.g. Keegan, *Face of Battle*, p. 48.

[102] See e.g. Croft, "A Company Commander," p. 25.

hatred against the enemy soldiers and were provoked to kill even helpless prisoners." Such battlefield dynamics shaped soldiers' actions on
both sides, contributing to an intensifying spiral of fighting and atrocity. John Randle described an incident in which a Japanese company
was expected to surrender. When one of his Indian soldiers was shot
dead instead, his Pathans went "fighting mad" and ignored his orders
to take prisoners, killing one hundred and twenty four Japanese: "I
found myself both exhilarated and appalled by this sheer animal lust
to kill," remarked Randle.[103]

Simmel's sociological premise of human commonality reminds us
that soldiers from very different societies had comparable capacities.
Amid the political, social, and organizational differences between the
opposing sides, the structure of battle led to reciprocal behavior, as the
discussion above has sought to show. Soldiers from both sides fought
to the end, or killed enemy wounded, or played dead to ambush their
opponents. Last-ditch resistance served to evoke a similar response
from the enemy. These actions did not simply reflect the social and cultural characteristics of the troops involved, or their political and racial
beliefs. These were reasonable, and understandable, responses to harsh
situations. Soldiers from different backgrounds came to behave in similar ways, whatever they thought about the matter. To excavate and analyze structural pressures created by the fighting does not entail denying
differences among the soldiers at war in Burma. But it does draw attention to self-generating, battlefield sources of combat behavior.

The Battle at Sangshak

The Japanese were not unique in their willingness to die. A look at some
of the fighting that preceded the siege of Kohima shows that such willingness, even in its suicidal, "Oriental" variants, was more widespread
than standard accounts allow. Though the Japanese remained virtu-
osos in the consistency with which they fought to the death, the differences with other armies and societies were relative, not absolute. If
these differences require explanation, so too do the commonalities and
overlaps. At times, the distinctions between the two sides blurred, even
in respect of supposed key markers of Japanese difference. The engagements dealt with below show some of the alternative paths down

---

[103] Randle, *Battle Tales*, pp. 67.

which combat could go, as soldiers facing stark choices made different decisions.

In March 1944, the Japanese 31st Division marched toward Kohima
as part of the U-Go offensive intended to cut the Allied supply route
from India to China and to destroy the forces preparing to invade
and re-conquer Burma. Aware an offensive was in the works, but not
of its details, 14th Army's IV Corps estimated that a single Japanese
regiment, at most, would head for Kohima. IV Corps sent the 50th
Indian Parachute Brigade, newly arrived for jungle training, as part
of a forward screen to the area around Ukhrul and Sangshak, a little over thirty miles east and south of Kohima. Commanded by a
young Brigadier, M.R.T. Hope-Thomson, the under-strength parachute
brigade was given little in the way of information, food, or ammunition. It continued with its training regimen. As the Japanese offensive
began to develop, despite radio links, neither divisional nor corps command informed Hope-Thomson of reports the Japanese were moving
in strength toward his brigade. On 18th March, he still believed the
nearest Japanese were forty miles further east. The next morning at
9:30, his most forward company on a position known as Point 7378
reported sighting 900 Japanese. These were soldiers from III Battalion, 58th Infantry Regiment, of the 31st Division's Left Raiding Column on its way to Kohima via Ukhrul. "C" Company of 152nd Indian
Parachute Battalion on Point 7378, and behind them the rest of 50th
Brigade, were in the way.[104] (See Map 6.1)

By 2 p.m. on 19th March, III Battalion had surrounded and put
under fire the 170 Indian paratroopers of "C" Company. Their commander, Major John Fuller, had orders to hold until relieved. III Battalion attacked at about 3 p.m. and was repulsed. Overnight, the Japanese
put in two more attacks. By dawn, Fuller and three of his officers were
dead, as were forty men, and many more wounded. The second-in-
command was seriously injured and ammunition was all but used up.
At mid-morning, according to the Japanese regimental narrative of the
action, "C" Company's fire slackened considerably. Out of ammunition and likely to collapse at the next attack, ordinarily speaking it
was time to surrender; no further military purpose would be served by
continued resistance.

---

[104] Allen, *Burma*, pp. 212–213; Latimer, *Burma*, pp. 199–201; Seaman, *Battle at
Sangshak*, pp. 63–64.

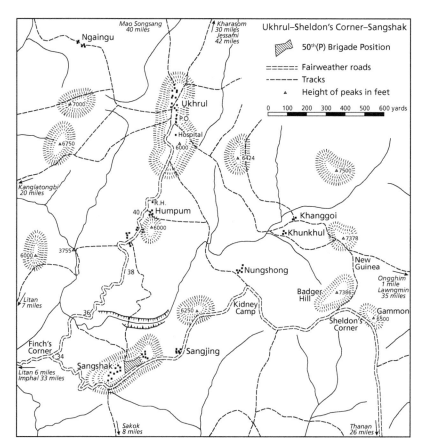

Map 6.1 Sketch map of Ukhrul-Sheldon's Corner-Sangshak Area.[105]

Instead, the Japanese were astonished to see a line of Indian para-troopers rise from their holes and charge down the hill, "firing and shouting in a counter-attack."[106] Not unlike the solitary Japanese rifle-man at Bastion, the remnants of "C" Company had opted for a "banzai charge" as a route out of their situation. Many were killed by Japanese fire. But an irony of war placed a wide ravine, unseen from "C" Com-pany's positions, between the Indian paratroopers and the Japanese. Some of the would-be suicides who had so far survived fell into the ravine, and were able to escape the battlefield. Others now surrendered.

---

[105] From Allen, *Burma*, p. 213.
[106] Quoted in Seaman, *Battle at Sangshak*, p. 64.

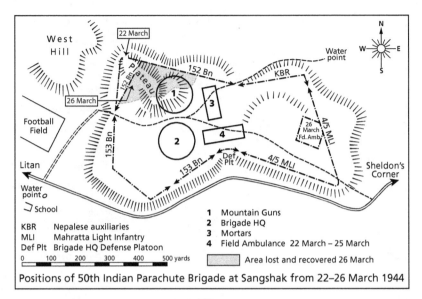

Positions of 50th Indian Parachute Brigade at Sangshak from 22–26 March 1944

Map 6.2 The perimeter at Sanghak.[107]

At this point, at the very top of the position on Point 7378, a British
or Indian officer rose. He put a pistol to his head and shot himself in
full view of the Japanese below. The Japanese narrative reports that
"[o]ur men fell silent, deeply impressed by such a brave act."[108] "C"
Company had been all but wiped out fighting to the last man, who
killed himself. The Japanese suffered 160 casualties, including a company commander and two platoon commanders killed and four other
officers wounded.[109]

The Left Raiding Column carried on to the village of Sangshak, near
where Hope-Thomson hurriedly concentrated his brigade out of fear it
would be destroyed piecemeal by the much-superior Japanese forces.
The best position he could find was a 800X400-yard plateau overlooked by nearby hills, lacking a water supply, and with stone just
under the topsoil that prevented digging in. This was a poor position indeed. (See Map 6.2) Hope-Thomson placed his battalion and a
half of paratroopers and the 4/5th Mahratta Light Infantry in scrapes

---

[107] From Seaman, *Battle at Sanghak*, p. 71.
[108] Quoted in Seaman, *Battle at Sanghak*, p. 65.
[109] On the fight at Point 7378, see Edwards, *Kohima*, pp. 70–73; Seaman, *Battle
at Sanghak*, pp. 63–66.

around the perimeter of the plateau. Major General Shigesaburō Miyazaki, the commander of the Left Raiding Column, arguably should have carried on to his main objective at Kohima, leaving 50th Brigade invested in his rear to be dealt with later. Instead, concerned about leaving such a strong position behind him, he attacked it. He lost precious time and suffered serious casualties among his first line infantry at Sangshak, sorely missed later in the failed effort to take Kohima.

Miyazaki did not wait for his artillery to come up, but instead launched a night assault early in the morning of 23 March with three companies from Major Nagata's II Battalion, 58th Regiment. He bet on routing Hope-Thomson's brigade before its defenses were prepared. Lieutenant Ban led the attack sword in hand screaming "Charge!" But the Gurkha and Indian paratroopers were ready. Their fire annihilated the lead Japanese company. Ban hacked down four Indian soldiers before being hit by machine gun bullets and shell fragments as he tried to slay a fifth. Japanese officers yelled "Don't let the company commander down!" before they too were hit, as their men hurled grenades at the Indian positions and fired their light machine guns from the hip. Lieutenant-Colonel J.H. Trim, commander of the 4/5th Mahrattas, heard the Japanese yelling to one another with shrieks that to him sounded barely human.[110]

Hope-Thomson's brigade held off the Japanese for four days and nights. By day, the thirsty defenders were subject to harassing fire from Japanese positions overlooking the plateau. They watched forlornly as many air-dropped supplies fell wide of the mark and floated down outside their lines. By night, the Japanese launched increasingly furious assaults, and 50th Brigade responded with desperate, costly counter-attacks to maintain their perimeter.

Over the night of 25/26 March, the Japanese finally managed to break into the northwest corner of the perimeter, threatening the entire position. A composite force of 150 men – the remaining fighting power of two Japanese battalions – was consolidating its toehold as dawn broke. One of 50th Brigade's staff officers recalled that "[t]hings got incredibly intense. The Japanese were then only 100 yards from Brigade Headquarters and we'd run out of grenades. However, our

---

[110] Allen, *Burma*, pp. 215–216; Nunneley and Tamayama, *Tales by Japanese Soldiers*, pp. 158–159; Thompson, *War in Burma*, p. 151.

men became even more ferocious and daring. Every man was fighting for his life."[111] The brigade's two remaining mountain guns were firing over open sights at enemy only sixty yards in front. The Japanese rushed the guns, taking one and knocking out the crew of the second, but for one Indian artilleryman who rose from the floor of the gun pit with a ramrod and set about beating the Japanese with it, who fled. The 50th Brigade now committed its reserves in desperate efforts to push the Japanese out of their toehold. First came the Brigade Defence Platoon, decimated in a frontal attack that killed its commander, after which were two scratch groups of fifteen men a piece, each under an officer.[112] These too were repulsed and both officers killed. The Japanese then overran the gun pits and killed the battery commanders, Majors John Locke and Jack Smith, as they tried in vain to retake the guns.

At this point, in a dangerous gamble, "A" Company of the 153rd Indian Parachute Battalion was pulled off its section of the perimeter and readied for an attack. The 153rd had been recruited from Gurkha regiments and "A" Company's commander, Major Jimmy Roberts, was a pre-war regular. Around the contested area, he could see the dead "sprawled singly in the open or heaped grotesquely near the strongpoints . . . filling all the forward trenches."[113] The stench of decomposing bodies of men and mules from the previous days' fighting enveloped the battlefield. Because the plateau was overlooked, and no one could dig in properly, the urge of soldiers under fire to hug the ground was intensified and visible. In a classic display of bravado intended to steel his troops' nerves as he prepared and directed the attack, Roberts moved from position to position with studied nonchalance, "his hat tipped onto the back of his head as usual, his binoculars tied up short under his chin."[114] His Gurkhas worked their way forward in rushes supported by machine gun and mortar fire. A Japanese warrant officer on the receiving end recalled, "[t]he Gurkha soldiers . . . rushed on and on though many had fallen, screaming as they advanced despite their wounds. Hand-to-hand fighting was everywhere and hand grenades flew everywhere. Our comrades encouraged us, the enemy screamed at us."[115]

---

[111] Captain Richards quoted in Edwards, *Kohima*, p. 86.
[112] Seaman, *Battle at Sangshak*, p. 94.   [113] Seaman, *Battle at Sangshak*, p. 95.
[114] Seaman, *Battle at Sangshak*, p. 97. Seaman was an officer in 153rd Battalion and present at Sangshak.
[115] Quoted in Seaman, *Battle at Sangshak*, p. 96.

Howling, the Japanese put in a counter-attack. Their "eerie and disconcerting" shouts were accompanied by bugles and cymbals meant to encourage themselves and dispirit the defenders.[116] Not to be outdone, and to support their soldiers fighting with the sounds of solidarity, two British officers who carried hunting horns as an affectation began blowing them. The Mortar Troop commander set his men to singing, recalling later that "[i]t made a dreadful din but served its purpose."[117] By late morning, "A" Company had re-established the perimeter but lost half its strength in doing so, including one platoon commander killed and two wounded. Roberts was lucky and came away unscathed. All of the Japanese officers involved were killed save one who was carried back with eleven bullet wounds. Only twenty Japanese, most wounded, survived of the force that had penetrated the perimeter.[118]

Recovering the bodies of officers was not only a Japanese desire; the Gurkha and Indian paratroopers also ran great risks to retrieve under fire their dead officers. The growing collection of officers' corpses from the fighting on 26 March was kept in a small space by brigade headquarters, the only place in the entire perimeter safe from sniper fire. Nearby, an "imperturbable Gurkha cook" served up a stew of decomposing mule, curry powder, and apple puree, the only food regularly available, which, however revolting, was "gulped down by famished men." For soldiers collecting food for their platoons, and others on errands to brigade headquarters, the corpses were "a macabre reminder of what the morning had cost."[119] Lt. Col. Trim was so reminded when he saw Major Smith, the battery commander, "lying by the path with his intestines spilled out."[120]

Late in the day on 26 March the decision was taken to withdraw. That night, at 10:00, 50th Brigade's mortars and other heavy weapons fired off their remaining ammunition to convince the Japanese the garrison was about to counter-attack. Leaving behind about 150 wounded who were unable to move, the paratroopers and the 4/5th Mahrattas moved off the plateau as silently as possible, initially to the southeast

---

[116] Seaman, *Battle at Sangshak*, p. 97.
[117] Quoted in Seaman, *Battle at Sangshak*, p. 98.
[118] Edwards, *Kohima*, p. 86; Keane, *Road of Bones*, p. 204; Nunneley and Tamayama, *Tales by Japanese Soldiers*, p. 161; Seaman, *Battle at Sangshak*, pp. 92–98.
[119] Seaman, *Battle at Sangshak*, p. 101.
[120] Quoted in Keane, *Road of Bones*, p. 203.

through some dense woodland avoiding Japanese staging areas. They broke into small parties and made their way back to British lines as best they could. Meanwhile, the three battalions of the Japanese 58th Regiment had suffered heavily and were preparing a final desperate attack on Sangshak over the night of 26/27 March, to be led by the regimental commander, Colonel Fukunaga, who expected to die. As the attacking Japanese came onto the little plateau after midnight, they soon realized the defenders were gone.

Both Fukunaga and Miyazaki had known Lieutenant Ban, and that morning they looked together for his body. They discovered that the Indian paratroopers had accorded Ban what respect they could manage for a fearless enemy. His sword was not looted, and he was buried with it neatly rolled in a blanket in a shallow grave (the only kind of grave the obsidian under the plateau allowed). Kameyama reported "Our men were all moved by this."[121] In response, Colonel Fukunaga ordered that the wounded paratroopers be cared for and that PoWs from 50th Brigade were not to be harmed. Miyazaki later released many of the Brigade's PoWs in their underpants near Kohima. The Japanese 58th Regiment had lost about 500 dead and wounded out of its 2,800 soldiers, and Japanese casualties overall were about 1,000 of 4,000 involved. Of the 3,000 men under Hope-Thomson's command in the Sangshak area, about 900 were killed, wounded or captured. The 152nd Indian Parachute Battalion suffered particularly heavily, losing 350 men of 600 while its officers put in a positively Japanese performance: eighteen of twenty-five were dead, and only two of the remainder had not been wounded.[122]

At Sangshak, then, Indian soldiers and their officers fought in putatively "Japanese" style, with banzai attacks and shouts. The experience of battle led both Japanese and Indian soldiers to adopt different practices. Crack forces, putting in virtuoso performances, earned each other's respect and demonstrated this through treatment of the dead and of prisoners. Racialized categories for soldiers' behavior were scrambled.

---

[121] Quoted in Nunneley and Tamayama, *Tales by Japanese Soldiers*, p. 162.
[122] Latimer, *Burma*, pp. 201–202, 483, n.96; Seaman, *Battle at Sangshak*, pp. 131–133. Several of these officers were contemporaries at Oxford in the 1930s of Richard Hillary, author of *The Last Enemy*, part of a set known as "the long-haired boys" critical of authority. Few of them survived the war.

The Japanese 31st Division would run into two more blocking positions before it reached the Kohima area, at Jessami and Kharasom, where the Assam Regiment, a war-raised Indian battalion, was dug in with orders to fight to the last man. At Jessami, the Indians held out for five days before withdrawing in small parties when ordered to do so. One of their officers described the fighting as they struggled to hold their perimeter:

Young and inexperienced sepoys were fighting like veterans; red-hot machine-gun barrels would be ripped off, regardless of burns in the process; Japanese grenades and cracker-bombs were picked up and thrown clear of the trenches with all the calmness in the world, and there did not seem to be a man in the garrison afraid to carry out any task given to him.[123]

At Kharasom, after three days of resistance, Captain Young realized that his company would not last through another attack. He was under orders not to surrender the position, but he came up with a different solution than had Fuller's "C" Company on Point 7378. On the night of 30 March, Captain Young had his troops withdraw in small parties through the jungle. In strict compliance with his orders, Young remained behind to defend the position with those wounded who could not leave. He was last seen stacking tommy-gun magazines and piling grenades in his bunker, and setting up a wounded soldier with a Bren gun. As his soldiers moved away through the night, they heard behind them sounds of heavy firing and then silence.[124]

From Structure to Representation

In reflecting on the qualities of the Japanese soldier after the war, Slim remarked: "If five hundred Japanese were ordered to hold a position, we had to kill four hundred and ninety-five before it was ours – and then the last five killed themselves."[125] The 50th Brigade's stand at Sangshak did not quite approach Japanese standards. There is something unique about the relative consistency with which Japanese soldiers fought to the last man in the Second World War. There is a place for national style. Nonetheless, especially if one focuses on the first 50 percent to die rather than the last 50 percent, there was a great

---

[123] Quoted in Edwards, *Kohima*, p. 95. [124] Edwards, *Kohima*, p. 96.
[125] Slim, *Defeat into Victory*, p. 538.

deal of shared ground in battlefield behavior between the Japanese and British imperial forces. Carfrae remarked of his Nigerian chindits that they were "brave enough" for the fighting at hand.[126] Common human capacities and potentials were actualized when soldiers from either side faced comparable circumstances, even as national styles were never fully effaced. Inhibitions and difficulties in surrendering in a war suffused with racially charged propaganda, and the dynamics of perimeter attack and defense in heavily forested terrain, led to similar behaviors all around. But this commonality can be difficult to grasp precisely because events and experiences are narrated through categories of difference and antagonism. The racism that suffuses Allied accounts of the war against Japan is the topic of the next chapter.

One consequence set in train by the foreclosure of surrender in Burma was that the Allies suffered further casualties mopping up Japanese remnants. Such "needless" deaths were a source of rage and frustration among Allied soldiers. This anger informed their accounts at the time and afterward. The structural properties and powers of battle shape not only soldiers' behavior, but also their thinking about and their representations of battle, the ways in which they discursively construct their experiences. Inquiry is faced with a difficult problem: the knowledge we have about battle which derives from participants is not exterior to an order of knowing and being created by battle itself.[127] Participant accounts must be positioned within a theory of battle and of the powers it exercises over representation.

---

[126] Charles Carfrae, IWM Interview, Reel 1, 10467, IWM.
[127] Cf. Barkawi and Brighton, "Powers of War," p. 135.

PART III

History and Theory

7 | *The Experience and Representation of Combat*

The Japanese – those hobgoblins of the forest, the enemy – were beyond easy reach of our imagination. They were men of a sort, of course, but men totally alien. Pitiless, inexorable, they seemed to lack all human warmth, giving no quarter and expecting none.

. . .

We were rational Europeans, not fanatics . . . how could we be expected to behave in such a way?

– Charles Carfrae[1]

Allied participants in the fighting in Burma, at the time and afterward, narrated it through orientalist and racist tropes, as they did the Asia-Pacific War more generally.[2] In their accounts, combats took the intense and pitiless form they did due to Japanese fanaticism and savagery. In *Defeat into Victory*, Slim wrote "our object became . . . to destroy the Japanese Army, to smash it as an evil thing."[3] How are we to interpret such representations, their assignment of blame and responsibility, their descriptions of events, their tropes and stock characters? Participant accounts are key but disputed sources in military history for what they tell us about the experience of, and motivation for, combat.[4] How should we interpret them?

The racial antagonism that pervades Allied narratives arose during the war itself, as a consequence of experience. Few British or American

---

[1] Charles Carfrae, "Dark Company," p. 128, 80/49/1, IWM.
[2] Dower, *War Without Mercy*.
[3] Slim, *Defeat into Victory*, p. 183. After characterizing as unchristian and irreligious communist commissars, the Japanese, and Nazi soldiers, he goes on of the 14th Army, "We fought for the clean, the decent, the free things of life." Ibid.
[4] See e.g. the debate between Linderman and McPherson: Linderman, *Embattled Courage*; *World Within War*; McPherson, *Cause and Comrades*. Cf. Moore, *Writing War*.

soldiers, much less Indian or African ones, knew or cared much about the Japanese before the war. The fighting generated the palpable hatred of the Japanese among participants. It offered occasions for the menagerie of epithets flung by Indian and imperial as well as by metropolitan soldiers. Narrations of fighting the Japanese are not sober reflections by soldier-agents with stable identities. They are emanations from people in the grip of war and its powers of transformation. Such representations offer significant evidence of soldiers' thinking at various removes in time. As Hynes comments, war memoirs are a species of "conversion literature."[5] So too are letters, diaries, and even memos from those dealing with the shock of war. Hynes remarks, "[No one] goes through a war without being changed by it, and in fundamental ways."[6] Soldiers' narrations in official documents, memoirs, and elsewhere provide windows on processes of change.

War throws people into alien orders where they play new roles, in which they may "no longer recognize themselves."[7] The experience of war tends to disintegrate categories and personalities.[8] Representations of war seek to reify, to provide taken-for-granted identities and narratives that account for the violence and suffering. For those who survive, battle's shocking events and fateful contingencies remain with them, with consequences for lives and personalities long after the fact.[9] In after-action reports and letters written in the immediate wake of fighting, as well as memoirs published decades later, soldier-writers try to make sense of, and order their experience, to make it cohere. As Martin van Creveld comments, "fighting itself was a rough, confused, primitive business very difficult to describe in any kind of coherent way."[10] Discourses of race war helped to stabilize battle, to sequence its events, and provide reasons for the awful things that were done and suffered.

Soldiers' observations and representations have to be situated against the changes they underwent and the pressures they faced. Before the war, many Indian officers, like other colonized elites, saw

[5] Hynes, *Soldiers' Tale*, p. 5.   [6] Hynes, *Soldiers' Tale*, p. 3.
[7] Levinas, *Totality and Infinity*, p. 21. Cf. Barkawi and Brighton, "Powers of War," p. 136.
[8] That war is a disintegrative experience for individuals, groups, and societies is a recurrent theme in historical and memoir literature. See e.g. Fussell, *Great War and Modern Memory*; Caputo, *Rumor of War*; Homer, *Iliad*; Leed, *No Man's Land*; Sajer, *Forgotten Soldier*; Watson, *Enduring the Great War*.
[9] See e.g. Shephard, *War of Nerves*.
[10] Creveld, *Culture of War*, p. 120.

Japan as a model to emulate.[11] Most of the soldiers they commanded were illiterate or had little education. The wartime army introduced literacy and education programs to train its Indian and African soldiers, and then "information" programs to counter Japanese and Indian nationalist propaganda, supplying the discourse of race war. Once caught up in the fighting, brown and black officers and soldiers came to think about and act upon the Japanese in similar terms as their Anglo-American counterparts. Race hate was war generated.

Of course the discourse of race war drew upon long-standing orientalist resources in Western culture, particularly regarding associations of Asians with vermin and simians. But it was adapted to, and made expressive of, battlefield experience in Burma. It provided soldiers and officers, in different but related registers, with a shorthand to describe, discuss, and analyze their experiences. In this way, shockingly racist ideas came to frame and inform commanders' and soldiers' actions, not so much as motivation for combat but as a way of conceiving operations and tactics, and of determining what the appropriate actions were.

The disintegrative and reordering dynamic set in train by the experience and representation of war can continue long into the "peace" for soldier-writers. They have written not only the primary documents in archives, but produced much of the secondary historiography of war. The chapter closes with a look at how the Battle of Sangshak carried on as veterans engaged in pitched combat over the historical record. Some sought to hold the "race war" line against any evidence to the contrary. Others deployed the voices of Japanese veterans met on post-war reconciliation visits. What war had wrought among its denizens continued to shape writing about it for decades to come. The transformative powers of battle constitute the very historical record we use to make sense of war.

"Why Fight Japan?"[12]

Why fight Japan? For the British in the Far East in the Second World War, the answer to this question was not self-evident. For their Indian and African troops, it was even less obvious. While in "political India,"

---

[11] Aydin, *The Politics of Anti-Westernism in Asia*, Chapters 4, 7; Khan, *Raj at War*, pp. 112–113.
[12] The title of a pamphlet produced for British troops in the Far East by the Directorate of Army Education. 1945 (59), NAM.

and among Indian commissioned officers, views differed about Japan and the Pacific War, most Indian and imperial soldiers began the war with very little idea of Japan. In this they were not so different from their British counterparts. Any consideration of the role of racial antagonism in shaping the battlefield actions and experiences of these soldiers must begin with their capacities to understand the ostensible political identities and purposes at stake in the war.

For Indian soldiers, the question of capacity begins with literacy. According to one estimate, 90 percent of Indian recruits were illiterate on joining the forces.[13] In 1943, 82 percent of infantry recruits in the Indian Army were illiterate.[14] Infantry soldiers for the most part were recruited from peasant communities and had very little in the way of formal education until their military service. In East Africa, the KAR also recruited peasants and distrusted skilled urban laborers or mission school graduates.[15] Charles Carfrae described using a map in orientation lectures on the war to his Nigerian troops training in West Africa. "This is where the Germans live. Here is Italy, there France...There would be smiles and pointed fingers. Ah yes, 'Frenchies' – a fair number of men came from Chad and Fort Lamy."[16] He had trouble keeping his soldiers awake for these sessions. (See Figure 7.1) Educated imperial recruits were more likely to be sent into the technical branches of service than to the infantry.

An Indian Army morale official noted that "it is only the small number of educated IORs who can have any real appreciation of the development of the war as a whole."[17] In 1943, officers responsible for propaganda and information for Indian troops realized that "extensive propaganda, in a geographical sense" was beyond most Indian soldiers.[18] The troops lacked the necessary education and breadth of experience. Ralph Russell asked one of his *naiks*, or corporals, who the enemy nations were? "The Italians," came the answer.[19] Thimayya recalls of his Ahir company before the war: "They were a simple

[13] India Command Weekly Intelligence Summaries, L/WS/1/1506, OIOC.
[14] Report of Infantry Committee, L/WS/1/1371, OIOC.
[15] Parsons, *African Rank-and-File*, p. 115.
[16] Charles Carfrae, "Dark Company," p. 56, 80/49/1, IWM.
[17] Morale Reports, August, September, and October 1944, L/WS/2/71, OIOC.
[18] Quoted in Bhattacharya, "'A Necessary Weapon of War,'" Ph.D. diss., p. 68.
[19] Russell, *Findings, Keepings*, p. 236. Russell remarks, "It was not until much later that I came to see that I had no reason to expect that he would know these things. Why should he? Like most of the great number of war-time

Figure 7.1 East African troops receive a geography lesson.[20]

people. They asked for little. They arose early, worked hard and were asleep by eight in the evening... [they had] an unquestioning faith in simple but genuine values."[21] Indian soldiers were often described with variations of "simple country people."[22] This demeaning attitude reveals condescension from both British and Indian officers, and it discounted soldiers' intelligence. Nevertheless, peasant soldiers had relatively little exposure to the world beyond their villages. The politics of the world war were not a central concern, nor why they joined the army. Their dedication and bravery in these circumstances often surprised officers. Carfrae remarked of his Nigerian soldiers that they "fought against a nation they had never heard of a year or two before

recruits he had joined the army 'to fill his belly,' and wasn't in the least concerned with whatever it was that the army had recruited him to do." Ibid.

[20] K 8605, IWM.

[21] Evans, *Thimayya of India*, p. 104.

[22] Singh and Randle interviews; Aida, *Prisoner of the British*, p. 94; Auchinleck, quoted in Connell, *Auchinleck*, p. 948; Kaul, *The Untold Story*, p. 48; Toye, *Springing Tiger*, p. vii; Tuker, *While Memory Serves*, pp. 54, 66. See also Confidential Reports on VCOs and some NCOs of the 4th Battalion, Indian Grenadiers, Tighe Papers, 1945, 8206–83–20, NAM.

on a battleground equally unknown."[23] Cookson said of his Gambian soldiers that "[w]ithout a murmur of complaint they defended a country whose inhabitants they despised in a quarrel whose implications they did not understand."[24]

Given the backgrounds of their personnel and the technical requirements of modern warfare, Imperial militaries had to become vast centers of education. "[T]he army was the third largest educational institution in East Africa."[25] Recruits in the Indian Army began earning school certificates during their initial training. In 1942, the army developed a course for sixteen-year-old boys to receive eighteen months basic education before enlistment.[26] Promotions to NCO and VCO ranks were dependent on attaining school certificates.[27] But imperial military education was double-edged for the authorities, as soldiers had access to ever more information which could not be entirely controlled. Early in the war, many British and Indian officers observed a lack of interest in politics among the rank and file, indeed from their perspective the apparent lack of any political views at all.[28] By May 1944, Indian Army intelligence noted that it had become impossible for officers to avoid questions about politics from the troops.[29] In East Africa, too, army education played its part in contributing to the increasing political awareness among KAR soldiers.[30]

In response, officials developed a variety of information and propaganda programs.[31] In the wake of the retreat from Burma in 1942,

[23] Charles Carfrae, Dark Company, p. 181, 80/49/1, IWM.
[24] Quoted in Hamilton, *War Bush*, unpublished manuscript, p. 143. Cookson's soldiers were shocked at the poverty and small stature of the Indian civilian populations they encountered.
[25] Parsons, *African Rank-and-File*, p. 115.
[26] Perry, *Commonwealth Armies*, p. 112.
[27] India Command Weekly Intelligence Summaries, L/WS/1/1506, OIOC.
[28] Aynsley Delafield, Peter Francis, Tony Banks, and Peter Gadsdon, interviews by the author; Intelligence Summaries India – Internal, 1 October 1943, L/WS/1/1433, OIOC; "Note by EICO on measures to counter the Japanese sponsored attack on the loyalty of the Indian Army," INA and Free Burma Army, L/WS/1/1576, OIOC; Singh, *Soldiers' Contribution to Indian Independence*, pp. 40–41; author's correspondence with Col. S.C. Singha, 23 August 2001.
[29] Army Commanders' Conferences, 23–26 May 1944, L/WS/1/1523, OIOC. See also Bhattacharya's discussion, "'A Necessary Weapon of War,'" Ph.D. diss., pp. 76–78.
[30] Parsons, *The African Rank-and-File*, pp. 190–193.
[31] Bhattacharya, "'A Necessary Weapon of War,'" Ph.D. diss. See also Bolt, *Pseudo Sahib*.

the military authorities in India were concerned about "defeatism" and undertook a morale-boosting campaign. This involved print and radio propaganda, entertainments and comforts for the troops, and guidance and training on morale for officers. Another initiative was the "Josh" system. "Josh" means pep, spirit, or enthusiasm in Urdu. Specially trained officers in each unit were to meet informally with small groups of troops to discuss the war. A range of publications for Indian troops were produced and "Josh" officers briefed on the lines they were to take with the soldiers.[32] Reading rooms stocked with relevant publications were provided for the troops wherever possible. In the words of an instruction pamphlet for "Josh" officers, the purpose was to "build in every Indian soldier the knowledge and firm faith that the Japanese and everyone who represents the Japanese are his own personal enemies."[33]

Atrocity was central to these and other efforts. Horrors committed against Indian soldiers or Indian expatriates in Japanese-occupied areas filled publications and talks. Rapes of Indian women and Japanese disrespect for Indian religions figured prominently, with some reports claiming that Indian women had been raped inside places of worship. Propagandists invented conflicts between Indian cultural and religious practices and those of the Japanese. Hindu soldiers were told that the Japanese were cruel to cattle and that they desecrated temples. Variations included Sikh PoWs being forced to shave their beards and cut their hair or Hindu or Muslim troops being forced to handle or eat beef or pork respectively. Indian soldiers passing through the 14th (Training) Division, gathered in small groups, were asked "[d]id you know that Jap fathers sell their daughters into brothels and that this is a widespread custom in Japan?"[34]

These contrivances did not always convince. An intelligence report noted that "trying to make [Indian Army soldiers] hate Jerry or the Jap is somewhat artificial."[35] Front line soldiers in general tend to be

---

[32] See J.A.H. Heard, LH for a collection of such materials.

[33] "Instructions on Josh Work and Josh Group Organisation within Units," INA and Free Burma Army, L/WS/1/1576, OIOC.

[34] Major General A.C. Curtis, Report on the 14th Indian Division July 1943–November 1945, p. 9, P140, IWM; J.A.H. Heard, "Josh," Nos. 2, 3, 6, LH; Bhattacharya, "'A Necessary Weapon of War,'" Ph.D. diss., p. 68.

[35] India Monthly Intelligence Summary, No. 13, 5 January 1943, L/WS/1/317, LH.

focused on the far more immediate and absorbing concerns of a combat zone.[36] A report on British soldiers in India noted that they are "extremely suspicious of lectures and instructions on Current Affairs. It all sounds like official 'dope.'"[37] Information, propaganda, and morale programs were more in evidence in India in training and support facilities than at the front in Burma, and were more likely to be adequately organized and resourced closer to the end than to the beginning of the war.

From Ignorance to Hate

In their ignorance of Japan and the politics of the Asia-Pacific Wars, British soldiers were similar to Indian ones. A report on British infantry in India noted that "[b]efore the sudden entry of Japan into the war, the average British soldier knew little or nothing of the Japanese."[38] Gunner-Signaler Evritt Loseby remarked, "I don't think we gave one whit about the Japanese before the war."[39] The Royal Welch Fusilier Ron Thomas identified his geography class as the only place he had ever heard of Japan.[40] John Shipster, a wartime junior officer in the 7/2 Punjab, reports: "I cannot remember ever having been told anything about the Japanese during our training in India before we went to Burma. I was ignorant of the Japanese soldier's traditional background and culture."[41] "Of any widespread appreciation of a higher purpose in the war there is at present little sign," observed the writer of a morale report on British troops, "the most fundamental stimulus to action appears to be the desire to finish the war as soon as possible in order to get home."[42] As with the Indian soldiers and their material benefits, British troops abroad expressed more concern about the

---

[36] See e.g. Allport, *Browned Off and Bloody-Minded*; Farrar, "Nationalism in Wartime"; Linderman, *World Within War*, Chapter 8, pp. 300–344; Roy, "Discipline and Morale."

[37] India Command Weekly Intelligence Summaries, 22 June 1945, L/WS/1/1506, OIOC.

[38] Report of Infantry Committee, 56 (a), L/WS/1/1371, OIOC. See also *Shipster, Mist Over the Rice Fields*, p. 4.

[39] Evritt Loseby, interview by the author.

[40] Ron Thomas, interview by the author.

[41] Shipster, *Mist Over the Rice-Fields*, p. 4.

[42] ALFSEA Morale Reports, November, December 1944, and January 1945, p. 1, WO 203/2355, TNA.

fidelity of their wives, the conditions of repatriation, and their economic prospects after the war.[43]

Yet Loseby and Thomas came to passionately hate the Japanese during the course of the war.[44] Their experience in this regard was a common one. The report quoted above, written in 1943 by a committee of experienced infantry commanders, goes on to note that "while there is nothing wrong with the determination of the British Infantry soldier to fight and kill the Jap," it is only among those units which have already seen action that there is significant animosity toward the Japanese.[45] Whatever their state of ignorance regarding the Japanese before the war, many British soldiers developed a full array of racial attitudes toward them during it. For George Macdonald Fraser, "[i]t was disconcerting to find yourself soldiering in an exotic Oriental country which is medieval in outlook, against a barbarian enemy given to burying prisoners up to the neck or hanging them by the heels for bayonet practice."[46] Shipster reflected on his initial ignorance of the Japanese "psyche" and "ethos":

I knew nothing of the cult of Emperor worship, nor of the soldier's willingness to die rather than be taken prisoner, which accounted in part for the scorn and derision with which the Japanese treated all prisoners. As the months passed I did of course learn the significance of words such as banzai...and hara-kiri...[47]

Although his views are stereotyped, Shipster remained comparatively level-headed in comparison to some of his colleagues. Much closer in

---

[43] See India Command Weekly Intelligence Summaries, L/WS/1/1506, OIOC; SEAC Morale Reports, WO 203/4536 and /4537, TNA; ALFSEA Morale Reports, WO/203/2355, /4538, and /4539, TNA; Roy, "Discipline and Morale."

[44] Loseby remained convinced that the Japanese would undress the dead bodies of British and Indian soldiers, sever their limbs, and then put their uniforms back on over reassembled corpses. The purpose of this, he maintained, was to harm morale because when their comrades came to recover and bury the dead, the corpses would fall apart when they were lifted by the limbs. That bodies would fall apart when lifted is most likely an effect of wounds or of the rapid decay that occurs in the jungle (see Bergerud, *Touched with Fire*, pp. 84–87). Loseby attributed it to a dastardly and inhuman Japanese trick. Evritt Loseby, interview by the author. Similar stories about bodies circulated among American soldiers and marines fighting the Japanese. Linderman, *World Within War*, p. 159.

[45] Report of Infantry Committee, 56 (a), L/WS/1/1371, OIOC.

[46] Fraser, *Quartered Safe*, p. 26.   [47] Shipster, *Mist Over the Rice-Fields*, p. 4.

time to events than Shipster's memoir, the Chindit Captain Durrant wrote:

Somehow one can imagine [having] a drink and a cigarette with a German... but having once met the Japs one can only imagine kicking their heads in. They look like animals and behave like animals and they can be killed as unemotionally as swatting flies. And they need to be killed, not wounded for so long as they breathe they're dangerous... My only regret is that I didn't take up this sport earlier, the close season will be dull... [48]

Variations on phrases like "one round, one dead Jap," "the only good Jap is a dead Jap," and "vermin score" for body counts, were common in official paperwork and other accounts, as were analogies between Japanese soldiers and various animals and insects.[49] (See Figure 7.2) The Japanese were commonly figured as filthy, stinking, screaming, stupefied, trapped like a beast, etc.[50] "The Jap is cruel by nature."[51] "KILL THESE SWINE," wrote one general.[52] Fraser began his memoir with "[t]he first time I smelt Jap..."[53] The operation to repatriate Japanese troops to Japan after the war was known officially as "Operation Nipoff."[54]

For Indian troops as well, racial hatred was a product of fighting. Many developed racist and even exterminationist attitudes toward the Japanese once they were on campaign in Burma. While a 1943

[48] Captain N. Durant, typescript account of the "Wingate show," p. 20, 4885, IWM.

[49] See e.g. Lowry, *Infantry Company*, p. 51; Major H.C. Gay, Extracts from his memoirs, p. 127, 88/48/1, IWM; IWM Brig. K.H. Collen, letter of 12 December 1944, 79/21/1, IWM; Major General W.A. Dimoline, 11 (EA) Division Training Instruction No. 13, para (f), IX/1–2, LH.

[50] See e.g. Major General W.A. Dimoline, Ceylon to the Chindwin, pp. 43–44, IX/13, LH.

[51] "The Jap," Lecture, Jungle Warfare School, Shimoga, 7304-1-2, NAM.

[52] General Sir Douglas Gracey, Situation on Division Front, 17 November 1943, 1/8, LH.

[53] Fraser, *Quartered Safe*, p. 3. He continues: "I can no more describe the smell than I could describe a colour but it was heavy and pungent and compounded of stale cooked rice and sweat and human waste and... Jap. Quite unlike the clean acrid woodsmoke of an Indian village or the rather exotic and faintly decayed odour of the bashas in which the Burmese lived – and certainly nothing like the cooking smells of the Baluch hillmen and Gurkhas of our brigade or our own British aromas." National styles had olfactory dimensions.

[54] Operation NIPOFF: evacuation of Japanese surrendered personnel to Japan, WO 203/6338, TNA. Allen suggests "some wag" at Mountbatten's SEAC was responsible for the name of the operation. Allen, "Innocents Abroad," p. xxi.

Figure 7.2 "Killed like animals": A dead Japanese soldier in Burma with mines he intended to plant, 1945.[55]

report noted "there still existed a patent lack of basic conscious enmity amongst Indian troops toward the vaguely comprehended Jap," the increasing bitterness of the fighting began to produce its own effects.[56] "The Japs are most uncultured and cruel," one Indian soldier wrote home in late 1944 or early 1945, "[t]hey have got beastly characteristics. Such a nation should be totally destroyed for the good of the world."[57] In the wake of successful Allied offensive operations to

[55] IWM Photo SE 4042.
[56] Memorandum on the work done by the P.R. Central Group and its future, 10 Nov. 1943, INA and Free Burma Army, L/WS/1/1576, OIOC.
[57] ALFSEA Morale Reports, Nov. and Dec. 1944 and Jan. 1945, p. 15, WO 203/2355, TNA.

re-enter Burma, a morale report commented that "[f]irst-hand experience of the enemy's cruelty to the occupied populations has bred a genuine hatred of the Japanese."[58] "May God bring destruction to this oppressor nation," a *havildar* exclaimed of the Japanese in a letter home.[59] A *jemadar* reached somewhat unsuccessfully for world historical language to describe the meaning of the war: "This war raised by two brutal nations of the world challenges every human race to fight against it in connection to save the human culture, morale, civilisation, and what not."[60]

Harbakhsh Singh, an ICO captured at Singapore who refused to join the INA, devoted a chapter to the Japanese in his memoir. They come off as brainwashed, self-sacrificial ideologues determined to die for their country and to do so without a thought for their loved ones back home. All the stock characters are present, from Kamikaze pilots to the human tank mines who would lie in wait and detonate their devices when a tank passed over.[61] Shah Nawaz Khan, an ICO captured at Singapore who became an INA major-general, offered a more balanced account. Initially, the sight of "white soldiers fleeing for their lives before the Japanese, an Asiatic nation" undermined British imperial prestige and assisted Indians in overcoming their sense of racial inferiority.[62] But in Singapore, Khan observed the Japanese bayonetting prisoners. They also ordered Indian PoWs to bayonet British officers, and bayonetted the Indians who refused. He thought that "[t]he Japanese were trained in such a manner that they took pleasure in this sort of work and treated it as a good pastime."[63] He learned to hate the Japanese: "From the day that we first came in contact with the Japanese most of us developed a great dislike of Japanese methods of dealing with people whose cause they professed to champion. This dislike intensified when we saw with our own eyes the organised looting and raping indiscriminately indulged in by Japanese soldiers."[64] War experience generated race hate.

---

[58] Morale Reports, November 1944–January 1945, L/WS/2/71, OIOC.

[59] Morale Reports, November 1944–January 1945, L/WS/2/71, OIOC.

[60] Morale Reports, November 1944–January 1945, L/WS/2/71, OIOC. The "what not" may be the product of the writer of the report who chose not to translate the rest of the VCO's letter.

[61] Singh, *Line of Duty*, Chapter 17, pp. 161–165. See also Crasta, *Eaten by the Japanese*.

[62] Khan, *My Memories of I.N.A.*, p. 6.   [63] Ibid., pp. 10–11.   [64] Ibid., p. 48.

Battlefield Analogies

Indian and other soldiers made use of an array of demeaning analogies to describe the Japanese and their experiences in combat. An Indian major, mixing the ovine with the entomological, described the Japanese withdrawal after the defeat at Imphal in these terms:

Then happened ridiculous incidents when the rabble started withdrawing and every [company] like mine would see by first light hundreds of sheep like Japs trying to get past our positions where we had every infantry weapon sited ... even the [company commander] would push the bren gunmen aside and enjoy killing the Japs like insects, brutal ... [65]

For one VCO, the experience of shooting down Japanese was more like bowling: "It was a real pleasure to see the little yellow bollies being bowled over like nine pins."[66]

The Allies often used analogies involving animals or insects that lived underground to describe the Japanese, like "fanatical little rats."[67] Their ubiquity offers an opportunity to consider what work such analogies might do in soldiers' narrations, how else they may be read than simply as evidence of racial hatred. Slim was fond of an ant simile: "The Japanese were ruthless and bold as ants."[68] During the war he told his officers, "[p]icture yourself fighting man-sized ants ... [the Japanese have] all the qualities and faults of the fighting ant."[69] At Chatham House after the war, he told a conference that the Japanese were neither men nor animals but soldier ants.[70] Here, in addition to its racist connotations, the soldier ant functions as a way to think about how the Japanese actually operated and fought.

[65] Middle East Censorship Fortnightly Summary Covering Indian Troops, 14 June–27 June 1944, L/PJ/12/656, OIOC.

[66] Col. E.C. Pickard, "Boundary Point 39," 96/8/1–2, IWM.

[67] Major M.A. Lowry, *Infantry Company*, p. 51. See also Major H.C. Gay, Extracts from his memoirs, p. 127, 88/48/1, IWM; Brig. K.H. Collen, letter of 12 December 1944, 79/21/1, IWM; Major General W.A. Dimoline, 11 (EA) Division Training Instruction No. 13, para (f), IX/1–2, LH. For the full range of animal metaphors used to describe the Japanese, see Dower, *War Without Mercy*, Chapter 4; Cameron, *American Samurai*, pp. 95–96; Linderman, *World Within War*, pp. 168–173. In addition to rats and ants, monkeys and apes were the most common.

[68] Slim, *Defeat into Victory*, p. 537. See also pp. 239, 381, 485.

[69] Infantry: GHQ(I) Infantry Liaison Letters, Jungle Fighting in Burma, Appendix A, No. 14, 15 January 1945, L/WS/1/778, OIOC.

[70] Minutes of the Meeting at Chatham House on the Mentality of Japanese Troops, 8 September 1948, AL5304, IWM.

Figure 7.3 Living underground: A Sikh soldier resting in a captured Japanese bunker.[71]

The Japanese constructed elaborate bunker systems, skillfully camouflaged and often connected by tunnels. Due to Allied air and artillery superiority, they had to dig deep to survive. They often lived, fought, and died underground. Admiring their bunkers, one British officer thought of the Japanese as a colony of intelligent (but unclean) rabbits.[72] (See Figure 7.3) The Japanese failed to vary many of their

[71] IND 3226, IWM.
[72] Capt. D.M. Cookson, "With Africans in Arakan," p. 45, 82/37/1, IWM.

tactical procedures and routines, lacking flexibility and initiative.[73] In the view of many British officers, their march discipline and security arrangements were atrocious.[74] Many a noisy Japanese column was ambushed, or easily avoided, as desired. Accordingly, they could be thought of as a colony of ants that has fixed ways of going about things, and which is consequently vulnerable. Japanese "habits were consistent, and [their] reactions easy to gauge."[75] If one knew these vulnerabilities, the Japanese could be stomped on and killed as if they were ants.[76]

These constructions drew upon orientalist tropes to be sure, the Japanese a combination of the primitive and the modern, a breed of mechanized savages working in mindless, mass unison. At the same time, these analogies oriented officers and troops to elements of Japanese tactics and behavior, and provided an idiom to discuss battlefield events. For the Indian major quoted above, "sheep" seemed an adequate description for the weary, hungry, diseased, and defeated Japanese he saw pulling out of Imphal, who then fell like flies under his automatic fire. The result of one stratagem, another officer remarked, was a "glorious slaughter of Japanese who ran screaming from their coverts only to be shot down in scores ... like ... a rat hunt."[77] Observing the fighting for Mandalay Hill, General Pete Rees reported: "At first the Japanese resisted, very like hornets, but when they saw the game was really up, then they scattered and ran like rabbits."[78]

Imagery of this kind arose from battlefield experience. But it also worked to shape battle, as soldiers acted as if the Japanese were insects to be stomped on. More than just a propaganda construction or racist trope, the Japanese as ants, rats and so on formed part of a *lingua*

---

[73] Gen. Sir Douglas Gracey, "Suggestions for Training for and Conducting War Against the Japanese for Troops who have been Fighting in European Theatres of War," 2/24, LH; Ferguson, *Wild Green Earth*, pp. 209–213; Slim, *Defeat into Victory*, p. 537.

[74] Gen. Sir Douglas Gracey, "Report on New Features of Japanese Tactics," p. 3, 2/23, LH; Lt. Gen. Thomas J. Hutton, "Operations in Burma," p. 52, 3/6, LH; Slim, *Defeat into Victory*, p. 120.

[75] Ferguson, *Wild Green Earth*, p. 209.

[76] Slim, *Defeat into Victory*, p. 485; Infantry: GHQ(I) Infantry Liaison Letters, Jungle Fighting in Burma, Appendix A, No. 14, 15 January 1945, L/WS/1/778, OIOC.

[77] Major D.C. Rissik, "Forgotten Front," p. 98, 91/8/1, IWM; quoted in Thompson, *War in Burma*, p. 58.

[78] Quoted in Allen, *Burma*, p. 408.

franca for the British, Indian and imperial troops fighting in Burma, at once descriptive and prescriptive. Consider in this vein Calvert's idea of Japanese soldiers as cornered beasts, or Fergusson's slippery eels.[79] To see the Japanese in this way was practical advice for soldiers about to fight an enemy who often resisted until dead, and who fought on even when wounded or hopelessly outnumbered. At the same time, this language and way of thinking about the situation – commended to soldiers as battlefield guidance from their commanders – played its part in reproducing the no-quarter combat it warned about. Tipped off to regard their enemies as dangerous until dead, Allied soldiers were unlikely to offer the Japanese chances to surrender, or to succor their wounded, as the last chapter showed. The guidance impelled soldiers toward harsh but practical responses to tactical situations they were likely to encounter. The irony is that the advice helped reproduce the very structure of battle that made it necessary. As the Japanese knew they were going to be killed anyway, why not take an Allied soldier with them?

To the extent that authorized racisms ("orientalism") come to govern and influence battle and war, it is in large measure through providing a way to describe and think about, and so to act upon, the enemy. This may seem an obvious point. But it is an importantly different one than approaching racial ideology as evidence for the motivations of soldiers to fight. In Burma, British, Indian, and imperial troops developed much of their anti-Japanese racism after they were already fighting the Japanese. Their use of, and their imbrication within, racist discourses were occasioned by the war itself, and by the training and propaganda programs of their military institutions. British, African and Indian officers and soldiers all could be incorporated into wartime racial discourses. It was not necessary for the making of savage battle in the Asia-Pacific Wars that soldiers came from particular national or ideological contexts. In the perverse cosmopolitanism of war, *anyone* could come to enjoy killing the Japanese like flies or knocking them down like nine-pins, or hate them for their murderous stubbornness on the battlefield.

The language soldiers used reflected not only their different backgrounds, but also the ways in which their experiences changed them. Soldiers' narratives were not separate from battle and military

[79] Calvert, *Prisoners of Hope*, p. 237; Ferguson, *Wild Green Earth*, p. 206.

experience; they were products of them. The war evolved a way of thinking about and fighting the Japanese. This way of thinking shaped soldiers, how they were trained and how they behaved on the battlefield. It provided the language they used to conduct and describe the fighting. Additionally, racist constructions of the Japanese served in part as a handy outlet for anger at the unbearable situation that, it was believed, the Japanese had created by fighting with such determination. Racialized discourse named and blamed the perpetrator of all the suffering: the Japanese. As Simmel remarks, "we usually hate those whom we have caused to suffer."[80] In writing in these ways about their experiences, whether in documents at the time or in memoirs later, soldiers laid a trail that enabled others to construct after the fact the story of different nations and their soldiers at war, and of battlefields populated by essentialized characters with fixed identities and ways of behaving.

Representations of combat by participants are not exterior to combat; they are in various ways generated by it, by its demands, frustrations, and horrors. Combat is not a reality separate from those who participate in it, and upon which they can report "objectively." Combat and combat veterans are in co-constitutive relations.

From War to History

The question for inquiry should not only be, as it often is for military history and sociology, how did "Americans," "Germans," or other national subjects of a certain generation or generations perceive, experience, and report on war.[81] Of course such studies make important contributions and their findings have been widely used in this book. But in presupposing the nation and national soldiers, they risk reducing to national context actions and behaviors in war shared by many different people. In so doing, they reify the nation. If the experience of combat transforms participants *and* shapes how they write about it afterward, what are the implications for military historiography? Significantly, quite aside from wartime documents, diaries, and letters, a great deal of military history is itself produced by veterans. This includes not only the vast memoir literatures, but also the many campaign accounts and histories penned by retired commanders, officers,

---

[80] Simmel, *Conflict & the Web of Group-Affiliations*, p. 26.
[81] For recent efforts of this kind see Kindsvatter, *American Soldiers*; Rose, *Men of War*.

and other soldiers. This phenomenon is common to modern wars, and even many ancient ones. Wars can be waged discursively long into the peace.

For soldier-writers, different experiences of war produce demands for different kinds of war stories. A major divide among Anglo-American veterans of the Asia-Pacific Wars was the experience of Japanese captivity. Those who had been PoWs produced a stark memoir literature.[82] They tended to oppose postwar reconciliation initiatives and the normalization of relations with their former enemies. By contrast, those who had participated in defeating the Japanese, and who had helped annihilate their enemies in the war's final battles, were more open to and active in reconciliation. Much of their memoir literature emphasized war's adventuresome aspects.[83] Other veterans refought campaigns in dueling analyses of operational events, or considered the political and military significance of campaigns they had served in. These subjects held therapeutic value for veterans, providing a larger frame in which to find meaning for their war experience.[84]

In yet other ways, the nature of war experiences informed the political speech and activities of veterans and their associations.[85] Whether seeking state benefits, debating how a war should be remembered, what debts and obligations remained, or staking out a position on contemporary policy, veterans claim a particular meaning for their service. In so doing, they give meaning to that service. Many South Asian veterans of the Indian Army in the UK organized as the "Undivided Indian Ex-Servicemen's Association."[86] They advocated for the building of the Memorial Gates at Hyde Park Corner in London in order to recognize the contribution of imperial troops to the world wars. "Undivided" referred to the pre-partition Raj and enabled immigrants from India,

---

[82] Three chapters of Crasta's memoir have "torture" in the title. Crasta, *Eaten by the Japanese*. See also Durnford, *Branch Line to Burma*; Evans, *Roll Call at Oeyama*; Lomax, *Railway Man*.

[83] See e.g. Gilmore, *Connecticut Yankee*; Nunneley, *Tales from the King's African Rifles*; Randle, *Battle Tales from Burma*; Schlaefli, *Emergency Sahib*.

[84] See e.g. Seaman, *Battle at Sangshank*, Chapter 10 and Appendix B; Brigadier L.F. Richards, "To Redress an Injustice," 5 March 1986, 17/VII, Louis Allen Papers, DL.

[85] Mann, *Native Sons*.

[86] See e.g. Simon Rogers, "Soldiers of the Empire," *The Guardian*, 6 November 2002; R.S. Dhatt and M. S. Pujji, interviews by the author; "Memorial Gates," www.memorial-gates-london.org.uk/, accessed 26 March 2016.

Pakistan, Nepal, and elsewhere to join the association. Highlighting shared heritage over the present day divisions of South Asia, the theme of "undivided India" offered "higher meaning" for war service of a kind the veterans of national armies could take for granted. It was also useful for navigating immigrant politics and for gaining acceptance and support for British Asian communities.

Combat and Historiography in the Burma Campaign

Produced by soldiers and veterans, the materials through which we seek to understand war carry war's antagonisms; they are shaped by fighting, by specific battles, by old debts and lost arguments between commanders, invoiced in the lives of soldiers. In a way, military historiography is too close to its own subject matter. Clarity demands an exacting reflexivity, of a kind evident in the life and work of Louis Allen, a Japanese-speaking British military intelligence officer who participated in the Burma campaign and wrote its standard account, *Burma: The Longest War 1941–45*.[87] Between the first and second editions of that book, Allen became embroiled in historiographical disagreement with veterans of the Battle of Sangshak. He helps guide us through some of the ways in which history is a continuation of war by other means.

From Yorkshire, of Irish Catholic and Lithuanian Jewish parents and an impoverished upbringing, Allen became not only an important military historian but a prominent scholar of Japan and of Lafcadio Hearn.[88] He had embarked, before the war, on an education in French language and literature at Manchester University, having won a county scholarship. His talent for languages landed him in a wartime Japanese linguist training program at the School of Oriental and Asian Studies in London. He went on to serve as a translator and interrogator in India and Burma, including debriefing Japanese soldiers and officers after the war and investigating war crimes. He returned to his French studies in Manchester, and later pursued them at the Sorbonne and London, and took up an academic post in the subject at the University of Durham in the northeast of England. "But gradually the war and his own

---

[87] On Allen, see Nish, "Louis Allen, 1922–1991"; Purvis, "Louis Allen (1922–91) and Japan."
[88] Purvis, "Louis Allen (1922–91) and Japan."

experience as a participant in the war came to dominate his attention."[89] In his scholarship on the war, he made use of Japanese as well as English language sources. This involved not only Japanese official histories and other scholarship on the war, but also Allen's access to wartime documents and to Japanese veterans themselves, with whom he developed a variety of relationships.

Chapter 6 left off at the end of the battle, as the 50th Indian Parachute Brigade broke into small parties to make their way back to 14th Army lines.[90] When Brigadier Hope-Thomson came out, in a party led by the brigade major, he was promptly sent back to England as a battle exhaustion case, the euphemism for mental breakdown. In the preferred memory, and history, of many of the surviving officers, this was nothing more than a "black legend."[91] "Malicious" official reports at the time and "mischievous... semi-official histories" after the war had wrongly blamed the brigade, and its commander, for the disaster that had apparently befallen it.[92] Hope-Thomson was a casualty not of shell shock but of the corps commander's desire to displace blame. Corps had known about the oncoming Japanese, but failed to inform the brigade left in the way.[93] The first edition of Allen's *Burma* offers a substantial narrative of Sangshak, a battle that significantly delayed and disrupted the Japanese thrust on Kohima and produced important intelligence for Slim and his generals.[94] Allen reported on Hope-Thomson's mental condition: "he was on the edge of madness"; "Nerves on edge... squatted on floor of his trench"; "no fit state"; "grasped his tube of toothpaste, convinced it was his pistol."[95]

Allen's account aroused howls of protest from 50th Brigade's surviving officers. In lengthy invective, they peppered Allen with letters and refutations after *Burma*'s publication in 1984, challenging his narrative of the battle on several points. It was in part Allen's fidelity

---

[89] Nish, "Louis Allen, 1922–1991," p. xiii.

[90] See above, Chapter 6, pp. 35–43.

[91] Seaman, *Battle at Sangshak*, Chapter 10, pp. 118–122.

[92] Seaman, *Battle at Sangshak*, pp. 119, 120. The ambiguity of the significance of a battle, or even its outcome, is a characteristic feature of war. Often, only retrospectively, with careful study, might it become apparent how this or that engagement or happening helped determine the outcome of a campaign, or whether a particular battle was a "defeat" or a "victory" and in what sense.

[93] Seaman, *The Battle at Sangshak*, pp. 121–122.

[94] Allen, *Burma*, pp. 212–220 (1984 edition).

[95] Allen, *Burma*, pp. 216, 217, 219 (1984 edition).

to Japanese sources and voices, down to their reports of a curious snowfall at battle's end, which so agitated Allen's detractors.[96] They protested most of all his description of Hope-Thomson's mental condition. In their letters and accounts, 50th Brigade's officers claimed the brigadier could not have broken down during the battle because he had visited them on the perimeter, in calm and confident demeanor. He was spirited out of theater afterward so that he would not testify against the corps commander. One former officer, who had gone on to a career in the Royal Canadian Mounted Police, threatened to seek agents on Allen and his informers. Another, in a letter to Allen's editor, counted up the Japanese sources in Allen's meticulously researched work and accused Allen of being "pro Jap." "In God's name whose side is he on?" he asked.[97] (Allen's own intelligence fieldcraft and expertise had led to the ambush and slaughter of thousands of retreating Japanese at the Battle of Sittang in 1945.) The brigadier himself wrote, too. Hope-Thomson accused Allen of portraying him as "an incompetent, cowardly, hysteric," and of offering him up in his old age "as an object of scorn to my profession and the general public and of shame to my son."[98]

The 50th Brigade veterans provided elaborate justifications for apparently dubious decisions Hope-Thomson had made, contesting points of operational fact from events forty years past.[99] They objected to Allen's humanist perspective on Japanese accounts, in which he assessed and accredited or discredited them according to normal scholarly procedures.[100] They questioned taking seriously anything in the Japanese narratives.[101] Seaman (a veteran of the battle), in his effort at a definitive account, suggested there was a plot to label Hope-Thomson a nervous breakdown so that he would keep silent about

---

[96] As Allen remarked, "trying to tell the story from both sides makes me many enemies." Quoted in Nish, "Louis Allen, 1922–1991," p. xiv.

[97] Basil Manico to J.M. Dent and Sons, 20 May 1986, 17/VII, Louis Allen Papers, DL.

[98] Hope-Thomson to Allen, 5 September 1985, 17/VII, Louis Allen Papers, DL.

[99] See e.g. Brigadier L.F. Richards (ret'd) to Allen, 13 February 1986.

[100] Basil Manico to J.M. Dent and Sons, 20 May 1986, 17/VII, Louis Allen Papers, DL. As Allen remarked in a letter about his correspondence with the 50th Brigade officers, "I think they were incensed by the fact I'd used Japanese sources and described the Japanese effort at some length." Allen to [unknown], 30 August 1987, 17/VII, Louis Allen Papers, DL.

[101] R.D. Sylvester to J.M. Dent and Sons, 3 December 1985; Allen to Sir Leslie Glass, 31 March 1985, 17/VII, Louis Allen Papers, DL.

corps command's mistakes.[102] Allen responded with vigorous counter-correspondence and an appendix in his later edition detailing the points raised by 50th Brigade's officers. Confident in his sources, he did not back off on the main points of his narrative of the battle, although he worked in material that came to light as a result of his correspondence with 50th Brigade's officers and others.[103] For Allen, 50th Brigade's veterans were motivated by what they saw as a lack of recognition for their stand and sacrifice at Sangshak, at the time and afterward. From the perspective of corps command, Hope-Thomson had made a hash of it, choosing a poor position to fight on and failing to hold out as long as he should have.

Hope-Thomson's officers had wanted to remember him as he had been during the formation and training of their brigade, as their leader.[104] But Allen was right. Indeed, he and Hope-Thomson went on to have a lengthy, increasingly personal correspondence in which the retired brigadier candidly discussed his breakdown during the battle.[105] It had begun early on. An efficient and impressive officer, Hope-Thomson had risen rapidly but at the cost of time in combat commands. Amid the intensity of the fighting at Sangshak, he became progressively undone. By the end of the battle he was hiding in his trench, emerging periodically to yell "Fire the guns! Fire the guns!"[106] A few of 50th Brigade's officers knew about the breakdown. The senior officers tried to get the medical officer to declare him unfit for command.[107] Others, out on the perimeter during the fighting, had no

---

[102] Seaman, *The Battle at Sangshak*, pp. 121–122.

[103] If anything, Allen was more categorical in the revised edition about Hope-Thomson's mental state. He dropped some of the specific details, such as the toothpaste incident, but now stated that Hope-Thomson arrived back at 14th Army lines in a "state of collapse from battle exhaustion" and was admitted to hospital with a "nervous breakdown" (p. 219). Allen, *Burma*, pp. 212–220, 652–653; Allen to Peter Shellard, 5 February 1986 with enclosure "Proposed alterations to the text of *Burma: The Longest War* in respect of the chapter dealing with the battle of Sangshak; Allen to Mr. Sylvester, 6 February 1986; Allen to Sir Leslie Glass, 16 February 1986, 17/VII, Louis Allen Papers, DL.

[104] Allen remarks in a letter of 50th Brigade officers that "psychologically, the resentment at my narrative stems from causes that are often unsaid, and can't therefore be explicitly dealt with." Allen to Peter Shellard, 8 March 1986, 17/VII, Louis Allen Papers, DL.

[105] See in particular Hope Thomson to Allen, 11 September 1985; Hope Thomson to Allen, 17 February 1990, 17/VII, Louis Allen Papers, DL.

[106] Sir Leslie Glass, "The Brigade Major's Story," 17/VII, Louis Allen Papers, DL.

[107] He refused on grounds of the harm it would do to Hope Thomson's career. Sir Leslie Glass, "The Brigade Major's Story," 17/VII, Louis Allen Papers, DL.

idea about their commander's state of mind. Not long after the battle and his escape, the brigade major told the story to a British colonial official, Sir Leslie Glass, while drinking on a veranda in Delhi. The brigade major poured "forth without bitterness but in anguish."[108] Hope-Thomson recovered quickly and, although demoted, went on to serve with distinction in the European theater in 1944–45 as an adjutant and battalion commander. He remarked after the war that "I would go through the whole campaign in Europe again rather than that seven days in Sangshak. The tempo and the fierceness of the fighting did not compare."[109]

It was his scholarly rigor that enabled Allen to reconstruct what happened at Sangshak. He refused to take primary accounts at face value, whether British or Japanese.[110] As he remarked of his relations with Japan, "one of the privileges of friendship is criticism."[111] He took seriously, in precocious ways for his times, the problem of cultural difference and understanding others. His own wartime efforts to comprehend the Japanese and their language, in order to fight them, were practical precursors to his driving scholarly interests and ancillary activities. Allen was active in the Burma Campaign Fellowship Group and other efforts to sponsor visits and exchanges between Japanese and British veterans of the campaign.[112] These visits eventually produced some of the material used in this book, such as the publication of Japanese veterans' accounts in English translation.[113]

The reconciliation efforts were controversial among British officer veterans, including those interviewed for this book. Some refused to buy Japanese-made cars and other products, and had little interest in

---

[108] Sir Leslie Glass, "The Brigade Major's Story," 17/VII, Louis Allen Papers, DL.
[109] Quoted in Victor Brookes, Games and War, p. 5, Mss Eur CO770, OIOC. Brookes served in the 153rd Indian Parachute Battalion at Sangshak. He asked Hope-Thomson after the war how the fighting in the two theatres compared.
[110] See e.g. Allen, "A Personal Postscript by Louis Allen."
[111] Allen, "A Personal Postscript by Louis Allen," p. 202.
[112] Nish, "Louis Allen, 1922–1991," p. xv.
[113] See e.g. Grant and Tamayama, *Burma 1942*; Nunneley and Tamayama, *Tales by Japanese Soldiers*. In writing *The Battle at Sangshak*, Seaman used Japanese sources made available by the Burma Campaign Fellowship Group, including from a Japanese veteran of Burma who worked closely with Allen after the war, Masao Hirakubo. Seaman also participated in a visit to London in 1984 by Japanese veterans of the 58th Regiment, who had fought 50th Brigade at Sangshak. Seaman, *The Battle at Sangshak*, p. 130. Allen shared his hard-won access to Japanese sources with other scholars. See e.g. Nish, "Louis Allen, 1922–1991," p. xv.

meeting with those they had fought decades back. They cited Japanese battlefield behavior, things done to friends, as well as the treatment of Allied PoWs. They opposed trade and other diplomatic relations with Japan. Others were interested to go along on the reconciliation trips, feeling that scores had been settled: what hurt the Japanese gave out in 1942–43, they received back with interest in 1944–45.

However much Allen and his 50th Brigade critics might have differed on the course and meaning of events at Sangshak, and whatever the disputes among veterans over reconciliation, all shared a continuing involvement in the war. Some were still prosecuting its antagonisms on into the peace, while others were seeking to understand and overcome them. What they were trying to do with the war was shaped by their experience of it. Before being sent to Burma, Allen greatly feared the Japanese. During the war, seeing them in their diseased, emaciated, and defeated state in the later stages, he came to pity them. After the war, standing before a quaking Japanese serviceman who was probably a war criminal, he saw only a "human being" whom he had helped reduce to a "state of almost animal terror."[114] Allen's experiences of the war produced him as a veteran and scholar, with the questions and perspectives he had. "His historical writings stemmed as much from this personal experience as from archival research," remembered a historian who knew him.[115] Allen's histories were translated into Japanese by Japanese veterans, his allies in reconciliation and understanding, pursuing their own memory wars in Japan. Dying of cancer in 1991, in a wheelchair, Allen's last public act was to give a lecture on the Burma campaign at the Imperial War Museum in London. The war experiences of soldiers and veterans animate the production of materials for understanding war, and shape many of the histories and accounts we have of particular wars.

Disintegration to Reflexivity

The author of the epigram of this chapter, Charles Carfrae, helps summarize its themes. In the late 1940s, he wrote the lines from which the epigram was taken as part of a draft memoir about his time as commander of a Nigerian Chindit column in Burma. War memoirs

[114] Allen, "Innocents Abroad," p. xxxvi.
[115] Nish, "Louis Allen, 1922–1991," p. xiii.

and novels sometimes originate from drafts veterans write shortly after returning from war, but which are revised for publication or find publication much later in life, if at all, often after retirement.[116] When Carfrae had come out of Burma he was, by his own account, "intensely depressed... gloomy." He remained "very depressed" for about a year.[117] Writing out his experiences was one of the ways of working through them, of overcoming or finding a place for them. The Japanese, he wrote bitterly, "seemed to lack all human warmth," they "butchered wounded chindits."[118]

But in the version revised and published as *Chindit Column* forty years later, Carfrae backed off the emphasis on Japanese inhumanity, offering more unambiguous qualifications. He and his fellow officers only "thought" the Japanese lacked human warmth.[119] These reflections on Japanese inhumanity occur in the text after he relates an incident in which he ordered his troops to burn rather than bury forty dead Japanese. The job was bungled: "Expecting nothing but bones and ashes when the flames died, instead we found lumps of roasted, blackened flesh still recognizably human, grotesquely crowned with bleached steel helmets like inverted pots."[120] This failure to properly dispose of the remains of enemy soldiers became an occasion for commenting on the enemy's apparent lack of humanity. The Japanese were themselves somehow to blame for his actions.

At the same time, Carfrae used the passage to suggest that putative Japanese fanaticism showed up the Europeans, who were in comparison not so committed to their ideals or as ready to die for them as the Japanese were for theirs: "since we could neither comprehend nor equal [Japanese determination], we were indeed inclined to dismiss the enemy's preternatural, indeed sometimes useless bravery and spirit of self-sacrifice as 'fanaticism.'"[121] This dimension of the passage comes

---

[116] See e.g. Marlantes, *Matterhorn*. Marlantes wrote the first draft of the novel immediately after his military service in Vietnam while on a Rhodes scholarship in the early 1970s. It was then revised over many years before publication in 2010. *Matterhorn* Seminar with Karl Marlantes, London School of Economics, 13 March 2015.

[117] Charles Carfrae, IWM Interview, Reel 4, 10467, IWM.

[118] Charles Carfrae, "Dark Company," p. 128, 80/49/1, IWM.

[119] Carfrae, *Chindit Column*, p. 119.

[120] Ibid. Japanese dead were often left unburied in Burma. See Randle, *Battle Tales*, p. 68.

[121] Carfrae, *Chindit Column*, p. 120.

out with much greater clarity in the later, published version but is in both. His reflections on his enemy's humanity furthered a reflexive attitude toward his own. As Allen remarks of the qualities of a good war memoir, for the author there is "value in a retreat from immediacy, to take stock of what his experiences mean *now*."[122]

Carfrae could never quite leave the war behind. As he told an interviewer in 1985, he became "unwell" for about a week every year even though there was nothing physically wrong. "I recognize that this is a kind of hangover from my Burma days."[123] Carfare leaves us a finely observed war memoir, evidence of the nature of colonial armies and combat, of Chindit expeditions and the Burma campaign. But he produced it to make sense of his own war, and the text bears the marks. So does our evidence of war carry the scars of its participants.

---

[122] Allen, "A Personal Postscript by Louis Allen," p. 200. He goes on: "Not that he should alter them; but that he should put them down just as they were and then see them afresh."

[123] Charles Carfrae, IWM Interview, Reel 4, 10467, IWM.

8 | *Cosmopolitan Military Histories and Sociologies*

It was part of our Bushido code.

– A British officer[1]

What can we now do in military history and sociology as a consequence of the analysis in the preceding pages? What do we see when we situate soldiers and armies in cosmopolitan rather than national terms, when we make them at home in the world? We can begin with the 20th Sikh Anti-Aircraft Battery in Hong Kong, whom we last encountered mutinying over steel helmets.[2] They were captured in December 1941 and recruited into Japanese service. Sent to Burma, they engaged Allied aircraft during the second Chindit operation in the spring of 1944. Some of the Sikh gunners were captured again, this time by Brigadier Mike Calvert's Chindit columns battling for Mogaung. Calvert found the Sikhs "an emaciated, miserable lot, completely resigned to whatever fate was due to them."[3] They told him, variously, that they would have been shot had they not joined the Japanese, that they were led astray by Japanese promises, and that they had only volunteered in order get back to India and their families.

Short of personnel, Calvert decided to make use of the Sikhs. In line with the techniques used to raise the Indian National Army, he began by hinting they could recover their self-respect as soldiers, and moved on to the stick and carrot.[4] He told them he would temporarily give

---

[1] Michael Demetriadi, interview by the author.
[2] See above, Chapter 2, pp. 61–62.   [3] Calvert, *Prisoners of Hope*, p. 210.
[4] Calvert told the Sikhs that he had known their unit before the war and that they were efficient and accurate gunners. He went on: "I had noticed that under the Japs they had been very inaccurate when firing at us. I considered that this must be because in their hearts of hearts they did not want to shoot at us." Calvert, *Prisoners of Hope*, p. 210. Like Thimayya in the kidney soup episode and Randle in the elephant dung affair, Calvert provided a public narrative and a legitimation for compliance from the soldiers, regardless of whether they had actually been aiming at Allied aircraft. See above, Chapter 2, pp. 61, 73.

them the benefit of the doubt and not have them shot if they agreed to serve as stretcher bearers. Although they would still be tried for treachery after the war, he would put in a good word if they served. Calvert had neither the authority to nor the intention of shooting the Sikhs, which they may well have realized. But he secured their willingness to be put again under discipline and to function as soldiers in an ancillary if dangerous task. Calvert's brigade suffered heavily at Mogaung. The Sikhs "did serve us well, but they never smiled. I did put in a good word for them. They were treated leniently."[5]

Far from elite shock troops, the Sikhs provided the Japanese and the British with elementary forms of wartime military labor. Survival, self-interest, and relative comfort are likely motives for their moves from surrender, to Japanese service, to British service again. We would not look in the first instance to the political situation in the Punjab, or to religion or culture, that is, to "Sikh" sources to explain these decisions. That would be to risk ascribing common tendencies in stressful and life-threatening situations to a particular society. I have sought to argue something similar for military discipline and the will to combat. Militaries and battlefields are sites of limited choices and harsh constraints for everyone involved. Battle makes common demands, and generates similar responses, among those who participate in it. Battle is no respecter of nations.

That said, the fate of the 20th Sikh AA is demonstrably "Sikh" in all kinds of ways, if by that we mean attention to time and place, and to the question of how the soldiers of the 20th AA *experienced* their situation. Shaped by colonial society and economy, by Sikh culture and its masculinities, and subject to the Raj's invented traditions and politics, the Sikhs of the 20th AA navigated the undoing of British Asia. In letting go the "army vs. society" debate, the co-constitution of army and society comes into view. Armies and their articulations with social context are historical. They produce bodies of troops with a particular character. These bodies of troops go on to have histories of their own.

Co-constitution enables accounts that do not have to choose between "army" and "society" but which can put these fields into the same analytic frame, even when they are imperial and transnational in scope. Co-constitution positions national and other militaries, like the colonial ones largely considered here, on an equivalent analytic

---

[5] Calvert, *Prisoners of Hope*, p. 210.

footing. All armed forces are constituted out of social contexts for use in political projects of various kinds.

The first contribution, then, is an approach to military inquiry which reifies neither nation nor army. A second puts tradition and ritual at the center of modernity's leading institution. In rote instruction and drill, military practitioners have reliable procedures (variably and historically applied) for training soldiers, generating solidarity, and ensuring discipline, of an elementary kind. What makes armies work are their ancient techniques. Peoples around the world have experienced and conducted organized warfare; there are many historical variants and trajectories of drill and combat, a fact easily obscured by the global dominance of Western forms in recent centuries. From such a cosmopolitan standpoint, it becomes possible to see the common forces at work shaping soldiers' actions on the battlefield, and to strip away not only some of the chauvinism which governs military writing, but also the Western triumphalism.[6] Below, some Welsh "samurai" in the First Arakan help draw out and illustrate this postcolonial critique.

A third contribution concerns the politics of armed force. One of the outcomes of the methodological nationalism of military history and sociology is a kind of territorialization of violence. The assumption that armed forces and their histories come in trinitarian packages, of state, army and nation, allows national politics seemingly to underwrite and account for soldiers' violence. War becomes about peoples fighting for their homelands.[7] This book relates different military histories than those of the Western and national state. British imperial forces were part of the global military system of the British Empire. Armed force was organized on a transnational basis, from a variety of populations, to secure a world order project.

In such circumstances, the politics of the army took on different valence. Strategically interlaced with colonial society and designed to serve the interests of distant rulers, the army did not rely on politics for discipline or fighting spirit. For colonial soldiers, service in the army was not about the wars of peoples and homelands. World War II marked a transition from colonial armies directly officered by Europeans to the "advice and support" of client, proxy, and other subordinate armed forces characteristic of the Cold War and after. The politics

---

[6] Cf. Hanson, *Western Way of War*; *Carnage and Culture*.
[7] Barkawi, "Peoples, Homelands, and Wars?"

of anti-colonial nationalism, so evident in the final years of the British Indian Army, undermined one system for the transnational organization of armed force and made way for another. The simplicity and cosmopolitanism of army discipline made it adaptable to either. We are left with the irony that disciplined armed force, so crucial to politics, relies on elementary forms outside their realm.

Oriental Styles

In their classic military sociological account from the Korean War, Samuel L. Meyers and Albert D. Biderman ran into the problem of ascribing common human tendencies to a particular society. They were trying to account for the "unprecedented" and "strange" behavior of Chinese communist soldiers.[8] What puzzled them was the combination of spirited combat behavior and unwillingness to surrender, on the one hand, with a "docile and cooperative" disposition as prisoners, on the other.[9] Chinese PoWs expressed discontent with the communist regime. "What was there about the system of military-political control that could produce such excellent soldiers in the face of what seemed to be such widespread dissatisfaction?"[10] The same question might be asked about colonial armies.

Meyers and Biderman's solution was an orientalist combination of primary group theory and national style. The People's Liberation Army created strong primary groups which fought well, but the soldiers did not internalize communist values. When captured, they exhibited "the social behavior of the Oriental": they conformed out of a desire for social harmony, they wanted to avoid "loss of face," and they desired social recognition through group membership.[11] The Chinese soldiers were not "modern," according to Morris Janowitz, writing in his foreword to the Meyers and Biderman volume.[12]

---

[8] Meyers and Biderman, "Introduction" in Meyers and Biderman, *Mass Behavior in Battle and Captivity*, p. xvii.

[9] Ibid., p. xxvii.   [10] Ibid., p. xvii.

[11] Meyers and Biderman, "Introduction" in Meyers and Biderman, eds., *Mass Behavior in Battle and Captivity*, p. xxviii-xxix; Samuel Meyers and William Bradbury, "The Political Behavior of Korean and Chinese Prisoners of war in the Korean Conflict: A Historical Analysis" in Meyers and Biderman, *Mass Behavior in Battle and Captivity*, pp. 243–244, 317.

[12] Morris Janowitz, "Foreward" in Meyers and Biderman, *Mass Behavior in Battle and Captivity*, p. vi.

Biderman had pursued a different strategy in his companion volume on US PoWs in Korea, *March to Calumny*. There he was concerned to show that the cooperative behavior of US PoWs towards their captors did not reflect defects in US society. Rather, as Janowitz put it, "Americans in Communist prisoner-of-war compounds behaved very much like other human beings in terms of the amount of shock they experienced and the severity of the pressure applied."[13] American soldiers behaved like "other human beings," while Chinese behavior reflected the "social-psychological character of the Chinese."[14] Chinese PoWs bargaining for perks reflected a specifically Oriental propensity: "The Oriental assumes that he can make bargains with the representatives of power, trading his active assistance for personal security and small favors."[15] Resignation was yet another indication of the Oriental character of the Chinese PoWs.[16] Innate national character is invoked to account for common behaviors in extreme circumstances. This move both reinforces, and draws on, our image of the world as consisting of different territorial peoples and their styles of fighting. In this case, the military sociologists used the binaries of West/Orient and modernity/tradition to categorize and describe national styles.[17]

Needless to say, Western PoWs have been observed behaving very like Meyers and Biderman's Chinese. British PoWs in Germany during the First World War bartered for better conditions from their guards with food from their Red Cross parcels.[18] According to Henry Faulk, who studied PoWs in the UK during and after World War II, German prisoners tried to conform to group norms and were deeply desirous of group membership and acceptance. They were bewildered by defeat and capture. But, as one German officer wrote of his fellow prisoners, "Their basic rule is Not to Lose Face, no matter what the cost."[19]

Military inquiry, with its comparative national histories and sociologies, is particularly prone to reading common human capacities as

---

[13] Ibid., p. v.
[14] Meyers and Biderman, "Introduction" in Meyers and Biderman, *Mass Behavior in Battle and Captivity*, p. xxvii.
[15] Ibid., p. xviii.　　[16] Ibid.
[17] For Meyers and Biderman, the Chinese prisoners displayed "traditional orientations to authority." "Introduction" in Meyers and Biderman, eds., *Mass Behavior in Battle and Captivity*, p. xxvii; Cf. Said, *Orientalism*.
[18] Jones, *Violence against Prisoners of War*, pp. 267–268.
[19] Faulk, *Group Captives*, pp. 67, 73, 175, 198, 205.

national and cultural difference. Soldiers, like PoWs, are easy fodder for comparative national study. They are conveniently marked out by race, uniform, and the antagonisms of war. It can appear that their behavior derives from the specificities of the society they came from. Actions that might reflect wider commonalities with "other human beings" are instead reduced to effects of particular societies, cultures, and politics. Similarity is read as difference. Orientalism turns this gap between nations into a chasm: Western ones vs. the rest.

The Banzai Charge in Postcolonial Perspective

The answer to this problem is not the opposite mistake, to read historical difference as always evidence of underlying human commonality. If I have emphasized similarities among soldiers from different backgrounds, it is because of the tendency to national chauvinisms in military inquiry. What I want to do now is show the purchase postcolonial critique can offer on the problem of similarity and difference in military behavior. The "banzai charge" has been understood as a signature Japanese tactic, embodying Japanese national character. But the rush of infantry across ground swept by fire might be termed a "banzai charge" if conducted by Japanese, or instead the climax of a carefully planned attack if by Europeans. How do we tell the difference? What of infantry attacks on the Western Front in the First World War, for example?

Like their refusal to surrender, the Japanese preference for repeated costly frontal assaults – the banzai charge – was cited by Allied soldiers as evidence of Japanese courage but also of their rigidity and stupidity.[20] The Japanese were trying to overcome Allied material superiority with fighting spirit. But it is also the case that any infantry attack involves rushes across fire swept ground. At stake here is a tension between the group spirit required for such a rush, and the tactical rationality associated with organized warfare, especially its modern Western form. The banzai charge trope locates spirit on the Japanese side and retains rationality for the Allies.[21] But is this to project on to the Japanese dimensions of Western military behavior we choose to

---

[20] Bergerud, *Touched with Fire*, pp. 131–132; Fergusson, *Wild Green Earth*, p. 213; Linderman, *World Within War*, pp. 164–165.

[21] See Barkawi and Laffey, "Postcolonial Moment," pp. 335–336, on the "national-political approach" for a similar example.

obscure? What of rigidity and stupidity? Distinctions between the West and non-West can profoundly mislead when it comes to the nature of soldiering and warfare.

Here it is useful to go back to the First Arakan in 1942–43, discussed in Chapter 4, and in particular the fighting at Donbaik, a moment when the Japanese still appeared more adept at modern warfare than did the Allies. (See Map 4.1) In the invasions of Malaya and Burma, the Japanese had maneuvered even in densely forested terrain. Their columns would move around British Indian positions, through terrain the British commanders considered impassable, and set up blocks in the rear. When the British Indian forces went on the offensive in the Arakan, they limited their movements to the coastal strips on either side of the Mayu Peninsula, considering the mountainous central spine unsuitable for large formations. This allowed the Japanese to hold up the British Indian offensive by defending the coastal strips alone.

A mile north of Donbaik the coastal strip narrowed to a thousand yards, much of it consisting of open paddy. There the Japanese built a carefully sited, well-camouflaged, and skillfully constructed bunker complex, known to the British as Forward Defensive Locality (FDL) Chaung. (See Map 8.1) "In this spot, for fifty days," Allen wrote, "the Japanese stood off attack after attack by massed battalions of 14th Indian Division."[22] FDL Chaung was a mostly dry watercourse, in places nine feet deep, which ran from the jungle-clad foothills to the water's edge. A secondary *chaung*, running off to the northeast, intersected the main one 200 yards from the jungle, forming a triangle. The Japanese heavily fortified FDL Chaung with bunkers and slit trenches, and on the secondary *chaung* built two particularly strong positions known as Sugar 4 and Sugar 5. At Sugar 5, the Japanese hollowed out an existing mound, while at Sugar 4 they dug their bunkers into the banks of the *chaung*.[23] "We had made many bunkers in China," a Japanese soldier at Donbaik wrote, "but this time we made stronger ones by working day and night as we expected the British would have many big guns."[24] To the east, FDL Chaung was overlooked first by two foothills, the North and South Knobs, on which the Japanese prepared positions, and yet further on by two steep, densely wooded hills,

---

[22] Allen, *Burma*, p. 98.   [23] Thompson, *War in Burma*, p. 49.
[24] Senior Private Takeo Kawakami, quoted in Nunneley and Tamayama, *Tales by Japanese Soldiers*, p. 124.

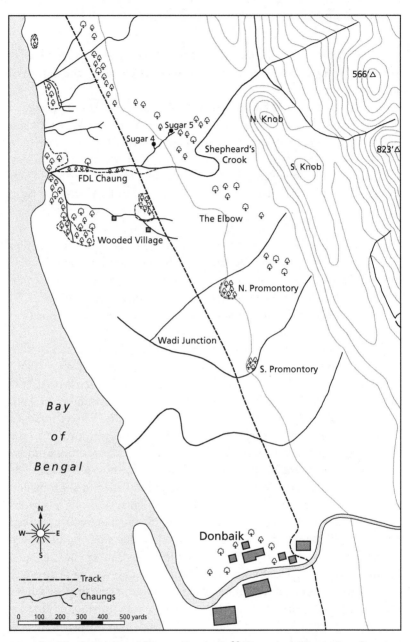

Map 8.1 The Japanese position at Donbaik:[25] Sugar 4 and Sugar 5 are between and just to the north of FDL Chaung and Shepheard's Crook. British Indian forces attacked from the north.

---

[25] Map from Thompson, *War in Burma*, p. 47 and from Kirby, *The War Against Japan*, Vol. II, facing p. 340.

where the Japanese placed mortars, field guns, and machine guns. The Japanese positions were mutually supporting, covering likely routes of advance with interlocking and overlapping fields of fire; "it was impossible for assaulting troops to reach a bunker without coming under fire from at least two others."[26] From Sugar 4 and Sugar 5 enfilading fire covered the ground in front of the main *chaung*. The bunkers were built with thick log and earth walls and ceilings four or five feet thick: "quite impervious to bombardment by field guns and even the direct hit of a medium bomb rarely penetrated."[27] Camouflaged expertly, their garrisons numbered between five and twenty men, armed with light and medium machine guns, rifles, and grenades.

Over the Top

The stage was set for a replay of the First World War. Many of the British generals involved, like Noel Irwin, the overall commander of the Arakan offensive, were veterans of the trenches. The first attacks on FDL Chaung were put in by 47th Indian Brigade on 7, 8, and 9 January 1943. They tried in company and then battalion strength, with artillery support, to take the position but failed at the cost of around a hundred casualties. The Japanese commanders resorted to a common tactic when faced by attackers with strong artillery. When the shelling preceding an attack began, a sentry was left in each position while the rest of the troops took shelter in specially prepared caves and stout bunkers to the rear. As the shelling lifted for the enemy infantry attack to be put in, the defenders rushed back to their frontline bunkers and awaited orders to begin firing.[28]

Lord Wavell, the Commander-in-Chief, India, impressed on Irwin and his division commander, Major General Wilfrid Lloyd, the need to take Donbaik. Supported by more artillery and a company of medium machine guns from the MG Battalion/9th Jats, 47th Brigade put in another attack on 18–19 January, led by 1/7th Rajput and 1/Inniskilling Fusiliers. "C" Company of the 1/7th Rajput was decimated attacking across open ground, while "A" Company managed to get atop the two knobs, only to come under withering fire from a previously unseen machine gun. Initially just twelve men came back from "A" Company, out of around eighty.[29]

[26] Slim, *Defeat into Victory*, p. 152.   [27] Ibid.
[28] Thompson, *War in Burma*, p. 48.
[29] Madan, *The Arakan Operations 1942–1945*, pp. 36, 39.

The battlefield began to offer up tropical versions of the horrors of the Western Front. On 18 January, a platoon of Inniskillings had tried to advance along the beach under cover of smoke. The Japanese put a heavy concentration of mortar and gun fire right into the middle of the smoke. Over the next two months the rotting corpses of this platoon remained where they fell, visible from the British and Indian lines.[30] As new units were brought in to replace 47th Brigade's shattered battalions, they saw their predecessors' dead strewn in front of the Japanese positions. Long-billed vultures tugged out guts through the bulging battledress worn by the corpses. Offshore, a British newsman spotted sharks feasting on a windfall of Inniskilling dead washed out to sea from the tidal *chaungs*.[31]

In 1941, the Commander-in-Chief of the Indian Army, General Sir Claude Auchinleck, had lambasted the "blind conservatism" of its infantry officers. The idea that frontal attacks across open ground on a dug-in enemy would be successful with just one more battery of artillery, just one more infantry battalion, was the forlorn hope of World War I. "The last war proved the fallacy and the uselessness of [this] method of attack, but many infantry would still seem to prefer to be killed than to think out or accept a looser, more skillful method of approach."[32] As if to prove Auchinleck's point, Irwin wrote afterward that the attacks failed to take Donbaik because "there were not enough troops following each other up." It was not "the frontages that were wrong, but the depths."[33] Irwin wished he had greater mass to throw at the Japanese defenses.[34]

In February, 55th Indian Brigade put in two more attacks, one with four infantry battalions. Both were frontal assaults lacking in tactical subtlety. At one point, the 2/1st Punjabis managed to get atop the bunkers at FDL Chaung but the Japanese called down mortar and artillery fire on their own positions. While the Japanese rode out the shelling inside their bunkers, the Punjabis suffered heavily out in the

[30] Major D.C. Rissik, "Forgotten Front," pp. 70, 75, 91/8/1, IWM.

[31] Rankin, *Telegram from Guernica*, pp. 226, 228, 234.

[32] Notes by His Excellency the Commander-in-Chief on the Training of Infantry, Army in India Training Memorandum, No. 6, April 1941, L/MIL/17/5/2240, OIOC.

[33] Lt. Gen. N.M.S. Irwin, 2/1, Irwin to Wavell, 20 March 1943, P139, IWM; quoted in Allen, *Burma*, p. 102.

[34] Lt. Gen. N.M.S. Irwin, 2/1, Irwin to Wavell, 9 and 20 March 1943; "Note on our capacity to operate offensively against Burma," P139, IWM.

open and were forced to withdraw. At this point, Irwin advised Wavell that the goals of the First Arakan campaign were "no longer practicable" nor worth the cost in casualties.[35]

Unaware of just how demoralized his own forces were, Wavell also underestimated the Japanese. He wanted to restore the shaken prestige of the Raj and its Indian Army. "I am more worried about the morale aspect both of the troops and to India as a whole than anything else," Wavell wrote.[36] Wavell pushed for further offensive operations on the Mayu Peninsula well beyond the point at which they were likely to succeed, while downplaying the threat posed by a Japanese counterstroke. Wavell ordered Irwin to overwhelm Donbaik by sheer weight of numbers, ironically the Western image of an Oriental strategy.[37] He wrote to Irwin on 7 March telling him to continue with his offensive efforts: "I should like to finish up this campaigning season with a real success which will show both our own troops and the Jap that we can and mean to be top dog."[38] Were the Japanese to have behaved in a similarly self-defeating way, they would have been accused of trying to "save face." One British officer in the Arakan reproached his generals with just this charge.[39]

The "Mighty Warriors from Wales"[40]

On the very same day that Wavell had written Irwin about being "top dog," the Japanese launched their counter-offensive in the Arakan. By 17 March, ten days later, they were well on their way to trapping British Indian forces in the Mayu Peninsula. In these circumstances, the 14th Indian Division's all-British 6th Brigade put in a final, futile attack at Donbaik on 18 March, led by the 1/Royal Welch Fusiliers (1/RWF).

Even if the attack had been successful, 6th Brigade would still have had to turn around and fight its way out of the Japanese block behind it. Lloyd had wanted a more creative plan of attack than hurling 6th

---

[35] Lt. Gen. N.M.S. Irwin, 2/1, Irwin to Wavell, 6 and 23 February 1943, P139, IWM.

[36] IWM P139, Lt. Gen. N.M.S. Irwin, 2/1, Wavell to Irwin, 9 April 1943.

[37] Kirby, *War Against Japan*, Vol. II, p. 334.

[38] Lt. Gen. N.M.S. Irwin, 2/1, Wavell to Irwin, 7 March 1943, P139, IWM; quoted in Allen, *Burma*, p. 101.

[39] Major D.C. Rissik, "Forgotten Front," pp. 84, 117, 91/8/1, IWM.

[40] A phrase used by West African troops to describe 1/RWF. Michael Demetriadi, interview by the author.

Brigade's battalions at FDL Chaung along the narrow frontage of the coastal plain. At Slim's suggestion, he considered using two battalions from 71st Indian Brigade to clear the high ground on the top of the Mayu range, removing Japanese positions from the hills overlooking FDL Chaung and opening up the Japanese flank. Irwin, however, disapproved of this plan. He was convinced that another overwhelming infantry attack on a narrow front would finally dislodge the Japanese from Donbaik.[41] Irwin wanted the "extreme of concentration" with "sufficient waves of troops" to "swamp" the enemy positions.[42] A "white peril," so to speak, would engulf the outnumbered Japanese defenders. Like Lloyd's own commanders Irwin believed that no troops could operate on the densely covered, almost perpendicular slopes of the Mayu Mountains.[43]

A.H. Williams, a schoolmaster and talented Territorial, or reserve, officer, was the commander of 1/RWF. Described as "very Welsh," he treated his soldiers like a fair and benevolent teacher and was "extremely loved by the men."[44] On 7 March, Williams surveyed the Japanese positions:

The line here is extraordinary. The Japs hold a *chaung* running from the jungle area to the sea . . . the two strong points are called Sugar 4 and Sugar 5, the latter being really formidable. All that can be seen is a mound of earth with a dead tree standing on the top . . . On the sea flank we face the enemy in the 1916 style at a distance of about 300 yards but on the jungle side we are at right angles to the *chaung* and only 60 yards from [Sugar 5] . . . From the Twin Knobs the whole battlefield as far as Donbaik can be seen very clearly. There is no difficulty identifying the Jap positions on many of which the camouflage of leaves has now turned brown. The gunners were busy shelling . . . their shells were falling [plum] on the target but they say they have no effect at all.[45]

---

[41] Allen, *Burma*, p. 101.

[42] Lt. Gen. N.M.S. Irwin, 2/1, Irwin to Wavell, 9 and 20 March 1943, P139, IWM.

[43] Lt. Gen. N.M.S. Irwin, 2/1, Irwin to Wavell, 9 March 1943, P139, IWM.

[44] Rankin, *Telegram from Guernica*, p. 234; Michael Demetriadi, interview by the author. Demetriadi was the intelligence officer for 1/RWF at Donbaik. Of Williams one of his soldiers remembered, "He was a good man . . . always walked about efficiently, always looked like a soldier." Ron Thomas, interview by the author.

[45] Diary of Lt. Col. A.H. Williams, 7 March 1943, 3722, RWF. The World War I analogy at Donbaik also struck David Rissik serving with 2/DLI. Major D.C. Rissik, "Forgotten Front," pp. 69–70, 91/8/1, IWM.

Williams and 6th Brigade's commander, Brigadier R.V.C. Cavendish, did not want any artillery preparation for their attack on 18 March, a view supported by artillery officers. They preferred the advantage of surprise. Preliminary bombardment would not destroy the Japanese positions and would alert them to an imminent attack. Irwin overruled Williams and Cavendish as he had Lloyd. "I have definitely lost my artillery battle," Williams noted in his diary after being called back to Indin to hear a talk by Irwin on 15 March. Irwin, like Wavell, was most concerned that the campaign end on an "advancing note."[46]

So it was that, in the manner of the last war, the Royal Welch Fusiliers went over the top on the morning of the 18th, after an impressive but ineffectual bombardment that had dumped 124 tons of shells on the Japanese positions.[47] Their job was to take the triangle area, including Sugar 4 and 5, formed by the junction of the main and secondary *chaungs*. 1/RWF's "A" Company got atop the strongpoints, but, as before, the Japanese called down fire on their own positions to clear off the attackers. "Our men were falling like flies but our targets had all vanished underground," remembered a Fusilier who survived the attack.[48] As in earlier attacks, previously unobserved Japanese machine guns opened fire at the decisive moment. "D" Company made it into the secondary *chaung* only to be pinned down in it by fire from all sides. "C" Company, held by machine gun fire, was unable to advance much beyond its start line. With "D" Company cut-off and the attack faltering, Williams committed his reserve, "B" Company, in an effort to link up with "D" Company and clear the Japanese machine guns holding back "C" Company. To communicate with his cut-off troops, Williams got hold of the loudspeaker from an Indian Field Broadcasting Unit normally used for propaganda broadcasts to the Japanese.[49] Williams' Welsh warbled over the battlefield and "D" Company answered with

---

[46] Irwin quoted by Williams, 15 March 1943, 3722, RWF. Irwin claimed that it was Lloyd who overruled the plans for no preparatory artillery bombardment for the 18 March attack. See Lt. Gen. N.M.S. Irwin, 2/3, Irwin to Woodburn Kirby, 4 January 1956, P139, IWM.

[47] Major D.C. Rissik, "Forgotten Front," p. 76, 91/8/1, IWM.

[48] Fusilier W.C. Smith, "1939–1945 The Unsung Heroes: A Personal Account," MS, pp. 21–22. Ron Thomas observed "A" Company's attack: "They were all out in the open, you could see some of the lads running back and to, you know, no cover. They were being fired on from positions they couldn't see." Interview by the author.

[49] Kemp and Graves, *The Red Dragon*, pp. 51–52. The Japanese also used loudspeakers for propaganda. At Donbaik they played well known tunes for

rifle shots to indicate its position and strength. But "B" Company only advanced about forty yards before it too was pinned down and then accidentally strafed by the RAF.

At this point Lieutenant David Graves, a platoon leader in "B" Company, tried to turn the tide of battle single-handedly, in a quixotic and suicidal display of valor. When his father, the poet, writer and First World War veteran Robert Graves, said "goodbye to all that," he did not mean the regiment in which he had served, the Royal Welch Fusiliers. For the elder Graves, who spent much of his life in Mallorca, the affectual bonds of military service exercised more power than those of national society.[50] Graves got his son a posting with the Royal Welch after the war had started.[51] Sent to a tragic and absurd re-enactment of his father's war in the Arakan, the younger Graves tried to take out the Japanese positions pinning down B Company. Williams observed much of the action:

Then David Graves decided to try his own hand. Taking with him Sgt. 81 Jones and Fus. 29 Jones he sallied forth with a handful of bombs. I saw Fus. Jones go over the top firing a Bren gun from the hip followed by David who bombed his way into a small trench whence he began to throw grenades into another trench about 15 yards further on. To my horror I saw a bomb being thrown at him but fortunately it landed short and David had already ducked.[52]

Both Sergeant Jones and Fusilier Jones were wounded. Graves returned to replenish his supply of grenades, remarking to Williams that he thought the opposition was small. Graves went forward again, apparently alone, to try and grenade his way into further enemy positions.

the homesick British soldiers and taunted them with the thought that American soldiers garrisoned in the UK were sleeping with their wives and girlfriends. See Davies, "Memories," p. 59.

[50] Robert Graves, *Goodbye to All That*. Unlike his friend and fellow officer Siegfried Sassoon, who rendered them the "Flintshire Fusiliers" in his autobiographical trilogy, Robert Graves maintained his ties to the Royal Welch. It was "[t]he only organisation I've been proud to belong to," he wrote to a fusilier who was with his son at Donbaik. Robert Graves to Reuben Jones, 9 June 1964. Copy provided to author by Rueben Jones. See also Sassoon, *Memoirs of a Fox-Hunting Man*; *Memoirs of an Infantry Officer*; and *Sherston's Progress*.

[51] He wrote to the Colonel of the Regiment asking him to take on his son as an officer. Major-General J.R. Minshull Ford to Robert Graves, 20 January 1940, 3635, Graves Collection, RWF.

[52] Diary of Lt. Col. A.H. Williams, 18 March 1943, 3722, RWF.

He was seen falling, possibly shot through the head, but his body was never recovered.

At this point, Williams withdrew his battered "C" Company and planned a night attack with two companies from 1/Royal Scots to link up with "D" Company trapped in the secondary *chaung*. The attack went in after midnight. Mortar and automatic fire exploded into darkness and pierced it with tracer rounds. The Scots NCOs could be heard encouraging their men forward, "Come on, you fuckers, get up!" But the Royal Scots did not make it far past the start lines of the Royal Welch. Williams' Welsh now went out over the loudspeaker a last time, instructing beleaguered "D" Company to make its way back under cover of the remaining darkness. Led by a lieutenant, they came out through the *chaung* arriving at their start lines at 4:50 a.m. Over the next few nights, more survivors from the attack made their way back to British and Indian lines. 1/RWF lost in their attempt on Donbaik thirteen officers and 162 other ranks killed, wounded, or missing, or about a fifth of the battalion in twenty-four hours.[53]

Military Orientalism

After the battle, Williams wanted to recommend Graves for the Victoria Cross (VC) but was advised to downgrade his recommendation to the Distinguished Service Order (DSO). The problem was that Graves was reported as "missing, believed killed" which meant there was a chance he was taken prisoner. Professional British officers, along with their counterparts in the Imperial Japanese Army, considered it a disgrace to be captured. As General Sir Francis Tuker told his troops, "Surrender is shameful as long as we have strength to bear arms."[54] The VC was given either posthumously or to those who survived their acts of gallantry and avoided capture. However, the DSO was only given to the living, and Graves was eventually listed as "assumed killed." Graves was thought too alive for the VC and too dead for the DSO. In the end, he received a Mention in Dispatches (MID), as there was no posthumous decoration at the time between the VC and MID.[55]

[53] Kemp and Graves, *Red Dragon*, pp. 52–53; Rankin, *Telegram from Guernica*, pp. 236–237.

[54] Sir Francis Tuker, Special Order of the Day, 4th Indian Division, 23 October 1942, 71/21/2, IWM.

[55] Colonel Michael Demetriadi, Author's Interview and Correspondence; Diary of Lt. Col. A.H. Williams, 30 March 1943, 3722, RWF; Kemp and Graves,

For many Anglo-Americans, the notion that surrender is shameful was a chief indicator of the irredeemable otherness of the Japanese.[56] While Japanese troops were more likely to actually fight to the last man than Allied troops, the value was shared in principle by officers in both armies. It was part of "our Bushido code" remarked one of Graves' fellow officers in the Royal Welch.[57] Tuker exhorted his men to fight to "the last man, the last round, the last bomb, *the last bayonet*." One of Slim's corps commanders wrote: "It cannot be too strongly emphasised that surrender to an oriental enemy is indefensible [therefore] the principle of 'the last man and the last round' MUST be fully understood and carried out by every soldier."[58] In an Indian battalion, the British commander told his regular officers that he would not recommend them for any decorations for valor no matter what they did. It was their job to be brave beyond the call; decorations were only for the wartime emergency commissioned chaps.[59] As with Cameron's "American Samurai," there was a curious mirroring of the values of the enemy, even amid racial othering.[60] While exhorting their troops to fight like the Japanese, British officers and Allied officials condemned the Japanese way of war as subhuman.[61] In excusing defeat, Irwin claimed that the British were "not so savage as a nation as the Jap is."[62] While finding in emperor worship and militarism evidence of Japanese backwardness and feudalism, bureaucratically calibrated relations of shame and disgrace governed the award of bits of ribbon and tin in the British and Indian armies.[63]

Relaxing assumptions that the Japanese were innately different helps draw out "traditional" and other subaltern aspects of British military

---

The Red Dragon, Appendix A; Glover, *That Astonishing Infantry*, p. 204. At the time the Military Cross was not awarded posthumously.

[56] See e.g. Cameron, *American Samurai*, pp. 112–115; Charles Carfrae, "Dark Company," p. 128, 80/49/1, IWM; Dower, *War Without Mercy*, p. 67; Fergusson, *The Wild Green Earth*, pp. 205–206; Linderman, *The World Within War*, pp. 163–167; Shipster, *Mist Over the Rice-Fields*, p. 4.

[57] Michael Demetriadi, interview by the author.

[58] General Stopford, "Some Notes on Warfare in Undeveloped Countries," Major General W.A. Dimoline, X/7, LH.

[59] John Randle, interview by the author.

[60] Cameron, *American Samurai*, pp. 104, 126.

[61] See e.g. Jungle Warfare School Shimoga, Lecture, "The Jap," 7304-1-2, NAM; J.A.H. Heard, "Josh" weekly newssheets, LH; Dower, *War Without Mercy*, pp. 140–144; Thorne, *The Issue of War*, pp. 124–131.

[62] Lt. Gen. N.M.S. Irwin, 2/1, "Rough shorthand note of Army Commander's press conference," P139, IWM.

[63] Dower, *War Without Mercy*, pp. 20–21.

experience. This is because orientalist constructions of Asians are primarily concerned with underwriting one-sided accounts of the West, as more modern, rational, and so on. Stripped away, what Western or Asian soldiers share in common, and what distinguishes them, appears anew. In postcolonial perspective, the strategic role of the military in sustaining distinctions between a rational and modern West and the non-European world starts to slip. Histories of armed forces and warfare that we thought we understood through reference to categories like the nation and modernity require reassessment.

Chapters 1 and 2 drew attention to a curious feature of imperial militaries: the mismatch between the ethnicized titles of regiments and the backgrounds of their soldiers. Notionally Muslim regiments in the Indian Army had Sikh and Hindu soldiers. Likewise, the Royal Welch Fusiliers were by no means composed only of Welsh soldiers. The regiment was known as the Birmingham Fusiliers because it had so many recruits from the English midlands serving in its battalions, and that was before wartime replacements who came from all over the British Isles.[64] Not everyone understood Williams' Welsh over the loudspeaker at Donbaik.[65] But on "Taffy Day" in the RWF, those Birmingham-born English "proved themselves as good Welshmen as could be desired."[66] Just like in the Indian Army, soldiers became attached to their unit identities through serving in those units, not because unit names "accurately" reflected the ethnicity of their soldiers.

Revealing comparisons run deeper. Caste is often seen as the defining feature of Indian society. Scholarship on the Indian Army often dwells on the subject, and for John Lynn it helps explain what makes Indian soldiers different from other ones.[67] "When thinking of India it is hard not to think of caste," Nicholas Dirks remarks.[68] But caste was not a rigid and immutable system of social hierarchy. It was transformed by British rule, becoming the central term in a colonial project of cultural control, "the precipitate of a powerful history" as Dirks

---

[64] Reuben Jones, interview by the author. On the loss of the local territorial connection of British regiments, see French, *Military Identities*, pp. 279–283.

[65] Ron Thomas, interview by the author.

[66] Frank Richards quoted in French, *Military Identities*, p. 98. Taffy is a derogative term for the Welsh. "Taffy Day" refers to St. David's Day, St. David being the patron saint of Wales.

[67] Lynn, *Battle*, Chapters. 2, 5, pp. 29–72, 145–177. The subtitle of Chapter 5 refers to the "native character" of Indian soldiers.

[68] Dirks, *Castes of Mind*, p. 3.

puts it.[69] As such, caste in India becomes more directly comparable to other "caste" systems constructed around heredity, status, and occupation, as for example in the historical role of European nobility in the officer corps. Caste does not appertain only to Indians. It can refer to any order of power and hierarchy based upon degrees of purity and pollution. Accordingly, not only can the British regimental system be thought of in caste terms – from the prestigious guards regiments down to the workaday county regiments – but so too can the regular officer corps, which maintained its aristocratic aura and customs, if not always its bloodlines or bank accounts, and was further divided and ranked by regimental affiliation, social class, and public school. "It was sort of a caste system," remarked one Indian cadet at Sandhurst in the 1920s, when trying to figure out the "pattern of groups based on schools, common interests, and old family friendships" among the British cadets.[70]

1/RWF's Welsh schoolmaster would not have been part of that pattern. Despite his evident military ability, Lieutenant Colonel Humphrey Williams lacked the appropriate origins and status. Not only was Williams Welsh in a regiment that was dominated by English "gentlemen" officers, he was a Territorial and not a regular or professional officer.[71] The first battalion of a regiment usually is the preserve of regular officers and the most prestigious of a regiment's battalions. But many of the regular officers in 1/RWF had been killed or captured in the 1940 campaign in France, where Williams commanded a company and was wounded in action, coming out at Dunkirk.

When 1/RWF shipped out to India, Williams went as the second-in-command. As the First Arakan got underway, the regular officer commanding the battalion was sent off to serve on a brigade staff and Williams took over. While Donbaik was a defeat, high command recognized that Williams and his battalion had done well. Williams was awarded the DSO.[72] All other things being equal, he should have

[69] Ibid., p. 8.

[70] J.N. Chaudhuri quoted in Barua, *Gentlemen of the Raj*, p. 58.

[71] During its time in Burma there was only one other Welsh speaking officer in the battalion besides Williams. On the attitude of regular officers toward territorials, see French, *Military Identities*, pp. 215–217.

[72] The day after the battle, 19 March 1943, Brigadier Cavendish wrote to Williams: "I would like to let you know how much I admired the way you commanded your Battalion during the action and the leadership you displayed." A.H. Williams, News Cuttings, Vol. 2, RWF.

carried on in command of the battalion. In the event, after returning to India with the battalion, Williams resigned, or "gave up" his command, as one of his obituary writers put it.[73] It is unclear precisely why Williams did so. He refers to a "true state of affairs" in his diary but never lets on exactly what this was.[74] His resignation was unpopular with many of the officers of 1/RWF, several of whom spoke derisively of their new commander and were promptly posted elsewhere.[75] These officers had come to respect Williams for his character and ability. But when Williams first had been appointed commander, he was poorly received by some of these same (English) officers.[76] Before Donbaik, he had worried about whether he would be accepted by them, whether he could be an effective commander, and thought about resignation.[77] Williams was a Welsh speaker, a trait he shared with many of the other ranks in the 1/RWF but not its officers. He may have been socialist or left leaning.[78] He certainly had a taste for the ribald, and a "delicious sense of humour," according to one of his officers.[79]

This was on display at a dinner for the officers of 1 and 2/RWF held in Poona, India after the First Arakan and before Williams resigned his command. The occasion was a few days of sports competitions between the two battalions. 1/RWF had got the better of the games, and in general had the reputation of being "rough and ready," burnished by their recent combat experience.[80] 1/RWF's NCOs had even managed to steal the prized stick of 2/RWF's commander, which turned up in the NCO's mess a week or so after the meeting of the two battalions.[81]

---

[73] No author, "Lt. Col. A.H. Williams, DSO, OBE, TD," *Y Ddraig Goch* [unknown date], p. 84, RWF.

[74] Diary of Lt. Col. A.H. Williams, 25 September 1943, 3722, RWF.

[75] Diary of Lt. Col. A.H. Williams, 22, 23, August, 22, 23, 25, 28, September, and 3 October 1943, 3722, RWF; Colonel Michael Demetriadi, Author's Interview; Bennett, *Memoirs of a Very Fortunate Man*, pp. 126–127.

[76] Diary of Lt. Col. A.H. Williams, 1, 25 February 1943, 3722, RWF.

[77] Diary of Lt. Col. A.H. Williams, 17, 31 January, 1, 2, 6 February 1943, 3722, RWF.

[78] A.H. Williams, News Cuttings, Vols. 2 and 3, RWF.

[79] Lt. Col. P.C. Dryland, "Humphrey Williams," *Y Ddraig Goch* [unknown date], p. 84, RWF. Dryland served with Williams in Normandy. An early wartime diary entry of Williams' refers to a lecture on venereal disease given by the medical officer to the troops: "M.O. very explicit and roundly cheered at end." Diary of Lt. Col. A.H. Williams, 5 October 1939, 3722, RWF.

[80] Colonel Michael Demetriadi, Author's Interview; Bennett, *Memoirs of a Very Fortunate Man*, pp. 123–124.

[81] Bennett, *Memoirs of a Very Fortunate Man*, p. 125.

Unduly swollen with regular officers because it had yet to see much action, 2/RWF was known as the "High Tea Battalion." Its officers toted the mess silver along on field exercises, and had a reputation for over-attention to proper comportment.[82] At coffee after dinner the officers of the two battalions were not mixing. Williams took to the piano and played a piece of classical music to applause. He then broke into a bawdy parody of a popular song, "Fascinating Bitch," about a beautiful young woman who puts herself through school as a high-priced call girl. It went in part: "And every once in a while I'd take a little rest,/Just to drive my customers wild./Oh, I wish I were a fascinating bitch."[83] Williams' officers joined in at the last line of the chorus, as ever misogyny uniting the band of combat veterans. After they had finished singing, a 2/RWF officer stood up and said "That was disgusting."[84] A brawl broke out.

Sometime afterward, a deputation of 2/RWF officers made representations to Brigadier Hugh Stockwell asking for Williams to be removed from command. Stockwell was an RWF regular who was commanding a brigade elsewhere in India. The 2/RWF officers had appealed to a senior officer of their tribe. Somehow, Stockwell effected Williams' resignation. Likely, Williams' own doubts about his acceptance and suitability for command were aggravated by Stockwell's efforts and by news of the 2/RWF deputation. For one of Williams' officers, all that mattered to Stockwell and his fellow regulars was that the commanding officer be of the right caste: "In the eyes of the officers of the pre-war regular army, they didn't really trust anyone who was not an 'officer and a gentleman.'"[85]

A regular officer serving with 2/RWF, Garnett Braithwaite, was sent to take command of 1/RWF. Braithwaite had never seen action and had a speech impediment, stuttering seriously. Over the next year, he demoralized the battalion.[86] In line with 2/RWF's aristocratic demeanor,

---

[82] From a note left by a former archivist for the RWF, Peter Crocker quoting an officer of the Manchester Regiment's MG Battalion who had served alongside both 1 and 2/RWF in Burma. Brian Owen, Curator for the RWF, correspondence with the author, 1 March and 2 April 2012.

[83] Bennett, *Memoirs of a Very Fortunate Man*, p. 124; Cray, *The Erotic Muse*, p. 353. The original song was called "Fascinating Lady."

[84] Quoted in Bennett, *Memoirs of a Very Fortunate Man*, p. 124.

[85] Michael Demetriadi, interview by the author.

[86] This was the conclusion reached by a the Divisional psychiatrist who investigated why 1/RWF had proportionately more psychiatric casualties than

he insisted on tables, chairs, and an officers' mess while in the field, whereas previously 1/RWF officers had eaten with their troops. 1/RWF officers began sarcastically referring to their unit as the "2nd/1st Royal Welch Fusiliers."[87] In the end even the battalion padre asked higher command to relieve Braithwaite.[88] Unfortunately, it took a rout after an ill-conceived attack on a well-planned Japanese defense at Aradura Spur in May 1944 before Braithwaite was finally relieved.[89] Meanwhile, Williams was sent back to the UK, taking over 7/Royal Welch Fusiliers in early 1944, a battalion more appropriate in caste terms for him to command. His war ended in Normandy where he was severely wounded in the stomach during a mortar barrage.[90]

Of the Royal Welch, one officer remarked, "They were rather a tribal lot."[91] As the war teetered in the balance, pomposities concerning reserve and professional officers, first and second battalions, and whether Welshmen could be gentlemen, led to the removal of an effective battalion commander and his replacement by a stuttering incompetent of the appropriate social class. This is a small affair in the scale of things, to be sure, but revealing on the question of difference between Western and other armed forces and societies. Irrational commitments regarding purity and pollution, and their entwinement in orders

other battalions at Kohima: "The reason for this was that [1/RWF] were commanded by an officer who was unpopular throughout the unit, and who had failed to win the respect of his subordinates either as a tactician or as a man before battle, and during battle failed in both roles, with the result that numbers of men broke down who should never have done so; it was not so much a matter of individual breakdowns as of a wholesale loss of group morale with numbers of anxious men turning back bewildered with feelings of helpless apathy, mixed with disgust at the lack of proper leadership." Maj. PJR Davies, Divisional Psychiatry: Report to the War Office, Psychiatrist attached to HQ 2 Div, Nov 1943-Nov 1945, p. 20, WO 222/158, TNA. See also Gwylm Davies, Michael Demetriadi, Reuben Jones, interviews by the author. Stockwell apparently took care to cover up some of the consequences of his intervention to remove Williams. When Williams died in 1983, Stockwell was Colonel of the Regiment. He ordered the regimental archivist to destroy notes that Braithwaite had left for the archive when he died. The archivist complied and left a note recording this fact in the RWF archives. Brian Owen, Curator of the RWF, conversation with author, Wrexham, Wales, 12 January 2012.

[87] Diary of Lt. Col. A.H. Williams, 12 October 1943, 3722, RWF.
[88] Michael Demetriadi, interview by the author.
[89] Kemp and Graves, *Red Dragon*, pp. 72–74. Latimer, *Burma*, p. 302.
[90] Williams recovered to work for BBC Wales as an Education Officer after the war.
[91] John Randle, interview by the author.

of power, were not the preserve of South Asians. "The British in India," observed one officer of his own kind, "were every bit as caste-ridden as the Hindus and our caste rules were just as strict."[92] Having "tribal" identities unites rather than divides Western and non-Western soldiers.

Crucially, the hierarchies at work in the Williams affair concerned conflicting militarized masculinities. Williams' everyman style of contemporary military leadership contrasted with the aristocratic traditions of the Royal Welch, and was presumably part of the occasion for his undoing. The 1/RWF lorded its combat experience over those who prided themselves on drinking tea out of fine china on exercise. In his absurdly English way, Braithwaite tried to have his officers strike a pose of imperturbability of the kind that supposedly won the Battle of Waterloo. Combat soldiering is a strategic site for the production of masculinity, which returns to shape army–society relations. In colonial armies, the relative military value of Western and non-Western masculinities was ranked in orientalist fashion, the natives brave but in need of leadership and organization.[93] Like civilizational trajectories of drill and discipline, organized warfare involved different models of military masculinity, which were connected and combined in the global histories of armed forces. Masculinity for soldiers concerned the disciplined capacity for violence; for officers, it was about organizing and directing violence. Masculinity provided a cosmopolitan basis for organized violence, shared by soldiers from different places and classes and on both sides of the battle lines.

Politics, Obedience, and Violence

Many scholars sharply differentiate national peoples in terms of their capacity to commit violence and, especially, atrocity. Politics and racism motivates perpetrators from Nazi Germany to Rwanda, according to scholars working in fields as distinct as Holocaust studies or discourse analysis.[94] What is obscured by this reduction of extraordinary violence to the realm of politics and the world of national or

---

[92] Col. H.B. Hudson, "A Backward Glance: A Personal Account of Service in the Indian Army 1932–1947," p. 34, CSAS.

[93] Streets, *Martial Races*.

[94] Goldhagen, *Hitler's Willing Executioners*; Mamdani, *When Victims Become Killers*.

ethnicized polities? One effect is to preserve the idea that, ordinarily speaking, human beings are pacific. It is from the political world that their willingness to engage in such violence arises, overcoming putative inhibitions and providing reasons for mutual slaughter. Political necessity, an extreme identity, or ideological fanaticism inspires those who do the work of war and atrocity. The turn to national politics provides a meaningful frame for war which both accounts for and contains war's extraordinary eruptions of violence.

The work of nationalizing and politicizing the making of combat and atrocity is particularly evident in debates over the *Wehrmacht*. For Omer Bartov, German soldiers were "devoted believers in a murderous ideology"; for Daniel Goldhagen, the members of the German reserve police battalions who shot Jews in Poland and the USSR "wanted to be genocidal executioners" and "considered the slaughter to be just," due to their "demonological anti-semitism."[95] A chain of cause and effect links political ideology to the practical making of wartime and genocidal violence by soldiers and others. This chain creates a self-reinforcing cycle between soldier and polity, in which each lends meaning to the other. Goldhagen's avowedly "monocausal" explanation requires no other "intervening variable."[96] State, nationality, and motivation are aligned isomorphically in a political and cultural geography composed of nation states. For Goldhagen, "[t]he notion that ordinary Danes or Italians would have acted as the ordinary Germans did strains credulity beyond the breaking point."[97]

In reducing violence to politics, and in sourcing its motivations to collective identities, reasons for the violence can be identified, and this is in its own way reassuring. Mahmood Mamdani makes the point succinctly in his account of the Rwandan genocide: "Violence cannot be allowed to speak for itself, for violence is not its own meaning."[98] Mamdani shows how the genocide was made possible through the construction of the Tutsi as a racialized, nonindigenous other. For him, it is vital to understand the specific politics behind violence. "To be made thinkable, [violence] needs to be *historicized*."[99] How did the

---

[95] Bartov, *Hitler's Army*, p. viii; Goldhagen, *Hitler's Willing Executioners*, pp. 279, 392–393.
[96] Goldhagen, *Hitler's Willing Executioners*, p. 416.
[97] Goldhagen, *Hitler's Willing Executioners*, p. 408.
[98] Mamdani, *When Victims Become Killers*, pp. 228–229.
[99] Mamdani, *When Victims Become Killers*, p. 229.

agents involved understand the situation such that violence was the only course of action? Peoples are historical authors of their violence, and the reasons for it are to be found in histories and discourses of identity politics.

In turning to organizational routine and bureaucratic dehumanization to account for the everyday making of the Holocaust, Christopher Browning, Zygmunt Bauman, and others relaxed the hold of national society and politics on the perpetrators of atrocity.[100] In Browning's hands, the feelings, beliefs, and actions of the middle-aged police reservists he studied become comparable to those of other people, rather than exceptional. They found the work of gunning down Jews and other victims physically revolting. They did not like shooting babies, required alcohol and grew demoralized. Later as the killing process was institutionalized in camps and the policemen mostly used in rounding up and deporting victims, they gave foreign auxiliaries the most distasteful jobs.[101]

Regarding the supposed unwillingness to participate in slaughter of Danes and Italians, Browning's riposte to Goldhagen involved some particularly willing Luxembourgers in Police Battalion 101.[102] It turns out that soldiering in Nazi Germany – a failed empire – was a more cosmopolitan affair than one might imagine.[103] As in Burma, nationality did not necessarily determine who was capable of what. Many of the paramilitary battalions involved in the Holocaust were composed of Ukrainians, Latvians, and Lithuanians.[104] By 1945, foreigners outnumbered Germans in the *Waffen SS*.[105] More Danes died fighting in *SS* Divisions *Wiking* and *Nordland* than against the Nazi invasion and occupation of their homeland.[106] West European *SS* formations were

---

[100] Bauman, *Modernity and the Holocaust*; Browning, *Ordinary Men*; Kelman and Hamilton, *Crimes of Obedience*.

[101] Browning, *Ordinary Men*, pp. 59, 61, 76, 77.

[102] Browning, "Ordinary Men or Ordinary Germans," pp. 60–62.

[103] Baranowski, *Nazi Empire*; Mazower, *Hitler's Empire*.

[104] Browning, *Ordinary Men*, p. 52; Stein, *The Waffen SS*, p. 112.

[105] Stein, *The Waffen SS*, p. 137.

[106] Approximately 2,000 died of the 6,000 Danes in the *Waffen SS*. Danes also served in the *SS*-sponsored Danish Legion. Around nine hundred Danes died in the resistance movement. See Chistensen *et al.*, *Under Hagekors og Dannebrog*, pp. 491–494; Petersen, *Faldne i Danmarks Frihedksamp 1940–1945*. When losses in the Danish merchant marine are included, however, the deaths in Allied service approach equivalence. Thanks to Lars Bangert Struwe for assistance on these points.

"formidable fighters" and the "backbone of the defense" in the Battle of Berlin in 1945, where a battlegroup of Danish, Norwegian, French, and Latvian *SS* mounted some of the last organized resistance around the Reich Chancellery.[107]

The ubiquitous presence of foreign troops in modern war poses problems for the careful pairing of the national and ideological commitments of soldiers with their wartime objects of violence. Goldhagen addresses it by arguing that the principal "national groups who aided the Germans in slaughtering Jews" were as anti-Semitic as the Germans. Those who joined them were "animated by vehement hatred of Jews."[108] He has a point, but the ubiquity of anti-Semitism makes his German subjects that much less exceptional in character.[109]

Turning to other national histories in the way Goldhagen does exposes unexamined premises. If the world is populated with potentially warring nation-states, each with their separate histories and societies, than soldiers and other agents of violence are rooted in the national. Organizational or psychological factors are at best an intermediate level of analysis, not a primary explanation. Confronted by the presence of foreigners in the Nazi war and genocide machine, the question becomes why members of these other national groups might have sided with Hitler, what were their politics and national histories? The world consists only of territorially discrete, national societies each with their own armed forces with their stock characteristics and motivations. In politics as in scholarship, organized violence and its representation are critical to establishing this image of the world, a nation-state ontology of the globe.

Foreign Soldiers in Past and Present

The Indian Army and other British imperial forces were part of the globalization of Western forms of military discipline. What made the army global-izable was its cosmopolitan character and the adaptability of its sturdy and robust techniques to different social and political contexts. Many armed forces today began their institutional histories in colonial context or under imperial tutelage. The Kenyan Army was

---

[107] Beevor, *Berlin*, p. 258; Stein, *The Waffen SS*, p. 164.
[108] Goldhagen, *Hitler's Willing Executioners*, p. 409.
[109] Snyder, *Bloodlands*, pp. 191–194.

formed out of the Kings African Rifles. The Nigerian Army started as part of the Royal West African Frontier Force. The story is similar in much of former French Africa and in the successor states to the British Raj in South Asia and elsewhere. Other armies have mixed or informal imperial parentage. The South Korean Army and national police began in Japanese imperial service and then developed into national armed forces in the late 1940s under American occupation. The United States has trained, advised, and supported Latin and Central American armies and other security forces for over a century. Armies may appear to be the principal national – even nationalist – institution, but their histories are very often imperial and global in one way or another.

It is often observed that in the decades after 1945 the number of international wars declined while civil wars rose.[110] Armed forces were being used inside sovereign states, for purposes of "internal security." Foreign powers – often former imperial patrons – provided "advice and support" to one side or another in many of these "civil" wars.[111] Much like in the era of European empire, local armed forces were organized by great powers for regional and global projects of order making.[112] The military legacy of empire left in place a global coercive infrastructure for purposes of power projection, along with the modalities – shared colonial military histories, advice and support programs – to make use of it.

Rejiggered for new times after 1945, an imperial military order functioned beneath the veil of state sovereignty. It is this order that made it possible to fight the Cold War in Indochina using primarily "Asian boys," or to suppress popular armed challenges in Third World countries with client armies and death squads rather than First World expeditionary forces.[113] Even at the height of the US deployment to South Vietnam, heavily US-supported South Vietnamese forces outnumbered US forces by two to one, and they suffered many times the number of dead. These kinds of military relations continue in the first decade of the twenty-first century with the training of Iraqi and Afghan forces

---

[110] Holsti, *The State, War and the State of War.*
[111] Barkawi, "State and Armed Force in International Context."
[112] Barkawi, "Political Military Legacies."
[113] "[W]e are not about to send American boys 9 or 10,000 miles away from home to do what Asian boys ought to be doing for themselves." Lyndon B. Johnson, Remarks in Memorial Hall, University of Akron, 21 October 1964, available online at www.presidency.ucsb.edu/ws/?pid=26635, accessed 30 September 2014.

to secure governments set up by foreign powers. The War on Terror has led to a renewed proliferation of advice and support programs and other forms of security assistance.

Foreign forces have been normally used to exert power over colonized populations and the Third World or Global South. But their significance is not limited to the fates of subordinate states and societies in world politics. They have direct implications for the character of civil–military relations in Western states and for the kinds of imperial and foreign policies they have sustained. Imperial intervention and rule continually encountered and generated armed resistance. The expansion of Europe from the early modern period onward, which connected the globe and made possible the capitalist world system of our own day, relied on the availability of armed force. Arraying brown and black men in disciplined order to kill and violently repress other brown and black people was and remains central to the making of the modern world. The cosmopolitanism of the regular army enabled these histories.

Sources

I Archives

British Empire and Commonwealth Museum
  Oral History Interviews
  Empire at War
Churchill College Archives
  Papers of Field Marshall Sir William Slim
  Papers of Lt. Gen. Thomas Corbett
Cambridge Centre of South Asian Studies
  Papers of Col. H.B. Hudson
  Papers of Eric Stokes
Durham University Library
  Papers of Louis Allen
Firepower
  Brig. Crowe
  HKSRA
  Christopher Close
  21st Mountain Battery, RIA
  Lt. Col. H.J. Thuillier
Gurkha Museum
  Papers of Major Gajendra Malla
  Papers of 4/9th Gurkha Rifles
  Papers of 2/5th Royal Gurkha Rifles
  Papers of Eric Neild
  Papers of 3/2th Gurkha Rifles
  Papers of 1/6th Gurkha Rifles
  Papers of 5/9th Gurkha Rifles
  Papers of Brig. Godfrey Proctor
  Loose Archives 1/7th Gurkha Rifles
  Papers of 3/4th Gurkha Rifles
  Papers of 2/2th Gurkha Rifles
  Loose Archives 1st, 2nd, 3rd, 4th, and 5th Gurkha Rifles
Imperial War Museum
  Personal Papers:

Colonel J. F. Adye
Charles Carfrae
Colonel B. J. Amies
Maj. Gen. A.C. Curtis
Brig. P.J. Jeffreys
Pte. Isaac Fadoyebo
Col. RBG Bromhead
Lt. Col. J.E.M Bland
Capt. J.C Bolton
Bill Harding
Maj. Gen. T.H Birkbeck
Lt. Col. E.L. Sawyer
Lt. Col. W.L. Farrow
Lt. Col. P.G Cane
Major J.A. Chapman
Major R.J. Bower
Brig. K.H. Collen
Major. M.S. Clarke
Capt. D.M. Cookson
Major F.G. Commings
Gian Singh
Col. A.L. Craddock
D. Elvet Price
Capt. N. Durrant
Lt. Gen. Sir Geoffrey Evans
Major R.O. Garne
Capt. P. Collister
Sir Reginald Dorman-Smith
Lt. Col. A.F. Harper
Major H.C. Gay
Major P.H. Gadsdon
Capt. P. Griffin
D. Peter Wilson
Lt. Col. John Peddie
Col. E.C. Pickard
Lt. Gen. Sir Francis Tuker
Lt. Gen. N.M.S. Irwin
Major Parkash Singh
Major D.C. Rissik
Major I.F.R. Ramsey
Dipesh Chandra Misra
Col. F.K. Theobald

AL Series
7th Gurkha Rifles Regimental Journal
The Piffer
Misc Series
Journal of the 2nd KEO Goorkha Rifles
Journal of the 10th PMO Gurkha Rifles
Liddell Hart Centre for Military Archives
  Personal Papers
  J.A.H. Heard
  Lt. Col. V.E.O Stevenson-Hamilton
  Col. Rex C. Mace
  Maj. Gen. W.A. Dimoline
  Lt. Col. S.P. Fearon
  Brig. Brian Mortimer Archibald
  Brig. Arthur Blair Gibson
  Gen. Sir Douglas Gracey
  Gen. Sir. Frank Messervy
  Lt. Gen. Thomas J. Hutton
  Lt. John Pitt
  Maj. Gen. DNH Tyacke
  Lt. Col. Donald P. Bryce
  Lt. Col. A.C. Moore
  Gen. Sir Hugh C. Stockwell
  Brig. W.F. Jeffries
  Maj. Gen. James Scott-Elliot
  MFF6 Wartime Translations of Seized Japanese Documents
  JAMBO East African Services Magazine
National Army Museum
  Brig. GHB Beyts
  9/14th Punjab
  Y Ddraig Goch: The Journal of the Royal Welch Fusiliers
  Winifred Beaumont
  Japanese in Battle
  Stephen Cohen
  Major M.A. Lowry
  Clive Branson
  FAE Crew
  Antony Brett James
  2/13th FFR
  INA Leaflets
  John and Helene Scott
  B.L. Raina

  8/6th Rajputana Rifles
  Tighe Papers
  5/2nd Punjab
  Jungle Warfare School Shimoga
  5/11th Sikhs
Oriental and India Office Collection
  War Staff
  Military Department
  Political and Judicial
  European Manuscripts
  Registry
The National Archives
  WO 208
  WO 106
  WO 203
  WO 222
  WO 172
  CO 968
Royal Welch Fusiliers
  1/RWF in Burma
  A.H. Williams
  Graves Collection
  J.G. Bennett
  Gen. Sir. Hugh Stockwell
  M.A. Demetriadi
  Donbaik Materials
  6th Brigade
South Wales Borderers
  Alun Lewis
  Lt. Thomas Hugh Harries
  William Cecil Proll
  6th Battalion
  Pte. P. Thomas
  Military Training Pamphlets Far East
  D.F. Karaka

II Interviews

Major John Bagshawe and Major Robin Schlaefli. 23 February 2004, in Poole, Dorset, UK. Wartime officers in MG/11th Sikhs.

Major Maurice Biggs. 25 April 2000 in the Gurkha Museum, Winchester, UK. Wartime officer in 2/4th Gurkha Rifles.

George Coppen. 24 April 2001 in Rownhams, Southampton, UK. Wartime officer in 14/13th Frontier Force Rifles.

Gwylm Davies. 28 August 2000 in Penparcau, Aberystwyth, Wales, UK. Other rank in 1/Royal Welch Fusiliers.

Major Aynsley Delafield. 5 April 2001 in Bucknell, Shropshire, UK. Wartime officer in 2/13th Frontier Force Riles.

Rajinder Singh Dhatt. 13 April 2002 in Hounslow, London, UK. Havildar Major in the Royal Indian Army Service Corps.

Colonel M. A. Demetriadi. 16 October 2000 in Brandeston, Suffolk, UK. Served in various capacities in 1/Royal Welch Fusiliers.

Lt. Col. W. L. Farrow. 19 April 2004 in Farnham, Surrey, UK. Wartime officer in 1/11th Sikhs.

Peter Francis and Tony Banks. 19 January 2001 in Sollers Hope, Hereford, UK. Both wartime officers in MG Bn/9th Jat.

Major Peter H. Gadsdon, MBE, MC. 17 October 2000 in Seaford, Sussex, UK. Wartime officer in 4/14th Punjab.

John Hamilton. 26 April 2001 in Leatherhead, Surrey, UK. Wartime officer in 81 (WA) Division.

Graham Jenkins. 27 February 2001 in Ferryside, Dyfed, Wales. Wartime officer in 2/13th Frontier Force Rifles.

Reuben Jones. 11 October 2000 in Mackworth, Derby, UK. Professional soldier and NCO in 1/Royal Welch Fusiliers.

Lt. Col. Tony Mains. 11 April 2000 in Farnham, Surrey, UK. Professional officer in the 9th Gurkha Rifles.

Clifford Martin. 1 April 2001 in Henley-on-Thames, Oxon., UK. Wartime officer in 7/10th Baluch.

John Nunneley. 15 June 2000 in London, UK. Wartime officer in 36 KAR.

Mohinder Singh Pujji. 6 February 2002 in Gravesend, Kent, UK. Wartime pilot in RAF and RIAF.

Helen Price. 17 November 2000 in Edinburgh, Scotland, UK. Physiotherapist attached to an Indian Army hospital.

Kamal Bahadur Pursa. 3 May 2000 in the Gurkha Museum, Winchester, UK. Serving other rank in 1/Royal Gurkha Rifles.

Brigadier John Randle. 31 January 2001 in Wellisford, Somerset, UK. Wartime officer in 7/10th Baluch.

Gian Singh. 15 November 2000 in Skewen, Wales, UK. Other rank in Sikh Light Infantry.

Ron '25' Thomas. 4 September 2000 in Wrexham, Wales, UK. Other rank in 1/Royal Welch Fusiliers.

J. R. Wallis. 25 April 2001 in Hayling Island, Hampshire, UK. Wartime officer in 14/13th Frontier Force Rilfes.

Wigston and District Branch of the Burma Star Association. 4 May 2000 in the British Legion, Wigston, Leicester, UK. Present: Len Prior, other rank 2/Norfolks; Brian Bisiker, wartime officer, 1/Gambia; Evritt Loseby, other rank, 28 Jungle Field Regiment.

III Ph.D. Dissertations

Bhattacharya, Sanjoy. "'A Necessary Weapon of War': State Policies towards Propaganda and Information in Eastern India, 1939–45." Ph.D. diss., School of Oriental and African Studies, University of London, 1996.

Davis, Shelby Cullom. "Reservoirs of Men: A History of the Black Troops of French West Africa." Ph.D. diss., The University of Geneva, 1934.

Des Chene, Mary Katherine. "Relics of Empire: A Cultural History of the Gurkhas 1815–1987." Ph.D. diss., Stanford University, 1991.

Narain, Namrata. "Co-option and Control: The Role of the Colonial Army in India 1918–1947." Ph.D. diss. University of Cambridge, 1992.

Bibliography

Addison, Paul and Angus Calder, eds. *Time to Kill: The Soldier's Experience of War in the West 1939–1945*. London: Pimlico, 1997.

Agnew, John and Stuart Corbridge. *Mastering Space: Hegemony, Territory, and International Political Economy*. London: Routledge, 1995.

Aida, Yuji. *Prisoner of the British: A Japanese Soldier's Experiences in Burma*. London: Cresset, 1966.

Alavi, Seema. *The Sepoys and the Company: Tradition and Transition in Northern India*. Delhi: Oxford University Press, 1995.

Albrow, Martin. "Accounting for Organizational Feeling" in Larry J. Ray and Michael Reed, eds., *Organizing Modernity: New Weberian Perspectives on Work, Organization and Society*. London: Routledge, 1994.

Allen, Louis. "Innocents Abroad: Investigating War Crimes in South-East Asia" in Nish and Allen, eds., *War, Conflict and Security in Japan and Asia-Pacific, 1941–52*.

  Burma: The Longest War 1941–1945. London: Phoenix Press, 2000 [1984].

  "A Personal Postscript by Louis Allen" in Aida, *Prisoner of the British*.

Allen, N. J., W. S. F. Pickering, and W. Watts Miller. *On Durkheim's Elementary Forms of Religious Life*. London: Routledge, 1998.

Allport, Alan. *Browned Off and Bloody-Minded: The British Soldier Goes to War 1939–1945*. New Haven: Yale University Press, 2015.

Ambrose, Stephen E. *Citizen Soldiers: The U.S. Army from the Normandy Beaches to the Bulge to the Surrender of Germany June 7, 1944–May 7, 1945*. New York: Simon & Schuster, 1998.

Amin, Samir. *Eurocentrism*. New York: Monthly Review Press, 1989.

Anderson, Benedict. *Imagined Communities: Reflections on the Origin and Spread of Nationalism*. London: Verso, 1983.

Anderson, Fred. *Crucible of War: The Seven Years' War and the Fate of Empire in British North America, 1754–1766*. New York: Vintage, 2000.

Anderson, M. S. *War and Society in Europe of the Old Regime 1618–1787*. 2nd Rev. Ed. Stroud: Sutton Publishing, 1998.

Andreyev, Catherine. *Vlasov and the Russian Liberation Movement*. Cambridge: Cambridge University Press, 1987.

Appadurai, Arjun. *Modernity at Large: Cultural Dimensions of Globalization*. Minneapolis: University of Minnesota Press, 1996.

Arnold, David. "Bureaucratic Recruitment and Subordination in Colonial India: The Madras Constabulary, 1859–1947" in Ranajit Guha, ed., *Subaltern Studies IV: Writings on South Asian History and Society*. Delhi: Oxford University Press, 1985.

Asad, Talal, ed. *Anthropology and the Colonial Encounter*. New York: Humanities Press, 1973.

Genealogies of Religion. Baltimore: The Johns Hopkins University Press, 1993.

Audoin-Rouzeau, Stéphane. *Men at War 1914–1918: National Sentiment and Trench Journalism in France during the First World War*. Oxford and Washington, D.C.: Berg, 1992.

Avant, Deborah. *The Market for Force*. Cambridge: Cambridge University Press, 2005.

Aydin, Cemil. *The Politics of Anti-Westernism in Asia: Visions of World Order in Pan-Islamic and Pan-Asian Thought*. New York: Columbia University Press, 2007.

Baig, M. R. A. *In Different Saddles*. London: Asia Publishing House, 1967.

Balkind, Jon. "A Critique of Military Sociology: Lessons from Vietnam." *The Journal of Strategic Studies*, Vol. 1, No. 2 (1978): 235–259.

Bandyopadhyay, Sekhar. *From Plassey to Partition: A History of Modern India*. New Delhi: Orient Longman, 2004.

Baranowski, Shelley. *Nazi Empire: German Colonialism and Imperialism from Bismarck to Hitler*. Cambridge: Cambridge University Press, 2011.

Barat, Amiya. *The Bengal Native Infantry: Its Organisation and Discipline 1796–1852*. Calcutta: Firma K.L. Mukhopadhyay, 1962.

Barkawi, Tarak. "Peoples, Homelands and Wars? Ethnicity, the Military and Battle among British Imperial Forces in the War against Japan." *Comparative Studies in Society and History*, Vol. 46, No. 1 (January 2004): 134–163.

"State and Armed Force in International Context" in Alex Colas and Bryan Mabee, eds., *Mercenaries, Pirates, Bandits and Empires: Private Violence in Historical Context*. London: Hurst, 2010.

"Empire and Order in International Relations and Security Studies" in Robert A Denemark, ed., *The International Studies Encyclopedia*, Vol. III. Chichester: Wiley-Blackwell, 2010.

"Political Military Legacies of Empire in World Politics" in Sandra Halperin and Ronen Palan, eds., *Legacies of Empire: Imperial Roots of*

Contemporary Global Order. Cambridge: Cambridge University Press, 2015: 27–45.

Barkawi, Tarak and Mark Laffey. "The Postcolonial Moment in Security Studies." *Review of International Studies*, Vol. 32, No. 4 (2006): 329–352.

Barkawi, Tarak and Shane Brighton. "Powers of War: Fighting, Knowledge and Critique." *International Political Sociology*, Vol. 5, No. 2 (June 2011): 126–143.

Barth, Fredrik, ed. *Ethnic Groups and Boundaries*. London: Allen and Unwin, 1969.

Bartov, Omer. *Hitler's Army: Soldiers, Nazis and War in the Third Reich*. Oxford: Oxford University Press, 1992.

    The Eastern Front, 1941–45, German Troops and the Barbarisation of Warfare. 2nd ed. Basingstoke: Palgrave, 2001 [1985].

Barua, Pradeep P. *Gentlemen of the Raj: The Indian Army Officer Corps, 1817–1949*. Westport: Praeger, 2003.

Bauman, Zygmunt. *Modernity and the Holocaust*. Cambridge: Polity Press, 1989.

Bayly, C. A. *Empire and Information: Intelligence Gathering and Social Communication in India, 1780–1870*. Cambridge: Cambridge University Press, 1996.

    "Eric Thomas Stokes 1924–1981." *Proceedings of the British Academy*, Vol. 97 (1998): 467–498.

    The Birth of the Modern World 1780–1914. Oxford: Blackwell, 2004.

    "Eric Stokes and the Uprising of 1857" in Biswamoy Pati, ed., *The 1857 Rebellion*. New Delhi: Oxford University Press, 2007.

Bayly, Christopher and Tim Harper. *Forgotten Armies: The Fall of British Asia, 1941–1945*. London: Allen Lane, 2004.

    Forgotten Wars: The End of Britain's Asian Empire. London: Penguin, 2008.

Beetham, David. *The Legitimation of Power*. Atlantic Highlands, NJ: Humanities Press International, 1991.

Beevor, Antony. *Stalingrad*. New York: Viking, 1998.

    Berlin: The Downfall 1945. London: Viking, 2002.

    Ardennes 1944: Hitler's Last Gamble. London: Viking, 2015.

Bell, Catherine. *Ritual Theory, Ritual Practice*. New York: Oxford University Press, 1992.

Ben-Ari, Eyal. *Mastering Soldiers: Conflict, Emotions, and the Enemy in an Israeli Military Unit*. New York: Berghahn Books, 1998.

Bennett, Capt. J. C. *The Memoirs of a Very Fortunate Man*. Royston: Rock Road Books, Ltd., n.d.

Berger, Peter L. and Thomas Luckmann. *The Social Construction of Reality: A Treatise in the Sociology of Knowledge.* New York: Anchor Books, 1967 [1966].

Bergerud, Eric. *Touched with Fire: The Land War in the South Pacific.* New York: Penguin Books, 1996.

Betham, R. M. *Handbooks for the Indian Army: Marathas and Dekhani Musalmans.* Calcutta: Government of India Central Printing Office, 1908.

Beyts, Brigadier G. H. B. *The King's Salt.* Southwold: Southwold Press, Ltd., 1983.

Bhambra, Gurminder. *Rethinking Modernity: Postcolonialism and the Sociological Imagination.* Basingstoke: Palgrave, 2007.

Bhattacharya, Sanjoy. *'A Necessary Weapon of War': State Policies towards Propaganda and Information in Eastern India, 1939–45.* Ph.D. Thesis, School of Oriental and African Studies, University of London, 1996.

Bhuyan, Arun Chandra. *The Quit India Movement: The Second World and Indian Nationalism.* New Delhi: Manas Publications, 1975.

Biddle, Stephen. *Military Power: Explaining Victory and Defeat in Modern Battle.* Princeton: Princeton University Press, 2004.

Biderman, Albert. *March to Calumny: The Story of American PoW's in the Korean War.* New York: Macmillan, 1963.

Bidwell, Shelford. *Modern Warfare: A Study of Men, Weapons, and Theories.* London: Allen Lane, 1973.

The Chindit War: The Campaign in Burma, 1944. London: Hodder and Stoughton, 1979.

Black, Jeremy. *War and the World: Military Power and the Fate of Continents 1450–2000.* New Haven: Yale University Press, 1998.

Rethinking Military History. London: Routledge, 2004.

Bloch, Maurice. "Symbols, Song, Dance and Features of Articulation: Is Religion an Extreme Form of Traditional Authority?" *Archives Européenes de Sociologie*, Vol. 15 (1974): 55–81.

Bloch, Maurice and Jonathan Parry. *Death and the Regeneration of Life.* Cambridge: Cambridge University Press, 1982.

Bobbitt, Philip. *The Shield of Achilles: War, Peace and the Course of History.* London: Penguin, 2003.

Boëne, Bernard. "How 'Unique' should the Military be? A Review of Representative Literature and Outline of a Synthetic Formulation." *European Journal of Sociology*, Vol. 31 (1990): 3–59.

Bolt, Sydney. *Pseudo Sahib.* Aylesbeare: Hadinge Simpole, 2007.

Bond, Brian. *War and Society in Europe 1870–1970.* Stroud: Sutton Publishing Limited, 1998.

Bose, Sugata. *His Majesty's Opponent: Subhas Chandra Bose and India's Struggle Against Empire.* Cambridge: Belknap Press, 2011.

Bourke, Joanna. *An Intimate History of Killing: Face-to-Face Killing in Twentieth-Century Warfare.* London: Granta Books, 1999.

Branson, Clive. *British Soldier in India: The Letters of Clive Branson.* London: The Communist Party, 1944.

Brayne, F. L. "The Teaching of Urdu." *The Journal of the United Service Institution of India,* Vol. LXXIII, No. 312 (July 1943): 355.

Breckenridge, Carol A. and Peter van der Veer, eds. *Orientalism and the Postcolonial Predicament: Perspectives on South Asia.* Philadelphia: University of Pennsylvania Press, 1993.

Brett-James, Antony. *Report My Signals.* London: Hennel Locke, Ltd., 1948.

Browning, Christopher. *Ordinary Men: Reserve Police Battalion 101 and the Final Solution in Poland.* New York: HarperCollins, 1992.

"Ordinary Men or Ordinary Germans" in Robert R. Shandley, ed., *Unwilling Germans? The Goldhagen Debate.* Minneapolis: University of Minnesota Press, 1998.

Burton, Antoinette. "On the Inadequacy and the Indispensability of the Nation" in Burton, ed., *After the Imperial Turn: Thinking with and through the Nation.* Durham: Duke University Press, 2003.

Cadell, Patrick. *A History of the Bombay Army.* London: Longmans, Green & Co., 1938.

Caesar. *The Civil War.* London: Penguin, 1967.

Caforio, Giuseppe, ed. *Handbook of Military Sociology.* New York: Kluwer, 2003.

Callahan, Raymond. *Burma 1942–1945.* London: Davis-Poynter, 1978.

Calvert, Michael. *Prisoners of Hope.* London: Leo Cooper, 1996.

Cameron, Craig. *American Samurai: Myth, Imagination and the Conduct of Battle in the First Marine Division, 1941–1951.* Cambridge: Cambridge University Press, 1994.

Caplan, Lionel. "Martial Gurkhas: The Persistence of a British Military Discourse on 'Race'" in Peter Robb, ed., *The Concept of Race in South Asia.* Delhi: Oxford University Press, 1995.

Caputo, Philip. *A Rumor of War.* New York: Holt, Rinehart, and Winston, 1977.

Carfrae, Charles. *Chindit Column.* London: William Kimber, 1985.

Carruthers, Susan. *Cold War Captives: Imprisonment, Escape and Brainwashing.* Berkeley: University of California Press, 2009.

Chakrabarty, Dipesh. *Rethinking Working-Class History: Bengal 1890–1940.* Princeton: Princeton University Press, 1989.

Provincializing Europe: Postcolonial Thought and Historical Difference. Princeton: Princeton University Press, 2000.

Chandra, Bipan. *India's Struggle for Independence*. New Delhi: Penguin, 1989.

"Charles" [pseudonym]. "The Sepoy Overseas – and at Home." *Journal of the United Service Institution of India*, Vol. LXXV, No. 320 (July 1945): 298–303.

Chatterjee, Partha. *Nationalist Thought and the Colonial World: A Derivative Discourse*. London: Zed Books, 1986.

The Nation and Its Fragments: Colonial and Postcolonial Histories. Princeton: Princeton University Press, 1993.

Chodoff, Elliot P. "Ideology and Primary Groups." *Armed Forces and Society*, Vol. 9, No. 4 (1983): 569–593.

Christensen, Claus Bundgaard, Niels Bo Poulsen, and Peter Scharff Smith. *Under Hagekors og Dannebrog: Danskere i Waffen SS 1940–1945*. Copenhagen: Aschehoug, 1998.

Clausewitz, Carl von. *On War*. Edited and Translated by Michael Howard and Peter Paret. Princeton: Princeton University Press, 1976.

Clayton, Anthony. *France, Soldiers and Africa*. London: Brassey's, 1988.

Clifford, James. *Routes: Travel and Translation in the Late Twentieth Century*. Cambridge: Harvard University Press, 1997.

Close, H. M. *A Pathan Company*. Islamabad: National Book Foundation, 1994.

Cohen, Eliot. *Citizens and Soldiers: Dilemmas of Military Service*. Ithaca: Cornell University Press, 1990.

Cohen, Hannah. *Let Stephen Speak*. London: Sylvan Press, 1943.

Cohen, Stephen P. *The Indian Army: Its Contribution to the Development of a Nation*. Berkeley: University of California Press, 1971.

Cohn, Bernard S. *Colonialism and Its Forms of Knowledge: The British in India*. Princeton: Princeton University Press, 1996.

Colas, Alejandro and Bryan Mabee, eds. *Mercenaries, Pirates, Bandits and Empires: Private Violence in Historical Context*. London: Hurst, 2010.

Collins, Larry and Dominique Lapierre. *Freedom at Midnight*. London: HarperCollins, 1975.

Collins, Randall. *Interaction Ritual Chains*. Princeton: Princeton University Press, 2004.

"Does Nationalist Sentiment Increase Fighting Efficacy? A Skeptical View from the Sociology of Violence" in John A. Hall and Sinisa Malesevic, eds., *Nationalism and War*. Cambridge: Cambridge University Press, 2013: 31–43.

Condon, Brigadier W. E. H. *The Frontier Force Rifles*. Aldershot: Gale & Polden Ltd., 1953.

Connell, John. *Auchinleck A Critical Biography*. London: Cassell, 1959.

Wavell: Supreme Commander. London: Collins, 1969.

Cook, Haruko Taya and Theodore F. Cook. *Japan at War: An Oral History.* London: Phoenix Press, 2000.

Cooper, Frederick. *On the Waterfront: Urban Disorder and the Transformation of Work in Colonial Mombasa.* New Haven: Yale University Press, 1987.

Colonialism in Question: Theory, Knowledge, History. Berkeley: University of California Press, 2005.

Cooper, Frederick and Ann Laura Stoler, eds. *Tensions of Empire: Colonial Cultures in a Bourgeois World.* Berkeley: University of California Press, 1997.

Cooper, Randolf G. S. *The Anglo-Maratha Campaigns and the Contest for India: The Struggle for Control of the South Asian Military Economy.* Cambridge: Cambridge University Press, 2005.

"Culture, Combat, and Colonialism in Eighteenth- and Nineteenth-Century India." *The International History Review,* Vol. 27, No. 3 (2005): 534–549.

Cooper, Raymond. *'B' Company: One man's war in Burma 1942–1944 recalled in hospital in 1945.* London: Dennis Dobson, 1978.

Coronil, Fernando. "Beyond Occidentalism: Toward Nonimperial Geohistorical Categories." *Cultural Anthropology,* Vol. 11, No. 1 (1996): 51–87.

Crasta, John Baptist. *Eaten by the Japanese: The Memoir of an Unknown Indian Prisoner of War.* New York: Invisible Man Press, 2012.

Cray, Ed, compiler. *The Erotic Muse: American Bawdy Songs,* 2nd ed. Urbana: University of Illinois Press, 1992.

Creveld, Martin van. *Fighting Power: German and US Army Performance, 1939–1945.* Westport: Greenwood Press, 1982.

The Transformation of War. New York: The Free Press, 1991.

The Culture of War. New York: Ballantine, 2008.

Croft, John. "A Company Commander at Imphal 1944." *Journal of the Society for Army Historical Research,* Vol. LXXII, No. 289 (Spring 1994): 19–34.

Dandeker, Christopher. *Surveillance, Power & Modernity: Bureaucracy and Discipline from 1700 to the Present Day.* Cambridge: Polity Press, 1990.

Davies, G. H. "Memories." *Y Ddraig Goch: The Journal of the Royal Welch Fusiliers,* Vol. XXII, No. 4 (March 1982): 58–59.

De Normann, Roderick. "Infantry Regiment 950 – Germany's Indian Legion." *Journal of the Society for Army Historical Research,* Vol. 75, No. 303 (1997): 172–190.

Delbrück, Hans. *Warfare in Antiquity.* Lincoln: University of Nebraska Press, 1975.

The Barbarian Invasions. Lincoln: University of Nebraska Press, 1980.

Dhavan, Purnima. *When Sparrows Became Hawks: The Making of the Sikh Warrior Tradition, 1699–1799*. Oxford: Oxford University Press, 2011.

Dirks, Nicholas B. *Castes of Mind: Colonialism and the Making of Modern India*. Princeton: Princeton University Press, 2001.

Doty, Roxanne. *Imperial Encounters: The Politics of Representation in North-South Relations*. Minneapolis: University of Minnesota Press, 1996.

Douds, Gerard. "'Matters of Honour': Indian Troops in the North African and Italian Theatres" in Paul Addison and Angus Calder, eds., *Time to Kill: The Soldier's Experience of War in the West, 1939–1945*. London: Pimlico, 1997.

Dower, John W. *War without Mercy: Race and Power in the Pacific War*. New York: Pantheon Books, 1986.

Drinnon, Richard. *Facing West: The Metaphysics of Indian-Hating and Empire-Building*. Norman: University of Oklahoma Press, 1997 [1980].

Du Picq, Ardant. *Battle Studies: Ancient and Modern Battle*. New York: Macmillan, 1921.

Durkheim, Emile. *Suicide: A Study in Sociology*. New York: The Free Press, 1951.

The Elementary Forms of the Religious Life. New York: The Free Press, 1965.

Durnford, John. *Branch Line to Burma*. London: Four Square, 1966.

Dyer, Gwynne. *War*. London: The Bodley Head, 1986.

Echenberg, Myron. *Colonial Conscripts: The Tirailleurs Sénégalais in French West Africa, 1857–1960*. Portsmouth: Heinemann, 1991.

Edgerton, Robert B. *Warriors of the Rising Sun: A History of the Japanese Military*. New York: W.W. Norton & Co., 1997.

Edwards, Leslie. *Kohima: The Furthest Battle*. Stroud: The History Press, 2009.

Ehrenreich, Barbara. *Blood Rites: Origins and History of the Passions of War*. London: Virago, 1997.

Eisenhart, R. Wayne. "You Can't Hack It Little Girl: A Discussion of the Covert Psychological Agenda of Modern Combat Training." *Journal of Social Issues*, Vol. 31, No. 4 (1975): 13–23.

Eley, Geoff and David Blackbourne. *The Peculiarities of German History: Bourgeois Society and Politics in Nineteenth-Century Germany*. Oxford: Oxford University Press, 1984.

Ellis, John. *The Sharp End*. London: Windrow & Greene, 1990 [1980].

Elphick, Peter. *Singapore: The Pregnable Fortress*. London: Hodder and Stoughton, 1995.

Enloe, Cynthia. *Ethnic Soldiers: State Security in Divided Societies*. Athens: The University of Georgia Press, 1980.

Bananas, Beaches and Bases: Making Feminist Sense of International Politics. Berkeley: University of California Press, 2000 [1989].

Evans, Frank. *Roll Call at Oeyama: P.O.W. Remembers.* Llandysul: J.D. Lewis, 1985.

Evans, Humphrey. *Thimayya of India: A Soldier's Life.* New York: Harcourt, Brace, and Co., 1960.

Fahmy, Khaled. *All the Pasha's Men: Mehmed Ali, his Army and the Making of Modern Egypt.* Cairo and New York: The American University in Cairo Press, 2002.

Falcon, R. W. *Handbook on Sikhs for Regimental Officers.* Allahabad: Pioneer Press, 1896.

Farrar, Jr., L. L. "Nationalism in Wartime: Critiquing the Conventional Wisdom" in Frans Coetzee and Marilyn Shevin-Coetzee, eds., *Authority, Identity and the Social History of the Great War.* Providence and Oxford: Berghahn Books, 1995.

Farrell, Theo. *The Norms of War: Cultural Beliefs and Modern Conflict.* Boulder: Lynne Rienner, 2005.

Farwell, Byron. *The Gurkhas.* New York: W.W. Norton, 1984.

Fassin, Didier. *Humanitarian Reason: A Moral History of the Present.* Berkeley: University of California Press, 2012.

Faulk, Henry. *Group Captives: The Re-Education of German Prisoners of War in Britain 1945–1948.* London: Chatto & Windus, 1977.

Fay, Peter Ward. *The Forgotten Army: India's Armed Struggle for Independence 1942–1945.* Ann Arbor: The University of Michigan Press, 1993.

Feldman, Allen. *Formations of Violence: The Narrative of the Body and Political Terror in Northern Ireland.* Chicago: The University of Chicago Press, 1991.

Fergusson, Bernard. *The Wild Green Earth.* London: Collins, 1946.

Ferguson, James. *The Anti-Politics Machine: "Development," Depoliticization, and Bureaucratic Power in Lesotho.* Minneapolis: University of Minnesota Press, 1994.

Fernandez, James W. "Symbolic Consensus in a Fang Reformative Cult." *American Anthropologist,* Vol. 67 (1965): 902–929.

Fernandes, Leela. *Producing Workers: The Politics of Gender, Class, and Culture in the Calcutta Jute Mills.* Philadelphia: University of Pennsylvania Press, 1997.

Foucault, Michel. *Discipline and Punish: The Birth of the Prison.* New York: Vintage Books, 1995 [1975].

Society Must Be Defended. London: Penguin, 2004.

Fox, Richard G. *Lions of the Punjab: Culture in the Making.* Berkeley: University of California Press, 1985.

Fraser, David. *And We Shall Shock Them: The British Army in the Second World War*. London: Hodder and Stoughton, 1983.

Fraser, George MacDonald. *Quartered Safe Out Here: A Recollection of the War in Burma*. London: HarperCollins, 1995.

French, David. *Military Identities: The Regimental System, the British Army, and the British People, c.1870–2000*. Oxford: Oxford University Press, 2005.

Fritz, Stephen G. *Frontsoldaten: The German Soldier in World War II*. Lexington: The University Press of Kentucky, 1995.

Frost, Gerald, ed. *Not Fit to Fight: The Cultural Subversion of the Armed Forces in Britain and America*. London: The Social Affairs Unit, 1998.

Fujitani, T. *Race for Empire: Koreans as Japanese and Japanese as Americans during World War II*. Berkeley: University of California Press, 2011.

Fujiwara, Lt. Gen. Iwaichi. F. *Kikan: Japanese Army Intelligence Operations in Southeast Asia during World War II*. Hong Kong: Heinemann Asia, 1983.

Fussell, Paul. *Wartime: Understanding and Behavior in the Second World War*. Oxford and New York: Oxford University Press, 1989.

   The Great War and Modern Memory. Oxford and New York: Oxford University Press, 2000 [1975].

Gat, Azar. *War in Human Civilization*. New York: Oxford University Press, 2006.

Geertz, Clifford. *The Interpretation of Cultures*. New York: Fontana Press, 1993 [1973].

George, Alexander L. *The Chinese Communist Army in Action: The Korean War and its Aftermath*. New York: Columbia University Press, 1967.

Gerth, H. H. and C. Wright Mills, eds. *From Max Weber: Essays in Sociology*. New York: Oxford University Press, 1946.

Ghosh, Amitav. *The Glass Palace*. London: HarperCollins, 2000.

Ghosh, K. K. *The Indian National Army: Second Front of the Indian Independence Movement*. Meerut: Meenakshi Prakashan, 1969.

Giddens, Anthony. *The Nation-State and Violence*. Cambridge: Polity Press, 1985.

   The Consequences of Modernity. Cambridge: Polity Press, 1990.

Gilmore, Scott and Patrick Davis. *A Connecticut Yankee in the 8th Gurkha Rifles: A Burma Memoir*. Washington, D.C.: Brassey's, 1995.

Girard, René. *Violence and the Sacred*. Baltimore: The Johns Hopkins University Press, 1977.

Glover, Michael. *That Astonishing Infantry: Three Hundred Years of the History of the Royal Welch Fusiliers (23rd Regiment of Foot)*. London: Leo Cooper, 1989.

Glubb, John B. "The Conflict Between Tradition and Modernism in the Role of Muslim Armies" in Carl Leiden, ed., *The Conflict of Traditionalism and Modernism in the Muslim Middle East*. Austin: University of Texas Press, 1966.

Godfrey, Arthur. *Copies of the Proclamation of the King, Emperor of India, to the Princes and Peoples of India, of the 2nd day of November 1908, and the Proclamation of the late Queen Victoria of the 1st day of November 1858, to the Princes, Chiefs and People of India*. London: HMSO, 1908.

Goffman, Erving. *Asylums: Essays on the Social Situation of Mental Patients and Other Inmates*. New York: Anchor Books, 1961.

Goldhagen, Daniel Jonah. *Hitler's Willing Executioners: Ordinary Germans and the Holocaust*. New York: Alfred R. Knopf, 1996.

Gommans, Jos J. L. and Dirk H. A. Kolff, eds. *Warfare and Weaponry in South Asia 1000–1800*. New Delhi: Oxford University Press, 2001.

Gould, Tony. *Imperial Warriors: Britain and the Gurkhas*. London: Granta, 1999.

Government of India. *Statistics Relating to India's War Effort*. Delhi: Manager of Publications, 1947.

Grant, Major General Ian Lyall. *Burma: The Turning Point*. Barnsley: Leo Cooper, 2003.

Grant, Ian Lyall and Kazuo Tamayama. *Burma 1942: The Japanese Invasion*. Chichester: Zampi Press, 1999.

Graves, Robert. *Good-Bye to All That*. New York: Anchor, 1998 [1929, 1957].

Gray, J. Glenn. *The Warriors: Reflections on Men in Battle*. New York: Harper and Row, 1970.

Greenough, Paul. *Prosperity and Misery in Modern Bengal*. Oxford: Oxford University Press, 1982.

Griffith, James. "The Army's New Unit Personnel Replacement and Its Relationship to Unit Cohesion and Social Support." *Military Psychology*, Vol 1, No. 1 (January 1989): 17–34.

Griffiths, G. C. "The Railway Corridor and Before: With the 2nd Battalion in Burma." *Y Ddraig Goch: The Journal of the Royal Welch Fusiliers*, Vol. XXII, No. 4 (March 1982): 56–57.

Guha, Ranajit. *Dominance without Hegemony: History and Power in Colonial India*. Cambridge: Harvard University Press, 1997.

Elementary Aspects of Peasant Insurgency in Colonial India. Durham: Duke University Press, 1999.

Gupta, Akhil and James Ferguson. *Culture, Power, Place: Explorations in Critical Anthropology*. Durham: Duke University Press, 1997.

Gupta, Partha Sarathi. "The Debate on Indianization 1918–39" in Gupta and Deshpande, eds., *The British Raj and Its Indian Armed Forces 1857–1939*: 228–269.

Gupta, Partha Sarathi and Anirudh Deshpande, eds. *The British Raj and Its Indian Armed Forces 1857–1939*. Delhi: Oxford University Press, 2002.

Gurfein, M. I. and Morris Janowitz. "Trends in Wehrmacht Morale." *Public Opinion Quarterly*, Vol. 10, No. 1 (1946): 78–84.

Hackett, Sir John W. *The Profession of Arms*. London: Times Publishing, 1962.

Hall, Catherine. *Civilising Subjects: Metropole and Colony in the English Imagination 1830–1867*. Cambridge: Polity, 2002.

Hamilton, John A. L. *War Bush: 81 (West African) Division in Burma 1943–1945*. Norwich: Michael Russell, 2001.

Hanson, Victor Davis. *The Soul of Battle: From Ancient Times to the Present Day, How Three Great Liberators Vanquished Tyranny*. New York: The Free Press, 1999.

　The Western Way of War: Infantry Battle in Classical Greece. Berkeley: University of California Press, 2000 [1989].

　Carnage and Culture: Landmark Battles in the Rise of Western Power. New York: Anchor Books, 2002.

Harlow, Barbara and Mia Carter, eds. *Archives of Empire Volume I: From the East India Company to the Suez Canal*. Durham: Duke University Press, 2003.

Harries, Patrick. *Work, Culture and Identity: Migrant Laborers in Mozambique and South Africa c. 1860–1910*. Portsmouth: Heinemann, 1994.

Harrison, Mark. *Medicine and Victory: British Military Medicine in the Second World War*. Oxford: Oxford University Press, 2004.

Hauser, William L. *America's Army in Crisis: A Study in Civil-Military Relations*. Baltimore: Johns Hopkins University Press, 1973.

Hawkins, Jack. *Anything for a Quiet Life: the Autobiography of Jack Hawkins*. London: Elm Tree Books, 1973.

Helmer, John. *Bringing the War Home: The American Soldier in Vietnam and After*. New York: The Free Press, 1974.

Henderson, William Darryl. *Why the Vietcong Fought: A Study of Motivation and Control in a Modern Army in Combat*. Westport: Greenwood Press, 1979.

　Cohesion the Human Element in Combat: Leadership and Societal Influence in the Armies of the Soviet Union, the United States, North Vietnam and Israel. Washington, D.C.: National Defense University Press, 1985.

Herman, Ellen. *The Romance of American Psychology: Political Culture in an Age of Experts.* Berkeley: University of California Press, 1995.

Hevia, James. *The Imperial Security State: British Colonial Knowledge and Empire-Building in Asia.* Cambridge: Cambridge University Press, 2012.

Hickey, Michael. *The Unforgettable Army: Slim's XIVth Army in Burma.* Staplehurst: Spellmount, Ltd., 1998.

Hill, Richard and Peter Hogg. *A Black Corps d'Élite: An Egyptian Sudanese Conscript Battalion with the French Army in Mexico, 1863–1867, and its Survivors in Subsequent African History.* East Lansing: Michigan State University Press, 1995.

Hirst, Paul. *War and Power in the 21st Century.* Cambridge: Polity, 2001.

Hobsbawm, Eric and Terence Ranger, eds. *The Invention of Tradition.* Cambridge: Cambridge University Press, 1983.

Hobson, John M. *The Eastern Origins of Western Civilization.* Cambridge: Cambridge University Press, 2004.

Hollier, Denis, ed. *The College of Sociology (1937–39).* Minneapolis: University of Minnesota Press, 1988.

Holmes, Richard. *Firing Line.* London: Pimlico, 1994.

Holsti, Kalevi J. *The State, War and the State of War.* Cambridge: Cambridge University Press, 1996.

Homer. *The Iliad.* London: Penguin, 2003.

Hopkins, A. G., ed. *Globalization in World History.* London: Pimlico, 2002.

Howard, Michael. *War in European History.* Oxford: Oxford University Press, 1976.

Hubert, Henri and Marcel Mauss. *Sacrifice: Its Nature and Function.* London: Cohen and West, 1964.

Hull, Isabel V. *Absolute Destruction: Military Culture and the Practices of War in Imperial Germany.* Ithaca and London: Cornell University Press, 2005.

Huntington, Samuel P. *The Soldier and the State: The Theory and Politics of Civil-Military Relations.* Cambridge: Harvard University Press, 1957.

Hutchins, Francis. *India's Revolution: Gandhi and the Quit India Movement.* Cambridge: Harvard University Press, 1973.

Hynes, Samuel. *The Soldiers' Tale: Bearing Witness to Modern War.* London: Pimlico, 1998.

Inden, Ronald B. *Imagining India.* Oxford: Blackwell, 1990.

Isaacman, Allen. *Cotton is the Mother of Poverty: Peasants, Work and Rural Struggle in Colonial Mozambique, 1938–1961.* Portsmouth: Heinemann, 1995.

Jackson, Ashley. *Botswana 1939–1945: An African Country at War.* Oxford: Clarendon Press, 1999.

The British Empire and the Second World War. London: Hambledon Continuum, 2006.

Janowitz, Morris, ed. *The New Military: Changing Patterns of Organization*. New York: Russell Sage, 1964.

The Professional Soldier: A Social and Political Portrait. New York: The Free Press, 1971.

Janowitz, Morris and Stephen D. Wesbrook, eds. *The Political Education of Soldiers*. Beverly Hills: Sage, 1983.

Jarvie, Ian. "Fanning the Flames: Anti-American Reaction to Objective Burma (1945)." *Historical Journal of Film, Radio and Television*, Vol. 1, No. 2 (1981): 117–137.

"The Burma Campaign on Film: 'Objective Burma' (1945), 'The Stilwell Road' (1945) and 'Burma Victory' (1945)." *Historical Journal of Film, Radio and Television*, Vol. 8, No. 1 (1988): 55–73.

Jeffery, Keith. "The Second World War" in Judith M. Brown and Wm. Roger Louis, eds., *The Oxford History of the British Empire*, Vol. IV, *The Twentieth Century*. Oxford: Oxford University Press, 1999: 306–328.

Jeffords, Susan. *The Remasculinization of America: Gender and the Vietnam War*. Bloomington: Indiana University Press, 1989.

Jeffries, Charles J. *The Colonial Police*. London: M. Parish, 1952.

Joas, Hans and Wolfgang Knöbl. *War in Social Thought: Hobbes to the Present*. Princeton: Princeton University Press, 2013.

Johnston, Alastair Iain. *Cultural Realism: Strategic Culture and Grand Strategy in Chinese History*. Princeton: Princeton University Press, 1995.

Jones, Heather. *Violence against Prisoners of War in the First World War: Britain, France, and Germany, 1914–1920*. Cambridge: Cambridge University Press, 2011.

Jones, Robert Alun. "Practices and Presuppositions: Some Questions about Durkheim and Les Formes élémentaires de la vie religieuse" in Jeffrey C. Alexander and Philip Smith, eds., *The Cambridge Companion to Durkheim*. Cambridge: Cambridge University Press, 2005.

Josephus. *The Jewish War*. London: Penguin, 1981 [1959].

Jünger, Ernst. *The Storm of Steel: From the Diary of a German Storm-Troop Officer on the Western Front*. New York: Zimmermann & Zimmermann, 1985.

Kamtekar, Indivar. "A Different War Dance: State and Class in India 1939–1945." *Past and Present*, Vol. 176, No. 1 (August 2002): 187–221.

"The Shiver of 1942" in Kaushik Roy, ed., *War and Society in Colonial India 1807–1945*. New Delhi: Oxford University Press, 2006.

Katzenstein, Peter J. *The Culture of National Security: Norms and Identity in World Politics*. New York: Columbia University Press, 1996.

Kaul, Lt. Gen. B. M. *The Untold Story*. Bombay: Allied Publishers, 1967.

Kaul, Vivien Ashima. "Sepoys' Links with Society: A Study of the Bengal Army 1858–95" in Gupta and Deshpande, eds., *The British Raj and Its Indian Armed Forces*.

Kaviraj, Sudipta. "The Imaginary Institution of India" in Partha Chatterjee and Gyanendra Pandey, eds., *Subaltern Studies VII*. Delhi: Oxford University Press, 1992: 1–39.

Kaye, John William. *A History of the Sepoy War in India 1857–1858*. Vol. I. London: W.H. Allen & Co., 1864.

Keane, Fergal. *Road of Bones: The Epic Siege of Kohima 1944*. London: Harper Press, 2011.

Keane, John. *Reflections on Violence*. London: Verso, 1996.

Keegan, John. *The Face of Battle: A Study of Agincourt, Waterloo and the Somme*. London: Penguin, 1978 [1976].

Kellett, Anthony. *Combat Motivation: The Behavior of Soldiers in Battle*. Boston: Kluwer, 1982.

Kelly, John D. and Martha Kaplan. *Represented Communities: Fiji and World Decolonization*. Chicago: The University of Chicago Press, 2001.

Kelman, Herbert C. and V. Lee Hamilton. *Crimes of Obedience: Towards a Social Psychology of Authority and Responsibility*. New Haven and London: Yale University Press, 1989.

Kemp, Lieutenant-Commander P.K. and John Graves. *The Red Dragon: The Story of the Royal Welch Fusiliers 1919–1945*. Aldershot: Gale & Polden, 1960.

Kempton, Chris. *Valour and Gallantry: H.E.I.C and Indian Army Victoria Crosses and George Crosses 1856–1946*. Milton Keynes: The Military Press, 2001.

Kertzer, David I. *Ritual, Politics, and Power*. New Haven: Yale University Press, 1988.

Khan, Lt. Gen. *Gul Hassan. Memoirs*. Karachi: Oxford University Press, 1993.

Khan, Mohammad Ayub. *Friends Not Masters: A Political Autobiography*. London: Oxford University Press, 1967.

Khan, Major-General Shah Nawaz. *My Memories of I.N.A. & Its Netaji*. Delhi: Rajkamal Publications, 1946.

Khan, Yasmin. *The Raj at War: A People's History of India's Second World War*. London: Bodley Head, 2015.

Kier, Elizabeth. "Homosexuals in the U.S. Military: Open Integration and Combat Effectiveness." *International Security*, Vol. 23, No. 2 (1998): 5–39.

Kiernan, V. G. *Colonial Empires and Armies 1815–1960*. Stroud: Sutton, 1998 [1982].

Killingray, David and R. Rathbone, eds. *Africa and the Second World War*. London: Macmillan, 1986.

Killingray, David and David Omissi. *Guardians of Empire: The Armed Forces of the Colonial Powers c.1700–1964*. Manchester: Manchester University Press, 1999.

Killingray, David and Martin Plaut. *Fighting for Britain: African Soldiers in the Second World War*. Woodbridge: James Currey, 2010.

Kindsvatter, Peter S. *American Soldiers: Ground Combat in the World Wars, Korea, & Vietnam*. Lawrence: University Press of Kansas, 2003.

King, Anthony. "The Word of Command: Communication and Cohesion in the Military." *Armed Forces & Society*, Vol. 32, No. 4 (July 2006): 493–512.

The Combat Soldier: Infantry Tactics and Cohesion in the Twentieth and Twenty-First Centuries. Oxford: Oxford University Press, 2013.

Kinkead, Eugene. *In Every War but One*. New York: W.W. Norton, 1959.

Kirby, Maj. Gen. S. Woodburn *et al. The War Against Japan: India's Most Dangerous Hour*. Vol. II. London: HMSO, 1958.

The War Against Japan: The Loss of Singapore. Vol. I. London: HMSO, 1957.

Kolff, Dirk. *Naukar, Rajput, and Sepoy: The Ethnohistory of the Military Labour Market in Hindustan, 1450–1850*. Cambridge: Cambridge University Press, 1990.

Krebs, Ronald R. *Fighting for Rights: Military Service and the Politics of Citizenship*. Ithaca: Cornell University Press, 2006.

Kundu, Apurba. *Militarism in India: The Army and Civil Society in Consensus*. London: I.B. Tauris & Co Ltd, 1998.

Laband, John. *Kingdom in Crisis: The Zulu Response to the British Invasion of 1879*. Barnsley: Pen & Sword, 2007 [1992].

Latimer, Jon. *Burma: The Forgotten War*. London: John Murray, 2004.

Lawrence, Henry. *Essays on the Indian Army and Oude*. Serampore: Friend of India Press, 1859.

Leathart, Scott. *With the Gurkhas: India, Burma, Singapore, Malaya, Indonesia, 1940–1959*. Durham, UK: Pentland Press, 1996.

Lebra, Joyce C. *Jungle Alliance: Japan and the Indian National Army*. Singapore: Asia Pacific Press, 1971.

Japanese-Trained Armies in Southeast Asia: Independence and Volunteer Forces in World War II. New York: Columbia University Press, 1977.

Leckie, Robert. *Strong Men Armed: The United States Marines Against Japan*. Cambridge: Da Capo Press, 1997 [1962].

Leed, Eric J. *No Man's Land: Combat and Identity in World War I*. Cambridge: Cambridge University Press, 1997.

Lewin, Ronald. *Slim: The Standardbearer*. London: Leo Cooper, 1976.

Leyin, John. *Tell Them of Us: The Forgotten Army – Burma*. Stanford-le-Hope, Essex: Lejins Publishing, 2000.

Levinas, Emmanuel. *Totality and Infinity*. Pittsburgh: Duquesne University Press, 1969.

Lincoln, Bruce. *Discourse and the Construction of Society: Comparative Studies of Myth, Ritual, and Classification*. Oxford: Oxford University Press, 1989.

   Death, War, and Sacrifice: Studies in Ideology and Practice. Chicago: The University of Chicago Press, 1991.

   Authority: Construction and Corrosion. Chicago: The University of Chicago Press, 1994.

Linderman, Gerald F. *Embattled Courage: The Experience of Combat in the American Civil War*. New York: The Free Press, 1987.

   The World within War: America's Combat Experience in World War II. New York: The Free Press, 1997.

Lomax, Eric. *The Railway Man*. London: Vintage, 1996.

Lorge, Peter. *The Asian Military Revolution: From Gunpowder to the Bomb*. Cambridge: Cambridge University Press, 2008.

Lowry, Major M. A. *An Infantry Company in Arakan and Kohima*. Aldershot: Gale and Polden, 1950.

Lunn, Joe. *Memoirs of the Maelstrom: A Senegalese Oral History of the First World War*. Portsmouth: Heinemann, 1999.

Lynn, John A. *The Bayonets of the Republic: Motivation of Tactics in the Army of Revolutionary France, 1791–91*. Urbana: University of Illinois Press, 1984.

   "Heart of the Sepoy" in Emily Goldman and Leslie Eliason, eds., *Diffusion of Military Knowledge, Technology, and Practices*. Stanford: Stanford University Press, 2003.

   Battle: A History of Combat and Culture. Boulder: Westview Press, 2003.

Machiavelli, Niccolo. *The Prince*. Cambridge: Cambridge University Press, 1988.

Mack, Andrew. "Why Big Nations Lose Small Wars: The Politics of Asymmetric Conflict." *World Politics*, Vol. 27, No. 2 (1975): 175–200.

MacMunn, Lt. Gen. Sir George. *The Martial Races of India*. London: Sampson, Low, Marston & Co., n.d. [1933].

   The Armies of India. London: Adam and Charles Black, 1911.

Madan, Lieutenant-Colonel N. N. *The Arakan Operations 1942–1945*. Delhi: Combined Inter-services Historical Section (India and Pakistan), 1954.

Mamdani, Mahmood. *When Victims Become Killers: Colonialism, Nativism, and the Genocide in Rwanda*. Princeton: Princeton University Press, 2001.

Manchester, William. *Goodbye Darkness: A Memoir of the Pacific War*. New York: Dell, 1982 [1980].

Manela, Erez. *The Wilsonian Moment: Self-Determination and the International Origins of Anticolonial Nationalism*. Oxford: Oxford University Press, 2007.

Mann, Gregory. *Native Sons: West African Veterans and France in the Twentieth Century*. Durham: Duke University Press, 2006.

Mann, Michael. *States, War and Capitalism*. Oxford: Blackwell, 1998.

　The Dark Side of Democracy: Explaining Ethnic Cleansing. Cambridge: Cambridge University Press, 2005.

Marcus, George E, ed. *Rereading Cultural Anthropology*. Durham and London: Duke University Press, 1992.

Marlantes, Karl. *Matterhorn*. London: Corvus, 2010.

Marshall, S. L. A. *Men Against Fire: The Problem of Battle Command*. Norman: University of Oklahoma Press, 2000 [1947].

Marston, Daniel P. *Phoenix from the Ashes: The Indian Army in the Burma Campaign*. Westport, CT: Praeger, 2003.

　The Indian Army and the End of the Raj. Cambridge: Cambridge University Press, 2014.

Mason, Philip. *A Matter of Honour: An Account of the Indian Army Its Officers and Men*. London: Jonathan Cape, 1974.

Massad, Joseph A. *Colonial Effects: The Making of National Identity in Jordan*. New York: Columbia University Press, 2001.

Masters, John. *Bugles and a Tiger: A Personal Adventure*. London: Michael Joseph, 1956.

　The Road Past Mandalay. London: Michael Joseph, 1961.

Mazower, Mark. "Military Violence and Nationalist Socialist Values: The *Wehrmacht* in Greece 1941–1944." *Past and Present*, Vol. 134 (February 1992): 129–158.

　Hitler's Empire: Nazi Rule in Occupied Europe. London: Penguin, 2009.

Mazumder, Rajit K. *The Indian Army and the Making of the Punjab*. Delhi: Permanent Black, 2003.

　"From Loyalty to Dissent: Punjabis from the Great War to World War II" in Roy, ed. *The Indian Army in Two World Wars*. Leiden: Brill, 2012: 461–491.

McNeill, William H. *The Pursuit of Power: Technology, Armed Force, and Society since A.D. 1000*. Chicago: University of Chicago Press, 1982.

　Keeping Together in Time: Dance and Drill in Human History. Cambridge: Harvard University Press, 1995.

McPherson, James M. *For Cause and Comrades: Why Men Fought in the Civil War*. New York: Oxford University Press, 1997.

Menezes, Lt. General S. L. *Fidelity and Honour: The Indian Army from the Seventeenth to the Twenty-first Century*. New Delhi: Oxford University Press, 1999.

Menon, V. P. *The Transfer of Power in India*. New Delhi: Orient Longman, 1957.

Merridale, Catherine. *Ivan's War: Life and Death in the Red Army, 1939–1945*. New York: Metropolitan Books, 2006.

Mershon, Sherie and Steven Schlossman. *Foxholes & Color Lines: Desegregating the U.S. Armed Forces*. Baltimore: The Johns Hopkins University Press, 1998.

Metcalf, Thomas R. *Ideologies of the Raj*. Cambridge: Cambridge University Press, 1994.

Meyers, Samuel L. and Albert D. Biderman, eds. *Mass Behavior in Battle and Captivity: The Communist Soldier in the Korean War*. Chicago: The University of Chicago Press, 1968.

Milgram, Stanley. *Obedience to Authority: An Experimental View*. New York: Harper and Row, 1974.

Moon, Penderel. *Wavell: The Viceroy's Journal*. Karachi: Oxford University Press, 1997 [1973].

Moore, Aaron William. *Writing War: Soldiers Record the Japanese Empire*. Cambridge: Harvard University Press, 2013.

Moore, Bob and Kent Fedorowich, eds. *Prisoners and their Captors in World War II*. Oxford: Berg, 1996.

Moran, Lord. *The Anatomy of Courage*. Garden City Park, NY: Avery Publishing Group, Inc., 1987 [1945].

Moreman, T. R. *The Jungle, the Japanese and the British Commonwealth Armies at War, 1941–45: Fighting Methods, Doctrine and Training for Jungle Warfare*. London: Frank Cass, 2005.

Morillo, Stephen with Michael F. Pavkovic. *What is Military History?* Cambridge: Polity, 2006.

Morris, Rosalind C., ed. *Can the Subaltern Speak? Reflections on the History of an Idea*. New York: Columbia University Press, 2010.

Moskos, Charles C. *The American Enlisted Man: The Rank and File in Today's Military*. New York: Russell Sage Foundation, 1970.

Moskos, Charles C., John Allen Williams, and David R. Segal, eds. *The Postmodern Military: Armed Forces after the Cold War*. New York: Oxford University Press, 2000.

Mosse, George L. *Fallen Soldiers: Reshaping the Memory of the World Wars*. Oxford: Oxford University Press, 1990.

Narain, Namrata. *Co-option and Control: The Role of the Colonial Army in India 1918–1947*. Ph.D. Thesis, University of Cambridge, 1992.

Narayan, B. K. *General J.N. Chaudhuri: An Autobiography*. New Delhi: Vikas Publishing House, 1978.

Neitzel, Sönke and Harald Welzer. *Soldaten: On Fighting, Killing, and Dying*. New York: Alfred Knopf, 2012.

Neumann, Peter. *The Black March*. New York: Bantam, 1967 [1958].

Nietzsche, Friedrich. *Beyond Good & Evil: Prelude to a Philosophy of the Future*. New York: Vintage Books, 1989.

On the Genealogy of Morals and Ecce Homo. New York: Vintage Books, 1989.

Nimis (pseudonym). "What Shall We Talk?" *Journal of the United Service Institution of India*, Vol. LXXII, No. 309 (October 1942): 356–360.

Nish, Ian and Mark Allen, eds. *War, Conflict and Security in Japan and Asia-Pacific, 1941–52: The Writings of Louis Allen*. Folkestone: Global Oriental, 2011.

Nish, Ian. "Louis Allen, 1922–1991: Formidable Character and Scholar."in Nish and Allen, eds. *War, Conflict and Security in Japan and Asia-Pacific, 1941–52*.

Nunneley, John. *Tales from the King's African Rifles*. London: Cassell & Co., 1998.

Nunneley, John and Kazuo Tamayama. *Tales by Japanese Soldiers of the Burma Campaign 1942–1945*. London: Cassell, 2000.

Omissi, David. "Europe Through Indian Eyes: Indian Soldiers Encounter England and France, 1914–1918." *English Historical Review*, Vol. CXXII, No. 496 (April 2007): 371–396.

Indian Voices of the Great War: Soldiers' Letters, 1914–18. London: Macmillan, 1999.

The Sepoy and the Raj: The Indian Army, 1860–1940. London: Macmillan, 1994.

Overmans, Rüdiger. Deutsche militärische Verluste im Zweiten Weltkrieg [*German Military Losses in World War II*]. München: Oldenbourg, 2004.

Palit, Maj. Gen. D. K. "Indianisation: A Personal Experience." *Indo-British Review*, Vol. XVI, No. 1 (1989): 59–64.

Major General A.A. Rudra: His Services in Three Armies and Two World Wars. Delhi: Reliance Publishing House, 1997.

Palmer, J. A. B. *The Mutiny Oubreak at Meerut in 1857*. Cambridge: Cambridge University Press, 1966.

Pandey, Gyanendra, ed. *The Indian Nation in 1942*. Calcutta: K.P. Bagchi, 1988.

Pandey, Gyanendra. *The Construction of Communalism in Colonial North India*. New Delhi: Oxford University Press, 1990.

Parker, Geoffrey. *The Military Revolution: Military Innovation and the Rise of the West, 1500–1800*. Cambridge: Cambridge University Press, 1988.

ed. *The Cambridge History of Warfare*. Cambridge: Cambridge University Press, 2005.

Parsons, Timothy H. *The African Rank-and-File: Social Implications of Colonial Military Service in the King's African Rifles, 1902–1964*. Portsmouth: Heinemann, 1999.

Peled, Alon. *A Question of Loyalty: Military Manpower Policy in Multiethnic States*. Ithaca: Cornell University Press, 1998.

Percy, Sarah. *Mercenaries: The History of a Norm in International Relations*. Oxford: Oxford University Press, 2007.

Perry, F. W. *The Commonwealth Armies: Manpower and Organisation in Two World Wars*. Manchester: Manchester University Press, 1988.

Petersen, Ib Damgaard, ed. *Faldne i Danmarks Frihedskamp 1940–45*. Copenhagen: Gyldendal, 1970.

Philllps, Barnaby. *Another Man's War: The Story of a Burma Boy in Britain's Forgotten African Army*. London: Oneworld, 2014.

Place, Timothy Harrison. *Military Training in the British Army, 1940–1944: From Dunkirk to D-Day*. London: Frank Cass Publishers, 2000.

Porter, Patrick. *Military Orientalism: Eastern War through Western Eyes*. London: Hurst, 2009.

Posen, Barry. "Nationalism, the Mass Army, and Military Power." *International Security*, Vol. 18, No. 2 (1993): 80–124.

Prasad, Sri Nandan. *Expansion of the Armed Forces and Defence Organisation 1939–1945*. Official History of the Indian Armed Forces in the Second World War 1939–45. Combined Inter-Services Historical Section India and Pakistan, 1956.

Praval, K. C. *Valour Triumphs: A History of the Kumaon Regiment*. Faridabad, Haryana: Thomson Press (India), 1976.

Prendergast, John. *Prender's Progress: A Soldier in India, 1931–1947*. London: Cassell, 1979.

Purvis, Phillida. "Louis Allen (1922–91) and Japan" in Hugh Cortazzi, ed. *Britain and Japan: Biographical Portraits*, Vol. V. Folkestone: Global Oriental, 2005: 344–357.

Pyle, Ernie. *Last Chapter*. New York: Henry Holt and Company, 1946.

Ralston, David B. *Importing the European Army: The Introduction of European Military Techniques and Institutions into the Extra-European World, 1600–1914*. Chicago: University of Chicago Press, 1990.

Ram, Moti, ed. *Two Historic Trials in Red Fort: An Authentic Account of the Trial by General Court Martial of Captain Shah Nawaz Khan, Captain P.K. Sahgal and Lt. G.S. Dhillon and the Trial by A European Military*

Commission of Emperor Bahadur Shah. New Delhi: M.L. Sabbarwall, 1946.

Randle, John. *Battle Tales from Burma.* Barnsley: Pen & Sword, 2004.

Rankin, Nicholas. *Telegram from Guernica: The Extraordinary Life of George Steer, War Correspondent.* London: Faber and Faber, 2003.

Richardson, Frank M. *Fighting Spirit: A study of psychological factors in war.* London: Leo Cooper, 1978.

Ricks, Thomas E. *Making the Corps.* New York: Scribner, 1997.

Riemer, Jeffrey W. "Durkheim's 'Heroic Suicide' in Military Combat." *Armed Forces & Society,* Vol. 25, No. 1 (Fall 1998): pp. 103–120.

Robertson, Roland. *Globalization: Social Theory and Global Culture.* London: Sage, 1992.

Rogers, Clifford J., ed. *The Military Revolution Debate: Readings on the Military Transformation of Early Modern Europe.* Boulder: Westview, 1995.

Rose, Alexander. *Men of War: The American Soldier in Combat at Bunker Hill, Gettysburg and Iwo Jima.* New York: Random House, 2015.

Rosen, Stephen Peter. *Societies & Military Power: India and Its Armies.* Ithaca: Cornell University Press, 1996.

War and Human Nature. Princeton: Princeton University Press, 2005.

Roy, Kaushik. "Military Synthesis in South Asia: Armies, Warfare, and Indian Society, c. 1740–1849." *The Journal of Military History,* Vol. 69 (July 2005): 651–690.

Brown Warriors of the Raj: Recruitment and the Mechanics of Command in the Sepoy Army, 1859–1913. New Delhi: Manohar, 2008.

"Discipline and Morale of the African, British and Indian Army units in Burma and India during World War II: July 1943 to August 1945." *Modern Asian Studies,* 44, 6 (2010): 1255–1282.

Warfare in Pre-British India – 1500 BCE to 1740 CE. New York: Routledge, 2015.

Roy, Kaushik, ed. *The Indian Army in the Two World Wars.* Leiden: Brill, 2012.

Royle, Trevor. *Orde Wingate: Irregular Soldier.* London: Phoenix Giant, 1995.

Rudolph, Susanne Hoeber, Lloyd I. Rudolph, with Mohan Singh Kanota. *Reversing the Gaze: Amar Singh's Diary, A Colonial Subject's Narrative of Imperial India.* Boulder: Westview, 2002.

Russell, Ralph. *Findings, Keepings: Life, Communism, Everything.* London: Shola Books, 2001.

Rutherford, Jeff. *Combat and Genocide on the Eastern Front: The German Infantry's War, 1941–1944.* Cambridge: Cambridge University Press, 2014.

Said, Edward W. *Orientalism*. New York: Vintage Books, 1979.

    Culture and Imperialism. New York: Vintage Books, 1993.

    Covering Islam: How the Media and the Experts Determine How We See the Rest of the World. New York: Vintage, 1997 [1981].

Sajer, Guy. *The Forgotten Soldier: War on the Russian Front – A True Story*. London: Cassell, 1999 [1971].

Sareen, T. R. *Select Documents on Indian National Army*. Delhi: Agam Prakashan, 1988.

Sassoon, Siegfried. *Memoirs of a Fox-Hunting Man*. London: Faber & Gwyer, 1928.

    Memoirs of an Infantry Officer. London: Faber and Faber, 1930.

    Sherston's Progress. London: Faber and Faber, 1936.

Savage, Paul L. and Richard A. Gabriel. "Cohesion and Disintegration in the American Army: An Alternative Perspective." *Armed Forces and Society*, Vol. 2, No. 3 (1976): 340–376.

Scarry, Elaine. *The Body in Pain: The Making and Unmaking of the World*. Oxford: Oxford University Press, 1985.

Scheler, Max. *On Feeling, Knowing, and Valuing*. Chicago: The University of Chicago Press, 1992.

Schlaefli, Robin. *Emergency Sahib*. London: R.J. Leach, 1992.

Scott, James C. *Weapons of the Weak: Everyday Forms of Peasant Resistance*. New Haven: Yale University Press, 1985.

Scott, Joan W. "The Evidence of Experience." *Critical Inquiry*, Vol. 17, No. 4 (Summer 1991): 773–797.

Seaman, Harry. *The Battle at Sangshak: Burma, March, 1944*. London: Leo Cooper, 1989.

Searle-Chatterjee, Mary and Ursula Sharma, eds. *Contextualising Caste: Post-Dumontian Approaches*. Oxford: Blackwell, 1994.

Sethna, Lt. Gen. A. M. and Lt. Col. Valmiki Katju. *Traditions of a Regiment: The Story of the Rajputana Rifles*. New Delhi: Lancers Publishers, 1983.

Sharma, Lt. Col. *Gautam. Nationalisation of the Indian Army (1885–1947)*. New Delhi: Allied Publishers, Ltd., 1996.

Shaw, Martin. *War and Genocide: Organized Killing and Modern Society*. Cambridge: Polity, 2003.

Sheehan, Neil. *A Bright Shining Lie: John Paul Vann and America in Vietnam*. New York: Vintage Books, 1988.

Shephard, Ben. *A War of Nerves: Soldiers and Psychiatrists 1914–1994*. London: Jonathan Cape, 2000.

Sherman, Nancy. *Stoic Warriors: The Ancient Philosophy Behind the Military Mind*. Oxford: Oxford University Press, 2005.

Sherry, Michael S. *The Rise of American Airpower: The Creation of Armageddon*. New Haven: Yale University Press, 1987.

Shibutani, Tamotsu. *The Derelicts of Company K: A Sociological Study of Demoralization*. Berkeley: University of California Press, 1978.

Shilliam, Robbie. "Modernity and Modernization" in Robert A. Denemark, ed. *The International Studies Encyclopedia*, Vol. VIII. Oxford: Wiley-Blackwell, 2010: 5214–5232.

Shils, Edward. "Primordial, Personal, Sacred and Civil Ties." *British Journal of Sociology*, Vol. 8 (1957): 130–145.

Shils, Edward A. and Morris Janowitz. "Cohesion and Disintegration in the *Wehrmacht* in World War II." *Public Opinion Quarterly*, Vol. 12, No. 2 (1948): 280–315.

Shipster, John. *Mist Over the Rice-Fields*. Barnsley: Leo Cooper, 2000.

Simmel, Georg. *Conflict and the Web of Group-Affiliations*. New York: The Free Press, 1955.

Sinha, Mrinalini. *Colonial Masculinity: The 'Manly Englishman' and the 'Effeminate Bengali' in the Late Nineteenth Century*. Manchester: Manchester University Press, 1995.

Singer, P. W. *Corporate Warriors: The Rise of the Privatized Military Industry*. Ithaca: Cornell University Press, 2003.

Singh, Gajendra. *The Testimonies of Indian Soldiers and the Two World Wars*. London: Bloomsbury, 2014.

Singh. Lt. General Harbakhsh. *In the Line of Duty: A Soldier Remembers*. New Delhi: Lancer, 2000.

Singh, Khushwant. *A History of the Sikhs: 1839–1964*. Vol. II. Princeton, NJ: Princeton University Press, 1966.

Singh, General Mohan. *Soldiers' Contribution to Indian Independence: The Epic of the Indian National Army*. New Delhi: Army Educational Stores, 1974.

Sledge, E. B. *With the Old Breed at Peleliu and Okinawa*. New York: Oxford University Press, 1990.

Slim, Field Marshal Sir William. *Defeat into Victory*. London: Cassell, 1956. *Unofficial History*. London: Cassell, 1959.

Smith, M. Brewster. *For a Significant Social Psychology: The Collected Writings of M. Brewster Smith*. New York and London: New York University Press, 2003.

Smith, Philip. "Meaning and Military Power: Moving on from Foucault." *Journal of Power*, Vol. 1, No. 3 (December 2008): 275–293.

Smurthwaite, D. *The Forgotten War: The British Army in the Far East 1941–1945*. London: National Army Museum, 1992.

Snyder, R. Claire. *Citizen Soldiers and Manly Warriors: Military Service and Gender in the Civic Republican Tradition*. Lanham: Rowman & Littlefield, 1999.

Snyder, Timothy. *Bloodlands: Europe Between Hitler and Stalin*. London: The Bodley Head, 2010.

Sondhaus, Lawrence. *Strategic Culture and Ways of War: An Historical Overview*. Milton Park and New York: Routledge, 2006.

Southern, Pat and Karen Dixon. *The Late Roman Army*. New Haven: Yale University Press, 1996.

Spector, Ronald. "The Royal Indian Navy Strike of 1946: A Study of Cohesion and Disintegration in Colonial Armed Forces." *Armed Forces and Society*, Vol. 7, No. 2 (Winter 1981): 271–284.

Stein, George H. *The Waffen SS: Hitler's Elite Guard at War*. Ithaca: Cornell University Press, 1966.

Steinmetz, George. "German Exceptionalism and the Origins of Nazism" in Ian Kershaw and Moshe Lewin, eds. *Stalinism and Nazism*. Cambridge: Cambridge University Press, 1997: 251–284.

Stewart, Nora Kinzer. *Mates & Muchachos: Unit Cohesion in the Falklands/Malvinas War*. McLean, VA: Brassey's (US), 1991.

Stokes, Eric. *The Peasant Armed: The Indian Revolt of 1857*. Oxford: Clarendon Press, 1986.

Stouffer, Samuel A. *et al*. The American Soldier: Adjustment During Army Life. Vol. I of *Studies in Social Psychology in World War II*. Princeton: Princeton University Press, 1949.

The American Soldier: Combat and Its Aftermath. Vol. II of *Studies in Social Psychology in World War II*. Princeton: Princeton University Press, 1949.

Strachan, Hew. *European Armies and the Conduct of War*. London: Unwin Hyman, 1983.

"Training, Morale and Modern War." *Journal of Contemporary History*, Vol. 41, No. 2 (2006): 211–227.

Street, Brian V. *Literacy in Theory and Practice*. Cambridge: Cambridge University Press, 1984.

Streets, Heather. *Martial Races: The Military, Race and Masculinity in British Imperial Culture, 1857–1914*. Manchester: Manchester University Press, 2004.

Subrahmanyam, Sanjay. "Connected Histories: Notes towards a Reconfiguration of Early Modern Eurasia." *Modern Asian Studies*, Vol. 31, No. 3 (1997): 735–762.

Sundaram, Chandar S. "A Paper Tiger: The Indian National Army in Battle, 1944–1945." *War and Society*, Vol. 13, No. 1 (May 1995): 35–59.

Tan Tai Yong. "Maintaining the Military Districts: Civil-Military Integration and District Soldiers' Boards in the Punjab, 1919–1939." *Modern Asian Studies*, Vol. 28, No. 4 (1994): 833–874.

The Garrison State: The Military, Government and Society in Colonial Punjab, 1849–1947. New Delhi: Sage, 2005.

Tanaka, Yuki. *Hidden Horrors: Japanese War Crimes in World War II*. Boulder, CO: Westview Press, 1996.

Taussig, Michael. "Culture of Terror – Space of Death: Roger Casement's Putumayo Report and the Explanation of Torture." *Comparative Studies in Society and History*, Vol. 26, No. 3 (July 1984): 467–497.

Taylor, Charles. "Interpretation and the Sciences of Man" in *Philosophy and the Human Sciences: Philosophical Papers 2*. Cambridge: Cambridge University Press, 1985.

Thompson, E. P. *The Making of the English Working Class*. Harmondsworth: Penguin, 1968.

Thompson, Julian. *The Imperial War Museum Book of the War in Burma 1942–45: A Vital Contribution to Victory in the Far East*. London: Sidgwick & Jackson, 2002.

Forgotten Voices of Burma. London: Ebury Press, 2009.

Thomson, Janice E. *Mercenaries, Pirates, and Sovereigns: State-Building and Extraterritorial Violence in Early Modern Europe*. Princeton: Princeton University Press, 1994.

Thorat, Lieutenant-General S. P. P. *From Reveille to Retreat*. New Delhi: Allied Publishers Private Limited, 1986.

Thorne, Christopher. *Allies of a Kind: The United States, Britain, and the War Against Japan, 1941–1945*. Oxford: Oxford University Press, 1978.

The Issue of War: States, Societies, and the Far Eastern Conflict of 1941–1945. New York: Oxford University Press, 1985.

Tilly, Charles. *Coercion, Capital, and European States AD 990–1992*. Cambridge: Blackwell, 1992.

Todorov, Tzvetan. *The Conquest of America: The Question of the Other*. Norman: University of Oklahoma Press, 1999.

Tomlinson, B. R. *The Indian National Congress and the Raj, 1929–1942: The Penultimate Phase*. London: Macmillan, 1976.

Toye, Hugh. *The Springing Tiger: A Study of a Revolutionary*. London: Cassell and Co., 1959.

Trench, Charles Chenevix. *The Indian Army and the King's Enemies 1900–1947*. London: Thames and Hudson, 1988.

Tuker, Lieutenant-General Sir Francis. *While Memory Serves*. London: Cassell and Co., 1950.

Turner, Victor W. *The Forest of Symbols: Aspects of Ndembu Ritual*. Ithaca: Cornell University Press, 1967.

The Ritual Process: Structure and Anti-Structure. New York: Aldine Publishing Company, 1969.

Verma, Lt. Gen. S. D. *To Serve with Honour: My Memoirs*. Dehradun: Natraj Publishers, 1988.

Voigt, Johannes H. *India in the Second World War*. New Delhi: Arnold-Heinemann, 1987.

War Office, The. *Statistics of the Military Effort of the British Empire During the Great War 1914–1920* (London: HMSO, 1922).

Ware, Vron. *Military Migrants: Fighting for Your Country*. Basingstoke: Palgrave Macmillan, 2012.

Watson, Alexander. *Enduring the Great War: Combat, Morale and Collapse in the German and British Armies 1914–1918*. Cambridge: Cambridge University Press, 2008.

"Culture and Combat in the Western World, 1900–1945." *Historical Journal*, Vol. 51, No. 2 (2008): 529–546.

Watson, G. R. *The Roman Soldier*. Ithaca: Cornell University Press, 1969.

Weber, Eugen Joseph. *Peasants into Frenchmen: The Modernization of Rural France, 1870–1914*. Stanford: Stanford University Press, 1979.

Weber, Max. *The Methodology of the Social Sciences*. New York: The Free Press, 1949.

Economy and Society, 2 Vols. Berkeley and Los Angeles: University of California Press, 1978.

The Protestant Ethic and the Spirit of Capitalism. London: Unwin Hyman, 1990 [1930].

Wedeen, Lisa. "Conceptualizing Culture: Possibilities for Political Science." *American Political Science Review*, Vol. 96, No. 4 (December 2002): 713–728.

Wesbrook, Stephen D. "The Potential for Military Disintegration" in Sam C. Sarkesian, ed. *Combat Effectiveness: Cohesion, Stress, and the Volunteer Military*. Beverly Hills: Sage, 1980.

Wheeler, Lt. Col. G. T. "Bombing: The Worm's-Eye View," *The Journal of the United Service Institution of India*, Vol. LXXII, No. 309 (October 1942): 297–304.

Wilkinson, Steven. *Army and Nation: The Military and Indian Democracy since Independence*. Cambridge: Harvard University Press, 2015.

Winter, Jay. *Sites of Memory, Sites of Mourning: The Great War in European Cultural History*. Cambridge: Cambridge University Press, 1995.

Wolf, Eric R. *Europe and the People Without History*. Berkeley: University of California Press, 1982.

Wong, Leonard *et al*. *Why They Fight: Combat Motivation in the Iraq War*. Carlisle: Strategic Studies Institute, U.S. Army War College, 2003.

Zimmerman, Andrew. "Africa in Imperial and Transnational History: Multi-Sited Historiography and the Necessity of Theory," *Journal of African History*, Vol. 54 (2013): 331–340.

Index

CPSIA information can be obtained
at www.ICGtesting.com
Printed in the USA
BVHW041252070420
577094BV00012B/309

9 781316 620656